Conducting Concerti

A Technical and Interpretive Guide

David Itkin

with generous assistance from
Carter Brey
Misha Dichter
and
Robert McDuffie

University of North Texas Press
Denton, Texas

Printed in the United States of America.

10 9 8 7 6 5 4 3 2 1

Permissions:
University of North Texas Press
1155 Union Circle #311336
Denton, TX 76203-5017

The paper used in this book meets the minimum requirements of the American National Standard for Permanence of Paper for Printed Library Materials, z39.48.1984. Binding materials have been chosen for durability.

Library of Congress Cataloging-in-Publication Data

Itkin, David, author.
Conducting concerti : a technical and interpretive guide / David Itkin. -- First edition.
pages cm
Includes index.

ISBN 978-1-57441-570-4 (cloth : alk. paper) — ISBN 978-1-57441-583-4 (ebook)
1. Conducting. 2. Concertos—Interpretation (Phrasing, dynamics, etc.) 3. Performance practice (Music) I. Title.
MT85.I85 2014
784.2'3145—dc23
2014019784

The electronic edition of this book was made possible by the support of the Vick Family Foundation.

For all those who continue to inspire great music,
my teachers, my students, my parents, and Stasia Belle

Contents

II. Violin Concerti

III. Cello Concerti

IV. Other Works

Introduction

Part 1: Conducting Concerti

Outstanding concerto conducting begins with the mastery of a variety of technical, analytical, aural, and intra-personal skills. These include all capabilities that we normally expect in the arsenal of the professional conductor, but also include some technical skills and specific matters of gestural nuance that are almost entirely the province of the conductor/accompanist. A considerable portion of this book is devoted to the understanding and development of these particular skills and their specific application in the repertoire.

In each chapter of this book, one concerto is discussed from many perspectives, including the specifics of accompanying, the conductor/soloist relationship, interpretation, score study, errata, balance, study of the solo part, orchestration, ensemble, and, of course, orchestra/soloist coordination. Although this is not fundamentally a book on conducting technique, technical issues are also discussed in detail in each chapter. These discussions focus primarily on the specific application of those conducting techniques and gestures that are particularly useful in the concerto (and other accompanying) repertoire.

Throughout this book I frequently use the terms "passive gesture" (or "passive beat") and "active gesture" (or "active beat"). While I am certain that both the intellectual and practical differences between a passive and an active gesture are already thoroughly understood by anyone reading this book, it is important to emphasize the enormous importance of this knowledge, and its practical application, when dealing with this repertoire. The importance of this issue lies less in the excellent execution of these techniques (which is a given) than in the conductor's growing knowledge and instinct for where each of these kinds of gestures is to be used in any given musical circumstance. With growing experience, both generally and in the specific accompanying repertoire, the use of these two very different types of gestures becomes second nature, and no longer needs to be a specific part of the score study or rehearsal preparation process. For younger or less experienced conductors, however, specific planning regarding which type of gesture will be most helpful, efficient, and musically productive in any given circumstance is often the difference between smooth, elegant, professional music making and a series of awkward transitions and small "train-wrecks."

Another important subject that is mentioned several (though perhaps not enough) times in this book is one to which I sometimes refer in my class as the "brain/hand schism." This is mostly a problem that affects younger or less experienced conductors, but it is not unheard of to see it afflict more experienced professionals. This "schism" is the accidental disconnect that takes place when the conductor is carefully following the soloist's activities (with his ear) but then fails to continue his own gesture (whether active or passive) in a logical and musically communicative manner. This most often occurs at moments when the task of the baton is to mark "empty" bars or flow through sustained harmonies in the orchestra while the soloist continues with more complicated material, or in some musically similar situation. When the "schism" occurs, the conductor's ears and brain are so focused on not losing track of complicated material in the solo part that the baton simply fails to accomplish even the simplest of tasks, and either sits frozen in space or moves rather vaguely, in a manner largely incomprehensible to the orchestra. When this happens, the conductor eventually finds himself ready to give the next required active gesture, cut-off, etc., but cannot effectively do so because he has failed to clearly mark or move through certain beats or bars that should have preceded that next active gesture. At that point, the orchestral musicians are likely to be confused and tentative, as they cannot reasonably be expected to understand what is meant by this next gesture. This problem is, of course, unconscious, as no one would knowingly allow the orchestra to be left without leadership in this way. The word "unconscious" is particularly appropriate here, since I have on many occasions pointed out this problem to student conductors who are quite certain that they marked every beat and/or bar in a given passage, only to discover on viewing a video of the event, or repeating the passage in rehearsal, that they did not. If one is an occasional victim of the "schism," overcoming this problem is largely a matter of being aware that it is, in fact, an issue. Identifying, during score study, the passages in a particular work that may offer the opportunity for a problem puts the conductor already half way to solving it. Experience also plays a part here, as the "frozen baton" that results from this problem is usually the result of the fear that one will not coordinate well with the soloist. Excellent study and a bit more experience with a given work, and with the repertoire in general, are also vital elements in putting the problem to rest.

In addition to achieving flawless technical coordination, seamless accompanying, and general orchestral and musical excellence, there is another subject that is of paramount importance when conducting this repertoire. The subject to which I refer can be best described as a quality of "effortless excellence" in the music making of two individuals (the soloist and the conductor). The qualities necessary to achieve this "effortless excellence" can be divided into two parts: (1) complete intellectual and musical command of the score and all orchestral issues (by the conductor), and (2) thorough, virtuosic technical command (by both soloist and conductor) that does not just meet but exceeds the demands of the work in question.

When the technical and intellectual demands outlined in the previous paragraph are met with ease, then the conductor and soloist can begin to approach a kind of music making that is consistently fresh and spontaneous. When each has complete trust in the other's knowledge, technical command, focus, professionalism, and musical integrity, then a new kind of freedom for the performance process is born. This freedom allows each performance to move beyond a fairly strict recounting of what has been rehearsed or previously performed, allowing the music to grow and be shaped uniquely and spontaneously, as one experiences in outstanding solo and chamber music performance.

Projecting this level of technical and intellectual expertise and inspiring the resulting trust, ease, and freedom in both the soloist and the musicians of the orchestra are the ultimate goals of the conductor in the concerto setting. Having accomplished this, the conductor has set the stage for a performance that is not only technically excellent but also a joyous and inspiring experience for both the audience and his musician collaborators.

The repertoire examined in this book was chosen from the vast array of great concerti, and is by no means intended to represent a precise selection of *the greatest* concerti, suggesting that any works not included here do not qualify in that category. On the contrary, the concerti that I discuss in this volume represent only a small portion of this great repertoire. The works examined here represent a combination of those concerti that student and young professional conductors are likely to encounter in their advanced study and early concert assignments, along with a number of personal favorites of mine. In examining the table of contents, it cannot have gone unnoticed that most of the major concerti by Beethoven and Brahms are not discussed in this book. Obviously, this is not an indication that they do not belong to this group of important and often performed concerti. The principal reason that I chose not to discuss those works (the piano and violin concerti by both composers) in this book is that a detailed discussion of all nine of these pieces can already be found in the works of Norman Del Mar (*Conducting Beethoven* and *Conducting Brahms*), and I saw no virtue in attempting to duplicate his brilliant work in this volume. Also, because space in any book is limited, I felt that this volume would be more valuable to the student and young professional conductor if I addressed works that have not already been so ably covered by Maestro Del Mar. Nonetheless, I have included the Triple Concerto by Beethoven and the Double Concerto by Brahms, even though these are discussed in the Del Mar volumes. This is for no better reason than the fact that these works are both particularly dear to me, and I could not imagine their omission.

Introduction

Part 2: The Soloist's Perspective

As is apparent by glancing at the title page, three extraordinary artists have generously assisted me in the preparation of this book: cellist Carter Brey, pianist Misha Dichter, and violinist Robert McDuffie. (From this point forward I will, for reasons of space and repetition, refer to them as C.B., M.D., and R.M., respectively.) I will not even attempt to list the accomplishments and credentials of these three colleagues here, because any attempt to do so would either require its own chapter or be insultingly incomplete, and I must assume that anyone reading this book is familiar enough with the careers of these three gentlemen to make that recital unnecessary in the first place.

I sat down for lengthy conversations with each of these artists to discuss their perspectives on the conductor/soloist relationship, what they need and want from an outstanding musical collaborator, their experiences with various conductors throughout their careers, the specific repertoire covered in this book, and many related topics. Their detailed comments regarding specifics in the repertoire are found within each relevant chapter, but I have reserved this section for their thoughts on these more general topics. In addition to discussing many valuable ideas about the various aspects of the conductor/soloist relationship, each of them shared some specific anecdotes from their own experience, and I have related some of these stories below. It might be suggested that these anecdotes are offered merely for entertainment, but that is not my purpose in including them. I have included a few of the many interesting stories that were shared with me to illustrate that the difference between becoming the conductor who is esteemed and appreciated by his soloist colleagues and one who is merely tolerated or even dismissed has a great deal to do with the technical, analytical, intellectual, and intra-personal skills that are discussed in this book.

When I first opened up the general subject of the conductor/soloist relationship, both M.D. and R.M. mentioned age and career position as significant factors influencing that relationship. M.D. said, "Age is a big factor. In my 20s when I played with all these great conductors I wanted to learn from them. You are with Ormandy or Leinsdorf, they make a suggestion, of course I want to hear it. Now it's different, I can accept a wise remark from anybody, but now I'm pretty hard to move in any direction." R.M. talked about three phases of a soloist's career and how, in each phase, the soloist's relationship to conductors changes. "Early on, we looked at our careers as more of a game, a business, a competition, than as an artistic endeavor. It was, 'Which conductors have hired you,' 'Where are you playing,' etc., instead of 'Why don't we really think and search for what Stravinsky was trying to achieve in his violin concerto?' That was secondary to the game. A lot of that was drilled into us by Dorothy DeLay. We were so grateful to be hired by these conductors that the relationship was a little skewed. It took a while to get to the point that it's an artistic partnership. Who cares who hired whom? We're trying to make music. But in your early to mid-twenties you have that cloud over you. There's a reason rental car companies wait until you are twenty-five before they'll rent you a car … you just aren't ready … a lot of us wanted to be famous before we wanted to be artists. Then you get to the second phase, you are more established, but the 'getting work' thing is still kind of a barrier to a complete music making experience. But now I'm at the point in my career where I don't give a ---- what the conductor thinks or what the audience thinks. If he disagrees with me we'll work it out and we'll do it on a beautiful level. It's a sense of security and confidence where you can hash out your differences on an even playing field. It's more of an audience thing than a conductor thing ... everyone wants to be liked. With success came a sense of security ... to be comfortable on stage and get your musical point across, and you really don't care what anyone else thinks. Now it's the rehearsal process that is more gratifying for me. Now I enjoy my experiences with conductors a lot more in this third phase of my career. I'm not ashamed to get my point across."

I have often discussed this age or "point in career" subject with my own students, because it is a double-edged sword. What the conductor can say to a soloist and how it ought to be said varies greatly depending on the relative ages and career positions of the two individuals. This is not to suggest, of course, that the conductor should *ever* speak to a soloist (even, for example, a teenaged local competition winner) in a manner that is disrespectful or condescending (on one end of the spectrum) or that the conductor should ever feel the need to be so thoroughly deferential (on the other) that his ability to lead and collaborate is compromised. But one of the many important intra-personal skills required of the conductor is to assess the relative career positions of the soloist and himself and to set an appropriate and productive tone for the relationship. When discussing a thorny moment in a concerto when the conductor needs a very specific approach or response from the soloist, or if their two ideas of tempo or interpretation seem dangerously different, I have often had students ask, "how do I ask that?" or, "how do I tell the soloist that?" Almost invariably, my answer begins with, "it depends on the person to whom you are speaking." My answer usually continues in this way: If you are working with a young person who is not yet a significant soloist you are probably in a position to teach a bit, so go ahead and do so; when you are working with a lateral colleague you should feel free to speak your mind as long as you do it in a respectful and affable way; when you are working with a soloist who is clearly above your station you should make your request with reasonable deference, and if the soloist doesn't want to change what she is doing you close your mouth and do the best you can.

As we moved forward in our conversations to include specific experiences with various conductors, C.B. began by saying that, while all conductors are not created equal, he felt very fortunate to have had very few negative experiences in a career as soloist that has run the gamut from community orchestras to the New York Philharmonic. He did, however, single out one experience as a cautionary tale about how style, rather than substance, can also create a poor musical experience for everyone. The story involved playing the Schumann concerto with an orchestra and conductor he asked not to be named here. Realizing that he and the guest conductor were staying in the same hotel, C.B. contacted him to ask if he'd like to get together to talk or work through the piece before the rehearsal, but the conductor declined, saying that he "needed a nap." Once at the concert hall, the conductor's first words to C.B. were, "Some soloists don't know how to follow a conductor at all, I hope you're not one of them." Understandably nonplussed by this rude remark, C.B. proceeded to an orchestra rehearsal that consisted of running through the piece, without stopping, twice. The conductor didn't ever actually *rehearse* the piece, nor did he seek C.B.'s input, ask if he was pleased or had any requests, or anything of the kind. "A very self-aggrandizing and unpleasant person" is how C.B. finally characterized him, "cold, with no human connection." Even if (with no real rehearsal) the performance turned out to be technically competent, one can only imagine the complete void of inspiration that must have been present. The intra-personal skills that I discuss throughout this book are not important just to make sure things "fit together"; they are important because music is made by human beings, and great music is made by human beings who trust and respect one another.

These intra-personal skills do not apply only to the conductor/soloist relationship, of course. R.M. reflected on the relationship between the overall musical experience and the sense of engaged music making he feels from both the conductor and the musicians in the orchestra. "Sometimes my best experiences have been with conductors of lesser known orchestras that have more rehearsal time. You can have a journey. It's also different in these orchestras because the musicians and the conductor are more on the same journey than in 'brand name' orchestras." He then continued with a personal reflection from one of our performance experiences together: "I noticed a real affection for you [from the musicians] outside the rehearsal itself, and that translated into the work. It's a different kind of satisfaction, but in many ways it's much more meaningful." His sentiments reflect my own, in many ways. While I have been fortunate to conduct a number of supremely expert orchestras during my career, and notwithstanding the fact that musical and technical excellence are always among our primary goals, I have often found that my most cherished musical experiences are with outstanding regional orchestras like those for which it has been my privilege to be Music Director. As R.M. said, there is a certain sense of shared musical and personal journey in the music making process in these ensembles that is often not present at the "brand name" level.

R.M. also offered anecdotes about two conductors who inspired him to reach a higher level in similar ways, but with very different consequences. In the "second phase" of his career R.M. toured South America with Michael Tilson Thomas (MTT) conducting. "We didn't get along that well," he said, "he [MTT] likes to 'tweak' the soloist to let them know who's in charge, to set the pecking order." After criticizing R.M.'s intonation in the first movement of the Tchaikovsky concerto ("you're a little out there") he then stopped an orchestra rehearsal and called a piano rehearsal during break in the Barber concerto, a work for which R.M. was already well-known, giving R.M. detailed instructions about bow use and other matters. Although angry about it at the time, R.M.'s thoughts in hindsight were, "I hate to admit it, but he was right, and now I do what he asked in the Barber." On the plane trip home, R.M. says that MTT admitted, "I knew that if I made you mad you'd play better." R.M.'s observation to me was simply, "I hated him for being right, and I hated him for being such a jerk." By contrast, R.M. tells of a similar situation much earlier in his career (and this temporal distinction is, in part, critical) with Yehudi Menuhin conducting. Touring the Mendelssohn concerto "somewhere in Switzerland, he stopped rehearsal and took me into his dressing room, and said, 'no, no, no, no … what are you doing?' But he was my mentor, so that was totally cool. To him, I just said 'thank-you.'"

I mentioned above that the most important reason I have included some of these anecdotes is to illustrate that, even at the higher levels of our business, the skills of great concerto conducting are not always well understood and executed. I appreciated the fact that R.M. was extremely frank with me on that subject, highlighting the importance of rigorous score study, as well as aural skills and conducting technique. A few of his remarks were as follows: "[I was the soloist for] Donald Voorhees' last performance with the Allentown Symphony. I didn't know anything about him and the Bell Telephone Hour … all those things he had done earlier in his career. I had to keep repeating things because he was so far behind. And Sarah Caldwell, doing Barber at Grant Park … I had to keep waiting because she was behind. There have been several times in the early days when I had to wait for people to catch up. Claudio Scimone … I did a lot of waiting for him [in the] Introduction and Rondo Capriccioso. These guys just didn't know the pieces and didn't know how to keep up."

Finally, I want to mention a few of the anecdotes that were shared with me by M.D. These tales illustrate many angles from which a soloist might view the conductor, from respectful awe to hubris to disappointment to folksy humor to plain old incompetence. "The worst ever was a man who, thankfully, is dead, [Thomas] Michalak with the New Jersey Symphony. [In] Brahms D minor, every so often I would just stop playing [in rehearsal], he didn't even know I wasn't playing. By the end of the rehearsal I went off stage and said, 'You don't need me, you don't even need a pianist in this concert.' Years later I heard that he came out and told the orchestra, 'Mr. Dichter is cancelling because he doesn't like the way you play.' That was the lowest of the low." "[Pierre] Boulez' and my debut with Cleveland, the weekend that Szell died in 1970, the second Brahms D minor in [my] life. Boulez starts rehearsal [much too slowly] in 6, and conducts the entire opening *tutti* that way, while the musicians are looking at each other not knowing what to make of the tempo. I enter playing just as slowly, but then move the tempo forward, and Boulez says 'pardon, pardon,' and starts it over again in two, but now much too fast." "The best of the best was a man like [Eugene] Ormandy. Rach[maninoff] 2 and Rach[maninoff] 3 were unforgettable. He was like your custom Hong Kong tailor: one rehearsal and I walk on stage and it was like my custom made suit." "[Robert] Shaw used all these colored pencils. When he appeared at our first piano rehearsal with his stopwatch and colored pencils, I didn't know what to make of him. But he soon became one of my favorite musicians and dearest friends. He listened like crazy, but he needed, for himself, to have those pencils." "Leinsdorf was one of the easiest … Bernstein was the very easiest … Giullini I just tried to live up to every night."

I. Piano Concerti

Frederick Chopin

Piano Concerto No. 1 in E Minor, Op. 11

1st movement.

The considerable orchestral exposition of this movement presents some interesting musical challenges. First, and perhaps most important, is the subject of Chopin's orchestrating, which is an issue throughout his works for orchestra. In this exposition, as well as many other places in his concerti, his elegant and charming musical ideas are somewhat undermined by his less than expert skills in orchestration. This subject cannot help but lead us to consider the more immediate question: how do we keep this lengthy exposition engaging and musically relevant in spite of a certain orchestral "lumpiness."

Most conductors, of whom I am certainly one, shy away from exhibiting such hubris as to re-orchestrate the works of great composers. However, this exposition may be a place for some delicate helpful touches. One of the "fixes" that can be beneficial is to reinforce the first violins with a portion of the second violin section during the first twelve bars. The same technique can also be employed in other similar passages that are heavily orchestrated but have left only (or nearly only) the first violins taking the major melodic material. In such passages, the conductor must either choose to make the adjustment suggested above or, alternatively, must adjust the dynamics in the remainder of the orchestra quite significantly. In reality, the best solution may be to employ both strategies simultaneously.

The conductor should be aware of some extra time that is often taken by the soloist nineteen bars after **C**, on the third beat of the bar. It is only of particular note because it occurs precisely on the cello entrance, and on the final beat of a bar, so it is easy for the conductor to become involved in coordination of the following cello figure and fail to adequately anticipate the *rubato* in the piano.

In the twenty-third bar after **C**, we encounter a typical moment in Chopin's work, where the twenty-one-note figure in the right hand glides above the static eighth-note accompaniment in the left. In order to reach the following downbeat in good precision with the piano, the conductor either needs to be psychic or, preferably, needs to have paid extremely good attention to the soloist's habits during rehearsal. The potential problem is that a bar like this one is sometimes played with some *rubato* during the last beat, but equally often is played in strict tempo through to the following downbeat. The conductor's gesture (on the third beat) will be very different depending upon which musical shape the pianist prefers, and the conductor absolutely must know in advance which of these interpretive choices the pianist will take. If the conductor makes a slight pause on the third beat to allow for some freedom in the pianist's right hand, but the pianist plays in tempo across the bar-line, there is no possible way for the conductor to recover in time to have the orchestra's first beat match the pianist's. Likewise, if the conductor assumes a continuing pulse in tempo and the pianist suddenly takes some *rubato*, the conductor will find himself on the following downbeat well before the pianist, again with no way to recover. As in many places in Chopin's concerti, visually observing and listening for the pianist's left hand is an important tool, but in a case like this one it is not enough. Nothing can substitute here for foreknowledge of the pianist's intentions.

Thirty-two bars before **D** there is often a *subito pianissimo* inserted.

Some of the most treacherous moments in Chopin's concerti occur during passages that appear quite simple. This is not because they are especially difficult, but ironically because they may appear to present no difficulties or accompanying issues at all, and therefore we may let down our intellectual guard. The four bars beginning twenty-one bars before **E** are such a passage. There is often some *rubato*, or even a very slight lift, before each of the grace notes. Being aware of this is half the battle, but feeling the pianist's pace instinctively and not allowing the simplistic appearance of the passage to lull one into a lack of concentration are also very important.

I'll repeat myself here by saying that I am usually very hesitant to re-orchestrate the work of a great composer, even slightly. Once again, however, another arguable exception to that rule presents itself just after **E**. The important flute line that begins twenty-two bars after **E** works far better if played up one octave from where it is written. As written, even performed as loudly as the instrument can play in that register, it is all but impossible for this line to be heard over the piano. Just before that, the moving bassoon line needs be marked at least *mezzo forte* for similar reasons.

Eight bars before **G** the celli, and only the celli, should mark their part *mezzo-piano ed espressivo*, so that this important interior line calls attention to itself while all other string lines stay well in the background.

The passage beginning at **G** offers a perfect example of the type of writing for the piano that can make Chopin's concerti rather tricky to accompany for some conductors. The complete freedom of rhythm and tempo that is so important to a stylish performance is precisely the quality that can make the experience unnerving for the conductor. In passages like this one it is not only the conductor's ears, but also his eyes on the pianist's left hand, that will be very important for good coordination. I mention eyes on the left hand particularly in a passage like this one, as often the soloist's voicing choices will make the precise rhythm of the left hand difficult to hear clearly. Another reason that visual attention to the keyboard is often so important, as those who are not conductors will probably never had considered, is that the lid of the piano is situated between the piano's hammers and strings and our ears. In this set-up, the piano's sound is being directed out into the concert hall, and some passages like this one may sound quite muddy from our vantage point, while they sound perfectly clear in the hall.

As earlier in the movement, the flute line beginning sixteen bars after **H** is best played up one octave. This should last only until the end of the twenty-second bar after **H**. The rest of the passage (beginning on the dotted-quarter note E-natural) should be played as written, as it is rather impractical to continue in the higher octave, and any other solution would mean changing octaves in mid-phrase. As also mentioned earlier, clarinet and bassoon lines in the following section (seven bars before **I** through eighteen bars after **I**) need to be performed at higher dynamic levels than indicated.

In the bar directly before **M**, we observe (in most scores and parts) what we must conclude to be an error. In this bar, the second violins have a quarter note (C-natural) and rests (with *fermata*) for the remainder of the bar, while the rest of the strings have a half note with the *fermata* on the note. Clearly, the second violin part needs to match the rest of the strings. There is no reason that the 7th of the chord should not be sustained with the other voices, especially since that same pitch (middle C) is sounded by the solo piano on the second beat of the bar.

The last beat of the bar directly preceding **N** is usually best treated with a complete pause of the baton, as though there is a *fermata* on this beat. This not only allows the conductor to have sufficient flexibility to wait for the soloist to finish the figure at leisure, but also puts the conductor in a physical position to give a preparatory beat that will accurately reflect the faster tempo of the following bar.

The final two bars of this movement can feel a bit artificial, as though the composer felt the need to put a final *fortissimo* signpost at the end of the movement to make sure there was an unambiguous and perhaps more satisfying conclusion for the audience. One could compare this to the end of the final movement of Beethoven's Sixth Symphony where, to some, the final *forte* seems out of character and artificial. However, the two situations are not at all the same: Beethoven's conclusion puts a dignified, and only *forte*, punctuation mark at the end of a major symphonic work, while Chopin artificially attaches a completely inorganic, *fortissimo* "tuh-duh" and the end of a first movement that would probably have been better served by two *pianissimo* E-minor chords as a conclusion. Nonetheless, we have what the composer gave us, and no matter how much we may disagree it is not for us to drastically re-make the work in our own image. All that can respectably be done to soften this incongruous ending is to ask the orchestra to take care that the attacks, general sound quality, and even the dynamic of these chords lean toward the gentler, more dignified end of the spectrum.

2nd movement.

Chopin only specifies that the violins are *con sordino* at the beginning of the movement. However, for uniformity of sound it is best if the viole (and perhaps the celli and basses) are also muted.

Three bars before **B** the conductor should treat the second half of the fourth beat as a brief *fermata*, not moving toward the following downbeat until he hears the soloist begin the last three notes (D-sharp, C-sharp, B) of the bar. This is necessary not only for good ensemble, but also to give a clear preparation for the second horn entrance on the following downbeat.

In the seventh bar after B the strategy previously described of listening to (and watching) the pianist's left hand during passages of *fioratura* will be of no help at all. The baton arrives at the fourth beat of the bar, remaining paused as for a *fermata*, and then the ears take over entirely. If the conductor cannot, by listening to the progress of the upward scale, accurately anticipate when to give the preparatory gesture so that orchestra and soloist arrive together at the following downbeat, then the passage simply cannot be managed.

In many editions there is a tie in the right hand of the piano connecting the last note of the sixth bar after C to the first note of the following bar. Most pianists and scholars believe this to be an error, and therefore the octave A-sharp is repeated on the following downbeat.

Beginning in the eighth bar of C the solo bassoon must play at a higher dynamic than indicated in order to achieve reasonable balance with the piano.

Contrary to what is indicated, four bars before E it is best if the second horn treats the tied note not as a quarter note, but as an eighth-note, *staccato*. In this way the horn finishes the phrase in coordination with the piano rather than appearing to make an error by sustaining through the entire first beat of the bar.

The conductor should be careful during the last beat of the sixth bar after E, as many soloists will take the slightest lift on the barline. This is another example of the type of situation where it is best to pause on the fourth beat rather than flow slowly through it, as the latter solution severely limits the conductor's options and clarity.

For clarity of ensemble, as well as clarity of purpose, the turn in the first violins seven bars before the end is usually performed as an eighth note (G-sharp) followed by four thirty-second notes (A, G-sharp, F-sharp, G-sharp).

3rd movement.

In spite of the fact that Chopin specifically wrote *attacca* at the conclusion of the second movement, the conductor needs to remember to allow time for the strings to remove the mutes. The commotion and squeaking caused by forcing the musicians to do this in haste is, in reality, far more disturbing to the performance than a couple of extra seconds' pause that allows the process to proceed calmly.

The tempo at **C** is usually set rather *meno mosso* as compared with the opening tempo of the movement, with perhaps a slight subdivision just before **C** to aid clarity. Often, six bars before **D** there is an *accelerando* just significant enough to return to Tempo I by the beginning of the second bar before **D**.

The eleventh and twelfth bars after **E** (the two bars preceding the key change) need particular attention from the conductor. It is very important that the conductor have clearly in mind the harmonic context of the scale in order to be certain that the B-flat in the basses is placed correctly. This moment usually requires a subdivision of the second beat of the bar directly before the key change, depending on the amount of *rallentando* in the piano.

As earlier, a *meno mosso* is usually observed at **I**, with Tempo I returning two bars before **K**.

At the timpani entrance nineteen bars after **L** most scores and parts show half notes with two slashes across the stem. In modern nomenclature this indicates that the timpanist is to play measured sixteenth-notes, but to assume that this is what Chopin intended makes no sense, as this reading would clash gravely with the rhythmic structure of the solo piano. (If anyone is in doubt, observe the final bar of the movement where the notation is the same!) Surely these are intended to be unmeasured rolls in these and later bars, and any timpanist observed playing sixteenth notes should probably be quietly instructed as such.

ᔓᔕ

Frederick Chopin

Piano Concerto No. 2 in F Minor, Op. 21

1st movement.

The first gesture made by the conductor (the third beat of the bar) must convey not only the delicacy and lightness of the opening figure, but should also be sufficiently precise to allow for confident performance of an opening phrase that can be unnerving to some violinists. Also, the first violins must be careful that this phrase is not *pianissimo*, but only *piano*, warm and expressive.

A nice phrasing can be achieved by placing a slight break after the first beat of both the seventeenth and eighteenth bars before **A**. This creates two parallel phrases, each beginning on the second beat of a bar and continuing through the following downbeat. Failing to create such phrasing results in a more plodding, pedantic reading. For similar reasons, a more elegant shape for the phrase is created by placing a slight break after the first note of the following bars: three before **A** (all strings), two before **A** (all strings), and one before **A** (second violins, viole, and celli), as well as twenty bars before **B** (all strings), nineteen bars before **B** (all strings except second violins), eighteen bars before **B** (all strings), seventeen bars before **B** (violins only), thirteen bars before **B** (all strings), and twelve bars before **B** (first violins only).

A strongly articulated dot-dash reading works well for the quarter notes marked *sforzato* eight and nine bars before **B**. Five bars before **B** the strings often need to be cautioned not to play too softly. The dynamic here is still only (slightly less than) *piano*, and the sound must remain sufficiently full and warm to allow for a complete, mysterious sonic change at the *pianissimo* one bar before **B**.

As already mentioned, when conducting the Chopin concerti it is often important to pay critical attention to the pianist's left hand, as this usually provides the most concrete evidence of the soloist's intentions and progress through a given bar. Although the eleventh bar after **B** is not difficult to accompany, it provides another good example of this idea. Clear visual observation of the left hand in this bar allows for easy coordination between the piano and the orchestral strings.

The twenty-third bar after **B** provides another good opportunity for the use of a conducting technique that is vital in Chopin. (For many conductors, the problem in a musical situation like this one is neither the understanding of the technique nor the ability to execute it. The stumbling block for some is a combination of the secure knowledge regarding where to apply the technique and, importantly, the confidence to use it, which means fearlessly allowing the baton to come to a complete stop in the middle of a phrase, something that makes many younger conductors very uncomfortable.) In this bar, the fourth beat is usually noticeably longer than any of the three previous beats, as the soloist will often linger a bit over the delicious last three notes of the *fioratura* (C-natural, E-flat, D-flat) before proceeding to the final thirty-second note (C-natural). The usual gesture to indicate a bit of *ritard* on the fourth beat (slowing the rebound and slightly elongating the point of rest at the zenith of the beat before progressing downward toward one) is nearly useless here, and an entirely different gesture is called for. The baton arrives at the fourth beat and stays entirely still, as though a *fermata* is written on this beat, and gives the preparatory gesture only as the pianist completes the three notes mentioned above.

The bar twenty-one after **C** provides another example of the importance of the conductor taking her cues from the pianist's left hand during complex passages of *fioratura*. Depending on the choices made by the soloist, a slight subdivision may be required on the final beat of this bar.

Nine bars before **D** the first note in the celli is B-natural (not the often printed B-flat). Thirty-nine bars after **D** the first beat in the first bassoon part should read eighth-rest, sixteenth-rest, sixteenth-note (E-natural).

The eight-bar passage beginning thirty-seven bars after **D** generally has a very free, *rubato* feel, making it all the more important that the conductor be intimately familiar with the soloist's ideas about the twists and turns of Chopin's unique writing. As mentioned earlier, attention to the progress of the left hand is also critical.

Twenty-nine bars before **E** all strings should have *piano* indicated on the fourth beat of the bar (paralleling the passage four bars later), making the *piano* indication in the next bar unnecessary.

In the passage beginning twenty-four bars before **E** all woodwind solos need to be played at dynamics considerably higher than indicated in order to be heard clearly over the dense piano writing. This is true through **E**.

In the eleventh and twelfth bars after **E** a gentle *rallentando* is appropriate, as this gracefully sets up what is likely to be a somewhat slower tempo in the passage that follows.

2nd movement.
Some conductors will find the opening wind statements in this movement frustrating in terms of intonation. If so, they are not alone. Chopin's sparse writing, unusual voicing, and open texture can make the passage rather difficult to tune. A consistent, disciplined, harmonically based approach that regularly emphasizes the principle that higher is not always the solution is the best way to improve the intonation in a passage like this one.

Although it is not precisely what the composer indicated, the most logical place to cut off the strings in the sixth bar is after the piano arrives at the E-flat (*fermata*), but before the piano continues with any of the following thirty-second notes.

One bar before **F** the preparatory gesture should be given as the pianist plays the G-natural, beginning the last five downward notes before the bar-line. In the second bar of **F** the baton should pause on the third beat of the bar, waiting for the progress of the piano into, and even beyond, the beginning of the fourth beat. Only when the soloist reaches the five final notes of the bar (in the right hand) should the conductor make the quick but gentle preparatory gesture for the next bar. As mentioned earlier, this is precisely the type of musical situation in which the baton should not explicitly follow the solo part throughout the bar. To do so forces the conductor into long, extremely slow quarter-note beats which may result in a lack of security and good ensemble at the beginning of the following bar.

In the bars sixteen, seventeen, and eighteen after **F** a small lift after each first beat encourages a nice sense of phrasing. This allows for the creation of a phrase from the second beat of one bar through the downbeat of the next. By placing accents on each second beat the composer has essentially already indicated this idea, but some orchestras still insist on continuing the sound in complete *legato* in these spots, which does not allow the musical line to properly breathe.

In the extended *recitative* passage (twenty-seven bars before **G** through **G**), the conductor must walk a thin line between the twin duties of accompanying the soloist with great flexibility and providing precise leadership for the *pizzicato* basses. The dilemma, of course, is to provide a concrete rhythmic structure for the bass section without imposing one's own will on the pianist, therein robbing the soloist of the appropriate degree of freedom. Some conductors "solve" this problem by moving through each of these bars with a mushy *ictus* that is the result of insecurity: not knowing exactly where the soloist is headed within each phrase. Obviously, this "solution" results in tentative performance, poor ensemble, and lots of *pianissimo* playing from the basses. Instead, the conductor needs first to be certain to separate clearly those beats that are virtually without *ictus* (when only following the forward progress of the solo during continuing tremolo with no bass section involvement) from those beats which will have a very sharp, if small, *ictus*, showing either preparation or entrances for the basses. Next, the conductor needs to have the courage and certainty of knowledge to clearly place each beat in each bar. This is one of those moments when the orchestra depends totally on the knowledge, skill, and leadership of the conductor, and abdicating responsibility here is not an option. Finally, the woodwind entrances eleven and thirteen bars before **G** and the horns' entrance four bars before **G** must be clearly cued. This must be done not with just a motion of the baton in the appropriate direction, but also with a clear look in the eye beginning at least a couple of beats in advance. These musicians have not played in some time, and the nature of the preceding passage can create considerable insecurity for them that must be overcome by the conductor's calm and clarity.

3rd movement.

Once the conductor is certain that the soloist and strings are ready (usually immediately following the last note of the second movement), the conductor's preparatory gesture puts the third movement into motion. It is usually not practical here for the conductor to follow the soloist.

It is common for the orchestral passage beginning sixteen bars before **I** to be played *meno mosso*. There is really no good reason for this, however, and the composer certainly does not indicate it. This passage flows charmingly when kept in the original tempo. A graceful bit of *rallentando* at the conclusion of the flute solo is all that is necessary, moving immediately back into tempo four bars before **I**.

The first thirty-two bars at **I** require a supple exchange between beating in one and beating in three. Depending on the amount of *rallentando* employed by the soloist in various places, a possible plan for this section is as follows: **I** in one; five bars after **I** in three; nine bars after **I** in one; thirteen bars after **I** in three; fifteen bars after **I** in one; twenty-three bars after **I** in three; twenty-five bars after **I** in one; thirty-two bars after **I** in three (if the pianist's *ritard* seems to suggest it); the following bar in one.

At **K** the second violin part should read as follows: a quarter note (D-flat) followed by a half note (D-natural). The D-natural occurring on the first beat of the bar (in some scores and parts) clearly cannot be correct.

Thirty-seven bars after **K** the slurring pattern (in some scores and parts) in the first violins is incorrect. The previous slur should end in this bar (on G-natural) and the next slur begins in the following bar, encompassing four bars total.

The various strings entrances that are found twenty-four, twenty-five, and twenty-seven bars before **L** need to be carefully cued. This is another situation in which the passing of many recent bars of rest, in one, can cause some insecurity in the orchestra about the following entrance.

Conductors who might tend to get aurally tangled in the descending passage that follows, preceding the string entrance sixteen bars before **L**, will find it very helpful to simply follow (aurally and visually) the downward chromatic scale in the lower voice of the left hand. Listening in particular for the B-flat on the downbeat four bars before the orchestra re-enters makes the passage less confusing.

The horn signal just after the key change can be successfully handled in several different ways, depending on the taste and preferences of the conductor and the principal horn. This is often shaped with the first phrase rather quick, and the second phrase slower and with some *ritard.* To me, however, this seems counterintuitive, as we are heading back toward the original tempo in the next bar. Consequently, I prefer for the first phrase to be a bit slower, with a more noble character, while the second has a bit of *accelerando* that leads logically back toward Tempo I. In either case, these bars can be conducted in three or merely marked; in the latter case the hornist is allowed to play without specific leadership, but in a manner already rehearsed.

Even though the composer does not indicate it, a slight *rallentando* is rather appropriate in the two bars of *tutti* just before **O**. This gives the phrase a more *Maestoso* character, and keeps it from feeling like it "ran into a wall."

ও

Manuel de Falla

Nights in the Gardens of Spain

1st movement.

Despite the rather slow basic pulse of the opening section of this movement, concerns of music making and atmosphere make it preferable to remain in two, throwing in a subdivision here and there only when absolutely necessary for clarity or in a slight *rallentando*. The composer gives a metronome marking of ♩. = 50, but it is fairly rare to hear a performance as fast as that. It was my privilege to conduct this work for the first time with its quintessential interpreter, the late Alicia De Larrocha, and her tempo for this passage was more in the neighborhood of ♩. = 38. This slower tempo allows for a significant difference in tone and meaning for this music, as contrasted with a performance that adheres more strictly to the composer's metronome marking.

Just before **2**, it is rather traditional to allow the English horn some time at the end of the solo. Whether extra time is given, and how much, are surely matters of personal taste, not of right and wrong.

The entrance of horns in the third bar after **4** is an example of the musical situation to which I referred in the first paragraph of this chapter. Specifically, with such a slow main pulse, a subdivision will probably be needed for clarity and security of the entrance. The same applies four bars later in the woodwinds.

At **5**, and following, the composer is not specific about moving from $\frac{6}{8}$ to $\frac{3}{4}$, but the musical substance, his beaming choices, and the indication ♪ = ♪ all clearly indicate a change. The most logical solution is to make the change in the fourth bar after **5**, as there are no bars following this point that might be questionable as to their metric structure.

At **8**, we find the indication *Poco stringendo* (sino ♩ = 104). This *stringendo* will need to be *poco* indeed, as the tempo at **8** (based on the previous metronome marking) is already ♩ = 99. At **9**, the composer offers *Tempo giusto* and ♩ = 104, the tempo that is the completion of this very modest *stringendo*.

Approaching the downbeat at **12**, the conductor usually needs to be patient to allow the grace note in the left hand of the piano to be sounded before placing the orchestral entrance with the following chord. In most cases, the preparatory gesture can coincide with the placement of the grace note, or just before.

Following the piano through the arpeggios at **13** is a fairly easy matter. The conductor needs only to follow the progress (in the entire piano texture) of this rhythm, ♩♩ 3 ♪ ♩ 3 ♪, in the first and third bars, and this rhythm, ♩ 3 ♪ ♩ 3 ♪ ♩ 3 ♪, in the second and fourth bars, to make what may appear rather thorny at first glance into something fairly simple.

In the first, third, and sixth bars at **16**, it is fairly traditional to take a bit of time in the last, decaying beat of the bar. This will usually require a subdivision in the final beat of each of these bars. At **17**, one has to hope that the pianist will provide a bit of polite body language that allows the conductor to place the downbeat with the clarinet accurately. If, at the previous cut-off, the pianist is sitting with the left hand poised over the F-sharp and offers nothing in the way of leadership but to simply depress the key, then the conductor cannot possibly show the clarinetist the entrance properly.

The tempo at **19** is still ♩ = 58, and nowhere does the composer indicate that this passage should speed up toward the new tempo at **20**. Unfortunately, some conductors who are either bored with this passage or believe that the similarity of material (i.e., similarity with the passage that follows) indicates a necessary similarity of tempo choose to move the music at 19 forward so that the tempi match by the time they reach 20. I find this to be absolutely contrary to the intention of the music. At 20, the half-step figures in solo winds and *tutti* strings are re-interpreted in a new tempo, with the figurations in the solo piano added. These two passages are not identical twins; they are fraternal twins with very different personalities.

2nd movement.

Beginning in the fifth bar after 4, it is easy for the conductor to inadvertently coordinate the orchestra with the piano one sixteenth-note off from where the orchestra really should be. The line in the piano to which the ear naturally gravitates is, of course, at the top. If the conductor carelessly tunes into the top voice without clear analysis, he is likely to hear the principal rhythm of each bar as two quarter notes followed by two eighth notes, which will put the entire orchestra perpetually behind. A solution (in addition to being better acquainted with the intricacies of the solo part) is rather obvious: if the lowest voice of the piano is not clearly audible from the podium, then the conductor needs to be sure to visually observe the left hand for good coordination.

The composer does not ask for *subito più mosso* at 9, but this is a common, though careless, choice made by some conductors. This much easier but far less interesting choice is sometimes made in spite of the composer's admonition that the *accelerando* is to be *pochissimo e gradualmente*. The conductor has eight bars to move from ♩ = 120 to ♩ = 144, so there is no need to come shooting off the blocks at 9, so to speak.

Anyone doing their math carefully may be a bit stumped by the tempo relationships between 10 and 13. At 10 the composer gives us ♩ = 144, but at 13 asks that the tempo be exactly half of that,

Doppio meno vivo, but specifies ♩ = 84; rather obviously, 84 is not half of 144. Clearly, something has to give. There are lots of ways to solve this. The three most obvious solutions are (1) to go faster than indicated at **10**, (2) to go slower than indicated at **13**, or (3) to abide by his metronome markings exactly but don't worry about **13** being precisely half tempo. A fourth solution, and my preference, is to take the composer's metronome markings literally, but to add a slight *incalzando* at **12**, getting the tempo moving forward just enough by **13** to make cutting it in half come out correctly as ♩ = 84.

In the third bar after **20** the composer asks that we use the next two bars to move from ♩ = 120 to ♩ = 84 by means of *rall. poco a poco*. For some reason, many conductors and pianists take the new tempo *subito* at this point, and this is not at all what the composer asked. There is considerably more drama created by charging into the figure in celli and basses still at ♩ = 120, and then letting the weight of the sound naturally slow the forward motion, exactly as de Falla wrote.

3rd movement.

Even though there is not a world of difference between the metronome marking at **22** (♩ = 126) and that given the beginning of the third movement (♩ = 132), it is clear that by being so specific the composer wanted to be sure that an extra jolt of energy be applied in the first bar of this movement. Acknowledging this, it is odd that one usually hears these tempi performed identically, with no change at all where the third movement begins. Making this happen as the composer asked, however, is largely out of the conductor's hands, as the soloist alone is in charge of the tempo at **22**. If the soloist can be convinced to set the tempo a bit more modestly at **22**, so that there remains room for the conductor to inject this extra bit of energy at the first bar of the third movement, then the problem is solved. If not, the conductor will probably need to be content with the usual outcome: *lo stesso tempo* at the beginning of the third movement.

If the composer's instructions at **27** (*Calmando appena e gradualmente*) are followed precisely, then making this connection between the soloist's downward scales and the following orchestral entrance is no issue at all. However, many conductors begin at **27** already somewhat *meno mosso*, so that the first few beats of the orchestra's material do not seem rushed or frantic. When this is the musical decision, then the conductor must completely separate herself from the tempo she hears in the piano, giving a preparation that is truly in the desired new tempo at roughly the mid-point of the second beat of the bar before **27**.

The passage between **30** and **31** (with the exception of the fourth and fifth bars, where the solo piano is absent) will have an improvisatory feel. In spite of this, it is not stylish for the conductor to "follow" the solo part here, as this will make the accompaniment uneven, and lacking any logical, steady sense of pulse. The conductor will probably need to accommodate the soloist at the end of each phrase (the first two beats of the fourth bar and last beat of the seventh bar), but can usually keep the tempo steady throughout the remainder of the passage. (For a more developed discussion of this subject, see the chapter on *Concierto de Aranjuez*, second movement.)

The transition to *Tempo I* (one beat before **32**) works well if the new tempo is exactly *doppio movimento* (the previous eighth note being equal to the new quarter note), and this is the most common practice heard in performance. The math doesn't work very well, since the previous eighth note (approx. mm168) clearly doesn't equal the new quarter note (stated as mm120), but the music does.

Between **41** and **43**, the composer throws in an occasional bar that appears (by its essential rhythmic construction) to be in $\frac{3}{4}$, and he does this without ever giving us clear instructions; specifically, these are the fourth and twelfth bars after **41** and the eighth bar after **42**. These bars should be conducted in three, rather than remaining in two and treating the rhythms as hemiolas, because they are not, in fact, hemiolas. These bars represent the common rhythmic construction in Spanish music of alternating between $\frac{6}{8}$ and $\frac{3}{4}$ while maintaining a constant eighth note. (See the composer's *Three Cornered Hat*, etc.) Eight bars before **43** we remain in three.

At **43**, the composer gives us a bit more information than we really need. Solely his reassurances that the previous ♩ = the new ♩., and that this tempo should be ♩. = 58, are more than sufficient. For some reason, he insists on muddying the water with his additional explanation *a tempo, ma quasi doppio più lento*. The tempo at **43** is only (roughly) "slower by half" (*doppio più lento*) when compared with the last metronome marking (at **42**), but is not intended to be half of the "current" tempo (found in the several beats directly preceding **43**). Focusing solely on the information that is found in the second sentence of this paragraph makes knowing what to do here simple.

The tempo instruction at **44** should be read in two parts. The first half of the sentence (*Sempre lo stesso tempo*) applies to the orchestra and the second half (*ma un poco libero*) refers to the solo piano. The conductor must not attempt to accommodate the soloist's rhapsodizing in this passage, or he will make nonsense out of the celli/bass (later including viole and second violins) figures. These figures are a canvas on which the soloist paints. As mentioned above regarding the passage between **30** and **31**, if you keep moving the canvas the picture starts to look pretty strange.

Five bars before the end, the composer is very explicit and clear in his explanation regarding the transition into $\frac{12}{8}$. In spite of this, instead of the requested ♪ = ♪, one more commonly hears (old) ♩ = (new) ♩., completely ruining his intended rhythmic juxtaposition.

In the bar before $\substack{12\\8}$, he brilliantly sets up the dotted quarter note pulse, appearing here as a hemiola in $\substack{3\\4}$, making the task of following his instructions both easy and logical. Observing all of this, it is hard to understand why some conductors insist on keeping the *major pulse* the same, instead of the *eighth note* as the composer asked. Not only will following his instructions precisely create the correct metric relationship, but it will also allow the final five bars to settle logically into the intended tempo. When the incorrect relationship is used, the tempo at which one arrives at $\substack{12\\8}$ is considerably faster than intended: approximately ♩. = 60 instead of the intended ♩. = 40.

❧

George Gershwin

Concerto in F

1st movement.

The opening metronome marking in the first movement (𝅗𝅥 = 69) will seem problematically slow to some conductors. However, before abandoning Gershwin's instruction in favor of a faster tempo, one should at least attempt to understand the logic behind it, as there are several good reasons to stick to his indication. First, this tempo allows the important motive in the timpani to ring out with proper weight and importance, while a faster tempo diminishes these qualities. Second, in the passage beginning at bar 5 Gershwin's tempo keeps the syncopated figures weighty and sexy, rather than having them sound rushed and sarcastic. Third, the composer's stated tempo keeps the bassoon solo (later bass clarinet) properly playful, without feeling frantic or in any way drawing virtuosic attention to itself. Finally, this tempo allows the violin figure at **1** to feel weighty and dramatic, rather than hysterical.

As will be discussed further in the next chapter (Rhapsody in Blue), no work by Gershwin can be properly prepared for performance without a thorough understanding of the central rhythmic question: which eighth notes and/or sixteenth notes (the latter usually in the context of a dotted eighth-note/sixteenth-note figure) are to be played "swung" and which are to be played as written? This is a fairly complicated subject that has no fixed answer for all situations. Each situation must be judged by the musical needs and logic of that particular moment, because a solution that makes sense in one portion of a piece may not make sense in another, seemingly similar passage.

In addition, because the decision "to swing or not to swing" is, in places, rather subjective, all conductors, soloists, and orchestral musicians will not necessarily agree on all solutions. Let's consider, for example, the famous trumpet solo (and all similar music that follows) at **57** in "American in Paris." Some trumpeters (and conductors) are ardent in their belief that this music should be played as written, with straight eighth notes. Others are equally certain that it should be played with the eighth notes swung, and one can hear many fine performances and recordings with either solution employed.

This question is somewhat less difficult and subjective when considering the first movement of the Concerto in F, as the cut-time meter eliminates a few of the variables. Specifically, a figure like the one in bar 5 does not really open up the question of a swung or not-swung eighth-note. In this figure, at this tempo, the eighth-note can be played straight, with no discussion necessary, as the difference between straight and swung is negligible.

This is not so, however, for the eighth note following the third beat in bars 7 and 8. Playing this note straight, when it is followed by a triplet, results in a forced and unstylish performance. It feels logical to play it swung, as though it is the third part of a triplet on the third (quarter-note) beat of the bar.

Passages of repeated dotted eighth/sixteenth figures (bassoon solo 4 bars before **1**, bass clarinet solo 6 bars after **1**, tutti 6 bars before **2**, and woodwinds at **2**) usually fall into line of their own accord. However, if the question is asked, it will result in the most natural and stylish performance if the orchestra is told to swing this figure. Instructing the orchestra to play these figures as written will result in a "tight" and academic-sounding performance, something more like Berlioz than Gershwin.

It was mentioned earlier that the cut-time meter removes some of the questions about "swing" in this movement. This is largely because passages containing entirely eighth notes (or at least containing no sixteenth notes), such as those 5 bars before **2** and at **7** are always played as written, without swing.

The passage at **5** presents a new twist on this question. In every performance that I can recall hearing, and every performance that I have conducted (until recently), this passage is played straight, with no eighth notes swung. The style and expression of this passage are such that, in all honesty, it had never occurred to me to do it any other way. The fact that the melody contains both eighth notes and the dotted-eighth/sixteenth combination as integral components makes me believe that this should be played straight. Otherwise, how would eighth notes and sixteenth notes be differentiated from one another, since usually, in swing style, those rhythms are executed identically?

However, a 2009 performance in Las Vegas that I conducted with the outstanding young pianist Joel Fan caused me to re-think this question, or at least to be open to more than one possibility. Joel plays this passage with the eighth note swung throughout, which gives it an entirely different, and quite charming flavor. In this reading, the sixteenth notes (as at the end of the first bar at **5**) must be played literally, as sixteenths. Otherwise the sixteenth and the eighth will have the same value, both sounding as swung eighth notes. In the more "traditional" reading (with eighths played straight), the first note six bars before **6** in first violins, flute, and oboe, will be played straight, but in this interpretation it must be swung with all other similar rhythms. The only exceptions within this interpretation are the final four eighth notes preceding **6**. Even when adopting the swing approach for this passage, these four *staccato* notes should probably remain straight, as playing them swung destroys the logic of the end of this phrase. (Because it contains the same essential musical content, the passage at **11** should be played in whatever style [eighth notes swung, or not] is chosen at **5**.)

At **7**, the eighth notes are straight, differentiating them clearly from the triplets at the end of the second, fourth, sixth, and eighth bars. Even though the eighth notes at **8** are executed without swing (as in the fifth bar of the movement), the sixteenth note at the end of the third beat of each bar is swung (executed as the third part of a triplet).

Some materials contain an error in the fifth bar after **12**. The last note in the bar in first clarinet and first trumpet should be (concert) D-natural.

At **13**, it is important to observe the quarter note in the horns, as contrasted with the half note in all other instruments. The conductor should gently indicate the second beat of the bar (with the baton only) as a cut-off for the horns, while indicating with the left hand that all other instruments continue to sustain. The baton then remains inconspicuously paused in the second beat, and the *fermata* is sustained with the left hand until the piano reaches the G-flat in the middle of the bar, signaling the appropriate moment to release the orchestral chord. At that point a gentle cut-off with the left hand is all that's needed.

At **14** the musical substance is, of course, much like the material in bar 5. It is important to note, however, that here the composer indicates the tempo 𝅗𝅥 = 88, giving the passage a considerably different feel than earlier in the movement. This is yet another reason to adhere strictly to the tempo given at the beginning of the movement, in order to insure that these two passages do not have nearly identical *tempi*.

Why the composer places the words "in two" at **16** is a bit puzzling. We were already in two (since *Alla breve* at **14**) and nothing of the music at **16** implies something contrary to that.

The bar before **17**, marked *calando*, can be a bit trickier than it looks at first glance. It is not specifically this bar, but coordination in the following bar, which may cause a problem for some conductors. The possible lack of coordination at **17** is the result of the conductor not being able to accurately anticipate the degree of *rallentando* at the end of the previous bar. As the soloist executes the last two triplets, the conductor must commit to a clear and unambiguous gesture as preparation for the *pizzicato* on the following downbeat, as well as setting clear tempo for the bass clarinet, whose figures are awkward and exposed (despite being marked *pianissimo*). In order to confidently and accurately make this preparatory gesture, the conductor must be certain of the soloist's intentions as the pianist approaches the double bar. Some soloists slow nearly to a stop, lingering lovingly over the last triplet, while others, still slowing, move the triplet line more organically toward the E-flat on the following downbeat. Knowing which of these things (or perhaps some version that combines them) will occur, and using this knowledge to place the preparatory gesture accurately, is the difference between a seamless, musical result and a minor scuffle.

The new section at **20** is conducted, as indicated, in four. The eighth note in this passage is usually not swung. Whether or not the dotted eighth/sixteenth figures are played swung or as written is a subjective judgment. Playing them swung gives a natural, organic feel, as that rhythm matches the triplets appearing in the same bars (e.g., five and seven bars before **21**). On the other hand, the juxtaposition, within the same bar, of the strict dotted rhythms and the triplet has its own kind of charm.

The transition into **26** can be handled in one of two different ways, depending on the degree of *ritard* employed by the soloist. If the soloist takes a modest *ritard* then the preparatory gesture can coincide naturally with the beat directly preceding **26**. If the *ritard* is more considerable then the preparation lines up with the final eighth note before the bar-line. In either case, it is imperative that the conductor be keenly aware of the exact tempo intended by the soloist at *Pochissimo meno mosso*, as there is little or no opportunity during the first beat of the bar to comfortably adjust to an unexpected tempo, while keeping the winds and strings together with the soloist and with each other. Due to the nature and style of the music, this entire section of the piece is played with the sixteenth notes executed as written, without swing.

At **29**, the question "to swing or not to swing" rears its head once more. Here, however, the solution is fairly simple, as the decision must be the same as at **5** and **11**, whatever that may have been. To some ears, this section presents a different variable (specifically the triplets in the solo piano) that may require a different solution. Although there is a certain empirical logic to this argument, I don't agree. If the choice at **5** and **11** is to play the eighth note straight, then the addition of the triplets here is a charming rhythmic complexity that does not require changing anything else. Indeed, this is one of my favorite passages in the piece precisely because of this slightly uncomfortable rhythmic "tug" throughout. On the other hand, if the previous decision was to play the eighths swung, then that solution fits perfectly with the piano part here.

2nd movement.

While the conductor sets the general mood and tempo for the first three bars of the movement, it is best to allow the principal horn considerable freedom in the execution of the phrase generally, as long as that musician's choices are not so extravagant as to mar the opening of the movement. This approach not only contributes to a more musical, less rigid result, but allowing principal musicians to be as personally expressive as possible in solo passages contributes greatly to both general and individual musician morale.

Executing all eighth notes literally best portrays the elegiac character of the opening section of this movement. Not only does this convey the proper character, but it also allows the sixteenth notes to be played without confusion (with regard to being swung, or not; in this case, not).

The indication *poco accel.* in bar 5 is not thoroughly explained by the composer. More specifically, he doesn't really explain how we are to get out of this *accelerando*. The indication *a tempo* appears at the beginning of the following bar, but surely we are not intended to increase the tempo and then revert to the original tempo so suddenly. The conductor should either slow the pace gradually during bar 6, or slow down somewhat toward the end of bar 5 if it is deemed important to re-establish the original tempo precisely at the beginning of the next bar.

It is common to allow the principal trumpet some leeway (read "*ritard*") at the end of the seventh bar before **1**. (The same is true in later, similarly structured bars: 3 bars before 1 and 5 bars before 3.) In this case, the conductor should follow the trumpeter as a soloist (within reason). When any more than the most modest *ritard* is taken it is usually advisable to subdivide the final beat for coordination with both the fourth horn entrance and the continuation of strings into the following bar.

At 1, creating the proper atmosphere depends largely on the dynamics being precisely executed by the clarinets, basses, and solo oboe. The oboe must be allowed to play *piano*, and in order for this to be effective the clarinets and basses must play a true *pianissimo*.

Three bars before 4, the baton should flow through the third and fourth beats of the bar following the renewed tempo in the piano, but without a defined *ictus* on either beat. In the following bar, the baton shows small, sharp *icti* with virtually no rebound to facilitate accurate placement of the woodwind chords. One bar before 4, the second half of the bar is handled very differently than two bars earlier. After the soloist concludes the second beat, the baton accelerates forward toward a small but sharp *ictus* on the third beat of the bar, confidently re-establishing tempo. This gesture must be placed geographically so that it is clearly visible to the soloist, as the conductor is leading, not following, at this delicate juncture.

At 7, it is most polite and respectful to merely mark the downbeat of each bar, following the concertmaster's solo as one would any other soloist while using the left hand to encourage a beautiful sustained sound in the accompanying strings. In the fourth bar, the baton remains passively on the first beat (after marking the bar), waiting for the solo violin to arrive at the harmonic on the fourth beat. After the harmonic sounds, the conductor shows the fourth beat in the desired tempo for *Più mosso*, as preparation for the woodwinds' entrance.

At 8, as in similar music earlier in the movement, all eighth notes are executed literally. This allows the sixteenths to also be performed as written. In the fourth bar after 9, it is clearest for the trumpet and woodwinds if the final beat of the bar is subdivided, particularly because most conductors add a bit of *ritard* at this point to round out the phrase gracefully.

From this point until the middle of the first bar at 10, there is no need to mark the empty bars. Doing so, even discreetly, can distract from the focus that should be entirely on the pianist. A simple explanation in rehearsal that the next bar conducted is at 10 is sufficient to avoid any confusion. Then, at 10, after the downbeat is passively and unobtrusively marked, the baton flows with equal passivity to the left, pausing there to indicate the passage of the second beat, and finally accelerates with considerable energy and expressivity toward the third beat.

3rd movement.

The musical text in the sixteenth bar after 4 contains a discrepancy that needs to be resolved between conductor and soloist. The D-flat (second note) in the piano and the same pitch sounding simultaneously in the woodwinds are transcribed with different rhythmic values. In discussion with the soloist, a decision should be reached before the orchestra rehearsal as to which reading will be adopted.

One bar before 15, after marking the downbeat (as has already been done in each bar since 14) the baton moves almost unnoticed to the right (in the second beat position) before lifting to prepare the downbeat at 15. This is one of thousands of moments in the concerto repertoire where neither soloist nor conductor is precisely leading or following. The conductor needs to be sure to catch the eye of the soloist as the baton is raised, to allow the soloist to follow the baton. But, at the same time, the conductor follows the soloist's body language so that the downbeat is easily played together.

The solo passage occupying the twenty-two bars preceding **20** does not need to be marked bar by bar with the baton. Again, explaining to the orchestra where the next downbeat will be shown is sufficient and far less distracting.

The unexpected, enigmatic stroke of the gong one bar before **22** is a watershed moment in the work. While the conductor should never interpose himself as an actor in the drama, this is a moment in which the conductor should be particularly careful of his gestures and body language so as to avoid disturbing the moment. Once the gong sounds on the downbeat, the conductor should be completely, but unobtrusively still from head to toe. This is the kind of moment in music when the listener should be afraid to draw breath, lest one disturb so important an event. The conductor's body language should also reflect this respect for the moment, without becoming part of it or trying to add to it in any way. When the tension of the decaying gong cannot be endured any longer, the conductor, with one eye on the soloist and one on the orchestra, gives a decisive, *fortissimo* preparation for the following downbeat.

The swell from *piano* to *mezzo forte* and back to *piano* that begins four bars before the end needs to be carefully controlled, particularly as it concerns the sound cresting no higher than *mezzo forte*. The orchestra's swell should seem a caress that follows the line of the solo piano, and not a tidal wave against which the soloist must battle. This gentle swell settles comfortably back at *piano* in the penultimate bar (though the composer does not specify this dynamic), allowing for a long, slow *crescendo* toward the final chord.

☙

George Gershwin

Rhapsody in Blue

When first studying this score, one notices two unique elements in the orchestration. These elements are, of course, the inclusion of three saxophones and a banjo. In re-orchestrating this work for symphony orchestra, Grofe wisely included the saxophones so that the jazz band flavor of the original is, to some degree, preserved. In some orchestras, acquiring the saxophonists is considered a particular difficulty and/or expense. Because of this, some conductors and administrators are tempted to do without them, as there is no solo playing in these parts and virtually every note is doubled somewhere else in the orchestra. This is a very poor idea, however, as the saxophones are quite audible within the orchestral texture, and their sound is important to lending the correct atmosphere for the work. The same issue (difficulty and/or expense of acquiring personnel) is likely to be under consideration in some orchestras regarding the banjo, though here the situation is somewhat different. Though the color of the banjo adds a unique charm and character to the piece, it is by no means as essential as the saxophones. In addition, the banjo is virtually inaudible a great deal of the time (unless amplified, a choice bringing with it its own set of potential problems), and it can be quite difficult in some cities to locate a banjo player who can read music and follow a conductor.

Continuing the discussion from the previous chapter regarding rhythmic execution (specifically, “to swing, or not to swing”), the entire opening passage of this work (as well as other similar passages) should be executed with eighth notes as written.

At **12**, the composer writes *a tempo* and *Tempo giusto*, so it is easy to overlook the fact that this moment demands a faster tempo than any in the piece up to this point. But to clarify the matter, the composer also writes 𝅗𝅥 = 76, which is likely to be a good deal faster than any previous *a tempo*. Even though Gershwin expresses the tempo in relation to the half note, this passage is usually conducted in four.

Though there is not a new metronome marking, *Con moto* (at **14**) will be faster than the tempo at **12**, and is conducted in two as the composer indicates. The bar marked "Broadly" (four bars after **14**) is usually best if the beat remains in two, with a tempo that is only modestly slower; this approach keeps this particular bar from becoming a musical event of more importance than was intended. The only reason to conduct this bar in four is if the soloist insists on a tempo so slow that it becomes unmanageable in two. Conversely, the single bar marked *rubato* (five bars before **16**) is best controlled in four, returning to two in the following bar.

The only bars that need to be conducted between **18** and **22** are those containing the horn solo. The orchestra needs only the explanation that, following **18**, the short, conducted horn solo follows a brief solo piano passage, and that the next conducted passage is the pick-up to **22**.

Careful control of dynamics is of the highest importance in the passage beginning at **28**. The atmosphere, as we hear this important theme for the first time, should have not even a hint of the grandeur to come. On the contrary, part of the brilliance of this melody is that it functions here as something intimate and introspective, while later appearing as something grand and extroverted. In order to achieve this, orchestral execution with appropriately delicate sound and dynamic at **28** is paramount. In addition, it is important not to overdo the *crescendi* that begin in the third bar of each phrase.

At 28, an unprinted, but nonetheless pervasive, tradition has taken hold; this tradition involves playing the "answering" phrases in the *Andantino* section (the third through eighth bars after 28, the eleventh through fourteenth bars after 28, and the analogous passages after 29) at a tempo approximately twice as fast as the actual *Andantino* theme. As much as I dislike this tradition (mostly because it takes the instruction *poco rubato* and turns it into a simple mathematical doubling), this particular example can't be placed in the same category as other questionable interpretive practices that have attached themselves, kudzu-like, to significant musical works. In his recording (as pianist) of the original version, with the Paul Whiteman band, the composer makes essentially this exact doubling of time, so to say that doing so in a modern performance is somehow ridiculous or out of bounds is not fair. On the other hand, M.D. pointed out that Gershwin's piano roll rendition of the work does not double the time. In that version, the composer plays the first two bars of the *Andantino* a bit faster, so that no doubling of the tempo afterward feels necessary and the gentle push and pull of *poco rubato* is again present. Regardless of both what is above and the ubiquitous "tradition," I still prefer these passages to be played as he wrote them, *poco rubato*, with a gentle pushing forward of the tempo (beginning at *Andantino*) followed by a logical pulling back.

For practical balance with the piano, the dynamics beginning in the third bar after 30 usually need to be altered somewhat. The beginning of this bar needs to be adjusted downward to approximately *mezzo piano*, with each of the following swells cresting at no more than *mezzo forte*. Otherwise, the pianist is performing for no one but himself.

While it is not universal, it is quite common for the pianist to add a short *pausa*, just enough to place the hands, on the bar-line preceding 34. When this is the case, coordination at the following downbeat is quite easy. When the pianist goes forward without this breath the conductor can place the downbeat based on the pacing of the preceding triplets.

It is most dramatically effective if there is no silence (or virtually none) on the bar-line at **37**. Gershwin and/or Grofe went out of the their way here to make sure that almost no instruments sustaining the *fermata* before **37** are playing on the following downbeat. This allows for at least the possibility of a clean, strong entrance at **37** without any real need for extra space that was not requested.

The four thirty-second notes that precede **39** are often executed as four sixteenth notes in the new, *Grandioso* tempo, rather than exactly as written. There are reasonable arguments for each solution, and each conductor must adopt the one that makes the most musical sense to him. Clearly, the first reason to play the downward scale as thirty-second notes (in the new tempo) is simply because that's what is in the score. Although it is not marked in the score in this way, it is reasonable to assume that the scale before the bar-line belongs in the new tempo, as it is clearly part of the next section of the piece. Also, playing it as written with a headlong, downward rush lasting only one-half of a beat creates a very exciting moment, propelling us into the *Grandioso* passage. Reasons to play this scale as though they are sixteenths (in the new tempo) include (1) that the *ritard* of the preceding several bars makes sixteenth-notes in the new tempo virtually identical to thirty-second notes in the old tempo (a rationale that is not entirely convincing to me, personally, but is certainly very creative), and (2) that the motion of sixteenths better reflects the overall rhythmic structure of the passage it introduces (again, creative but not thoroughly convincing). This discussion may seem strangely familiar even to those who are studying this piece in depth for the first time. If so, it is probably because the issue so closely resembles the never-ending conversation regarding the four thirty-second notes at the end of the introduction to the first movement of Beethoven Symphony No. 1. There, also, it can be said that there are reasonable arguments on both sides, but that's an entirely different book.

The *tutti* triplet that functions as the pick-up to *Molto allargando* (last beat of the first bar at **40**) can be taken in one gesture if the desired result is to press the triplet forward with energy moving toward the downbeat, or subdivided into three parts if the desired expression is to achieve more dramatic emphasis on each chord. The decision is entirely a matter of the result desired by the conductor and soloist.

Both three bars and two bars before the end, only the downbeats need to be marked with the baton. After arriving at the *forte/piano* on the downbeat three bars before the end, the baton can remain motionless while only the left hand traces the arc of the *crescendo-diminuendo* figure. This effect should climax at no more than *mezzo forte* before beginning its decline, to be certain that the solo piano is always heard clearly. When the piano arrives at the downbeat of the penultimate bar, the baton clearly but gently marks this event, again remaining motionless afterward, while the conductor's left hand and general body language convey the *crescendo* toward the final downbeat. The preparatory gesture for the final downbeat can be placed with the fourth beat of the penultimate bar if the pianist remains reasonably in tempo across the final bar-line. However, if the penultimate bar contains considerable *allargando*, especially in the third and fourth beats, then the preparatory gesture is given after the fourth beat, as a quick, out-of-tempo gesture, while maintaining eye contact with the soloist.

ೞ

Edvard Grieg

Piano Concerto in A Minor, Op. 16

1st movement.

The *tutti* chord in the second bar should be played only *forte*, as marked, and with appropriate attention to creating a beautiful and majestic opening for the work. The common, ungainly "thump" that is the result of the chord being overplayed should be avoided.

In bars seven through ten, the printed articulation is rarely played as marked. The string figures here are most effective when played exactly as the composer asked, with the quarter notes *staccato*, exactly the same length as the eighth notes. (M.D. also mentions that he appreciates it when the orchestra plays the rhythm of this theme precisely, with an exact sixteenth note following the dotted eighth note, with no "over-dotting" or "double dotting," since that is how he will play it at A.)

At B it is most in keeping with the new theme in the piano for the string articulation to be quite *legato*, with essentially no space at all between the eighth notes. This articulation allows the oboe and piano to be highlighted while keeping the string sound unobtrusively in the background.

In the fourth bar after C a slight subdivision on the fourth beat of the bar is not only very helpful for the strings (as a cut-off), but also helps to accurately set up the new, slightly faster tempo in the following bar.

Twenty bars before E (and following) the choice of articulation for the triplets in the violins is a matter of taste. I prefer that this be played on the string, well into the upper half of the bow, as this provides a more subtle and delicate accompaniment. As the *crescendo* grows a few bars later, I ask the strings to move more to the middle of the bow, still staying on the string but becoming slightly more separated.

Six bars before the *cadenza* (one bar before the key change), it is very important that the conductor have the soloist's intentions well in mind. If the soloist moves forward through the fourth beat with relatively little *rallentando* then the conductor can show the preparation precisely where the pianist plays the fourth beat. On the other hand, if the pianist takes substantial time with the last beat, the last three notes in particular, then the preparation needs to wait until the pianist is already executing those last three notes. Otherwise the conductor risks a preparatory gesture that is out of tempo and lacking in clarity.

The orchestral entrance following the *cadenza* is marked *Tempo I*, but in spite of this clear instruction many conductors take these four bars at a tempo closer to *Lento*. In addition to setting a mood that is unnecessarily funereal, the result of this choice is either that the following *Poco più allegro* is too slow (a situation that M.D. mentions he appreciates not having to deal with) or that the tempo change is not "a little" but a lot faster. The tempo shift here should feel fairly subtle, and this is not possible when the *Tempo I* passage is played too slowly.

The *forte-piano* in the strings two bars before *Poco più allegro* should be handled gently. Even the marking *forte-piano*, which seems to imply specific dynamics (namely *forte*), should be executed relative to the surrounding dynamics and, in particular, the overall musical context. As I'm fond of saying to orchestras in a moment like this one, this *forte-piano* should have the effect of a sigh, or a gentle embrace, not a sharp stick in the eye.

M.D. particularly asked me to call to the attention of younger conductors the *diminuendo* in the orchestra seven bars before the end. For less experienced orchestral musicians, the soloist's simultaneous, rocketing *crescendo* can be the cause of, as Alan Greenspan put it, "irrational exuberance."

2nd movement.

In the opening orchestral passage of this movement it is very important that the dynamics be adhered to strictly (in terms of their placement in the bar), and that they not be overplayed. On the latter subject, clearly the zenith of each expressive *crescendo-diminuendo* cannot be more than *mezzo-piano*, at the very most, as a dynamic higher than this risks making a caricature of this extraordinary moment. In terms of placement in the bar, the conductor (and the orchestral musicians) should look carefully for the point in each bar where the zenith occurs. (Some scores and parts are poorly laid out in this regard, and may need to be corrected and/or clarified.) For example, in both the first and second bars, the climax is on the second beat, meaning that the entirety of the second beat is in *diminuendo*, and this is by no means clear in all materials. Perhaps more important, however, is the execution of these figures. It is the downward slope of each of these *crescendo-diminuendo* combinations in which the true beauty of the phrase is to be found, and musicians often need to be encouraged to give as much intellectual and physical effort to the *diminuendo* as they do to the *crescendo*.

The *forte-piano* eight bars before **A** should be played with some delicacy. This is not only because it is proper under the musical circumstance, but also so that it is starkly differentiated in orchestral color (and volume) from the *sforzato* that appears ten bars before the end of the movement. In the latter instance, the narrative has risen to a highly dramatic pitch, and in the former it is only a hint of emotions yet to come.

Three bars before the end of the movement it is most effective to subdivide the triplet for the horn. This allows for maximum flexibility in coordinating the horn with both the conclusion of the grace notes in the piano and the downbeat in the strings. A slight lifting of the sound before the final downbeat adds considerable emotion and charm to the conclusion. Such noticeable breaks should not, therefore, be made between each of the notes in the penultimate bar, as this creates a phrase that is pedantic and unnecessarily lumpy.

3rd movement.

Grieg's omission of a "final" bar-line at the end of the second movement, giving us only a double bar and the key change, clearly indicates that we are to move on to the finale without any unnecessary pause. The *fermata* on the double bar gives us a chance for a settling breath following the cut-off, but no more.

The twenty-seven-note scale in the bar before *Poco animato* can be handled a number of ways, and it is very important that the conductor know ahead of time what the soloist plans to do. Some pianists take this bar entirely *a piacere*, without any real sense of relationship to the original, or the following, tempo. When this is the case, the conductor must be guided by the general pacing of the scale, and by the proximity to the bottom A-natural, in deciding when to begin the preparatory gesture. Other soloists organize the bar for themselves in either three or four beats (on odd occasions, two beats) of the *Poco animato* tempo. (M.D. counsels both conductors and pianists that "three beats are best.")

Likewise, the bar before **A** is generally executed in three beats of the prevailing tempo. Assuming this is the case, the conductor must discipline herself not to indicate a bar containing three beats, but should show only the downbeat (as the last in a series of *ictus*-less passive gestures that indicate "empty" bars) and the preparation for the following downbeat. (M.D. offers, "If the pianist insists on playing this bar in a different way ... just tell him '*do it in three beats*!' " His point is well-taken, but, as always, younger conductors should consider to whom they are speaking before giving instructions.) All of this is similarly applicable to the bar before **F**.

Bringing the orchestra back in after the short *cadenza*-like passage seventeen bars after **C** is considerably less daunting than it may appear. The final two octaves of the upward scale generally take exactly two beats in tempo. As such, they offer an easy opportunity for placement of the preparatory gesture, on the G-sharp at the beginning of the final octave.

At **E**, the (extremely *pianissimo*) entrance of the strings should be coordinated with the top note of the arpeggio in the piano. Knowing this, the conductor should not indicate the second beat of the previous bar where it is played in the piano, or he risks an endless, meaningless upward gesture. After passively marking the downbeat of the bar before **E**, the baton should remain motionless until the soloist has begun the arpeggio at **E**. Then, a fairly quick but delicate preparation is all that is necessary for both good coordination and appropriate atmosphere.

In like manner, the string chords found two bars and four bars before *Tempo I, animato* should coordinate with the top note of the soloist's arpeggio. Usually this means that the preparatory gesture coordinates (roughly) with the bottom note of the arpeggio.

If the passage two bars before **H** becomes too blurred (due to pedaling and/or hall acoustics) for the conductor to accurately follow the progress of the sextuplets to a coordinated downbeat at **H**, then he will find it helpful here (and in hundreds of other passages in the repertoire) to turn and directly observe the soloist's hands. This should be done with some subtlety, turning the body the least amount possible, and being careful to keep the baton in roughly its normal position so as not to hide the beat from the right side of the orchestra.

In the empty bar preceding *Quasi presto*, the conductor should give a quick look to make certain he has the soloist's eyes before proceeding to the preparation and downbeat. It is usually best here if the conductor leads.

In this next section, the conductor must carefully show the first *arco* entrance of the strings. Both the five-bar introduction (instead of the expected four) and the fact that the strings enter on the fourth bar of a phrase (rather than in the following first bar of a new sub-phrase) places all responsibility on the conductor to be clear and confident.

Achieving precise execution (in the violins) of the passage found four and five bars before the end may take a moment of rehearsal. These figures are both strictly *misurato*, but are based in entirely different mathematics from one another. Some violin sections need to be cautioned to prepare the mathematics properly in order to cleanly and clearly execute the strict thirty-second notes four bars before the end after playing the quarter-note triplets (each divided into four parts) five bars before the end. This is a truly wonderful effect when executed precisely and with a minimum of *ritard* or unwritten *rubato*, and it is excruciating both musically and visually when done poorly. (M.D. adds, and I concur, that in the coda of the work [from **K** to the end] nothing is gained by a tempo that is slower than the composer indicated and/or one that is constantly slowing from **K** to the end. On the contrary, a good part of the nobility of this passage is found in its masculine forthrightness and lack of syrupy excess. After all, the composer gives us both a metronome marking he desires and, much more importantly, the relationship between the previous tempo and this one [𝅗𝅥. = ♩], so there is no reason not to take him at his word.)

Aram Khachaturian

Piano Concerto

1st movement.

The fact that the composer marks the opening bass drum solo *fortississimo* is not to be taken lightly. This brutal, violent opening to the work should nearly shock members of the audience out of their seats. Although the value given to this note is a dotted half, I prefer for the percussionist to dampen the sound after the initial impact, rather than letting it ring, as this adds additional weight and drama to this already rather shocking moment.

Many of the quarter notes in the first ten bars (violins and viole in bars 2 and 3, and winds bars 6 through 10) are not marked with any specific articulation, and the angular nature of the music may tempt musicians to play them *staccato* or nearly so. The drama and heft of the music are best served, however, if these figures are played with considerable weight, as though with dashes, not dots, with a slight separation between each note.

The severity of the opening of the work should not be diminished by the orchestra's marking of *mezzo piano* at the entrance of the solo piano. The conductor should be careful of two issues here: first, that the strings do not play too softly at bar 11 in a misguided effort to "accompany" and, second, that the muscular character of the opening ten bars of this passage is not emasculated by an overly precious approach to the sound at bar 11. This latter issue is partly a subjective matter of sound production and partly the quality of the *staccato* quarter notes remaining quite *secco*.

At bar 20, the celli and basses may need to be cautioned to play precisely the rhythm in their parts, and not to imitate the similar, but not identical rhythm in the upper strings. The completely *legato* line in the low strings, lacking the rests found in violins and viole, better communicates both the *crescendo* and the drama in this bar. The same situation can be found in bars 35 and 316.

The quarter notes in the strings from bar 42 to bar 45 are not marked *staccato*, as they are earlier in the movement. Following (here) the famous axiom of law that "the absence of one thing implies the presence of others" (that is, implies the presence of its opposite), we should feel free to have these quarter notes played quite long, as this *sostenuto* style better supports the piano's sound. This is also true in the upper strings when playing the melody at bar 46. Here the eighth notes have no articulations at all, but the presence of slurs in the same material in the woodwinds compels us (in my opinion) to play this passage completely *legato*.

Many of the eighth notes in bars 50 and 52 (violins, viole, and woodwinds) have no articulations. To aid in the penetration of the sound through the brass and solo piano, as well as to heighten the drama, I ask that these eighth notes be played extremely *staccato*. (Unfortunately, this seems to violate the principle to which I referred in the previous paragraph, but nearly all musical decisions are subjective within the context of the musical moment at hand.)

Bar 59 contains a misprint in the celli and/or basses in some materials. All three notes in this bar should be B-flats, although some parts show some or all of the pitches as A-natural.

It is curious that in bar 60 the clarinet is marked *forte* while the flute and oboe have *mezzo-forte* remaining from two bars earlier. This may be because the composer wanted to make certain that the upper octaves did not too severely dominate in this woodwind trio, or it may simply be an error. Subdividing the last beat of this bar helps to create a pleasing conclusion to the phrase, but is by no means absolutely necessary. Following the final notes of the bar, the conductor should not proceed to the following downbeat, but should allow the baton to remain suspended following the final beat. Once the pianist begins the following passage, the baton can begin to gently mark the bars that follow. In this way the conductor does not allow his movement to intrude on the silence indicated by the breath mark.

Some conductors, as well as a few pianists, insist that the metric relationship between bars 71 and 72 is ♩. (in bar 71) = ♩ (in bar 72), but this makes absolutely no sense whatsoever. First, this solution makes the transition into bar 73 quite awkward, as that relationship could no longer be ♩ = ♩., as it clearly must be. Second, this idea contradicts the entire rhythmic set-up of the rest of the movement.

In bars 74 and 75, a more exciting shape can be made of the three note phrases in the strings by placing a slight breath mark after each quarter note. As before, the eighth notes (and, of course, the quarter notes) are played completely *legato*, but with a somewhat physical, slightly *marcato* attitude.

Though one does not wish to make a major issue of it from the audience's perspective, it is important to clearly indicate the second beat of bar 86, so that the viole and celli are not left to fend for themselves. These same string sections should be cautioned not to accent this second beat, as drawing attention to this rhythm was surely not the composer's intention. These instruments join the *tremolo* chord on the second beat only because they needed to complete their previous descending line, not because the composer wanted to hear the chord re-attacked on the second beat. A complete lift of the sound is appropriate at the end of bar 87, preceding the significant dynamic change in the following bar. During bars 88 and/or 89, it is advisable to make eye contact with the bass clarinetist, as she plays for the first time in the piece in bar 90.

The eighth notes in bars 100 and 101 should be played long, as indicated, but with a slight separation and always with *vibrato*.

In the passage from bar 106 to bar 113 the celli are marked "2 soli," but following the composer's directions precisely is not a good idea. As a young conductor, I received some very fine advice from the veteran conductor and teacher, and consummate gentleman, Paul Vermel, on this subject. He suggested, as others have, that the *only* number of strings that one wants to avoid playing the same part is two. In case the reasons for this are not obvious, we should explore them briefly. Two strings alone will sound to the listener as two solo voices, and except in the case of truly extraordinary players and/or incredibly simple music, they will never be absolutely in tune with one another. Three or more players, however, begin to take on the characteristic of an orchestral string section, where minor disagreements in intonation begin to disappear to the ear through the perception of an aggregate pitch. The *vibrato* of multiple players also tends to mask intonation disagreements, while the differing vibrato of only two players can sound quite jarring. In the particular instance under consideration, there is also the chromatic nature and rather high register of the passage to be considered, making it all the less likely that two celli will play perfectly in tune with one another. For all these reasons, it is best to have either three celli or one solo cello play this passage.

It is neither necessary nor musically appropriate to take any *ritardando* in bar 116. The charm of the moment is found in the surprising, sudden interruption of the phrase. Hinting at this interruption beforehand by adding a *ritard* ruins the surprise.

For no reasons other than personal preference, I ask the violins to add the following articulation details: bars 231, 233, and 245, completely *legato*; bar 237, the A-sharp *staccato*.

The six successive down-bows in all strings in bars 238 and 239 are missing in some parts. When they are missing (or have been changed in the bowing process by principal players) I strongly suggest that they be added back, as they add an irreplaceable moment of drama that is otherwise missing.

Though some concertmasters and/or conductors insist on changing it, there is no reason not to follow the composer's articulation and bowing instructions at bars 292 and 301. At bar 292 he specifically asks for a *ricochet* bowing, three notes per bow (not two notes *ricochet* down-bow and the third note up-bow, as some insist). At bar 301 he specifically asks for the similar figure to be played with separate bows, and there is no reason not to take him at his word.

Bars 307 through 309 are, again, a passage where the composer leaves us without concrete information about articulation. Without evidence to the contrary, the violins should play completely *legato* through the downbeat of bar 310. Bars 310 through 313, however, are most dramatic when the quarter notes are played with a slight space between them, as though there is a dash on each quarter note.

Complete *legato* is called for in violins and viole in bars 334 to 337. (In some scores, the bar numbers are incorrect here.) This entirely lyrical approach acts as a musical counterbalance to the angular nature of the figure in the solo piano.

It is of particular note that there is no *diminuendo* written in the celli or bass parts in bars 345 and 346. Nonetheless, both the *ritardando* and, more importantly, the transition to the following *pianissimo* passage suggest that adding a *diminuendo* is appropriate and more musical. On the other hand, allowing the basses to continue *fortissimo* through the downbeat of bar 347 has its own unique and quirky charm. I have done it both ways in different performances, but remain unconvinced that either is necessarily a superior reading.

In order to execute bars 366 and 370 exactly as written, the third beat should be subdivided. By doing so, the celli are able to sustain (along with the piano) while the upper strings are released as indicated, leaving the mild discomfort of the exposed 9th clearly audible without the softening quality of the rest of the string harmony.

In the passage from bar 391 to bar 400, the same principle that was discussed above with regard to the celli applies here to the basses. Though the intonation dangers are by no means as thorny here (as there is only one pitch in the passage), it is still better to use three basses rather than two. Though the articulation in the basses should be completely *legato*, a bit of extra bow speed at the beginning of each new note helps to define the rhythm, and keeps the listener from thinking that this is just one long note that lasts for eleven bars.

Some soloists make a slight pause at the end of bar 480 before proceeding to the downbeat at *Tempo I*. When this is the case, coordination with the soloist is not an issue. However, in the less common circumstance that the soloist continues in tempo, the easiest manner of coordinating with the piano is by thinking harmonically, rather than metrically. Following the whole-tone scales in D-flat in the left hand (three complete octaves followed by a final four-note fragment, beginning on the third beat of bar 477) is the most logical way to arrive in coordination with the piano at the downbeat of bar 481. When the soloist *does* make a slight pause before attacking bar 481, then the conductor can also utilize the rhythm of the passage for good coordination. In this case, there are usually four even beats, each beginning on a D-flat. The beats will usually be of nearly equal duration because, even though the final (fourth) scale is only two-thirds the length of the previous three, the addition of the slight pause makes up the additional time, making the four scales (each beginning on D-flat) of approximately equal duration.

The passage from bar 481 through bar 486 is another which, lacking specifics of both articulation and phrasing, requires the conductor's input for uniformity of expression. I ask the upper strings and winds to place a comma following the third beat of each bar, setting off each bar as an individual sub-phrase.

For similar reasons, I ask for a breath mark to be placed at the end of the fourth bar before the end of the movement. In the penultimate bar, the conductor should resist the temptation to add any *rallentando*. On the contrary, the muscular nature of the final statement of the theme requires that the tempo drive relentlessly through to the final bar.

2nd movement.

At the opening of the movement (as well as in similar passages throughout this movement), the intended articulation for the upper strings needs clarification from the conductor. The quarter notes with dashes, three notes per bow, can be reasonably interpreted as long notes with a bit of space between them, or as completely *legato*. I always ask the strings to play completely *legato* in this and all similar passages in this movement, as any space between the quarter notes creates an unnecessarily "lumpy" accompaniment for the bass clarinet and, later, for the solo piano. On the contrary, the goal for this passage should be to create a texture that is seamless and effortless.

The passage from bar 49 to bar 80, featuring the flexatone solo, is one of the most unique and mysterious moments in the concerto literature. This passage does, however, present a number of issues to be resolved by the conductor. First is the question of whether or not this solo was really intended for the flexatone in the first place. It has been suggested that the designation of this instrument was an error on the part of the original editor, and that the instrument played at the premiere was, in fact, a musical saw. We may never know for certain, but performance of this passage on a bowed saw does create a more singing line, removing from the equation the sound of the strikers on the flexatone. Whether one chooses to use a saw or a flexatone, the next issue to confront is that of balance. For the flexatone (or saw) to have any chance of being heard clearly over the rest of the ensemble, all other instruments (including the solo piano) must play strictly *pianissimo*. Even when this is done, hearing the flexatone (or saw) as one might like is usually still a challenge. If adjustments in dynamics do not provide sufficient improvement in balance, then discreet amplification might be considered. (Having written the preceding sentence of my own free will, I must be completely honest by adding that the idea of such electronic support in an acoustic performance makes my skin crawl.) For all the reasons that make the flexatone (or saw) solo complicated in its execution, intonation, and balance, it should also be noted that some conductors have chosen to substitute either a synthesizer or a solo soprano voice. Although neither of these alternatives is by any means what the composer had in mind, either can solve the balance issue while also providing a uniquely expressive musical quality. Bypassing the obvious issue of willfully altering the composer's orchestration, the vocal alternative should only be chosen when a soprano soloist with extraordinary control of dynamics, vocal weight and color, and vibrato is available.

Two issues are worthy of notice at bar 100. First is the unique and often overlooked articulation in the first violins, where the composer places dots, not dashes, over the first two quarter notes. All too often, the articulation in this and the following bar are identical, and something much more interesting is implied by the composer's instructions. The other common error here is to mistake the indication *a tempo* for *Tempo I.* The tempo at bar 100 is the *Poco più mosso* tempo initiated in bar 84, or something reasonably like it, and the same is true for the *a tempo* indications found at bars 112 and 118. The composer carefully distinguishes these moments from the point at which the original tempo returns, where he indicates *Tempo I* at bar 126.

Pianists often take a slight pause at the end of bar 172, before placing the following downbeat. When the soloist makes this choice, the orchestra needs to work to sustain the drama by consciously continuing the *crescendo* through the soloist's pause, and being careful not to break the sound at the bar-line.

At bar 209, the composer's carefully marked dynamics need to be as carefully observed. Three different dynamics are present simultaneously, most notably the *forte* in the viole, and the moment works beautifully when everyone in the orchestra plays, as I am fond of saying, what they see and not what they hear.

Between the beginning of bar 224 and the middle of bar 229, the bass clarinetist will probably have to take an additional breath. It is important that the conductor and the bass clarinetist agree in advance on the location of this extra breath, as it may be necessary for the conductor to add some additional time at that point. Following the final note of bar 225 is one possible location for this breathing point. If this point is chosen for the breath, the conductor may elect for the strings to also place a comma in the same place in the bar, but I ask the strings to sustain the sound at the bottom of their *diminuendo* to create a more seamless moment.

Younger or less expert bass clarinetists may need to be cautioned regarding control of the pitch three bars before the end of the movement. This delicious, *pianissimo* clash between the B-flat in the bass clarinet and the A minor chords in the strings is made uncomfortable if, as sometimes happens, the B-flat leans to the lower side of the pitch. When this happens, the listener's impression may be that the bass clarinet is supposed to be playing an A-natural, coordinating with the A minor in the strings, but is rather unpleasantly sharp. Keeping the B-flat scrupulously to the high, but still accurate, side of the pitch helps to ensure that the listener immediately understands the intended pitch content of the moment.

3rd movement.

Some soloists request that the conductor make a slight *meno mosso* at bar 23. This request facilitates the figures that follow, but is usually based on the soloist's technical issues rather than musical substance. The composer specifically indicates ♪ = ♪, and changing the tempo at this moment renders nearly pointless the interesting change of meter. A better solution is to choose an opening tempo for the movement that allows for comfortable performance of the $\frac{3}{8}$ passage without a change of tempo.

It is usually best to take bar 29 in three, unless there is virtually no *ritard* at all. This choice has less to do with managing bar 29 than it has to do with placing the conductor in a position of control that allows him to be completely clear and accurate when re-establishing tempo in bar 30.

It is not terribly likely that the tuba or cymbal will miss their entrances in bars 48 and 49. However, these entrances are a bit tricky, and a look at each musician in places like this is a small part of what separates the conductors from the time-beaters.

In bars 109 through 112 there is a clear discrepancy in the articulation in flutes, oboes, and clarinets, as the sixteenth notes are without slurs in the first phrase and slurred in the second. This also raises a question of the articulation of the same passage in violins and viole. Assuming that both woodwind passages should be slurred, then the upper strings need to play the entire passage on the string.

If, however, the conductor comes to the less likely solution that the winds are to articulate (tongue separately) one phrase and slur the next, then the upper strings need to be instructed to play the first phrase off the string and the second phrase on.

The composer's indication of the tempo relationship at bar 157 is something of a mystery. The metric relationship indicated forces a logical *meno mosso* at this point, but fails to take into account the rather obvious relationship between the triplet at the end of bar 156 and triplets that follow. In order to create a musically pleasing transition, these triplets must match, taking into account the *ritard*, but this is not possible if we take Khachaturian's instruction literally. The most common solution (in fact, the only solution any soloist has ever utilized in a performance I have conducted) is to allow the new tempo to flow naturally from the *poco ritard*, with a ♩ = ♩ relationship, thus allowing the triplets to match across the bar-line.

The dynamics for solo winds between bar 304 and bar 336 may need some adjustment. The composer's goal is clearly to create a kind of echo effect between the first solo of each passage (horn at bar 304 and bassoon at bar 317) and what follows (clarinet at bar 307 and oboe at bar 320), which is why he marks the first solo at a higher dynamic than the second. Unfortunately, this effect doesn't really work in live performance because none of the woodwind solos will be heard at all over the solo piano unless they play *forte* or *fortissimo*. So the idea of downward terraced dynamics is rather impractical unless the soloist wants to play *mezzo piano*. In reality, all the woodwinds need to play *forte*, but the horn can play closer to *mezzo forte*, if desired, in order to balance the other solos.

During a break in a rehearsal for this work in Las Vegas, our very attentive apprentice conductor was pointing out to the soloist and me a few spots that needed balance attention. He specifically pointed out the *Maestoso* passage at bar 348 as being a problem in terms of hearing the solo piano. The pianist, Fabio Bidini, shrugged and laughed, as I think I did, too. And we told our apprentice conductor not to worry about it. Though we always want to be attentive to balance between soloist and orchestra, even when the major musical material is in the orchestra, this is one of those relatively rare moments where we have to throw caution (that is, our concern for balance) to the wind or risk losing the excitement of the piece. If the pianist cannot be heard well, or perhaps at all, between bars 348 and 359, then that's an acceptable sacrifice for the greater good.

In order to achieve the required weight of sound in bars 396 and 397 (and similar bars following), the violins and viole should play vigorously on the string. In the bars of static sixteenth notes between these passages (such as bars 398 through 402) the second violins and viole can be effective either on or off the string, but this decision changes the resulting sound of the passage, and therefore its intensity, quite significantly. Even if the sixteenth notes in passages like bar 408 (and following) are played off the string, it still leads to a more dramatic and better unified ensemble result if they are played strictly on the string beginning at bar 416.

☙

Franz Liszt

Piano Concerto No. 1 in E-Flat Major

In my conversation with M.D. about this concerto, he began by reflecting on the larger picture. I never fail to be amazed at how important it is to periodically step back from both the hectic schedule and the minute focuses of a life in music to appreciate and remember why we are doing this in the first place. While it is true that one of his first comments to me about this work had to do with a nuts-and-bolts sort of subject—"Not unlike Grieg, I try to remove the clichés and get back to the text"—his very first words were far more inspiring: "This piece has a special place for me. When I was twelve I had a record of this piece, and I sat listening to it day after day, thinking, 'I want to be a pianist.'"

Allegro maestoso. Tempo giusto.

After sustaining the *fermata* in the second bar, the next gesture with the baton is the upward gesture (fourth beat) as preparation for the following bar. Though the situation in bar 4 may appear to be the same, it is not. The cut-off for this *fermata* should be given with the left hand, while the baton lifts without *ictus* (as if in the fourth beat) and pauses, waiting for the (sometimes delayed) entrance of the piano. When the piano sounds the first beat of bar 5, the baton drops to indicate the downbeat (still without *ictus*), showing the second beat of the bar (in coordination with the piano) with considerable energy as preparation for the chord on the third beat.

Some conductors become perplexed during the end of the first *cadenza*, directly before **A**, and this confusion or hesitation can lead to a poor result in the first bar at **A**. What may, at first glance, seem chaotic in the final sub-bar before **A** (the passage between the fifth dotted bar-line before **A** and **A**) is, in fact, a well-organized passage containing ten distinct beats. These ten beats are neatly divided by the composer into five groups of two, each group separated by a dotted bar-line. Each of the ten "beats" contains four sonorities in the left hand, each one answered in the right hand. When this structure, and its attendant set of harmonies, is thoroughly analyzed and understood, this passage is not particularly difficult to follow with the ear, even when performed at considerable velocity.

Though it usually does not sound this way in practice, it is easiest for the conductor to hear the scale in the third bar after **A** as containing four beats. The first "beat" begins with the first note (C-natural in the right hand) and contains the first nine notes of the scale. Beats 2, 3, and 4 each begin on E-flat and contain one octave of the E-flat major scale. It is usually possible to place the preparation for the following bar on the E-flat that begins the fourth and final "beat" of this scale. (M.D. mentions that he thinks of the first three "beats" in this scale beginning on each of the C-naturals [in the right hand], with the fourth "beat" beginning on the D-natural nine notes before the end of the scale.)

It is not particularly difficult to get out of the brief *cadenza* that follows (the eighth bar after **A**). It is necessary, however, to be certain of the soloist's intentions regarding the *fermata* just before the end of the bar. Some soloists take a true *fermata* here, and others take essentially the equivalent of a double-dotted eighth rest, creating one complete beat when combined with the final thirty-second note. In the latter case, the conductor can comfortably show the preparation on the rest, allowing the soloist to follow the baton, flowing forward naturally into the cadence. If the soloist observes the *fermata* more literally, then the preparatory gesture is shown after that brief silence, usually following the pianist's body language.

Following the next four-bar phrase, it is important to continue to passively mark each bar for the orchestra, as the following entrances (between this point and **B**) can be a bit confusing. The baton marks one bar for the short *cadenza* (the thirteenth bar after **A**) and one more for the following bar as the piano begins the triplets in the right hand. In order to be certain that the principal clarinet is not confused, it is polite (in addition to making clear eye contact with the clarinetist at the beginning of the bar) to passively show the first two beats in the bar where the clarinet solo begins, with the third beat being a more active, preparatory gesture.

Likewise, several bars later, the soli first violins need eye contact one full bar before their entrance. It is usually inadvisable to follow the composer's instructions precisely here with regard to the number of violins playing this passage. (See page 59 for a more thorough discussion of this subject.) For this passage I have always used either three or four players, depending upon the acoustics of the hall and the playing style and weight of sound of the particular soloist.

Although it is only marked *A tempo*, at **B** the soloist usually launches immediately into a tempo that is markedly faster than any tempo up to this point in the movement. For perfect coordination with the second violins and viole (and all that follows) the conductor must not only remember the tempo that is likely to be taken by the soloist, but also listen carefully for the placement of the first three sixteenth notes (leading up to C-sharp in the right hand) to feel the exact pulse and placement of the second beat of the bar.

Just after **B** we find the indication *poco a poco stringendo*, leading to *animato* in the eighth bar. This surely implies that once we reach the eighth bar after **B** the tempo is to remain constant through, and beyond, the key change eight bars later. In reality, however, by the time the key change is reached (or just before that) most soloists desire a tempo that is faster than the one that concluded the *stringendo*. This simply means that the *stringendo* is continued after passing *animato*, usually requiring a beat in two approximately four bars before the key change.

The parenthetic indication *a tempo* in the fifth bar after **C** would be better stated as *Tempo I*. This passage (usually conducted in four) is clearly to be played at the tempo of the fourth bar after **A**, where similar music occurs.

Quasi Adagio.

To begin the second movement, it is not necessary to show any beats in the first bar other than the rebound of the third beat, as preparation for the entrance of the celli and basses on the fourth beat. However, when conducting less-experienced musicians it may important to explain that the celli/bass entrance occurs on the final beat of the first measure, and is not a pick-up into the first printed measure, so that musicians counting bars of rests at the opening of the passage are not constantly one bar behind in their counting. However the opening bars are handled, it is polite to clearly prepare and show the entrance of upper strings to alleviate any possible insecurity or confusion.

Obviously, it is unnecessary to any show beats other than the first beat of the bars in the *recitative* section that contain only sustained or *tremolo* chords. While following the soloist's *recitative* with the ear and marking the start of each bar with the baton, it is useful to keep the left hand involved (in a sustaining gesture) so that the drama of the tremolo and the sustained quality of the wind chord do not lose energy. In the passage beginning eight bars before **E**, it is crucial that every cue be given clearly. By this point in the *recitative* it is not uncommon for even experienced musicians to be second-guessing themselves and clear eye contact for celli and basses, oboes, clarinets, and second horn will be gratefully received.

In the second bar of **E**, coordinating the beginning of the flute phrase with the piano is by no means difficult, but requires a clear decision beforehand as to who is leading and who is following. It is really easiest if the conductor leads with a clear third beat and the soloist follows. However, if the soloist insists on leading, then he must lead with unambiguous body language that will allow the conductor to cue the flutist with no misunderstandings or unnecessary stress.

M.D. mentions, and I agree, the regrettable contemporary habit of doubling the tempo at the flute entrance. It is entirely possible, far more musical, and much more in keeping with the composer's instructions (or lack thereof) to find one tempo that suits both the preceding five bars of piano solo *and* the passage that begins with the flute solo. Clearly, the solution is for the pianist to take those preceding five bars somewhat less ponderously, allowing the following passage to flow forward at an unhurried *Andante* or *Andantino*, still in four. Pursuant to our conversation about this concerto, M.D. wrote me a note (intended, I believe, for the reader) that said, "Be the only conductor in the world to point out to the soloist that no *più mosso* is indicated for the entire section in C major and E major!!"

Allegretto vivace.

Selecting a tempo for this section can, in some cases, be a matter of deft negotiation. Many pianists want to perform this music considerably faster than the *pizzicato* triplets in the strings can possibly be played cleanly and clearly. (M.D. wrote in a note to me, "Point out to the soloist that it's not Allegro!"—and his point is well taken.) The best that can be done is to attempt to find a tempo that will reasonably suit all parties, as it is unfair to the orchestra to force upon them a tempo at which the notes cannot possibly be played accurately, simply to make the pianist happy. In order to facilitate both balance and velocity, some conductors have the first violins play the passage at **G** *arco* and *spiccato*, rather than *pizzicato* as indicated. When this change is made, the same change should be made (in first violins only) for the four bars beginning with the fourth bar after **H**. Though it may be tempting to conduct some parts of this section in one, it is usually most effective for good ensemble when the conductor stays in a small, controlled, elegant three throughout.

Once the soloist selects a tempo at *Allegro animato*, the conductor must continue in that tempo through the music at **J** (**I** in some materials), no matter what that tempo may be. Sometimes the tempo selected by the soloist does not take into consideration the musical or technical demands of the orchestral material at **J**, and M.D. suggests that the conductor clearly, but politely ask the pianist to take a tempo that allows **J** to be played *L'istesso tempo*.

The tenth bar after **J** is, of course, *subito meno mosso* and conducted in four. Twenty-two bars after **J**, or fairly soon thereafter depending on the pace of the *più animato*, the conductor will want to find his way into two. Four bars before the end of the movement one may wish to go back into four, even though there is no change in tempo, as the drama and articulation are enhanced by this choice.

Allegro marziale animato.

Unlike the beginning of the *Quasi Adagio* section, it is important to discreetly mark the downbeat of the first bar before gently preparing the third beat for the pianist and cueing the viole and winds on the following beat.

Even though it seems to have become a tradition, there is no reason for the orchestral material in the first six bars of **K** to be played in *allargando*. It seems to me that continuing in tempo keeps the excitement of the passage alive and does not inhibit the *strepitoso* feeling that the pianist is trying to achieve in each answering phrase. M.D. concurs.

At *a tempo* in the fourteenth bar after **K** one may choose to beat in two, as the tempo and the orchestral figures that follow flow together better in this way, and don't require beating in four. At **M**, as earlier, some conductors choose to have the first violins play *arco* rather than *pizzicato*, for balance with the piano and to accommodate the velocity of the triplets.

Four bars before the end, it is important that the figure in flutes, piccolo, and violins (in the first three beats of the bar) be played precisely as sixteenth notes, as written, so that it matches the final four sixteenths without hesitation. To accentuate this figure and foster better rhythmic accuracy in the violins, I ask them to slur the first twelve notes of the bar together (down-bow), then slur together the final four sixteenths plus the first note of the following bar in one up-bow.

ꕥ

Witold Lutoslawski

Paganini Variations for Solo Piano and Orchestra

I am very much indebted to the great pianist Vladimir Viardo for providing me with my first opportunity to perform this piece. With a concert already scheduled that included its more famous cousin (Rachmaninoff), Vladimir suggested that we remove the planned opening orchestral piece and instead play this work, following the Rachmaninoff, to close the first half of the program. While this piece has certainly been programmed in this fashion many times before, it was Vladimir's particular fondness for this composition that led me to program it for the first time. This seemingly unlikely pairing of two pieces based so literally on the same theme and utilizing the same form seems somehow wrong in theory, but works beautifully in practice.

Though it will be quite apparent to any conductor studying the work for the first time, one of the more difficult things about score study in this piece (and conducting it in performance) is the rather frustrating way that the full score is presented on the page. (I refer here to the Chester/Hansen score; CH55770.) Because of this problem, no matter how one usually marks one's scores during study, one should be particularly careful here to mark cues and other important indications with great care and clarity for easy location of these items under real rehearsal and performance conditions. The first and most easily remedied of these issues is the fact that the frequently recurring four-bar repeats are quite difficult to see at first glace, and are therefore easily missed when the eye is moving quickly across the page. While the form makes no sense without them, that doesn't mean that, in performance, one could not easily move the eye forward before realizing the mistake. Marking them clearly by hand will, of course, solve the problem. The other score layout issue will take quite a bit more time and busy-work to overcome. This is (as is obvious at first glance) the annoying habit of leaving empty space in the score (instead of continuing to show each empty bar in the line with a whole rest) and then dropping in a new, partial line at mid-system. See, for example, pages 4 and 5. On page 4, the brass are dropped in at mid-page, the strings are taken out, and bassoons and harp are dropped in for a few bars each, making the entire thing look like some sort of architectural drawing. On page 5, however, lies the real danger, as the indentation of the strings by one bar, combined with the lack of vertical lines that visually create one system, makes it entirely likely that, under the stress of performance, one will see the woodwinds, harp, and solo piano as one system and the strings as the next system. Again, some busy work with a pencil fixes all of this, but that really isn't supposed to be our job. I'm sure the copyist thought he was doing us a favor by removing all those annoying, empty bars, but he wasn't. This "help" by the copyist is rather similar to being presented with a score that is entirely at concert pitch. Some less experienced composers (and some publishers) apparently think that it will be helpful to the conductor if he doesn't have to deal with all those annoying transposing instruments. This method is, in fact, much more confusing to most of us, because we have spent so long looking at transposing instruments already transposed on the score. But I digress.

The theme and first two variations (beginning through **3**, **3** through **5**, and **5** through **7**) do not present any particular conducting or orchestral problems, and they generally flow nicely together with ease. In order to clearly establish the new tempo that begins Variation III (at **7**), it can be useful to take a slight pause on the bar-line. If this approach is chosen, the baton pauses on the second beat of the bar preceding **7**, without rebound, then lifts (after a moment's pause, perhaps roughly equal to one extra beat) to give the preparation in the new tempo.

In the first section of Variation IV (at **9**) the *piano* indicated for the scale figures in the first violins and viole should not be taken too literally, or these lines will not be clearly heard. One doesn't need to be too concerned about the dynamic contrast within the line (*piano* for the sixteenth notes and *mezzo-forte* for the concluding eighth note, which is marked haphazardly anyway), as the desired effect is achieved by the addition of other instruments on the last eighth note of each bar.

It is very important that the pianist move forward precisely in tempo to the first chord of Variation V (at **11**). If the pianist hesitates here without the conductor's prior knowledge, the conductor will already be on the way toward a sharp *ictus* on the first beat of the bar (to elicit a clean syncopation response from the strings) by the time he realizes extra time has been taken on the bar-line. Taking some time here, if the pianist either needs or just wants it, should not be a problem, but making the decision at the last moment will result in a considerable mess.

There is no good reason for Variations VII and VIII (**15** through **17** and **17** through **19**) to present significant ensemble problems, but that doesn't mean that they won't. The issue, if any, will be the discipline of tempo and execution among so many musicians (including the soloist) playing *staccato* sixteenth notes simultaneously. The charm and excitement of these variations lies in the machine-like precision of these chromatic sixteenths in so many voices. However, it is easy for a thrilling silk purse to rapidly become a tedious sow's ear when this passage is *almost* together and all musicians are playing *almost* the same articulation.

Another pause is often inserted on the bar-line before the beginning of Variation XI (at **23**). As before, this allows the pianist an extra moment to set up the new tempo and mood, and is particularly appropriate here. Though not indicated, I find it is nice to take some time in the final bar of this variation (one bar before **25**), subdividing the entire bar. This approach keeps the final woodwind phrase from feeling hurried and better sets up the string entrance that follows.

In the second half of Variation XII (**26** to **27**), the conductor must decide to take the composer's markings about woodwind phrasing (and breathing) literally, or not. Personally, I don't find the idea that the flutes and clarinets should repeatedly breathe on the bar-line to be particularly compelling musically. My objection is not based in the woodwind parts themselves, but rather in the fact that woodwind breaths at these points force the solo piano to change the shape of every phrase, making a *ritard* and/or pause at or near these bar-lines to allow time for these players to breathe. I prefer to ask the flutes and clarinets to breathe only in the middle of the second and fifth bars after **26**. In my opinion, this solution makes for a more natural phrasing, as well as avoiding musical complications for the soloist.

There is some question regarding errata two bars before **27**. The reading in the full score (in the woodwinds, the third sixteenth note before the end of the bar) is clearly not correct, as it shows an F-natural in the second flute against a (concert) F-flat in the second clarinet. The question, whether they should both play F-natural or F-flat, may be a bit up for grabs, and there are good arguments on both sides. Supporting the position that F-natural is correct is the clear outline of the G-flat major scale as well as the fact that all F's in woodwinds are clearly F-naturals (apart from the one in question) during this entire four-bar phrase. Supporting the F-flat position is the introduction of this pitch in the solo piano both directly before and directly following the woodwind notes in question, which seems to support the idea of a subtle harmonic shift that would allow the F-flat to make sense. Running contrary to this argument are both the F-naturals in the following bar, and the more subjective idea that the F-flats in the piano part are passing tones that do not necessarily have an effect on the overall harmony. Saving the obvious for last, the two-piano score clearly shows F-naturals in the accompaniment, and this fact probably makes the entire preceding argument moot.

In Variation XVII (**35** through **37**), coordination between woodwind entrances, syncopated string chords, and solo piano can be very tricky. If this passage is particularly problematic in the first reading, it simply needs to be taken apart. There is no magic trick to solving this, but it needs to be rehearsed slowly so that all musicians can figure out where they fit in relative to other parts around them. Particularly because this is a work that is not generally well known, allowing musicians to hear it slowly once or twice to understand the relationship of one part to another generally solves the problem. The issue continues into Variation XVIII (**37** through **39**), but the specific orchestration choices make the situation somewhat less problematic here.

In the second bar after **41** (the second bar of Variation XX), the third note of second violins is C-sharp, not C-natural. Also, there should be a flag on the first (tied) note in violins and viole, making it an eighth note.

The bar-line preceding Variation XXI (at **43**) is another place where the soloist may place a short pause to re-set the hands and cleanly establish the new tempo. At the beginning of Variation XXII (at **46**), the composer expresses the new tempo relative to the half note, but is not explicit about a new meter. Clearly, we are to be in two at this point.

At **50**, the composer indicates only a breath mark, so one does not want to overburden this pause. After completing the preceding bar with two subdivisions, the baton can pause very briefly on the final note and then, simultaneously getting the eyes of the soloist, proceed to an energetic preparation in the new tempo.

As not all accents, *sforzati*, or *forte*'s are created equal, neither are all *glissandi*. A *glissando* that is printed (or requested by the conductor) in Puccini is not executed exactly the same as one in Tchaikovsky, and probably neither is the same as will be desired in Lutoslawski. The fundamental questions for string *glissandi* in an orchestral context are those of timing and definition: at what point during the printed note does the *glissando* begin and how clearly do we want to hear every pitch along the way? When a more graceful effect is desired (as in Puccini), one that imitates the artful *portamento* of a great singer, the motion is delayed until relatively near the end of the written value and the bow is often lightened somewhat during the execution of the figure. When, as here in Lutoslawski (at **50**), the *glissando* is a dramatic sound effect as opposed to an element that adds vocal elegance to the phrase, I usually instruct the strings to begin the motion at the beginning of the note, moving at a steady pace during its duration, and to maintain the natural bow pressure throughout. In this way, the effect is one of oddness and unease, as was most likely intended.

ꟹ

Sergei Prokoffiev

Piano Concerto No. 2 in G Minor, Op. 16

1st movement.

The *Andantino* tempo of this movement is interpreted with considerable freedom by various artists, from as slow as ♩ = 42–44 to as relatively rapidly as ♩ = 62–64. This choice graphically alters the nature of the piece, and should be made by the soloist with considerable care. No matter what the tempo, the conductor must specifically choose and communicate an articulation for the clarinets in the opening phrase. One might choose a shorter articulation of the quarter notes to better match the *pizzicati*, or a longer one to give a heavier and more serious feel to the opening of the work.

The string phrase that begins three bars before **1** is marked *pianissimo*, with no expressive markings that alter this dynamic. It is extremely important for the mood and expression of the opening of the work that the strings adhere carefully to what is written. The slow tempo, length of the phrase, and hyper-expressive harmonies lead many string sections to inadvertently *crescendo* during the phrase. This can be avoided by (1) appropriate gestural choices by the conductor, (2) insistence (in rehearsal) on attention to the dynamics, and (3) an instruction that the entire passage should be played in the upper half of the bow. Although the phrase that follows does include an expressive *crescendo-diminuendo*, the composer was careful to write *un poco crescendo*, and this phrase should crest at no more than an expressive *mezzo-piano*. Careful attention to all these details allows the composer's intentions for these first three similar phrases to be clearly heard: the first phrase (three bars before **1**) entirely *pia-*

nissimo, the second (three bars before **2**) *pianissimo* with a delicate *crescendo-diminuendo*, and the third (three bars before **4**) beginning *pianissimo* but growing to a more substantive *mezzo-forte* as transition to the following section.

The transition from one tempo to another at **7** can be handled in a number of different ways, and which method is selected is largely dependent on the tempo desired at *Allegretto*. Whatever tempo is chosen, it is desirable for this transition to feel logical and organic, rather than sudden and jarring, despite the obvious and sudden texture and rhythm changes at this point. Some soloists will want the tempo at **7** to be on the more ponderous side, ♩ = 120–130, which means that this section will probably be conducted in four. In this circumstance, a slight *ritard* before the bar-line allows the previous eighth note to approximately equal the new quarter note, creating the kind of seamless transition mentioned above. If a faster tempo is desired at **7**, something more like 𝅗𝅥 = 72–76, then the next section is certainly best handled in two. In this case, the transition is most fluidly handled with no *ritard* before the bar-line (or perhaps even a subtle *accelerando*), allowing the previous quarter note to roughly equal the new half note.

Even when the *Allegretto* section is conducted in two, the conductor may want to conduct some brief passages in four, for rhythmic and dramatic emphasis. Sections like the first three bars at **8** and some or all of the passage between the pick-up to **10** and **13** work well in this way. When this latter passage is conducted in four, the conductor returns to a beat in two at **13**.

It is quite common to hear the bar preceding **17** played half tempo *subito*, rather than with a graceful *poco rit.* as indicated. I have always found this puzzling and musically illogical, though soloists have, on occasion, coerced me to pace the bar in this way. Having admitted this, I should also say that I always attempt to talk the soloist into a more gradual and, in my opinion, graceful, transition into the slower tempo at **17**. When this reading is possible, the first beat in the bar can be taken as a quarter note, beginning at the preceding tempo and slowing only slightly, with the second beat subdivided for more *ritard* and good coordination with the soloist.

A slight subdivision is often necessary in the last beat before **20**. This ensures that the soloist's likely *rallentando* here is accommodated and coordinated with the flutes in this beat and on the following downbeat.

Where to place the preparatory gesture for the orchestra preceding **21** can be perplexing on the first try. The major issue here is to understand the soloist's pacing in the final bar of the *cadenza.* Many soloists take considerable time through the last several beats, particularly with the sextuplet on the final beat of the bar. If this is the case, the preparatory gesture can coincide with the final or penultimate note in the piano. Although this gesture is unlikely to be precisely equal to one beat in the next bar, this is not critical since the first two beats at **21** do not contain any rhythmic structure in the orchestra. On the other hand, if the soloist plays through the final beats of the *cadenza* essentially in tempo, the preparatory gesture can be placed logically on the fourth beat of the bar.

The final note of the movement in the viole will probably need some specific instruction, or each member of the section will intuit a different length. While it might be tempting to have the viole play the final note short, to match the *pizzicati* below them and to end the tremolo without event, I prefer that they sustain the final G-natural full-length, in logical partnership with the solo piano.

2nd movement.

Like the opening of the first movement, this movement is also played at a fairly wide variety of tempi. Usual opinions range from as "slowly" as ♩ = 128–132 to as truly *vivace* as ♩ = 162–166.

Though this movement does not present specific conducting challenges, per se, it does offer a few consistent orchestral pitfalls. Principal among the recurring issues in this movement is the likelihood that certain figures will appear late at this velocity (as compared with the solo piano) by the time the sound reaches the podium. The most likely figures where this problem may occur are the upward leaps in trumpets and horn (29, 34, 35, and 45), snare drum entrances (31), and string quarter note and triplet figures (40 to 42).

The clarinet solo at 52 is marked *mezzo-forte*, but this is rarely enough sound to compete with the *fortissimo* solo piano. Also, the moment requires more hysteria than this modest dynamic suggests.

The scrupulous conductor/accompanist will be tempted to listen carefully to the upward scale in the first half of the penultimate bar and to make whatever tiny adjustment might be necessary for a perfect cadence. However, this is usually a bad idea, as any hesitation in the baton or attempt to add or take away time is rather likely to result in both a very messy entrance from celli and basses and a tentative and uncoordinated entrance on the final downbeat from the rest of the orchestra. It is sufficient here to be certain throughout the passage (beginning at 49) that soloist and orchestra are in comfortable, logical coordination and to ensure that the baton is visible in the soloist's peripheral vision when approaching the final bars.

3rd movement.

As mentioned regarding the first movement, many fine pianists interpret *Allegro moderato* with wide latitude in this movement. One can hear this movement begin as truly *pesante* as ♩ = 72 (Alexander Toradze) and as relatively fleet as ♩ = 104–108 (Gustavo Romero). No matter what the tempo, achieving the appropriately oppressive, quasi Industrial Revolution atmosphere is the issue of greatest importance.

At 60, and at passages of similar music, it is important to be specific about the articulation for those instruments playing the figure that reads: *staccato* eighth note, eighth rest, accented quarter note. In order for these figures to have their desired musical meaning and impact, the *staccato* eighth note should be followed by a full-length quarter note. This strong differentiation of articulation helps to accentuate the fact that the musical phrases run awkwardly contrary to the meter.

The composer does not explain the method of execution for the harmonics in the first violin part between 81 and 83. He writes only his desired pitches and tells us that he wants them sounding as harmonics. This is an odd bit of writing on two levels. First, it would have been simpler for all concerned if he had written out the artificial harmonic for each note rather than forcing the players to read one octave down from the printed note (since the written notes also have *8va* above them) and then add the touch point a perfect fourth above. Second, these harmonics, unless played by a very large, amazingly expert first violin section, are virtually inaudible in live performance due to the amount of sound created by the rest of the orchestra and the solo piano. In the spite of the latter issue, it is important that the first violins execute the passage with appropriate gusto.

4th movement.

The usual tempo for this *Allegro tempestoso* is around ♩ = 160. It is common to begin this movement with only the briefest pause following the third movement in order to accentuate the shocking opening. When this approach is taken, it is best not to remove one's focus from the soloist after the conclusion of the previous movement. Once the last note has sounded and cleared, the conductor should take a quick glance at the orchestra to make certain that everyone is prepared to begin the finale, then return her eyes to the soloist to make sure he is ready before launching into the movement.

It is important to mention that many fine conductors take the main material in this movement in two, others in four. Even though it violates what I consider to be one of the major principles of conducting (that the value of the beat is chosen by utilizing the largest functional value, using the next smallest value only when genuinely necessary), I conduct the opening musical material in four. This is, of course, not because it cannot be conducted successfully in two. The choice is driven by the overlapping rhythmic elements of the music, and by my desire to stay involved with these shifting relationships on a moment-by-moment basis.

The *Meno mosso* at **97** is usually played at approximately ♩ = 100. This tempo, rather than a slower choice that is sometimes heard, keeps the energy of the piece from dying completely in this transition, and allows the conductor to make an artful *ritard* on the last cello triplet without becoming absurdly slow. At the other end of the spectrum, I have heard this passage conducted much faster, somewhere around ♩ = 132; I find this choice much too fast, since it robs the cello figure of its intrinsic sense of stealth and mystery.

At **99**, the conductor should strive to set the same tempo that the soloist will adopt at **100**. (This tempo is usually faster than at **97** even though it is not marked as such, probably around ♩ = 112–116.) Strangely, this is trickier than it seems, as I have many times taken a metronome marking from the soloist as their desired tempo for the solo passage, then conducted that tempo precisely at **99**, only to find that there was still a tempo change at **100**. If the soloist noticeably changes the tempo at **100** it is, obviously, not an ensemble or coordination issue; it just hurts my feelings.

The transition into **108** is another example of a passage that is best handled with a musically seamless quality. Assuming the tempo of the preceding section to be approximately ♩ = 112, a slight *ritard* just before **108**, slowing toward the neighborhood of ♩ = 96, allows for a smooth transition of (previous) quarter note equals (new) half note. The passage at **108** is then conducted in two, at the resulting tempo of 𝅗𝅥 = c. 96.

The *Meno mosso* (subito) in the second bar after **116** is often handled not as *meno mosso* but as half tempo *subito*; 𝅗𝅥 = c. 96 becoming ♩ = c. 96. Though much simpler in execution, this is, in my opinion, entirely contrary to the text. The composer had several methods at his disposal for expressing to us that he desired this section to be played exactly half the previous tempo, but he did not. What is clearly intended to feel sudden and somewhat jarring should not be turned into an even mathematical transition that barely gets our attention. (There are times when the goal is, and should be, a seamless transition, as discussed in the preceding paragraph, but this is precisely *not* one of those moments.) A tempo of approximately ♩ = 140 works well as a starting point for the *meno mosso*, with some relaxation of the tempo in the second bar. This approach is more difficult, but much more effective.

In order to give a preparatory gesture that is precisely in the correct, new tempo (approximately ♩ = 160) at **127**, the preparation should not be given until just after the final note(s) in the left hand has sounded. This assumes the usual amount of *ritard* in the solo part, allowing for a quick, in-tempo (quarter-note length) gesture as the pianist approaches the bar-line. In the unusual circumstance that the pianist actually concludes the phrase as written, with only *un poco rit.*, it may be necessary to line up the preparatory gesture either with the penultimate note(s) in the left hand or between this point and the last note(s).

Coordinating the final downbeat with the solo piano is a task not unlike that described at the end of the second movement. The conductor cannot wait for or accommodate the soloist here without causing mayhem on the last note of the piece. The conductor does, however, need to carefully observe the endpoint of the final *glis-*

sando, making sure that this figure lines up perfectly with the third beat of the bar in the orchestra. With that accomplished, his only remaining responsibility it to keep the baton within the peripheral vision of the pianist during the last three beats of the piece.

ೞ

Sergei Prokoffiev

Piano Concert No. 3 in C Major, Op. 26

1st movement.

The beautiful, extended opening passage of this movement allows the conductor to begin with only a cursory check with the soloist. After quietly making certain that the soloist is ready, the gentlest of downbeats sets the clarinet solo in motion.

At **1**, two issues of musical importance present themselves. First is the quality of the string sonority on the downbeat. The sound here must be of the lightest, airiest sort, with the lightest possible bow pressure and the bow position rather near the fingerboard. As listeners, we want to feel that this chord appears out of nowhere, so that we might be, at first, not even entirely certain that it has occurred. The second issue concerns the articulation of the first violins. The first flute has the same line as the first violins here, of course, but the flute is marked in long slurs, while the articulation in the violins is one that creates a workable bowing. The utmost care needs to be taken by the violins to insure that the line is long and continuous, without being chopped up by changes of bow direction. This is particularly at issue in the second half of the first bar, if the C-natural and A-natural are taken in separate bows as written, where special care needs to be taken that these two notes appear entirely as part of the longer line, without any sense of attack and decay in each bow stroke.

Even if the desired *rallentando* preceding **2** is fairly modest, it is a good idea to subdivide the last beat before *Allegro*, as this allows for more control in setting the new tempo. Though the composer writes nothing more descriptive than *Allegro*, the tempo for this passage is often a rather brisk ♩ = 146, or even a bit faster. Once the tempo is comfortably established, the only real danger in the opening section of this movement (through **12**) is the possible tendency of both soloist and orchestra musicians to continue pressing the tempo forward. While not dampening the exuberance of the music, the conductor must always keep an ear to this issue, lest the movement begin to move forward out of control.

Through **18**, the piece moves easily together between soloist and orchestra. Even when things are moving blissfully forward, however, it is a good idea in a passage like this one to avoid complacency. The moment we let our intellectual guard down is precisely when something awkward tends to happen. From **15** through **18**, for example, where clearly the soloist's material is secondary in musical importance to that of the orchestra, it is easy to assume that the soloist is following the orchestral sound, coordinating his own part with the orchestra. While this is, to some degree, generally true, it is not a binding contract, and the conductor must still remain attentive to the precise location of the soloist on every beat of every bar.

The transition at **18** is not difficult to pick up with the ear, as the piano figures make each beat quite clear. A conductor new to this work may be surprised, however, if the soloist moves forward two beats before **18** as though he is already in the new tempo. When the conductor is aware of this ahead of time, it is important that the urgency of the gesture, though passive on the second and third beats, reflects this change of tempo, so that the musicians of the orchestra are not caught off guard.

An important question does present itself at **18**, with regard to the rhythm in the string section. It is clear that the upper strings are to play eighth notes in the second and fourth beats during the first and third bars of this passage. But the rhythm in the piano, as well as the exact correlation of pitches, can lead the strings to comfortably slide into triplets, and this must be avoided. Part of the brilliance of this passage is the contrast between rhythms in triplets and rhythms in eighths and sixteenths. The issue takes on even more importance at **20**, where both eighth notes and sixteenth notes in the upper strings might feel like they should line up with the triplets in the piano; obviously, they should not.

At the return of *Andante* (**26**), it is tempting for this tempo to be exactly half the preceding tempo: old half-note equals new quarter note. In my opinion, such accidental metric relationships should be avoided. For a new tempo to feel "new," it is best if no precise and immediately detectable relationship exists. In this case, a tempo that is a bit slower than precisely half of the previous tempo suits the moment well. If the soloist concurs, the conductor may want to take a slight *ritard* in the one or two bars preceding *Andante*. This allows for a more graceful, less "running into a wall" transition, and also makes the passage in violins and viole slightly less tricky.

As is no doubt obvious, the bassoon solo at **28** will probably not be sufficiently forceful to carry into a large hall, over the piano solo, when played at the indicated *piano*. Balance needs to be particularly attended to when the bassoon drops to the lower octave three bars before **29**, as this line remains important and is often lost in live performance. Coordination between the solo piano and the moving voices in the orchestra in this passage can be quite simple or quite complex, depending on the soloist's approach. Some pianists take the passage between **28** and **30** with only a few mild *ritardandi*, and no extravagant *rubati*, but others take considerable license here. In the latter case, the moving lines in the orchestra, particularly those in the solo clarinet and bassoon, will inadvertently take on somewhat different rhythmic shapes than originally intended by the composer, and both conductor and orchestral musicians will need to be very sensitive to the push and pull of the *rubato*. Without these subtle but important accommodations, the performance of this passage appears to be a battle of musical philosophies between pianist and conductor, with the composer and the audience coming out the losers.

In the passage beginning at **30**, there is a delicate balance to be maintained between accommodating the soloist and making certain that horn, trumpet, flute, and oboe entrances are properly prepared. Many soloists take considerable time approaching **30**, as well as at the end of each of the four bars following. (The usual exception to this is the third bar. This bar will often have little or no time taken on the final beat, as the eighth note in trumpets suggests that the phrase moves forward.) In the first, second, and fourth bars, the danger is that, as the sextuplets in the piano slow, the conductor gets "stuck" on the fourth beat. One may get "stuck" in this way by showing the fourth beat in coordination with the soloist, and this very long beat, with a gesture drifting ever higher, leaves the conductor with no clear, graceful method for preparing wind entrances that follow. On the fourth beat of each of these bars, instead of showing the beat and rebounding naturally, the baton gently pauses at the point of *ictus* (a fairly low position; in this case, very near the position of the *ictus* of the first beat), waiting for the soloist to draw out the expression of this last sextuplet. Once the soloist reaches the final, or penultimate, note (depending on the pace of the figure) the baton lifts clearly, with the conductor's eyes squarely on the wind player(s) entering next. Some soloists eschew such extravagant *rubati* here, however, playing the passage nearly in tempo throughout, as was again demonstrated for me in a recent performance with the brilliant young pianist Haochen Zhang (2009 Van Cliburn Gold Medalist). While the passage is quite different musically when played in this way, it certainly loses none of its charm and mystery.

Setting the tempo at **32** is not as simple as it seems. It is critical that the conductor remember the desired tempo precisely here, including the fact, if true in the particular case, that some soloists take this final *Allegro* faster than the one earlier in the movement. Though it makes life difficult, at times, for strings and woodwinds, this final section can easily fly forward at ♩ = 160 for some pianists.

Looking at the page, it appears clear that the goal one bar before **39** is for the *poco ritard* to ease back organically and precisely into the *Poco meno mosso* that follows. While this is a logical and musically appropriate idea, it rarely works in performance. The reason it doesn't often work as described is that the previous tempo is usually quite fast and the following tempo so moderate (often around ♩ =96–100) that one bar is simply not enough time to gracefully slow down to that degree. The usual result is that the tempo slows down where indicated as much as good music making and ensemble will allow, but the tempo at **39** will probably be even slower than the final beat before it. To make this work well, the conductor sets tempo at **39** with the best possible memory of the most recent rehearsal or performance. Then, having heard the pianist set the new tempo, the conductor makes whatever adjustment (little or none, one hopes) may be necessary on the second beat.

Locking orchestra and pianist together cleanly at the following *Poco più mosso* (the second bar after **45**) is quite easy. First, this is usually played at the tempo of the same music earlier in the movement, and everyone on stage should be able to fall into it logically.

In addition, the simplicity of the orchestration at this point removes what might otherwise be additional complicating factors.

The second and third bars after **49** can be more trying for the conductor (and the orchestra) than they might appear. Not all soloists pace the *glissandi* and chromatic scales literally, leaving the conductor with a dilemma when the bottom note of the scale (two bars before **50**) does not line up with the first beat of the bar in the orchestra. (Note that even two artists as significant as Alexander Toradze and Valery Gergiev have an entire beat missing here in their otherwise marvelous recording of the work.) The composer does not indicate any *accelerando* here, nor does one make sense, given the heavy, plodding affair continuing in the orchestra. None of that logic will matter, however, if the soloist rushes forward here; requiring the orchestra to essentially skip a beat in live performance is really not a realistic or desirable option.

The composer does not specify the tempo at **50** precisely, but we assume, by musical context, that it is to be played at the same pace as the most recent *Allegro*, and this is usually the result. This tempo should not be difficult to set, keeping good ensemble between the pianist and (at first) celli. It is very important, however, that the conductor not assume that whatever tempo he sets in the first several beats is absolutely perfect. Subtle adjustments, undetectable to the listener, may be required as the conductor tracks every note in the piano.

2nd movement.

No issues of technical consequence should arise in the *Tema* section for the orchestra. One interpretive issue may need attention, however. The composer went out of his way not only to mark each quarter note (in the strings) *staccato* (the first two bars of the passage and the first two bars at **54**) but to insist on successive up-bows as well. These two markings together give us a clear indication that the style in the strings should be very short, even *secco*. Some conductors insist, for some reason, on undoing the obvious, giving each string chord added length that is not indicated. This seems not only to run contrary to the markings on the page, but also to the spirit of the music. This theme has that typically Prokoffiev feel about it, creepy, mysterious, and a bit cranky, and the string articulation that he indicates fits the moment perfectly.

Though it is not indicated, the conductor may want to ask the strings to play with a slightly lighter dynamic on the second and third beats of the second, third, and fourth bars before **54**. This slight echo effect in the string phrasing is not only rather charming, but, more importantly, allows the bassoon solo to be heard clearly without having to force the sound.

There is no need to mark bars during the pianist's solo in Variation I. By good fortune or good planning, the fact that the orchestra's next entrance is one beat before a rehearsal number makes this unnecessary. As in many similar places in the repertoire, an explanation in rehearsal is sufficient.

The relationship between the tempo of Variation I and the tempo of Variation II is usually old eighth note = new quarter note. Assuming that this relationship, or something roughly similar, holds true, then a small but energetic subdivision of the final beat of Variation I shows the orchestra the new quarter note pulse.

There is no need to add a *ritard* at any point during the last four bars of Variation II. In fact, doing so disturbs the forward motion and creates too much of a sense of conclusion. The *fermata* on the rest is more than sufficient to separate one variation from another. The pick-up (in the solo piano) preceding **63** can be a little confusing at first glance. Because the composer utilizes quarter notes with accents at unusual points in the bar (in Variation III) to emphasize the rhythmic structure and phrase shape, the pick-up to **63** appears (at first glace) as a quarter note. It is, however, played as an eighth note in the new meter and tempo, as is apparent only by the beam that trails across the bar-line below the notes.

The articulation in the strings during the two bars preceding **65** is very clear, and these two bars are, equally clearly, not the same as one another. An almost *legato* articulation is appropriate in the first of these two bars (quarter notes with dashes), while the eighth notes in the next bar should be quite separated. In too many performances these two rather different ideas sound too much alike.

The major issue in Variation IV is somewhat similar to that discussed regarding the passage at **30** (first movement). Here, again, wind entrances in particular fall during or just after moments when the pianist is likely to stretch the final beat of a bar. Precise locations where the conductor needs to be aware of this issue include the last beats of the following bars: the second bar after **69**, two bars before **70**, and each of the first four bars at **70**. In each of these locations, a slight subdivision of the fourth beat increases clarity for members of the orchestra, while allowing the pianist the freedom to elegantly stretch the thirty-second-note figures.

Delicate but clear subdivisions may be in order beginning one beat before **72**. Some soloists take this passage slightly more slowly than what precedes it, making precise coordination more difficult if the conductor remains stoically in quarter note beats. Regardless of any change of tempo, however, these subtle subdivisions help to emphasize the sense of accent and release inherent in the orchestration and articulations in the passage. I mention this musical, rather than technical, justification for these subtle subdivisions particularly because some soloists actually increase the tempo slightly here, but I still gently subdivide for texture and shape. Any need to subdivide ceases, of course, with the end of the flute figures.

The indication *con sordino* in the first horn, appearing in the fifth bar after **73**, is not an error. Though rather tricky technically and in terms of its effect on intonation, the composer does want the sound muted *subito* at this point.

It is usually best for the conductor to lead into the new tempo at Variation V. The half beat pick-up is simply not enough time for the conductor to respond following a soloist's self-generated entrance. This *Allegro giusto* usually falls in the neighborhood of ♩ = 128. A certain amount of *affrettando* is often applied at **76**, resulting in a new tempo at **77** of around ♩ =140. Though there is no change of tempo, stylistic issues suggest a change to beating in two at **83**. (In fact, owing to a combination of tempo and musical content, some conductors are in two as early as **77**.) When a beat in two is adopted here (**83**), there is no need to return to a beat in four until three bars before the end of the movement.

3rd movement.

The playful but not particularly speedy passage that opens this movement requires a beat in three. This is usually around ♩ = 126–136. Apart from some rather rapid scales, no serious technical or accompanying issues present themselves between the beginning of the movement and **101**.

Particularly skilled sections of cellists and bassists will be able to accurately adapt to the new tempo at **101** if the conductor moves immediately into one. The tempo here is not usually so fast that beating in three is awkward, so beating a bar or two of the new tempo in three, then gracefully moving into one, may be found to be preferable in some orchestras.

The *Meno mosso* at **110** can conceivably work at wide variety of tempi. However, this tempo must match the soloist's desire at **114**, which is usually around ♩ = 108. It is not uncommon to hear the beautiful orchestral passage at **110** played at a slower tempo, with the soloist simply taking his own, faster pace at **114**. When this happens, it does not rise to the importance of becoming a capital offense, but the composer was very clear with his indication (*L'istesso tempo*), and we should be observing it. There is no reason that the music at **110** cannot be played a bit more swiftly, if that is required to match the soloist's tempo at **114**, and still retain all of its expressive elegance.

The conductor will probably find that the grace note in the solo piano preceding the downbeat at **119** will be somewhat sustained. It is not uncommon for this note to take the length of a quarter note, or even a dotted quarter note, in the new tempo. For obvious reasons, the celli will not want an insecure or tentative gesture as they begin this phrase, and the conductor's placement of the preparatory gesture is largely based on the pacing of the pianist's grace note.

The woodwind entrances on the downbeats at both **124** and **126** should be points of caution for the conductor. In both places, the final beat of the previous bar is likely to take extra time. Gestures and strategies of the types discussed earlier (regarding the passage at **30**) will probably be helpful here. Despite the chromatic quintuplets in the right hand, coordination with the pianist is quite easy at **124**, even though some pianists will take a new, faster tempo here. As is no doubt obvious, aural and/or visual connection with the pianist's left hand is very important in a passage like this one.

The tempo at **131** usually resembles the faster of the earlier, similar *tempi* in this movement (**101**). As before, it may be prudent to begin in three and then move into one. For some pianists, however, this is a faster tempo than either of the *tempi* earlier in the movement. If so, it is probably necessary to begin immediately in one.

At a critical moment in the piece, less than a minute from the end, the conductor must not allow the sudden hemiola shape of the piano part at **146** to cause any hesitation or second-guessing. The tempo does not change here, but the intricacy of the coordination between *staccato* winds, *pizzicato* strings, and the solo piano requires that the conductor remain confident in his knowledge of all rhythmic interplay, driving this joyous finale confidently to its conclusion.

Sergei Rachmaninoff

Piano Concerto No. 1 in F-Sharp Minor, Op. 1

This concerto exists in three versions: the original (sometimes call the "first") version (1891), the interim revised version (1917), and the final revised version (1919). Information about these three versions, their dates, and even whether there are, in fact, two versions or three, differs from one source to another, which can make a clear understanding of this subject a bit more complicated than it needs to be. (1) "State Publishers 'Music'" of Moscow (Izdatel'stvo "Muzyka") offers the original version in a clearly labeled 1971 publication. (2) The Dover score (a reproduction of the 1965 Izdatel'stvo "Muzyka" edition) contains the interim revised version. Unfortunately, this score erroneously mentions on the title page that there are two versions of the piece, 1891 and 1917 (apparently lumping the two revised versions into one), but then fails to explain which version is found in that volume. (3) The final revised version is published by Boosey and Hawkes (B. & H. 16425). In spite of the fact that the first page of the score reads "Revised Version (1917)," this is, in fact, the final version, and is not the same score as the interim revised version found in the Dover edition and elsewhere.

The differences between the original version and the two later versions are significant, and they demonstrate the composer's maturity in matters of composition, form, and orchestration. In the 1917 version, a considerable amount of music is removed from the original and a great deal more is substantially revised. The differences between the two later versions are relatively minor, however, and concern only details of orchestration and a few small details in the piano part. But it should be noted that these orchestral differences are not so trivial that the issue of which of the latter versions one intends to perform will not matter. The final revised version is currently the one most often performed, but conductors should always consult with the pianist well ahead of time to be certain that the orchestral materials (and the score studied) are correct.

1st movement.
The desired tempo at **1** (*a tempo*) appears to be the same *Vivace* as utilized in the first bar of the movement. This is seldom the case, however, as most pianists (including Rachmaninoff) desire a more deliberate tempo at **1**. This discrepancy of tempo should not dissuade the conductor from opening the movement with a brisk *Vivace* (perhaps ♩=132), even if the soloist desires something more majestic (possibly ♩=108) at **1**.

The *Moderato* at **2** works well at a tempo around ♩= 74. It is common to take expressive *rallentandi* at various points during these first six bars. Though unmarked by the composer, this kind of expressive stylization is necessary to create the type of phrasing demanded by this music. The soloist is likely to make similar expressive gestures when the same music returns four bars before **3**. The conductor must unobtrusively and skillfully accommodate these variations in tempo, particularly in the first two bars at **3**.

The following *Vivace* (six bars before **4**) is best handled in two. This passage usually flows forward at approximately 𝅗𝅥 = 80. At **5**, it is usually best to return to beating in four. This section is usually approximately ♩ = 88, while the following *Poco meno mosso* (at **6**) will be closer to ♩ = 74.

In some commonly used scores and/or parts, several conspicuous errors are found between **4** and **5**, as follows: first bar at **4**, the final note in the bar in oboe and clarinet is (concert) G-natural; sixth bar after **4**, the second note in the second horn is (written) F-sharp; seventh bar after **4**, second bassoon, celli, and basses should have G-natural.

At *Vivace* (four bars before **8**), the indication *Doppio movimento* (the previous ♩ = the new 𝅗𝅥) should be followed exactly, in spite of the fact that some scores misprint the rhythmic relationship as ♪ = ♪, which makes no sense whatsoever. In spite of the much altered mood, the tempo at **10** should return precisely to the preceding tempo (at **8**), approximately 𝅗𝅥 = 88. The tempo relationship at **14** is printed correctly, the previous 𝅗𝅥 = the new ♩, allowing this *Moderato* to proceed logically at approximately ♩ = 88, in four.

Both five bars and one bar before **15**, the pianist usually takes some time with the second beat, allowing the end of the phrase to come to rest with calm and elegance. In both of these bars it is best for the baton to come to rest on the second beat, with no rebound, while allowing the soloist to complete the phrase. When the pianist approaches the final notes of the phrase, the conductor can then move toward the third beat, being certain not to anticipate the final note. This is, of course, another of those instances in which a split-second late is of relatively little consequence, but a split-second early ruins the moment.

A tempo around ♩ = 90 works well at **16**, and a gentle expansion of the phrase in the second bar sets the right atmosphere for the entrance of the piano in the following bar. As earlier in the movement, the *Vivace* at **21** is best handled in two.

2nd movement.

The first passage in this movement that presents potential coordination problems appears in the first three bars of **32**. It is of critical importance that the sextuplets in the piano line up unerringly with the *pizzicato* triplets in the upper strings. In order for this to happen, three elements must be present: (1) the soloist must be able to see the beat clearly and not have it hidden by the conductor's torso, (2) the conductor must have an intimate knowledge of the solo part in order to be able to easily place each beat accurately, and (3) the sonic environment (hall acoustics, soloist phrasing and pedaling, etc.) must be such that it is possible for the conductor to hear, with clarity, the progression of the solo piano.

Three bars before **33**, a rather significant *rallentando* is common. Although the solo piano is marked *pianissimo*, and many voicing choices are possible (some of which make the conductor's job easier, and some more difficult), it is critical that the wind lines (D, F-sharp) line up perfectly with the similar rhythmic line (D, C-sharp) in the solo piano.

As at **32**, coordination between the soloist's sextuplets and (in this case) second violin *pizzicati* is critical at **36**. The task is particularly thorny at **36** because many soloists will take a bit of expressive time in the first beat of each of the first two bars, making the perfect coordination of the *pizzicati* more difficult. When the conductor slows the rebound of the first beat in each bar to accommodate this extra time taken by the soloist, the second violins are left to essentially guess where to place the note occurring at the end of beat one (G-sharp in the first bar, the upper G-natural in the second bar). The only solution to this dilemma (other than doggedly insisting that the soloist stay in tempo, which is probably not a good idea) is two-fold. First, the conductor must remember precisely how much expressive time the soloist usually takes, and lead confidently with that knowledge, rather than waiting so long into the first beat to flow forward that the second violins are, in fact, guessing. Second, conductors possessing sufficiently sophisticated technique can show the precise entrance of the second violins by indicating it with a subtle subdivision in the left hand. After that, it should be possible to flow forward into the second beat without further complications.

Three bars before the end of the movement, the final eighth note in the bar needs to be shown in subdivision and then sustained during the pianist's final triplet, in *ritard.* Coordinating with the soloist, the conductor can then indicate the following downbeat for low strings and horns.

3rd movement.

The only detail in the first several bars of this movement that may require particular attention is the execution of the two sixteenth notes in the middle of the first and third bars. Even in rather skilled orchestras this rhythm has a tendency to become stylized, which is a pleasant euphemism for "played late and too fast," and this is to be avoided.

Three bars before **39** (and in other similar passages), it is common for the soloist to interpret the indication *capriccioso* with a bit of stretch across the first beat of this bar. When this is the case, the conductor needs to prolong the rebound of the first beat slightly (so as to not rush forward to the second beat), waiting to hear the second principal note of the bar (A-natural). Once the pianist has played the A-natural, the baton accelerates swiftly to the second beat, impelling the remainder of the bar forward.

The four bars of solo piano preceding 40 can be aurally daunting for some conductors. The angular, hemiola figures are designed to deceive the ear of the listener into temporarily losing a sense of the $\frac{9}{8}$ meter, and a passage like this is surely one of the signatures of Rachmaninoff's brilliance. The conductor, however, must not be seduced by this trick into losing track of the pianist's progress through the passage. The easiest signposts are as follows: five and six bars before 40, the third beat of the bar; four bars before 40, the rest on the downbeat followed by what sounds like a quarter-note triplet figure in the left hand covering the second and third beats; three bars before 40, same as the previous bar in the left hand; one bar before 40, clear rhythmic delineation of the second beat.

The pianist's voicing choices, in addition to the conductor's disadvantageous sonic position, can make following the passages in the third and fourth bars after 40 rather unnerving. Fortunately, this is also a passage where visual observation of the left hand entirely solves any problem that might arise here. If the duple figures in the left hand cannot be heard clearly, then they should be easily observable from the conductor's vantage point. The same holds true for the third and fourth bars before 41.

Though the *ritard* is not indicated until the downbeat at 42, some pianists will begin this gesture during the final notes of the previous bar. Deftly controlling the orchestra to slow down across this triplet just enough to accommodate this subtle shift can be a bit tricky. But it is very important for this to be solved properly; otherwise the orchestra arrives at the downbeat of 42 ahead of the soloist, which will be quite obvious to any listener. This same *ritard*, as it continues into the second bar after 42, is often exaggerated to the point that the piece comes to a virtual standstill on the last eighth note of the bar, and this is both completely unnecessary and rather unmusical. The goal here should be to create a charming, elegant transition into the *Allegro*, not to bring the piece to a halt before again launching forward.

The following *Allegro* is usually best handled in two, as the tempo will be around 𝅗𝅥 = 78. No conductor should have even the slightest difficulty picking up the tempo from the soloist here, since it is made obvious by the descending line (A-natural, G-sharp, F-sharp, E-natural) in the thumb of the right hand. I change to a beat in four at **44**, as the somewhat heightened rhythmic intensity and drama benefits from this approach.

The transition into the *Andante ma non troppo* section (four bars before **46**) feels easy and logical as long as one follows the composer's indications with reasonable diligence. Preceding this key change we find the indications *Poco meno mosso* and *ritard* (six and eight bars after **45**). If these indications are executed logically and musically, then the piece flows naturally and seamlessly into the following *Andante ma non troppo*. If, however, the conductor belabors these instructions, then the tempo at *Andante ma non troppo* will feel like an energetic resurgence, rather than the logical settling point of what comes before.

As long as the conductor and the soloist have settled between them the desired tempo and general pacing of the *Andante ma non troppo* section, then the conductor does not need to be overly concerned with accompanying each note of the filigree in the solo piano. Instead, the conductor can set the desired pace and allow the pianist to fit these delicate wisps into the framework provided by the orchestra. In the short *cadenza* five bars before **47**, it is not uncommon to hear the orchestra re-enter on the last eighth note of the bar after the pianist has already completed the passage and arrived at the following downbeat. The reason for this is fairly obvious: the conductor gets tangled in the rapid movement of this bar and assumes, "better late than early." It is true that this bar can be a bit daunting, especially on the first hearing and/or under pressure, as it is likely to be played extremely rapidly and without much concern for the signposts that might help the conductor. This puzzle is quite solvable, however. The key lies in following the downward arpeggio in thirds in the uppermost voice of the solo line that begins with the fourth beamed figure in the bar. Beginning at this point, we see four groups of four notes each, the first note of each group comprising one note of this downward arpeggio: E-flat, C-natural, A-flat, F-natural. Already grounded in the sustained E-flat major harmony, our ear can easily follow this minor seventh chord toward its resolution on the G-natural that coincides with the (orchestra's) third beat of the bar. The four tones down the minor seventh arpeggio provide the conductor with a guide for moving through the second beat of the bar, easily arriving at the third beat when the pianist strikes the G-natural, then moving forward in tempo while the pianist finishes the figure.

Some scores (including Dover) contain misprints in the first and third bars of **49**. In both of these bars, in both first flute and first horn, the fifth note in the bar should be (concert) F-natural, not G-natural.

At the return of *Tempo I* (three bars before **50**), it is common to add slurs to the upper strings in the first bar. This change makes the wind and string articulations similar and keeps the string figures from becoming something that resembles an etude. The most natural slurring solutions are as follows: First violins: slur together four notes (up-bow), six notes (down-bow), then seven notes (up-bow) that include the eighth note B-flat; Second violins: slur together six notes (up-bow), including the eighth note B-flat; Viole: slur together four notes (up-bow), then seven notes (down-bow).

The *Allegro ma non troppo* (*Allegro ma non tanto* in the final revised version) section (four bars before **55**) is best handled in four.

This tempo is usually only modestly slower than the previous *Allegro* (perhaps ♩ = 142), but the more active nature of the rhythmic structure tends to lend itself best to a beat in four. The indication at **58**, *poco a poco accelerando a tempo vivace*, leads naturally to the *Allegro vivace* seven bars after **59**, where we transition into two.

Though there is certainly no slowing of the tempo, nine bars before the end of the work I change to a beat in four, as I feel that the repeated accents and general rhythmic drive require this added muscle. At this same point, many professional timpanists change the pitches in their part, which makes a great deal of sense. Having modern instruments that can be rapidly re-tuned, surely the composer would have desired the tonic, and not the dominant, sounding in the timpani during these final moments of the piece.

☙

Sergei Rachmaninoff

Piano Concerto No. 2 in C Minor, Op. 18

1st movement.

The opening ten bars of solo piano are not generally indicated by the conductor as empty bars in the usual way. It is more than sufficient to explain to a less experienced orchestra that you will begin conducting at **1**, as marking these bars is both unnecessary and potentially distracting.

In the opening orchestral passage between **1** and **2**, the conductor does not need to be overly concerned with the subject of balance between orchestra and solo piano. The major musical material here is, of course, in the orchestra, and the piano accompanies. The register of the arpeggios in the piano gives the instrument tremendous resonance here, and an appropriate balance usually occurs naturally. After reading what is above, M.D. said, "Did you write 'let the orchestra play as loud as they want to' during the opening of Rach 2? I don't agree with that." Of course, that's not what I'm suggesting, but M.D.'s point is still well taken. This passage does not generally present balance problems, but that doesn't mean that, as always, the conductor should not be attentive to the issue.

A slight *ritard* often occurs in the second half of the eighth bar after **1**. The combination of the orchestral sound, the register in which the piano is playing, and the use of the pedal can all combine to make this figure somewhat lacking in clarity from the conductor's perspective. Carefully observing the keyboard and pianist's general body language can be helpful for good coordination here.

The passage between **2** and **3** is a prime example of the reason that it is a good idea to position the piano so that the conductor has a view of at least the pianist's left hand. From the conductor's perspective, the sound of the piano in a passage like this one can be a bit muddy and indistinct, making it more difficult to clearly hear the pivotal points in the piano that make good coordination possible (i.e., bottom and top notes of arpeggios, etc.). When the conductor can see the pianist's left hand, however, the "mud" clears up quite considerably, and accompanying such a passage becomes fairly simple.

The first beat of the first bar at **3** often needs a rebound that is slightly larger and somewhat slower than might seem appropriate for this music generally. This altered rebound serves to get the attention of the orchestra, particularly the celli, basses, and first bassoon, who might otherwise stumble into playing the second beat of the bar too early. Many pianists take a bit of extra time during this first beat, and the orchestra needs clear leadership that suits the musical and technical needs of the moment.

At *Un poco più mosso*, the best method of being immediately coordinated with the pianist's new tempo is a two-fold approach. First, the conductor must simply rely on his memory from rehearsal or recent performance to set the tempo with confidence as closely as possible to that which the pianist most recently adopted. The tempo of a virtuosic passage like this one will, however, vary at least slightly from one playing to the next, even with a very secure and dependable soloist. The second technique is to be acutely aware of the movement, through each arpeggio, and from one harmony to another. In the case of the first bar, this means being very aware of the progress of the C minor arpeggio (plus ♯ 4 and ♯ 7 passing tones) in the right hand, using it a clear guide to the new tempo. This process continues in each of the next seven bars, using both the rhythmic alternation of triplets and single quarter notes in the left hand, and the general harmonic movement, to easily coordinate with the piano. It should also be mentioned that some soloists take a slight *accelerando* in the two bars preceding *Un poco più mosso*. This gesture is quite logical and helps to smooth the transition, but even pianists that take this *accelerando* do not generally get all the way to the new tempo during these two bars, and another shift upward in tempo will probably still occur on the downbeat following the double-bar.

Directly on the heels of a conversation about following the composer's intentions instead of blindly following known "traditions" (we were actually talking about Gershwin at the time), M.D. made an interesting observation about the unique opportunity we have (with Rachmaninoff) to hear one of the greatest pianists that ever lived play his own works on recordings. He noted that in the second theme of this movement (beginning nine bars after **4**) Rachmaninoff does exactly the opposite of what's in the score. The composer, as pianist, takes substantial liberties with this passage marked *a tempo*, particularly in the fourth and sixth bars, but maintains a strict *a tempo* precisely where he wrote *ritard* in the tenth bar. But this information does not fall under the (somewhat negative) heading of "tradition," since it comes directly from the composer, just by an unusual route.

It is sometimes necessary to beat in four in the two-bar passages found both two bars and twelve bars before 5. Whether or not this is necessary depends upon the degree of *ritard* employed by the soloist. Even when these brief passages are taken in four, the beat returns to two at 5.

I have discussed in several locations in this book the wisdom of being more concerned with the harmonic and rhythmic material in a pianist's left hand, rather than always focusing on the melodic material that is most likely located in the right hand (see various discussions in the chapters on works by Chopin). Those important discussions notwithstanding, the passage at 6 is, for the most part, not one that lends itself to this technique. In this passage, the melody is often quite flexible, sometimes even minimally detaching itself rhythmically from the left hand. For this reason, it is important to focus with considerable sensitivity on the pianist's approach to, and pacing of, this melody. When this is done correctly and naturally, it allows the original melody line in the woodwinds to compliment the echoed material in the piano as a partner, rather than stiffly fighting the soloist's *rubati*.

The *Più vivo* at 8 is another example (see three paragraphs above) of a situation where both tempo memory and more concrete accompanying techniques need to work together. Even before hearing the pianist at this point, the conductor is required to commit clearly to a new tempo. But this tempo is "checked" in the conductor's mind by the relationship he hears among the first notes of each of the first three (quarter note) beats of the bar. In other words, the rhythmic/mathematical relationship between the D-natural (first beat), E-flat (second beat), and the right-hand entrance (third beat) provide a perfect series of signposts for the pianist's tempo. Therefore, by the second (half note) beat of the first bar, the conductor is able to make any subtle shift in tempo required for seamless, apparently perfect, coordination.

Different conductors interpret the articulation in celli and basses at the following *Più vivo* (seventeenth bar after **8**) differently. The question is whether the dash above each dotted quarter note implies that the figure is to be played "hooked" or if the lack of a dot above each following eighth note means that each two-note figure is slurred. Clearly, it would have been better if the composer had either given us the dot on each eighth note (to definitively indicate a "hooked" bowing for a slightly separated articulation) or removed the dash above each dotted quarter note (to clearly show that the two notes are slurred). Lacking either of these improvements from the composer, however, we are left to assume a solution. Some musicians believe that the dash is simply for expressive emphasis, and therefore the figure is clearly to be slurred. Others believe that if the mark is only for emphasis and is not part of a larger articulation the composer would have placed an accent on the note instead (even though a dash and an accent do not really have the same meaning, even in *piano*). Both assumptions carry some musical logic and some pitfalls, but the important thing is that the conductor make this decision (beforehand) and communicate it clearly either to the librarian (to be marked into the parts) or to the celli and basses at the first rehearsal.

One bar before *Maestoso (Alla marcia)* (the eighth bar after **10**) most pianists simply continue the *ritard* incrementally toward the new tempo. Some pianists, however, choose to slow down in this bar, especially the second half of the bar, to a point where there is essentially a *fermata* in this final triplet. When this is the soloist's choice it affects both the conductor's choices and the specific playing of the strings. Obviously, for the conductor this means that on arriving at the second beat of the bar the baton will stop completely (again, as though a *fermata* appears here), and the gesture preparing the next bar will probably coordinate with the final note of the bar in the piano. For the strings, this extreme *ritard* means that their measured sixteenth-notes become a thing of the past, and the final half bar must be play as unmeasured *tremolo*.

Unlike some similar passages in other concerti, the long arpeggio of grace notes in the first bar at **15** is to be coordinated exactly as it appears on the page: the lowest note of the arpeggio occurs with the first beat of the measure in the orchestra. To do otherwise, coordinating the top note of the arpeggio with the first note of the bar in the orchestra, as is sometimes the case in Chopin, means allowing the soloist to play the entire C major arpeggio while the orchestra sustains the harmony of G^7. I have heard it performed this way, but I cannot condone it, as this makes no sense to me whatsoever. At **15**, the baton should remain entirely motionless after indicating arrival at the first beat of the bar, while the soloist completes the arpeggio at leisure. Only when the conductor hears the first of the three following eighth notes (E, G, E) does she move gently into the rebound of the first beat, clearly cueing the first violins when arriving at the second beat.

The conductor should also be aware of the likely *ritard*, at times extreme, in the second beat of the second and eighth bars after **15**. This is of particular concern in the first of these two bars, lest the pianist's *ritard* force the conductor into an unclear indication for the entrance of flutes and oboes in the following bar. When the conductor knows this situation is likely to occur he should, as always, stop the baton (without rebound) on the second beat of the bar, waiting to flow into the rebound gesture until the soloist is closer to completing the figure.

The tempo at **16** can vary from as slow as ♩ = 86 to as quick as the composer's indication of 𝅗𝅥 = 63. As is perhaps obvious by the preceding, the choice to conduct this section in two or in four will be entirely dependent on the tempo desired by the soloist. In either event, a slight pause of the baton one-half bar before **16**, as the pianist completes the second sextuplet in the bar, helps to set this new tempo clearly.

2nd movement.

In the brief, but magical, introduction to this movement, subtlety of dynamics, balance, and orchestral color are of paramount importance. The conductor should be concerned that, in the third bar, the *forte* is not overplayed, nor performed with an inappropriately aggressive color of sound. This G-sharp major chord, arriving miraculously from the preceding F minor and C minor, needs to blossom into view, rather than being forced upon us. Conversely, the *piano* on the downbeat of the fourth bar must be played with a full enough sound that a truly delicious *diminuendo* to *pianissimo* can still follow. One other concern is that the basses' last note in the third bar, an F-sharp that adds the 7th to G-sharp major, not be played so softly that the unprepared listener cannot fully appreciate this addition to the harmony.

Between **17** and **18** the piano is, for all practical purposes, accompanying the solo flute and solo clarinet. This being the case, most soloists understand that it is not their prerogative to alter the tempo or independently shape the phrase. As long as the pianist can clearly hear the clarinet and see the baton then this process works nicely. The only real exception in this passage is the sixth bar before **18**, where the piano briefly resumes the dominant voice, and the conductor may need to adapt to the pianist's wishes rather than entirely control the proceedings.

Between **18** and **19** the major melodic material returns to the piano. Although this passage looks quite simple on the page, it can, in reality, be somewhat uncomfortable. The possible discomfort stems from the soloist's logical desire to shape this luscious melody with some modest *rubato*, while the triplets in clarinet and *pizzicato* violins demand strict adherence to one tempo, lest they pull apart into a complete mess. If, in the first rehearsal, the soloist takes liberties in this passage that are too extreme or unpredictable to be managed cleanly and logically in the orchestra, then a delicate, private conversation with the pianist might be advisable.

The passage between **19** and *Un poco più animato* (*Un poco più mosso* in some scores) presents yet a different set of variables and priorities. The major melodic material is in the violins, but the soloist is, well, the soloist. In this setting, an agreeable musical collaboration needs to be established regarding who is leading, who is following, and how the phrases should be shaped.

In the eight bars preceding **20**, the solo bassoons do not really play *piano*, except in a recording situation. In this case, *piano* is a metaphor for the gentle, lyrical nature of the duet, but in most concert environments the bassoons need to play at least *mezzo forte*. Note, in fact, that at **21** the violins and viole are marked *mezzo forte* in what is otherwise precisely the same musical context.

I always ask the celli to add a tasteful but passionate and clearly audible *portamento* between the two C-sharps four bars before **21**. Without this, this important phrase seems sterile and angular to me.

Many pianists take a slight *più mosso* in the ninth bar after **21**, and this is a moment in which the acoustics and/or the pedaling choices may make the right hand of the piano somewhat unclear from the conductor's perspective. Watching the pianist's hands, in addition to listening carefully, can usually untangle this passage if it is in danger of becoming uncoordinated. If the sound is particularly muddy from the podium, the conductor may have to depend almost entirely on visual coordination with the soloist's left hand.

The rhythmic situation at the downbeat of **23** is quite similar to the situation at **15**, but the solution is usually exactly the opposite. While the downbeat in the orchestra at **15** is coordinated with the first note in the arpeggio of grace notes, the *forte* entrance of low brass and other winds at **23** is usually coordinated with the top note (the whole note, C-sharp) of the pianist's arpeggio. When discussing the situation at **15**, I mentioned that an important reason for this decision is to avoid a conflict between dominant harmony (G^7) in the orchestra and tonic (C) in the piano. This same situation, here a clash between sub-dominant harmony (D-sharp half-diminished 7th) and tonic (C-sharp major) exists at **23**, but there are subtle differences in the overall musical situation that lead to a different outcome regarding the placement of the orchestral chord on the downbeat. First, the arpeggio of grace notes (at **23**) is usually performed quite rapidly, lessening the pain of the conflicting harmonies. Second, the first note of the bar in the left hand is played when the top C-sharp is reached in the right hand, and placing the orchestral chord at a point other than with the entrance of the left hand would be awkward, to say the least. Third, and most obvious, at **23** the composer vertically aligns the orchestral chord with the top note of the (piano's) arpeggio, while at **15** it is clearly aligned with the first (bottom) note.

Placement of the *pizzicato* chord in the second bar after **25** should not be difficult. Even though the preceding material feels playfully improvised, the eight triplets directly preceding the *pizzicato* chord are usually performed in a reasonably strict and predictable rhythm, allowing the conductor to place the preparatory gesture with the seventh of the eight triplets.

Two bars before **27**, a tasteful *portamento* in the violins between the first two notes of the bar adds some passion and *slancio* to the moment.

3rd movement.

The feel of the opening of this movement, appearing to be a rough and tumble march, often leads to a reading in the orchestra that is itself rough and overly aggressive. Much to the contrary, the sense of military bristle in the music is counterbalanced by the rather light orchestration and the opening dynamic of *pianissimo*. These two musical ideas, the military and the more delicate, must join as equal partners in this introductory passage.

Approaching the entrance of woodwinds four bars before **29** should not ever be a moment for anxiety. Even if the triplets in the pianist's right hand become somewhat obscured from the conductor's perspective, tuning out the triplets and aurally following the left hand makes this a simple task.

The preparatory gesture for the orchestra's entrance at *Moderato* (sixteen bars before **31**) provides a perfect case study for a common accompanying situation. Less experienced conductors will be tempted to coordinate the gesture (a half-note preparation) with the last half bar before the orchestra's entrance, but this is usually a mistake. If the soloist's *ritard* in the half bar preceding the orchestra's entrance is significant (as it is likely to be), then the gesture just described will leave the conductor hanging aimlessly in limbo, waiting for the soloist to complete the four eighth notes in the final beat. The result is likely to be a downbeat that is difficult for the orchestra to interpret, as well as being generally awkward and uncontrolled. A better solution in this, and the many other similar situations that conductor's encounter, is to wait to begin the preparatory gesture until approximately the final quarter note of the preceding bar, as this gives the conductor considerably more control, accuracy, and flexibility.

The famous melody in the viole at *Moderato* requires careful, loving shaping from the conductor to ensure that it is not overplayed or self-indulgent. Whether or not a *portamento* is added between the first two notes is a matter of taste and style. I prefer to have the viole add this gesture, gracefully and tastefully, as it is certainly within the boundaries of appropriate style and expression.

The passage beginning at **32** can be handled successfully either in two or in four. The only determining factor is the tempo chosen by the soloist. If the tempo is at or below Rachmaninoff's marking (𝅗𝅥 = 48), then it will probably be necessary to either conduct in four or, if remaining in two, to at least toss in some helpful subdivisions. If the tempo is any faster than the composer's indication, however, the passage flows more musically in two.

The passage between **34** and **35** can be more perilous than it appears on the page. Even with a string section that can execute the passage easily and cleanly, there are still potential "train wrecks" here. The principal issue is coordination between the theme as expressed in the strings and its echo in the solo piano. Many soloists unintentionally rush in the scale passages, and when this happens it is not practical to "adjust" the orchestra in a misguided attempt to "accompany." If this happens in rehearsal, a private discussion may be required. Also, it is polite (as well as practical) in a passage like this to mirror the beat in the left hand somewhere within the soloist's easy field of vision. Clearly, during the scale passages the soloist will not be staring up at the baton, so bringing a clear beat into her line of sight may solve any problems quickly.

One other issue of which the conductor should be aware is the possible tardiness (by perhaps as much as an eighth note) of clarinets and bassoons. As the soloist's passagework flies forward, these woodwinds may need to rhythmically anticipate by a considerable distance in order for their sound to occur in coordination with the piano by the time that sound reaches the podium and the audience. This same dilemma can occur concerning the solo trumpet at **35**.

The reiteration of the second theme (sixteen bars before **37**) brings with it the same issues as discussed earlier. It is certainly logical to assume that the phrasing, as well as the decision regarding the *portamento*, will be as before. I prefer, however, for this passage to assume a lighter, less dramatic character, as suggested by the more delicate character of the instruments assigned to the melody: violins and solo flute here as contrasted with viole and solo oboe earlier. To this end, I do not add the *portamento* in the violins, and ask for their sound to be lighter in character, with a less intense vibrato.

Even though the composer indicates at **38** that the preceding ♩ = the new 𝅗𝅥, it is best to begin the passage in four, thinking of the metric conversion as old eighth note equals new quarter note. The conductor may want to change into two at or near a point ten bars before **39**, making the *accelerando* and the transition into **39** go more smoothly. Observant conductors will also note that the composer's math for the transition at **38** doesn't really make sense. At *Meno mosso* he gives us a metronome marking of 𝅗𝅥 = 48, and at **38** tells us that the ♩ = 116. But if, at **38**, the old ♩ = the new 𝅗𝅥, then the ♩ at this point will be 192, which is clearly too fast. The only way to make some sense of this is to assume that the "old" quarter note in his equation is the pace we have reached at the end of the *ritard*, just before **38**. The tempo at that point will often be approximately ♩ = 58, making the transition to the new tempo, new 𝅗𝅥 = 58 and therefore new ♩ = 116, exactly correct.

Considering the very grand musical context of the moment, the melodic line at *Maestoso* (after **39**) cries out for the previously discussed *portamento* between the first two notes of the phrase. Although the beat is still in two here, the conductor needs to be sensitive to the possible *rubati* made by the soloist in the third and fourth bars, as well as other similar passages. Eight bars before *Più vivo* the conductor may find that some or all of these bars need to be in four in order to accommodate some stretch in the piano line as well as a traditional, though not printed, *rallentando* moving toward *Più vivo*.

The penultimate bar of the work should not pose any problems whatsoever, as any change of tempo from the soloist (forcing the orchestra to do the same) is certainly to be avoided. Some soloists insist on a slight broadening in this bar, but when this happens I always try to gently talk the pianist out of this course, as the headlong rush of energy being built up to this point demands to be carried to the end without any let up. Unfortunately, when this conversation occurs after I have heard the soloist play this bar with a slight *allargando* or *maestoso* feeling, it usually goes something like this:

D.I.: I wonder if we could move forward through those last bars without taking any *allargando*. Would that be all right?

Soloist: Am I slowing down there? I really don't mean to. Let's do it again.

[The passage is repeated.]

D.I.: I still feel like it slows down slightly during the second half of that bar. Can we avoid that, do you think?

Soloist: Oh, I'm really not slowing down; I just want those chords to have a more *maestoso* feel. OK?

You can see that in this not-so-uncommon situation, the conductor is really caught in a difficult spot. We have clearly made our point, but what to one person is just playing the chords "a bit *maestoso,*" is to another person clearly slowing down. Sometimes this is the delicate diplomatic path that we tread.

☙

Sergei Rachmaninoff

Piano Concerto No. 3 in D Minor, Op. 30

1st movement.

The *diminuendo* at the end of the second bar and the arrival at *pianissimo* in the third bar are expressive issues to be taken seriously, as their color and expressive qualities set the tone for the entire opening of the movement. The sudden (only two beats' duration) decay of sound from what already appears to the listener to be quite soft (*piano*) to what must be an almost inaudible *pianissimo* should take the listener's breath away. This is not only important from an expressive and textural point of view, but also from a practical one, as many soloists play this opening passage almost invisibly softly.

Balance and color continue to be very important during this entire opening passage, affecting several separate issues. All playing marked *pianissimo* in the winds must match the delicacy of the strings, and, depending on the acoustics of the theatre and the technical sophistication of the players, this may not be so easy to achieve. Also, the winds need to make clear differentiations between *piano* and *pianissimo*. Passages in the former dynamic constitute important musical lines while those with the latter are purely accompaniment.

A sighing *diminuendo* is often added in the third bar after **1** in order to differentiate this part of the phrase from the similar fragment two bars earlier. The conductor should be aware whether or not the soloist intends to add this expressive dynamic, so that the orchestra responds in kind.

The *ritard* in the eighth bar after **1** should be fairly modest, though some soloists will not agree. This is an important, but delicate expressive moment, intended to allow a bit of extra time for a graceful, unhurried *diminuendo*. As in many music-making decisions, this is definitely an example of "less is more." Here, an understated gesture results in a more sophisticated and elegant reading. Even though the composer did not go so far as to write "*poco ritard*," he makes apparent by his orchestration that this gesture should be modest, since when it is exaggerated the repeated notes in the upper strings become expressively awkward and draw unnecessary attention to themselves. In addition, a greater slowing of the tempo in just these three beats makes the immediate return to (the original) tempo in the next bar rather sudden and unmusical.

In the first two bars at *Più mosso*, even if the pianist's articulation is not completely transparent or the sound (as heard on the podium) is muddy, it is still easy to catch the end of this phrase before the orchestra's entrance. This is done by carefully observing the rising five-note figure in eighth notes in the pianist's left hand in the second bar of the passage. If, as mentioned above, the sound is unclear up to that point, then it is easy enough to coordinate the baton with the third and fourth beats of that bar, utilizing a beat that becomes increasingly more specific as the orchestra's entrance in the following bar approaches.

Four bars before **3** it is important for the conductor to have a firm memory of the soloist's tempo from previous rehearsal or pre-rehearsal meeting. The first beat of the *Più vivo* must swing confidently forward from the baton at the new tempo in order to make it possible for the syncopated entrances in the orchestra (first violins and solo horn) to be properly coordinated with the same figures in the piano. If the conductor hesitates while waiting for the soloist to play the first four sixteenth notes of the bar (in which the piano clearly establishes the new tempo), it is likely that it will already be too late to clearly cue accurate entrances for the violins and horn. This is one of those circumstances, like so many in the concerto repertoire, when fortune favors the bold. It is probably appropriate to mention, however, that fortune also favors the extremely well prepared and those with excellent tempo memory.

The two bars preceding **4** should sound logical and easy to the listener, but they require considerable care from the conductor. This is because the *colla parte* bar (read "*rallentando molto*") is likely to slow down very suddenly from the previous quick tempo; it will then shoot forward, back to tempo, in the next bar. The possible problem here is not so much concerning coordination with the *rallentando* in the first bar as it is about anticipating the sudden return to tempo and having the orchestra moving forward soon enough. As mentioned in the preceding paragraph, this is also a situation in which a certain level of boldness is required for the best result. Making sure that the orchestra is flowing forward swiftly but calmly at *a tempo* means that the conductor is, to a certainly degree, anticipating the return to tempo with her gesture before she actually hears it.

Although it is not, in itself, difficult to conduct, the following *Allegro* (at **4**) provides an opportunity to mention the physical and mental discipline that is so important when conducting this repertoire. The virtuosic nature of the solo playing in a passage like this one, as well as the mental activity required from the conductor to be certain he is coordinating accurately, combine to cause many conductors to beat far too athletically in a passage like this one. It is important in such passages (of which there are a great many in the repertoire) to separate our intellectual activity from the messages we wish to send via the character and size of the beat. When the mental activity required by, and/or the anxiety caused by, a particular solo passage finds its way into the baton then we have failed to separate the very different parts of our task. The style here, for example, is light, delicate, and playful, and a bigger, heavier beat will elicit an inappropriately dense string sound that will overwhelm the solo winds, and possibly even the solo piano. A small, delicate beat, drawing the players' attention to the tip of the baton, is called for here, no matter what computations may be swirling in our own brain. In a passage like this one the mind has one set of tasks but the conductor's hands have very different ones, and it is important that we never confuse which is which.

The brief *Moderato* section that begins just before 5 is a lovely moment for the orchestra. It is not, however, made any lovelier by playing it *Adagio*. This short passage contains two specific moments (one bar before 5 and the fourth bar after 5) where the composer asks for an expressive decaying of the tempo, and a base tempo for this *Moderato* that is too slow makes these expressive *allargandi* feel stodgy and meaningless.

In the charming *pianissimo* figures six bars before 6, it is important that the strings execute precisely the articulations that the composer indicated. Even though they often arrive on a down-bow, the quarter notes in these figures that are marked *staccato* must be played *staccato*, without variation. Of course, the fact that the quarter notes in question are the final notes of a phrase, and will probably be played down-bow, means there will be a tendency for them to inadvertently be played longer than the other similar notes in the phrase. The easiest way to describe the desired length, if asked, is to say that all the notes in the figure, eighth notes and quarter notes, are to be played the same length. Only by careful execution of this passage do we allow the completely different and more expressive articulation of the quarter notes several bars after **6** (those marked with dashes and not dots) to make musical sense.

The first three bars of the *Allegro* (six bars before **10**) provide another moment to observe the necessary separation between the brain and the baton. When we arrive at the *Allegro* we have just come from a rather exciting *accelerando* in four, but the character of the beat (and therefore of the leadership) changes instantly at this downbeat. Although the ear is carefully following the solo piano through the sixteenth-note figures, the baton stops on the downbeat of *Allegro* without rebound, left hand extended to sustain the *pianissimo* woodwind chord. Without showing any other beats in these bars, the baton then passively marks (at the appropriate moments) the downbeats of the following two bars, finally showing a gentle cut-off of the winds with the left hand.

The *accelerando* that begins four bars before **11** leads logically into a beat in two at **11**. Usually a return to four is necessary in the seventh bar after **11**, to facilitate the *ritard* and return to *Tempo I.* One common error, both technically and musically, when the conductor returns to beating in four at this point, is returning to four with an immediately slower quarter-note pulse. This creates a *subito meno mosso* effect that is then followed by the printed *ritard.* This is to be avoided for two reasons: (1) it is not what the composer asked, and it is musically awkward and unnecessarily "lumpy," and (2) except with an extraordinarily skilled orchestra, it is likely to cause several beats of poor ensemble while the second violins and viole adjust to this suddenly slower tempo. (It is important to note that the marking *rit.* occurs on the third beat of the bar, not at the beginning of the bar, so the entire idea of making a *subito meno mosso* at the beginning of the bar is totally contrary to the composer's intentions.) The idea, of course, is to return gradually from the tempo established at **11** to *Tempo I.* This requires not only that the conductor avoid a sudden *meno mosso* in the seventh bar after **11**, but also that the *ritard* not be so extreme that returning to *Tempo I* now requires *più mosso*. A simple, gentle *ritard* for six beats, moving from the tempo at **11** down to (but not past) *Tempo I* is all that is required.

The conductor sets the *più mosso* tempo in the first bar (third beat) of **12** based on information obtained during rehearsal. The soloist, however, will set the exact tempo of this passage, beginning on the next sixteenth note, where the arpeggios begin. The conductor, therefore, sets tempo as already described, but must then listen intently during the remainder of that bar in order to make any minor adjustment in tempo required by the soloist's choices of the moment.

This entire passage (from the *più mosso* after **12** to the *più vivo* after **13**) can be handled successfully in beats of either quarter notes or half notes, depending on the preference of the conductor and the general rhythmic dependability of soloist and orchestra. I prefer to remain in quarter note beats here, as I find that this insures better coordination of woodwinds with the solo piano, as well as creating more rhythmic drive forward in these figures, but this is an entirely subjective, personal choice.

The *più vivo* passage (ten bars before **14**) is best handled in two. Although I have mentioned many times in this text that keeping one's ears (and eyes) on the pianist's left hand will often make more complex passages easier to accompany, this is not necessarily one of those passages. Even though the lowest voice of the left hand provides a rhythmic punctuation that is easy to follow for the conductor, most pianists will voice this passage in such a way as to keep this line rather subtle, emphasizing the upper voice of the right hand. It is easiest and most functional here to simply following the charming swing of the melody in the right hand.

Seven bars after **14** I return to beating in four, staying in four into the following *Allegro*. Although this passage can certainly be managed remaining in two, I prefer this passage in four because this helps to emphasize the more muscular nature of the texture, and invites a more precise and exciting *staccato*.

The following *Allegro molto* is to be conducted in two, as indicated. Depending upon the pace of the preceding *accelerando*, the conductor will want to begin beating in two somewhere between one and three bars before *Alla breve* is indicated, as this helps to achieve a smoother transition.

Beginning at **15**, it is quite common for the bass line in half notes (celli and basses), the shifting harmonies in whole notes and half notes (woodwinds and horns), and even the expressive line in the first violins to lag somewhat behind the baton, as the eighth note figures in the solo piano move relentlessly forward. When this occurs in rehearsal, making certain that the habit does not continue is extremely important, but it is usually no more than a matter of bringing the issue clearly to the attention of all musicians and making certain that the beat remains clear and easy to follow. Orchestras that play habitually behind the baton have particular difficulties coordinating this sort of passage, and the result is an unpleasant discontinuity of harmony between solo piano and orchestra.

Somewhere during the four bars before *Allegro molto* (*cadenza*), the conductor will want to begin beating in four as the *ritenuto* (that begins eight bars earlier) continues to progress. This choice depends on both the progression of the *ritenuto* and the possibility that the soloist may desire these four bars to be played *meno mosso subito*. The expressive quality of this passage depends to a large extent on the precision and subtlety of the *crescendo-diminuendo* figures. Each figure must climax and immediately begin its *diminuendo* precisely as written so that the overlapping quality of these waves of sound occurs as intended. In addition, the zenith of each of these figures needs to be no higher than *mezzo-piano*, as higher crests for these figures destroy the inherently mysterious quality of the moment.

At the end of the *cadenza*, the soloist establishes the new tempo four bars before **19**, and it is at this point that the conductor's attention needs to be fixed again on the soloist. The indication *Meno mosso* at **19** is somewhat misleading (the expression *Lo stesso movimento* might have been less confusing), but the parenthetic indication that follows (𝅗𝅥 = ♩) tells us precisely what the composer desired. The conductor must mark the beginning of the first bar at **19**, flowing passively through the remaining beats of the bar, and then clearly indicate the following downbeat as a preparatory gesture for the solo flute.

One bar before *Moderato* (the continuation of the *cadenza*) the conductor must carefully and clearly control the two half notes in the horn, being careful not to move ahead of the solo piano. In the second half of this bar the soloist usually employs a considerable *ritard*. Allowing the baton to remain in the fourth beat, as though sustaining a *fermata*, while the pianist completes the final octuplet, can comfortably accommodate this. Next, coordinated with either the final or penultimate note of the octuplet (depending upon the amount of *ritard* employed by the soloist in these last few notes), the conductor gives a clear but gentle preparatory gesture for the horn.

Just as at the end of the previous section of the *cadenza*, the conductor begins marking bars at **20**, clearly showing the entrance of bassoons and horns two bars later, taking this tempo from the soloist. (The composer is kind enough to explain all of this with his indication "dirigieren" at **20**.) A slight subdivision may be employed in the beat preceding *Tempo I* for good coordination between first horn and solo piano. However, this is not necessary if the *ritard* taken is less severe, and a less extreme *ritard* can also be helpful in creating a less jarring transition back to *Tempo I*.

Many soloists take a slight *più mosso* at 22. When this is the case, the first few beats at 22 present a situation similar to that already discussed at 12. Before hearing the soloist's exact tempo (in the sixteenth-note figure), the conductor must commit himself confidently and clearly to the new tempo. He must then listen carefully to the sixteenth-note figures in the solo piano in order to ensure perfect coordination of tempo, immediately making any necessary micro-adjustments.

The first bar at 23 can be managed musically in at least two different ways (strictly observing what is printed, or not), and each has its positive and negative qualities. The composer does not indicate *rall.* until the second bar, leaving us to assume that the figure in winds in the first bar of 23 is to be played in the preceding tempo without variance of any kind, leaving the *rall.* for the entrance of the solo piano. This is all well and good in theory, but there are a couple of practical concerns that intervene. Following two increases in tempo just before 23 (one that is printed four bars before 23 and another that often occurs spontaneously at 22), we are left (at 23) with a tempo that may be as quick as ♩ = 140. This tempo feels rather rushed for the fairly delicate wind figure at 23. This is, however, an entirely subjective and personal musical decision, regarding whether this bar (and the similar figure in strings two bars later) retains the appropriate character when played literally *a tempo*. Even though one wants to be sure that there is a clear distinction between the *a tempo* feel of the orchestra's statements (first and third bars of 23) and the *rallentando* feel of the answers in the piano (second and fourth bars), it is possible to find some middle ground that does not make the orchestra's statements feel unnecessarily hurried.

Six bars before the end of the movement, the composer writes only *poco a poco accelerando*, but does not tell us if we are to begin this bar within the *rall.* where the pianist left off, or if we are to return immediately to *a tempo* and then begin the *accelerando*. Fortunately, as conductors, the problem will be solved for us, inasmuch as the tempo six bars before the end will be whatever pace is taken by the soloist. From a more analytical perspective, however, it is clear that this bar should begin at something resembling *Tempo I*, proceeding forward in *accelerando*. This final pressing forward of the tempo extends all the way to the last note, and adding a final *ritard* on the last two notes does no service to the music. On the contrary, continuing the *accelerando* relentlessly through these last several beats, though in *pianissimo*, retains the hushed but breathless quality that the composer intended.

2nd movement.

The question of setting the "correct" tempo is not paramount during the opening *tutti* of this movement, since these first thirty-one bars contain a variety of tempi, and the entrance of the soloist will occur at a completely different tempo. What is important, however, is that the conductor sets the proper mood, allowing each phrase to expand and diminish at its own pace, without any sense of hurrying forward.

The other subject that is of great importance in this passage is the expressive quality of all *diminuendi*. The composer often gives the orchestra only one beat to make a potent and expressive *diminuendo* (bars 1, 2, 10, 14, 17, etc.). Even at an unhurried *Adagio* this means that the decay of sound must begin precisely where written and should take on a very expressive and rather extreme character. When the composer allows a bit more time for the falling portion of the phrase (bars 5, 8, 9, 12, etc.), the expression must be just as potent, but can be a bit less extreme in character.

Both one bar and five bars before **25** a slight *ritard* is often employed in the final beat. In both of these bars, a slight subdivision for clarity and ease of expression is wise, essentially dictating (for first violins and viole respectively) the last eighth note of the bar. When this subdivision is made one bar before **25**, it is even more important than usual that the conductor be extremely clear and insistent regarding the change of tempo (led by first bassoon and first horn) at **25**. When these triplets, particularly the one occurring on the first beat, begin sluggishly and lag behind the new tempo, coordination with the theme entering on the second beat (in second violins and first flute) becomes impossible.

Although it is not, on its face, a difficult passage to follow with the ear, the particular acoustics of a given concert hall, as well as the soloist's pedaling and voicing choices, can make the passage at **26** more difficult to following than it needs to be. From an accompanying point of view, this is a somewhat unusual passage inasmuch as the best strategy is not following one specific register or voice in the piano. In this passage, a somewhat more global and sophisticated approach is best, continually retuning one's ear in a series of shifting focuses. An overview of these shifting lines is as follows:

Bar	*Beat*	*Focus Point*
First bar of **26**	1	Bottom voice of RH (eighth rest, F, G-flat)
First bar of **26**	2	LH (triplet F, low D-flat, G-flat)
First bar of **26**	3	Upper voice of LH (triplet A-flat, B-double-flat, C-flat)
Second bar of **26**	1	Middle voice of RH (triplet D-flat chord, D-flat, E-flat)
Second bar of **26**	2	RH sextuplet, especially the change of harmony on third part of triplet
Second bar of **26**	3	RH sextuplet

Third bar of **26**	all	Upper voice of RH
Fourth bar of **26**	all	Upper voice of RH

The same approach can be taken in the similarly structured passages at **27** and **32**, allowing the ear to follow those lines with clear scale passages or obvious changes of harmony.

The bar preceding **27** is another example of how important it is not to assume that all preparatory gestures before a new entrance of the orchestra occur in coordination with the final beat of the preceding bar (when that bar is played by the soloist alone). Showing the preparatory gesture when the soloist arrives at the third beat (one beat before **27**) leaves the conductor incapable of giving a preparation in the new tempo. This is, of course, because that third beat, within a *rallentando* and containing a *tenuto*, will be much longer than one beat in the following tempo. In order to give a preparation in the new tempo, the preparatory gesture should occur just after the penultimate note (G-natural) in the right hand. This usually allows for good coordination and avoids the awkwardness of a long, lingering, meaningless preparatory gesture.

Subdivision (of the triplet) is sometimes necessary in the final beat of the fourth bar of **27** in order to accommodate the soloist's *ritard.* At the end of the sixth bar after **27**, after the figures in the piano are concluded, it is best to show the cut-off for strings, clarinet, bassoons, and horn with a gentle gesture of the left hand only, which, therefore, does *not* indicate the first beat of the next bar. By doing this, the conductor does not appear to be placing a fermata on the downbeat of a bar marked *Più vivo*, which can be confusing. After the cut-off just described, the conductor can then wait for the soloist to begin the following bar at her leisure, and it is easy for the baton to calmly "catch-up" by the time the second beat of the bar occurs, getting perfectly in the swing of the new tempo the soloist has established.

The entrance of winds in the second bar of *Più vivo* is marked *piano*, with the first violins marked *forte*. This makes perfect sense in terms of balance and ensemble, but the downbeat (precisely at the *piano* entrance of winds) must be very strong and crisp in order to overcome the natural hesitation of some violins at this awkward entrance; awkward for some musicians because it juxtaposes the triplet within triplet figures in the solo piano against the starkly duple construction of the theme in the violins. The dilemma is obvious, that the *piano* downbeat for winds may appear (by the conductor's stronger, encouraging gesture for the violins) to imply *forte*, and some winds may need to be asked to overlook the strength of the gesture. Without encouraging a sound from the first violins that is inappropriately aggressive, it is important that they be encouraged to play as *forte* as possible here. They are, of course, still muted, and even a large and mature first violin section is often nearly inaudible here, when pitted against the *forte* in the solo piano.

Subdivision (of the eighth note, not the triplet) is sometimes necessary in the final beat of the bar before **28** in order to accommodate the soloist's *ritard*. Because the soloist will proceed *meno mosso* at **28**, it is often best for the baton to remain in the position of the first beat of bar (as if in *fermata*) until the soloist clearly commits to the new tempo in the second beat of the bar. When the pianist reaches the G-flat at the beginning of the second beat, it is, once again, quite easy for the conductor to "catch up" gracefully while cueing the viole just ahead of the third beat.

Either from inexperience, nervousness, or the mistaken presumption that it's not necessary, some conductors will choose not to mark each bar in a solo passage like the one directly preceding **29**. Unless one is dealing with an orchestra that is so expert, and all musicians so experienced, that it is logical to assume that *all* the musicians have played a given work *many, many times*, then bars in a passage like this one should still be gently and unobtrusively marked for the security and calm of the orchestra. I recently observed a performance of one of the Rachmaninoff concerti with an orchestra of very skilled and experienced freelance musicians led by a rather young and inexperienced conductor. Even though the musicians were, as stated, quite experienced and capable, the conductor's failure to mark empty bars in passages like this one caused not inconsiderable consternation among the players. As I'm fond of saying to my students, a moment like this needs to be considered from the *orchestra's* perspective, not from yours. Expecting the musicians to know where they are in the piece (unless it's been explained in rehearsal) after the conductor stops conducting and then starts again is not at all reasonable, no matter how "easy" the conductor may think the passage sounds. From the conductor's point of view, this passage is not difficult to follow, so it's easy to make the mistake that the orchestra ought to be able to follow the number of bars passing by ear. But look, for example, at the music found eleven and ten bars before **29**. Without looking at the score, there's no way to know that this music covers two bars; the composer could easily have notated the same music in a way that covers three bars, four, or even just one. So, when the intervening bars are not marked, and the conductor simply begins conducting again one bar before **29**, it is not at all reasonable to think that the musicians know where to play next. Contrary to some beliefs, politely marking those empty bars isn't insulting … it's our job.

One beat before *Poco più mosso* (the fourth bar after **32**), the baton should rest on the third beat, indicating a subtle *fermata* for the orchestra, awaiting the conclusion of the pianist's sextuplet. This pause of the baton allows the conductor, following the third beat, to give a preparatory beat that more accurately reflects the new tempo just ahead. This tempo is fairly easy to pick up from the soloist, in spite of the complex passagework. Clear triplets in the left hand and the flatted 10th in the right hand (on the second part of the first beat triplet) provide sufficient guidance for secure leadership. Such musical security and clarity of *ictus* are vital in order to successfully cue the solo flute and second violins following the second and third beats. Any insecurity or lack of confidence shown in the baton during this bar will result in weak, poorly coordinated entrances, or no entrances at all.

At **33**, the metric relationship (previous beat = new bar) works easily and seamlessly, as does the reverse relationship at **36**. The bar preceding **35** is usually best conducted in three unless the soloist's *ritard* in this bar is unusually modest.

The third bar of **36** is best handled in much the same manner as described for the first bar at **28**. As before, the conductor waits (on the first beat) for the soloist to clearly commit to the new, slower tempo before moving forward into the second beat of the bar.

One bar before **37**, I ask all winds to breathe between the second and third beats, allowing a bit of extra time in the bar to allow the phrase sufficient space. This is particularly important for those winds with a half note followed by a quarter rest, as they must be particularly attentive to releasing the phrase in coordination with those players that must breathe and re-enter on the third beat. I repeat this same procedure in the fourth bar of **37**.

Just as discussed near the beginning of the movement, it is important that the viole begin their triplets at **38** precisely in the new, faster tempo. What may be even more important, however, is that the viole, and other instruments with *crescendi* during the first beat of the bar, create in the space of only one beat the emotional pressure required to make the entrance of violins on the second beat logical and inevitable.

It is extremely important that the conductor be certain how the soloist intends to approach the passage that crosses the bar-line at **39**. Some soloists move completely in tempo from the sixteenth notes before **39** to those after, while others stop abruptly for a short "breath" on the bar-line. Not knowing which is intended, and/or not being technically prepared, will be disastrous.

As the soloist concludes the upward arpeggio in the penultimate bar of the movement, the conductor, having already marked the empty bar for the orchestra, subtly prepares the baton for the orchestra (at the position of the third beat) while focusing his attention completely on the pianist. At this moment, soloist and conductor move together, neither one truly leading or following, in order to execute the two chords in the following bar not only with precision, but accurately setting the desired tempo for the following movement. The third movement then commences after precisely two beats' rest, in the proscribed relationship of old quarter note equals new half note.

3rd movement.

The indication *piano* just after the first note of the movement does not really work when executed literally, and saps the energy from the movement before it really gets going. The five woodwinds are really no match for, and certainly no acoustical threat to, the brilliance of the solo piano marked *forte*. Therefore, a dynamic shift to a modest *mezzo forte* (instead of *piano*) after the first note is sufficient diminishment of volume. In similar manner, the indication *pianissimo* in the first violins in the sixth bar (and following) is too soft for this important material to be heard as an equal partner with the solo piano. Both this line and other later scale passages in the violins need to be played out at a dynamic closer to *forte* in order to have sufficient acoustic penetration.

Whether to play or omit the woodwind figures marked *ad libitum* in this movement (two bars before **43** and following) is, obviously, a subjective discussion of preference, since the composer went out of his way to tell us that these lines are not obligatory. While I do not think it can be argued that the movement is somehow irrevocably damaged by the omission of these figures, I do think it is fair to say that without these woodwind interjections these passages lack the feeling of hysteria and wildness that is very important to the overall feel of the piece. It cannot go unmentioned that, at the usual tempo of this movement, some of the figures, particularly in the oboe, are so fast as to be virtually unplayable with complete accuracy. This being said, we must remember that, even though he was a virtuoso pianist, Rachmaninoff was not a foolish or uneducated man in matters of orchestration, and he surely knew and anticipated the wildness that would be the result of these figures moving at this velocity. Understanding this, and though it goes against the professional grain in so many ways, we need to accept that these woodwind passages may not have been intended to be executed with perfection so much as they are intended to convey the kind of emotional abandon illustrated throughout the movement. In addition, though they are all marked *piano*, they need to be played approximately *forte* in order to have any chance of being heard.

The transition into **45** can be tricky and potentially messy. Conversely, it can be quite simple and natural, depending upon the manner in which the soloist handles the preceding *ritard* (if any) and the new tempo. If the *ritard* in the preceding bar is gentle and leads logically into the *meno mosso* without any unnecessary manhandling of the *tempi*, then the conductor can flow logically and easily into the new tempo without having to be overly concerned about lack of agreement in the new tempo. However, if the *Meno mosso* is abrupt, and/or the soloist takes a bit of extra "lift" between the first and second quarters of the bar, then coordinating the new tempo in the piano with the material in the first violins and viole can be problematic. This potential problem arises, of course, from the fact that the violins and viole can only place the D-natural that begins the new phrase based on the tempo shown by the conductor in the first beat of the bar. If that first beat is subject to hesitation while the conductor waits to hear exactly where the soloist will place the beginning of the new phrase (on the second quarter of the bar) then the gesture in the baton will probably not be specific or logical enough to elicit a clean, confident start to the new phrase in the strings. If the soloist does not, or cannot be convinced to, keep this transition flowing naturally forward, then the only other solution is to (briefly) stop the baton on the first beat and make a slight subdivision as the pianist plays the first note of the new phrase, allowing the violins and viole to respond quickly afterward. To be honest, what I've just described isn't a great solution, but if the conductor is forced into that position by the soloist's choices it's better than no solution at all.

The *ritard* six bars before **48** should not be overburdened. First, this is not so important a musical moment that it needs to be lingered over so ponderously. Second, and more important, in order to correctly facilitate the new tempo at *Scherzando* as indicated, the pulse (of the half note) must not slow down to a pace slower than the intended quarter-note pulse after the double-bar. One often hears this passage performed with a *ritard* so great that the piece comes nearly to a halt just before the double-bar, requiring that the pulse speed up at *Scherzando*, which is not at all what the composer had in mind. To the ear of the listener, the figure in the horns (a dotted half note followed by a quarter note) is the same as the rhythm in the strings (a dotted quarter note followed by an eighth note) after the double bar, but this only works if the two tempi flow seamlessly together. As we've observed elsewhere, a gentle, logical transition from one set of musical ideas to another is what was requested. When a transition like this is handled deftly, the listener should be amazed that we are somehow, magically in a completely new musical world from just a few bars before. We can be amazed because no one beat us over the head with the severity of the transition, but allowed us to slowly realize that the world has taken on new shape and color.

Depending on the amount of *ritard* the soloist chooses to employ (even though none is marked), the last (quarter note) beat before **49** may need to be subdivided. When the *ritard* is sufficient to require it, this slight extra gesture allows for comfortable and precise coordination between the solo figure and the final note of the bar in the clarinet.

The beat directly preceding **50** is another where it is best to postpone the preparatory gesture until the final eighth-note pulse of the bar, rather than aligning the gesture with the pianist's fourth beat. This gives the orchestra a more secure foundation for their entrance, as well as better approximating the actual tempo of the next bar.

In the bar before **51** the soloist usually takes some *ritard.* As the conductor will have already been beating in six (in $\frac{3}{2}$), no further subdivision is necessary except on the final beat before **51**, where a subdivision for the final eighth note of the bar is often needed. This last eighth note usually needs to be shown with a gesture that implies a slight *fermata*, as the soloist usually takes an extra moment to finish the arpeggio and re-place the hands for the next bar. Sustaining this note for only the briefest extra moment, the conductor then looks to the soloist's hands in order to coordinate the downbeat of the following bar.

A cut is sometimes taken from the end of the second bar of **52** to the downbeat at **54**. When this is done, the *ritard* in the timpani in the second bar of **52** should not be nearly as dramatic as when the piece is played without the cut. Forgoing a more severe *ritard* when the cut is taken facilitates a smoother transition to the more flowing tempo at **54**. When the cut is not employed, a significant *rallentando* is appropriate (though unmarked) in the second bar of **52**, in order to create a transition to the new mood and tempo at *Meno mosso*.

It is often necessary to subdivide one beat, or even two, preceding **53**, in order to allow the flutes to play with complete confidence and good coordination with the soloist. After the last eighth note of the bar is indicated, the conductor must still wait (as though in *fermata*) while the pianist completes the final triplet. This will appear to the flutes to be an invitation to sustain this last eighth note in the bar, but they should be cautioned against this. Even though considerable extra time is likely to be added to this beat, only the strings and first horn sustain, while the flutes execute their final note *staccato*, as indicated.

Depending on the pace of the soloist's *ritard*, I subdivide either one or two beats directly preceding **54**. Making sure that the final note in the piano does not occur simultaneously with the final note in the flute and clarinet (which, of course, it should not) is entirely in the soloist's hands. Once the conductor has shown the subdivision of the sixth beat of the bar, the die is cast, and there is nothing more the conductor can do. Either the soloist will place the final E-flat slightly before the woodwinds' B-flat, as a precise triplet, or he will not. Unfortunately, care is not always taken in this moment, and in many performances these two notes sound at the same time.

Subdivision of the beat directly preceding **55** is also recommended. This subdivision will help to prevent a common error during this beat: the first horn and celli moving at virtually the same moment within such a long quarter note beat. The (concert) A-natural in the horn occurring precisely in coordination with the same pitch in the piano (LH) is critical, as is the E-flat in the celli coinciding correctly with the piano's C-natural.

In the passage from **57** to **58** it is extremely important that the conductor be thoroughly versed in the intricacies of the piano part. Though complex from a pianistic point of view, this passage is relatively easy to follow aurally, as the harmonies change clearly and logically. Moving from the final bar before **58** to the downbeat of **58**, it is quite helpful to be looking at the pianist's hands in order to coordinate this downbeat. Perfect coordination is often only possible by following the physical motion of the pianist's left hand toward the low E-flat, as there may be a modicum of extra time taken between the end of the chromatic scale and the following downbeat.

There is usually some *ritard* added toward the end of the sixth bar after **58**. When the *ritard* is modest, the conductor can simply flow passively through this bar, using the fourth beat (aligned with the fourth beat in the piano) as a preparation for the timpanist. However, when the *ritard* is more extreme the baton will need to pause passively in the third beat, waiting until after the pianist reaches the fourth beat to show the preparation for the following bar. In this situation, this preparation can usually be coordinated with the penultimate sixteenth note in the pianist's left hand.

The transition back to Tempo I at **59** can be handled in one of two ways, depending mostly upon the preference of the soloist. If the soloist wishes to slightly sustain the final note in the bar before **59**, then the preparatory gesture can be coordinated with that final note, either approximately or exactly in the new tempo. However, if the soloist intends to play that note in, or approximately in, the new tempo, the conductor should give a preparatory gesture in the new tempo after the pianist resolves the suspension in the left hand to D-natural. The soloist then follows the baton to the following downbeat.

As at the beginning of the movement, figures like those in the first violins two bars before and four bars after **61** need the dynamic increased to at least *mezzo-piano*, or even *mezzo-forte*, in order to be heard at an appropriate level as compared with the piano.

Some pianists take a slight *allargando* just before *Più vivo*, six bars before **67**. This gesture, not indicated by the composer, can cause a lack of coordination in the first bar of *Più vivo*, as the soloist begins the new tempo and the violins and viole must join immediately with the *staccato* figure. If possible, it is best if the bar preceding *Più vivo* does not slow down, but perhaps might even *accelerando* slightly to create the smoothest, most organic transition possible.

Some pianists will slightly stretch the triplet in the first half of the bar, four bars before **68**. The persistent *staccato* accompaniment throughout the orchestra makes this gesture, though musically charming, difficult to accommodate. When the soloist insists on this approach, the conductor must choose one of two approaches, and they are both bad. The conductor can accommodate the slight stretching of that beat by attempting to accompany the gesture, slowing the orchestra slightly and then returning to tempo with the soloist. However, in all but the most skilled orchestras this is likely to result in at least slight, if not considerable, ensemble discontinuity. The other solution is to simply ignore the pianist, maintaining a steady tempo in the orchestra, and assume that the soloist will catch up during the following one or two beats. I did say that neither of the options was good, and I wasn't joking. Sometimes we just have to make do with what the soloist sends our way.

The conductor should be careful that the first beat in the ninth bar after **69** is shown without a strong *ictus*, clearly indicating the change in the rhythmic pattern in the celli and basses. A similar issue presents itself both four bars and two bars before **70**. Subtle shifts in the character of the beat, even in such a simple passage, indicating which beats are more passive and which intend to impel playing, are one of the many things that separate the conscientious and skilled professional from conductors of lesser ability.

It is not uncommon for the soloist to create a slight *allargando* in the fourth bar after **74**. There is a certain logic to this gesture, because it both accentuates the last repetition of that figure and leads smoothly into the slower tempo that follows. When the soloist makes this musical gesture, obviously the brass and timpani must respond in kind. Of course, the same is true in the bar directly preceding **75**.

The *ritenuto* two bars before **78** is often so expansive as to require the conductor to beat in four. The *poco a poco accel.* at **78** is handled easily by beginning the passage, in two, at the same pulse as the previous quarter note. The preceding *ritenuto* tends to flow logically and musically toward a pulse where this relationship (previous ♩ = new 𝅗𝅥) will make sense.

The penultimate bar should not be expanded with any kind of *allargando*. Although this is sometimes done, the unnatural expansion of time at this critical moment disturbs the energetic forward motion toward the final bar, and should be avoided if at all possible.

☙

Sergei Rachmaninoff

Rhapsody on a Theme of Paganini, Op. 43

A sharply executed downbeat is all that is required to begin the work. Some conductors inadvertently also show an extra beat (what would be the second beat of a preceding bar), and this is both unnecessary and possibly confusing for the orchestra.

In the pick-ups to **1** and **2** (as well as in similar figures following **2**) considerable care needs to be taken to ensure that the three sixteenth notes are not executed late, essentially becoming a sixteenth-note triplet on the last eighth of the bar, rather than being executed precisely as written. Even excellent musicians often need to be reminded to begin the figure early enough, and without rushing, to avoid the figure becoming a triplet.

Two bars before **2**, the expressive *crescendo-diminuendo* must not be overdone. The beginning dynamic of the figure is *piano*, so its zenith is appropriately *mezzo-piano*. The same principle applies in the sixth and seventh bars after **2**.

The articulation in the fourth, eighth, and sixteenth bars of the *Tema* (in the violins) must be executed exactly as written, with a slur between the two notes. There is no dot on the quarter note, so the figure is not hooked, it is slurred, and the quarter note needs to be played full length. This figure is sometimes played down/up, instead of in one down-bow slur as indicated, in order to facilitate the down-bow beginning the following bar. When this bowing (down/up) is employed, it is even more important that the violins be cautioned to play the quarter note full length before changing to the up-bow on the eighth note, thus giving at least the illusion of a two-note slur, as the composer intended.

Owing to the distance from the back of the orchestra to the front, as well as some general execution issues in brass instruments, the horn and trumpet entrances in the first sixteen bars of Variation II are often behind the baton, and therefore behind the soloist. When this occurs it needs to be fearlessly corrected, since such lack of coordination makes the entire passage unstable.

Two bars before **6** and five bars after **6**, the flutist needs to adjust the dynamic to *forte*, as it can be very difficult to hear the flute prominently enough in this register.

In the first bar of Variation IV, the conductor needs to listen attentively to the first group of sixteenth notes in the solo piano, as the soloist will be setting a new tempo here. Showing the first beat of the first bar of this variation in the correct, new tempo is vital in allowing the viole to execute the second beat accurately. This change of tempo is another good example of the idea that the conductor must be "with," rather than "following," the soloist. Despite what is written in the first sentence of this paragraph, the conductor must be, for all practical purposes, *in* the new tempo right from the downbeat, which means that he has really no opportunity to hear these first sixteenth notes before committing himself to a significant degree. A moment like this works smoothly and easily when conductor and soloist share the qualities of experience, trust, calm nerves, and excellent tempo memory.

From **9** through the eighth bar after **10** the conductor can create a superior sense of line and phrasing by beating in one. The last four bars of the variation can remain in one if the winds are adequately responsive and the soloist's tempo remains constant. If either of those variables is not in place, then it is advisable to return to beating in two. If the conductor feels it is necessary to return to a beat in two for the last four bars of the variation, he does not need to be concerned that this will be musically disruptive, since he will probably beat in two for the opening of the next variation in any case.

In the fifth bar after **12** (and other similar bars), it is a good idea to consciously change the position of the beat between the first and second beats of the bar. The sharp *ictus* given on the first beat that impels the syncopated chord in the strings should remain in the lower part of the conducting field. The same type of gesture on the second beat, which cues the chord in horns and bassoons, should be given somewhat higher, to be certain that various sections of the orchestra feel secure for these syncopated, *staccato* entrances. Even more important than the position of the beat, however, is that the conductor's eyes lead from section to section of the orchestra. In a case like this, the gestures alone do not communicate sufficiently specific information for all musicians to feel entirely secure and for the conductor to be truly leading rather than simply beating time.

Simultaneous with showing the downbeat of Variation VI, the conductor should be certain to look at the soloist to ensure good coordination of entrance and tempo. Many soloists play this passage slightly slower than Variation V, even though it is marked *L'istesso tempo. Staccato* eighth notes in this variation in the upper strings need to be carefully controlled, as they will tend to rush in some ensembles. If the soloist takes a bit of *ritard* two bars before **15** then it is nice to continue that feeling in the clarinet one bar before **15**. The same is true of the relationship between piano and flute five and six bars before **17**. In both cases, however, if the soloist stays strictly in tempo then the woodwinds should do the same.

It is traditional to take some extra time during both English horn solos near the end of the variation. When this is done, extra care needs to be taken with the *pizzicati* in viole and celli within the *ritard*. In either event, it is best for these *pizzicati* to be taken *divisi*. It should also be mentioned that, in some materials, one or both of the English horn's solo phrases are either incorrectly transposed or not transposed at all. While appearing correctly (to my knowledge) in all scores, these errors are found in some English horn *parts*.

Extra time should not be taken in the one measure of rest at the end of Variation VI. The composer wrote neither a *fermata* nor a grand pause here, so one is not to be inferred. Simultaneous with the preparatory gesture for the beginning of Variation VII, visual communication with both the soloist and the second bassoon is vital. In Variation VII, dynamic contrast and strict adherence to the composer's dynamics are critical. In spite of the relatively delicate texture of the orchestration, the horns must play *mezzo-forte* and *marcato* as indicated. Dynamic contrast in violin and flute figures (*piano*, *pianissimo*, and *pianississimo*) is also very important to the overall flow and feel of this passage.

After dictating the final note of Variation VII (viole, celli, double basses, and bass drum) without any rebound, the baton should stay motionless, raised where it remained following the second beat of the last bar. At the same time, the conductor's attention goes to the soloist so that the baton can coordinate precisely with the new tempo established by the piano in the first bar of Variation VIII. This first bar should be marked precisely in the new tempo but without a strong *ictus* on the first beat of the first measure. This gesture establishes tempo without tempting any horns or bassoons to play early. The second beat of the first measure should have a more active *ictus* as a preparatory gesture for the following downbeat, combined with specific visual communication with bassoons and second and fourth horns. A similar type of gesture, clearly indicating tempo but nearly devoid of *ictus*, needs to be utilized in situations like the two bars directly preceding **23**. Very active beats in bars like these can be tempting to an orchestral musician, and do not appropriately communicate the conductor's knowledge of the orchestra's activity or inactivity. Next, a sharper downbeat at **23** indicates the re-entry of the orchestra.

During much of Variation IX, a small beat, with virtually no rebound, is best. This tends to keep the rhythm accurate, as well as discouraging the natural tendency for these figures to rush. Obviously, any forward pressure on the tempo makes coordination with the soloist's off-beats very problematic.

At the beginning of Variation X, the dashes under the clarinets' quarter notes do not necessarily imply significant space between the notes, which is often how they are performed. A nearly *legato* tonguing, with emphasis on each new quarter note, provides a better distinction between the clarinets' articulation and that of the bassoons, horns, and strings. As well as faithfully interpreting what the composer wished, this distinction of articulation directs the listener's ear to the important material without the necessity of the clarinets playing louder than indicated.

For coordination between the bells, harp, and soloist's left hand at **29**, the beat should remain concise and, again, virtually without rebound. It is also helpful if the conductor does not accidentally hide the baton from the soloist's field of vision. To this end, using the left hand to mirror the beat, positioned low, near the conductor's left hip, can be a significant and unobtrusive aid to the soloist. Three bars before the end of this variation the bassoon is marked *pianissimo*. This is precisely the right atmosphere, but not always practical, as the decaying sound in the hall from the *mezzo-forte* passage in the piano in the preceding bar will often render this important bassoon figure inaudible if it is not played somewhat louder than marked.

Extreme delicacy of gesture, a floating quality, and not too much concern for dictating tempo are required at the opening of Variation XI. In the bar before **31**, it is important to indicate clearly for the orchestra that, unlike the two preceding phrases, this phrase begins with a pick-up on the third beat. No matter how clear the conductor's gesture may be, however, it is common for one (or more) of the musicians that should play on the downbeat of **31** to accidentally play on the pick-up with the flute and English horn. It is sometimes necessary to remind the orchestra in rehearsal of this issue, and a gentle cautioning palm of the left hand in the direction of the celli and double basses while indicating the third beat to the winds is by no means out of order.

Arriving at the fifth bar after **31**, the baton should remain stationary in the first beat, waiting patiently while attentively following the progress of the solo piano. For those who find following such a passage difficult, and are therefore uncertain of exactly when to release the strings and cue the harp, it is best to direct the ear to the succession of A-naturals and F-naturals marked with accents in the left hand. These notes begin the last six groupings in the bar and lead the ear easily to the correct cut-off point. The baton (having remained still since the beginning of the bar) should move gently to the second beat on the beginning of the fifth grouping (on A-natural) and more actively to the third beat on the sixth grouping (on F-natural). Next, the baton shows a cut-off for the strings and a cue for the harp on the following down beat. The tempo established by the pianist during the six figures/groupings mentioned earlier in this paragraph is usually a tempo that can then be maintained for the following bar of harp *glissandi*.

Though Variation XII will often have some (unmarked) *rubato* sections, setting the correct tempo is very important, since it is very awkward to adjust the tempo, even slightly, after the entrance of the piano. An elegant tempo for this movement is around ♩ = 72, but, obviously, this is at the discretion of the soloist. Also important for the opening of this variation is strict performance of what is indicted in the *arco* strings: these single notes are eighth notes, not quarter notes, and they are *pianissimo*. The clarinet solos at **32** need to be played with more sound than *piano* in order to be heard in proper perspective with the solo piano. Though there may be some unwritten *rubato* in the solo piano that the conductor must negotiate, the violin figures that appear six bars after **32**, nine bars before **33**, two bars before **33**, and seven bars after **33** should under no circumstances be subject to any influences of such *rubato*. These figures represent a sobering influence on the delightfully playful attitude of the minuet in the solo piano, and their somewhat more stern and mathematical character should be maintained. In addition, subjecting those figures to any variations of tempo is likely to cause considerable ensemble difficulties.

The tempo for Variation XIII should not be too fast, despite being marked *Allegro*. Somewhere between ♩ = 132 and ♩ = 140 is more than sufficiently swift. A tempo any faster than this takes away from the muscular quality of the passage and makes the variation begin to sound *scherzando* instead of *molto marcato* as written.

In the accompaniment of Variation XIV it is important that the accents should be observed precisely and with considerable weight. The heroic nature of musical material in this variation requires the counterbalance of these weighty accents appearing in locations that seem unpredictable.

In the opening portion of the scherzo, Variation XV, the conductor can choose to either mark each bar for the orchestra in the traditional way or simply inform the orchestra that she will begin beating again at **40**. (When the latter choice is made, the first two beats at **40** are shown clearly, exactly in tempo, but absolutely passively, with a sharp *ictus* on the third beat to clearly indicate both the cue and the stylistic and dynamic elements.) In either case, it is almost always best to conduct the passage following **40** in three. Though this can be managed between **40** and **41** in one, it is only possible with an extremely skilled orchestra and a soloist who is extraordinarily reliable rhythmically. The trick, if one is needed, in staying with the soloist throughout this passage is to mentally tune out all of the arpeggiations and concentrate only on the progress of the melody in the uppermost voice of the piano. Depending upon the voicing choices of the soloist this can, at times, be easier said than done. However, under most circumstances it is not a difficult task.

Several orchestral pitfalls present themselves in the opening bars of Variation XVI. (The eighth rest on the downbeat of the fourth bar being among the more obvious. This may seem like a ridiculous subject to address, but I have, more than once, heard musicians in high quality orchestras play in this rest.) In the first four bars, the violins and viole need to play uniformly *staccato*. The usual bowing in each of the first three bars (down-up-up) lends itself to an articulation of long-short-short, and this cannot be tolerated. The bowing does not necessarily need to be changed; the strings simply need to be cautioned that all notes must be equally *staccato* regardless of bow direction. Some conductors add, or perhaps fail to inhibit, a *crescendo* across the first two bars, followed by a two-bar *diminuendo*, and this also should be avoided. The addition of these corny dynamics does nothing to benefit this moment; quite to the contrary, the unchanging *pianissimo* maintains the desired sense of mystery.

In Variation XVII, there is some question regarding exactly where the *cresendi* and *diminuendi* stop and start in the first two bars after **47**, and other similar passages. Scores do not all agree, and some scores do not even agree with their matching sets of parts. In the first two bars at **47** and the two bars directly before **48** I prefer to have the zenith of the phrase on the fourth beat, with three beats of *crescendo* and one beat of *diminuendo*. I find this not only the most satisfying reading, because it corresponds to the harmonic tensions, but it is also the most reasonable resolution of the conflicting information found in the Edition Tair score. Conversely, the last time this occurs (four bars before the end of the variation) it is clear in the score that the *crescendo* climaxes on the third beat of the bar.

As satisfying as Variation XVIII is to perform, it is important that the orchestra does not descend into uninterrupted *forte* as a result of their quite understandable, hedonistic enjoyment. The composer's dynamics are quite detailed, and achieving beautiful shapes within each phrase depends largely on following those dynamics religiously. When the melody begins, or continues, in the orchestra with four sixteenth-notes on the third beat of a bar (e.g., one beat before **50**), it is sometimes necessary to subdivide this beat. This, of course, depends on the exact amount of *rubato* in the solo piano. This will also be necessary, at times, in the middle of a phrase, as in the third bar after **51**.

M.D. became quite eloquent in our discussion of this variation, mentioning that he credited "[Sviatoslav] Richter for having planted a wonderful image in [his] mind." M.D. continued, "He came to a concert of mine of Rach-Pag in Vienna in 1974. He was very kind. The more we talked about music the more it became clear that he thought about music visually. He gave me a thought about the 18th variation. He said, 'you know, we're talking about the devil and a beautiful young lady—and in this variation the devil's wearing a mask—the mask falls at the *pizzicati* (next variation)—but somehow in that D-flat variation it can't seem as'—he didn't use the word 'pretty'—'but it can't be quite that simple; something has to lurking underneath to show that there's a devil wearing a mask.' Then I went back to the score and realized that the inner voice in the left hand has two's against three's … and now I try to find a sensible balance in bringing out that lower voice which I now have dubbed the devil underneath the mask, and I've convinced myself that it's more sinister because of that. Before, it was just a pretty tune on top."

The opening bars of Variation XIX (the six bars of $\frac{2}{4}$ time marked *a tempo vivace*) are a matter of some controversy and consternation in some orchestras. In order to facilitate the accurate execution of the rapid downward triplets in first violins and viole, some conductors and/or concertmasters ask that the instruments be held in the lap, guitar-style, during these bars. Playing these triplets accurately and with sufficient force while holding the instrument in the normal position is somewhere between fairly difficult and impossible; thus, the alternative suggestion. Some musicians find this request distasteful, but I have yet to hear of another solution that thoroughly solves the problem.

Changes of tone, harmonic speed, and other musical issues, make the composer's indication *alla breve* at the beginning of Variation XXII something not to be ignored. This passage should always be taken in two. Early in the variation in particular, it is important to cue each individual string and timpani entrance, as well as the first entrance of bassoons.

Beginning at the third bar after **64**, some soloists ask for, or indicate by their performance, a slightly faster tempo. Even though it is not requested by the composer, a slightly faster tempo here helps both the scales in the solo piano and the lyrical lines in the strings flow more effectively. Whether or not the tempo change is made, this is another spot where dropping the left hand to subtly mirror the beat within the pianist's field of vision is polite, helpful, and highly advisable. Even a slight discontinuity between solo and orchestra in this passage may result in the downbeat at **66** not being synchronized, and this can be musically disastrous.

Variation XXIII is most effective in one. The conductor should mark the first two bars of the variation for a clear indication of the tempo. (It can be challenging for some conductors to mark these two bars, in one and at such a brisk tempo, both clearly and completely passively, but it is quite important. An active beat moving toward either of these two bars will be very tempting to musicians who are waiting to play *fortissimo* only a split-second later. Even when the musicians are scrupulously attentive and professional, and are unlikely to make a mistake, beating actively in these two bars is simply rude and amateurish, as it transfers the conductor's responsibility for technique and leadership to the musicians. The first active gesture *follows* the baton's passive indication of the downbeat of the second bar, serving as active preparation for the orchestra's entrance.) The tempo at the beginning of the variation is derived directly from the last four figures in the brief *cadenza* passage directly preceding. As discussed in detail previously, these bars should be marked in a clear tempo, but without any sharpness to the *ictus* that might invite a musician to play early. The rebound out of the second bar, however, should have considerable energy to impel the weight of sound required in the next bar. At **70** and following, the conductor should direct the baton with sharp *icti* in the direction of the third and fourth horns (those playing the eighth rest/dotted quarter note figure) in order to insure secure, clean, on-time performance of that figure. Although a pattern in one can still be maintained at **72**, I find it preferable to beat in two at that point in order to better inspire the proper forward motion and weight required in this passage.

No matter how *piano* the soloist plays at the opening of Variation XXIV, the dynamic in the first flute must still be adjusted or the sound will not penetrate in this register. The section from **75** until *Più vivo* has a better feeling of forward motion if conducted in two. If this plan is chosen, some subtle subdivisions may be employed in the last four bars before *Più vivo* where the accents are on the off-beats. This choice (to conduct these four bars in two) also allows for a smoother transition to *Più vivo* (in one).

Quickly picking up the soloist's new tempo at *Più vivo* is relatively easy, following the harmonic and rhythmic progression downward in the left hand. Some care needs to be taken six bars before **79** that the horns are not late playing the eighth note that follows the dotted quarter note. When this happens, it is very awkward to re-establish proper coordination with the soloist.

From this point to the end, the beat should remain in one. The only possible exception to this is found in the last three bars of the work. Some soloists pull the tempo back slightly here to achieve a more graceful conclusion. Whether this is the case or not, it may be advisable to beat in two during these three bars in order to be certain of clean coordination with the soloist and a gentle *piano* throughout the orchestra.

෴

Maurice Ravel

Piano Concerto in G

1st movement.

Although the conductor's initial gesture should be clear enough to be self-explanatory, it is sometimes necessary to remark to the orchestra that the work begins on the second beat of the first bar. If there is any lingering doubt in this regard in the mind of any musicians, then the considerable number of players counting rests at the opening of the work are more likely to be confused by the time they reach their first entrance. All clarity of gesture and any explanations notwithstanding, the piccolo player always needs a clear and encouraging look in the eye on the downbeat of the second bar.

Two bars before **4** it is common to take a bit of *rallentando*. This is done to create a smooth transition to *Meno vivo* and to add elegance rather than haste to the English horn solo. Unfortunately, some conductors choose instead to simply move the *Meno vivo* two bars early. This solves potential technical and artistic problems for the English horn, but simply transfers the abrupt change of tempo from one place to another. Allowing the English horn to begin in the preceding tempo, followed by a gentle *rallentando* that takes the listener from one tempo to another, is far preferable.

The unaccompanied solo passages between **7** and **8** usually take on a more relaxed feel. However, it is common for the pianist's tempo to be slightly *affrettando* when the orchestra re-enters both two bars and six bars before **8**. The conductor should keep this in mind, making sure that the rebound on the downbeat of each of these bars communicates this information, making good coordination between the upper strings and piano (on the second quarter note of the bar) possible.

The bar before **10** is usually handled best with a slight subdivision in the second half of the bar. This gives a clear indication for the solo trumpet to move to the G-sharp at the end the bar. Without this subtle, extra gesture, the trumpeter is left to his own devices to place that final note, and the rest of the winds are left to jointly determine (a very audible) cut-off point on the half beat. The return to Tempo I at **10** is quite sudden, but is not difficult to follow. If the pianist's C-sharps on each beat are, for whatever reason, not clearly audible to the conductor, then this is another example of a good time to be looking at the soloist's left hand for guidance. This visual observation of the keyboard is a good idea here no matter what the sonic circumstances, as watching the left hand allows the conductor to place the first beat of the bar clearly and confidently rather than reacting to it after the fact.

The first several bars at **12** provide an excellent example of why, in all concerti at all times, it is critical that the conductor's score study involves intimate, detailed knowledge of the solo part. In this passage, an inexperienced conductor (or one who has not properly done his homework) will want to hear the lowest F-sharps as occurring on a beat. Of course, conducting with this erroneous mindset would create a considerable mess, and such lack of familiarity with the intricacies of the solo part is inexcusable.

The *cadenza*-like passage at **17** is easily brought under intellectual control by thinking of it as eleven bars of $\frac{2}{2}$ meter. In spite of this mental exercise, the baton must stay absolutely still until the piano reaches the final four notes before **18**, where the conductor gives a clean, energetic preparatory gesture. In particular, the conductor needs to make eye contact with the percussionist playing the bass drum, as well as celli and basses, just before and during this preparatory gesture and downbeat. Staring at the score as the ears follow the final notes of the solo part is not acceptable, and is a basic abdication of one of the conductor's fundamental responsibilities of leadership and communication.

The two bars before **20** present all the same issues as described earlier regarding the two bars before **4**; the musical solution here can, and should, be similar. It is important in this instance that the horns' and bassoons' need for absolute clarity within the *rallentando* be recognized and addressed.

Although it is not clearly marked in the score until the following staff, the three cellists who play initially at **22** are those occupying the fourth, fifth, and sixth chairs in the section. This is made clear in the next staff where the first three cellists enter. All the strings in this passage are clearly marked as solo voices, and they are never to be doubled under any circumstances. Though not technically rapid, the harp solo is a bit treacherous because it involves so many consecutive, exposed harmonics. Due to the visual requirements of executing this passage of harmonics, the harpist cannot reasonably be expected to look away from the harp to watch the conductor. Once tempo is set in the first two bars at **22**, the reality is that the conductor usually follows the harpist, as a soloist, through the end of the first bar of **23**. In the second bar of **23**, the conductor is again in control of the proceedings, and the harpist follows the baton as usual so that everyone arrives at the downbeat of the third bar of **23** with good coordination. In the third bar of **23**, the *fermata* on the (third beat) rest is at least as important as the *fermata* on the downbeat, and should not be rushed. As before, during the three bars preceding **24** the harpist will have her eyes on the instrument far more than on the conductor. Having already made eye contact with those musicians who enter at **24**, upon arriving at the last beat before **24** the conductor's eyes go to the soloist to ensure a secure entrance. It may also be wise to observe the keyboard for good coordination of tempo at **24**, as the sound of the orchestra can obscure the clarity of the triplets from the conductor's sonic perspective.

Once tempo is set at **25**, the conductor's main task is simply to cue the various woodwind entrances. The solo horn neither needs, nor likely desires, a great deal of artistic leadership in this passage. What this musician will want is to be left in peace to negotiate this notoriously treacherous passage.

The Durand edition of the printed score contains (or at least contained) several errors in the last few bars of this movement in the B-flat Clarinet part. Seven bars before the end the (transposed) part should read A-natural, G-sharp, F-sharp, G-sharp; six bars before the end should read A-natural, G-natural, F-natural, G-natural. The following two bars are identical to these. Three bars before the end the (transposed) part should read A-natural, C-sharp, B-sharp, A-sharp; two bars before the end reads G-sharp, F-natural, E-flat, D-natural.

2nd movement.

After a suitable pause, and the completion of any necessary instrument cleaning, etc., the soloist begins at her pleasure with no further indications from, or communication with, the conductor. If it is not already apparent in the parts, the orchestra should be informed that the conductor will not mark the bars between the beginning of the movement and **1**, and that the first downbeat will occur at **1**.

In a passage like the flute solo four bars before **2**, the solo piano is, for all practical purposes, accompanying the orchestra. In that role, it is appropriate for the pianist to be reasonably flexible to the desires of the conductor and flutist during this passage, and most soloists instinctively understand this exchange of roles. The soloist re-establishes control of tempo and *rubato* at 2.

Although neither the musical substance nor the nature of the piano writing resembles the passages of *fioratura* found in Chopin's concerti, a similar accompanying technique may be employed three bars before 6. If the soloist's pedaling and/or the general orchestral sound make clear hearing of the right hand impossible, it is just as functional to follow the left hand here. This is really not the case, however, in the passage beginning at 6. In the luscious cabaret music at 6, it is not sufficiently detailed accompanying to follow only the left hand. Here, as in so many passages in the concerto repertoire, it is thorough familiarity with all details of the solo part that is absolutely necessary. The subtleties of expressive *rubati* (in the right hand) must be intimately followed by the conductor in order to achieve not only excellent coordination but also, more importantly, integrated musical expression.

Also important in this passage is the partnership between the English horn and the (right hand of the) solo piano. Some pianists, in a misguided effort at good ensemble playing, so subjugate their own part to the English horn line that the charm of the passage is all but lost. While the melody in the English horn is, obviously, important, it is the French cabaret character of the piano writing that gives this passage its charm. These two voices should be heard as equals, and this is not difficult to achieve, especially with the sustained strings playing extremely *piano*.

The painful clash between G-sharp (celli and piano) and A-natural (viole) on the third beat of the fourth bar before the end of the movement is not an error. Some inexperienced conductors change or eliminate the G-sharp, and others merely ask the celli to play it *pianississimo* in order to avoid the subject altogether. While it may be prudent to ask the celli not to lean heavily on this note (the listener's ear should be following the line in the viole anyway), this last moment of delicious pain is a masterstroke, and should not be "corrected" out of the piece.

3rd movement.

As is the case in many concerto finales, this movement does not present any considerable technical challenges from a conducting or accompanying standpoint, as long as the conductor is prepared with thorough knowledge of the solo piano part. The challenges in this movement are focused more acutely on the members of the orchestra, many of whom are given very challenging material by the composer (e.g., bassoons 14 to 16, strings 16 to 21, etc.). As with the opening of the first movement, a quick downbeat is all that is required to begin the finale. As mentioned in the earlier instance, the baton should begin, motionless, in a raised position, proceeding swiftly downward toward one. Beginning with the baton lowered (as though at one or in a more natural resting position) forces the conductor to give first an upward motion before giving the downward motion toward the first downbeat of the movement. This additional gesture appears to have the effect of adding an extra bar to the piece. This type of confusing and unnecessary gesture should, of course, be avoided.

Scrupulously adhering to the pattern of accents (and non-accents) in the passage between 4 and 5 is pivotal to properly executing Ravel's bit of musical humor. As should be obvious, the phrase is exactly as previously performed by the piano, but offset by a half bar. The accents, however, make the string phrase appear (to the ear) to line up exactly as when the solo piano played it, beginning on the first beat of a bar. For this reason, it is not only imperative that the strings perform the accents precisely where indicated, but also, more importantly, that they avoid placing accents on downbeats where they are not indicated.

Two bars before **7**, the (concert) F-sharp in the trumpet is not an error.

ꕤ

Robert Schumann

Piano Concerto in A Minor, Op. 54

1st movement.

The composer gives a time signature of $\frac{4}{4}$, but states the metronome marking relative to the half note. Oddly enough, this lack of specificity perfectly reflects the fact that the first movement is conducted variously in four and in two, depending on the musical needs of the moment. The preparation for the first bar should be a quick (quarter-note length), sharp gesture, given only after careful eye contact is made with the soloist to insure that she is entirely ready. I have, on two memorable occasions, seen conductors give only a cursory glance at the soloist (what, in hindsight, was not nearly enough of a glance) before attacking the first bar, only to find that the soloist was, in fact, not ready to begin. On one occasion we (the audience) waited for what amounted to several extra beats before the soloist collected herself and began. On the other occasion, the soloist, though not ready, jumped in immediately, mangling the first several chords. Clearly this is a situation to be avoided, and such a gaffe surely comes under the heading of "enthusiasm getting the better of common sense." Stated less politely, it probably comes under the heading of "Maestro, exactly how stupid *are* you?"

The main theme in the winds at bar 4 should begin with a beat in two, in order to establish the flow of the line. If some expressive time is taken in bars 7 through 10, then those moments will probably require a beat in four. As the pianist finishes the first solo passage (bar 19), the conductor, making sure there is eye contact or at least that the pianist is observing the baton through his peripheral vision, gives the preparatory gesture (in two) that allows first violins and soloist to continue comfortably together.

When giving the preparatory gesture for the *pizzicato* chords seven, nine, and eleven bars after **A**, the conductor should be careful not to assume a doggedly mathematical approach. In each of the bars preceding these string chords, some pianists will intuit a breath mark before the fourth quarter of the bar, adding a tiny bit of extra time to that bar. If the conductor assumes the bar will be absolutely mathematical (when the soloists takes this expressive approach) then the following chords will be early and/or raggedly executed.

The baton should remain motionless after indicating the entrance of celli at bar 66 (one bar before *Animato*). The soloist's *ritardando* in the remainder of the bar usually allows the conductor to give a preparatory gesture (for *Animato*) on the fourth beat: a gesture that is reasonably equal to the new half note. The clarinet and oboe solos in the *Animato* section are marked variously *piano* and *pianissimo*, and this is usually not practical. In a modern concert hall with a seven- or nine-foot solo instrument, these woodwind passages need to be played closer to *mezzo-forte*.

The bar of *ritard* at **B** usually needs to be conducted in four. In fact, it is often played as slowly as half tempo *subito*. I cannot help but comment on how much I dislike the practice of playing this bar exactly half tempo. The composer indicates "*ritard*," meaning an expressive elongating of the rhythmic values relative to the previous bar. When the bar is played exactly half tempo, there is actually no feel of *ritard* at all, because the pulse stays the same (as though the previous half note equals the new quarter note), and the delightful discomfort found in the expressive stretch of the note values is entirely missing. Over many years and many performances of this piece I've made a bit of headway on this subject with some pianists with whom I have shared the stage, but I'm afraid it's been precious little. This tradition seems still well engrained, but I'm hopeful that conductors who read this book will press for a more sophisticated and musically satisfying reading of this bar in the future.

The pace of the *ritardando* preceding the key change to A-flat major (bars 152-155) is entirely at the conductor's discretion, since there is no direct relationship stated or implied between this tempo and the one that follows. However, one may want to consider this *ritard* being fairly modest, for two reasons. First, this is neither the end of the movement nor the transition to a cadenza, so a really significant *ritard* here seems to unnaturally inhibit the progress of the piece. Second, though the composer does not indicate it in any way, this transition feels a bit more organic when the pulse of the quarter note before the double bar is not drastically slower than the pulse taken by the piano. Though the quarter-note pulse will almost undoubtedly be quicker after the double bar than before it, minimizing this difference, to the extent that is reasonable and musical, avoids some of that uncomfortable "slow down so we can speed up" feeling.

The half bar before **C** will usually need to be subdivided into three quarter-notes. It is to be hoped, however, that the final eighth note of the bar can be coordinated between clarinet and piano without a further subdivision.

Although I'm sure some other conductors will have a different opinion, I believe that the passage between **C** and *Più animato* is best conducted in four. If conducted in two the rhythmic stresses will tend to lose some of their impact, and the *sforzati* will fall between beats rather than on them. At *Più animato* we return to beating in two.

The third bar after **C** contains a significant misprint in many scores and some parts. In some materials, the clarinets and bassoons are shown here playing on the first (a half note) and fourth beats. Obviously, this is an error on its face since there aren't enough beats in the bar. Unfortunately, some conductors correct this by adding a dot to the half note, when the proper correction is to add a quarter rest at the beginning of the bar so that the figure matches those that follow.

At the beginning of the ninth bar after **D**, it is helpful to know in advance the soloist's intentions regarding the execution of the grace note at the beginning of the bar. If the grace note is taken fairly rapidly, then the conductor must show the preparation in a normal, logical manner relative to the previous phrase, assuming that the soloist will observe that gesture and coordinate with it. If, as is not uncommon, that grace note is sustained a bit longer, then the preparatory gesture is actually coordinated precisely with that grace note. This allows a comfortable and unhurried approach to the downbeat, placing the string sound with the chord, of course, and not with the grace note. The conductor then shows the cut-off of the string sound in two, even though he is likely to have been in four previously, continuing to gently mark the intervening bars until bringing in the first violins, in two, at bar 274. A similar, though not identical, situation presents itself at bar 312 (key change to A major). Here, the pianist's need to move her hands to a different position on the keyboard between the grace note chord and the downbeat virtually ensures a somewhat more leisurely approach to the grace note. As before, showing the preparatory gesture as the grace note is played is the best way to ensure good coordination with the piano and a clean *pizzicato* chord on the downbeat.

Dynamics are of some concern in the passage beginning at bar 389 (*Accelerando poco a poco*). Each phrase begins at *piano*, with a *crescendo* toward a *sforzato*, and then decays back toward the starting point. As is often the case in phrases with this shape, the composer does not specify the dynamic at the crest of each swell, precisely at the point of each *sforzato*. A specific dynamic (which *sforzato* is not) would be helpful here, and would keep these phrases from being overplayed, completely overpowering the piano. Certainly, a high point of no more than *mezzo-forte* is appropriate for the first two swells, with the last *crescendo* having perhaps a bit more energy, leading to the final orchestral chord of the phrase. It is also to be noted that the brass and timpani have no dynamics at all, which is a subject that needs to be clarified for these musicians separately. The last dynamic given for these instruments is *forte*, but they cannot play that dynamic here where the rest of the orchestra is supposed to be *piano*. A good, solid *mezzo-piano*, and no more than *mezzo-forte*, works well for them at this point.

The *Allegro molto* coda is conducted in one, usually in the range of 𝅗𝅥 = 78–90. The major musical challenge of the section is to be certain that the orchestra remains *piano* throughout, without any *crescendo* (until it is printed) as the end of the movement draws nearer and nearer. This is by no means just a question of balance. The sustained dynamic is important because much of the thrill of this section lies in the hushed, contained excitement of these figures when they are played consistently *piano*.

2nd movement.

This incredibly charming movement is usually conducted in four throughout. This is dependant, however, on the tempo chosen by the soloist, and the tempo of this movement varies considerably from one pianist to another. Schumann asks that his *Andante grazioso* be played at ♪ = 120, but most pianists (and conductors) would consider this tempo much too fast to convey the expression and elegance of the music. A more commonly heard tempo is somewhere around ♪ = 100, and it is not unusual to hear it closer to ♪ = 88, or even slower.

Before delving further into this wonderful movement, I must digress to relate a conversation that took place recently during a rehearsal of this piece between pianist Alexander Schimpf (winner of the 2011 Cleveland International Piano Competition) and me. We were discussing our experiences (as audience members!) with conductor missteps at the beginning of the first movement, as I've discussed above, when Alexander shared with me the pianist's fantasy retaliation for such stupidity. It goes like this … Having been embarrassed by a conductor who started the first movement before he was ready, the pianist pulls himself together during the break between the first and second movements, and, as he does, beckons to the conductor, asking him to lean over so the soloist can speak to him. As the conductor puts down his baton and leans over the piano, the pianist quickly puts his hands on the keyboard and starts the second movement, making it impossible for the conductor to cue the opening bar in the strings, and suffering roughly the same embarrassment the soloist endured earlier. This is, of course, entirely fantasy, and, to my knowledge, it has never happened. But it does illustrate the importance of awareness and generosity on the podium, because, even for conductors, what goes around comes around.

One of the first things to note in this movement is the subtle difference in articulation between various iterations of the principal musical material. In the first two bars, the sixteenth notes (in the strings) that comprise the theme are marked with dots and slurs, while later (bar 17) they have only dots. Some conductors either misunderstand this as a bowing issue or do not notice or deal with the subject at all. While it is true that many orchestras play the occurrences with the slur under one bow and those without the slur separately, this is neither absolutely necessary nor the major issue here. Schumann's message in creating this subtle difference is one of articulation, style, and meaning. When the dots are also covered in the slur, the articulation should be longer. Sometimes this is heard as nearly *legato* and other interpreters ask for only "long dots" or "dashes." By contrast, the passages with dots only (which also happen to be marked *pianissimo* rather than *piano*) should be more *secco*, with a feeling that is a bit secretive and clandestine.

Though not indicated anywhere by the composer, it is common for the second "sighing" figure (four bars before **A**; bar 25) to be played *più piano* as compared with the previous bar. In the bar directly before **A** (bar 28), the celli need to clearly finish the two-note phrase with the rest of the orchestra before beginning the new phrase with the final note (A-natural) of the bar. This means adding a comma (breath mark) before the A-natural, and insuring that the section plays this final note of the bar "leaning forward" musically as the opening of a new phrase. This quality of "leaning forward" over the bar-line is particularly important both four and eight bars later, where the pick-up in the celli coincides with the end of the phrase (a dotted sixteenth note followed by a thirty-second note) in the piano. When handled with care and intention, these moments of contrary musical motion (the dying end of the phrase in the piano overlapping the first, *espressivo* note of the cello phrase) are particularly potent and beautiful.

Three bars before the end of the movement, it is best to postpone the preparatory gesture for the next bar until the final note of the pianist's last phrase. While the previous phrase (five bars before the end) usually lends itself to placing the gesture on the fourth beat of the bar, the continuing *ritard*, as well as Schumann's instruction *mit Verschiebung*, makes it inadvisable to do this here. The slowing tempo and unpredictability of the phrase (as the composer requested) makes placement of the preparation on the pianist's last chord by far the best and safest option.

3rd movement.

In the opening phrases of the movement (bar 117* and following), the conductor must sometimes caution the strings not to overplay the accents or *subito forte* chords that are used as punctuation. These chords are exactly that, punctuation for the purpose of giving rhythmic drive and shape to the phrase, and they should not be interpreted as major musical events or played with any kind of roughness or conspicuous athleticism. (*In most editions, the bar numbers in this movement continue from the second movement. Therefore the first bar of the third movement is bar 109.)

The major ensemble issue in this movement is, of course, the hemiola figure that permeates so much of this finale. For experienced, disciplined musicians these passages do not present any particular technical or ensemble challenges, but for younger or less experienced players, they can become nightmarish rather quickly. As is probably obvious, the potential problem is that the hemiola figure in the orchestra will rush slightly (or perhaps significantly), never quite allowing for three entire beats in any bar. When this happens, the soloist is either so rhythmically strangled that she cannot keep up, or the frenetic feel of the orchestral playing causes the soloist to also rush, creating a mad dash forward that can no longer be controlled by either soloist or conductor. One sadly memorable performance at the Aspen Festival many years ago featured a very talented, but rather inexperienced young pianist with a somewhat less capable up-and-coming conductor. When the orchestra rushed (because they did not control the length of each rest, and therefore the length of each bar), the soloist rushed even more to compensate, as described above. The predictable result was virtual chaos in nearly every repetition of this music, with orchestra and soloist often finishing the sixteen-bar phrase as much as an entire bar apart from one another.

In addition to simply maintaining good ensemble, this music needs to be carefully and artfully phrased in order to avoid the feeling that, as one might believe on first hearing, it is a starchy march in $\frac{3}{2}$ meter. A phrasing that avoids the feeling of $\frac{3}{2}$ meter can be achieved by a combination of the following: (1) a slight accent on the downbeat of every other bar (first, third, etc.), though this is likely to happen all on its own, (2) a clear de-emphasizing of the note on the third beat of these same bars, in order to avoid the feeling that this note is on the second beat of a bar in $\frac{3}{2}$ meter, and (3) a slight *crescendo*, a "leaning forward" of the phrase across the second and third beats of the opposite bars (second, fourth, etc.). A careful execution of this phrasing results in the intended swing of the hemiola instead of confusion about what meter is present.

Unbelievably, some conductors beat this passage in a three pattern, actually creating one $\frac{3}{2}$ bar across every two printed bars. Thus, managing to completely undo the composer's musical intentions. I imagine that, when this choice is made, it is because the orchestra is of a technical and experiential level that they simply cannot play the figures accurately with a beat in one, and/or because the conductor's physical technique and rhythmic discipline are so poor that he cannot maintain clarity and control. In such cases, I truly believe that the proper decision is to choose another piece rather than to mangle this one.

Beginning at bar 883, the melodic figure in upper strings and woodwinds needs to be executed at a considerably higher dynamic than indicated. These figures are the most important musical material of this passage, as well as constituting a charming harmonic variation on the original theme, and they need to be heard clearly. At least *mezzo-forte* is appropriate, particularly for the woodwinds.

The soloist will sometimes adopt a slight *ritenuto* in bar 911. When this is done to any significant degree, ensemble for upper strings on the third beat of the bar can be tricky, as the beat in one cannot communicate the location of this, now delayed, third beat with complete clarity. Despite this dilemma inherent to beating in one, the solution is not to beat in three, as that will be awkward and unmusical at this tempo. The best solution is to (verbally) alert the orchestra to the slight tempo change, and to slow, relax, and slightly broaden the rebound in this bar. While absolutely not doing anything that resembles a three pattern, one can also make a slight subdivision in the downward portion of the pattern (preferably with the left hand), clarifying the position of that elusive third beat.

The *crescendo* entrance of first violins nineteen and fifteen bars before the end of the movement adds considerable drama to the drive toward the final cadence. Unfortunately, the first violins alone do not usually provide enough sound to create the desired effect. Also problematic is the fact that, in most editions, the *crescendi* are not placed in identical locations in both phrases, and in neither are they placed at the beginning of the note. The least intrusive solution is to ask the violins to move the *crescendo* to the beginning of the note (third beat of the previous bar) and to bring a great deal of intensity to the sound. The next line of defense is to simply add the second violins, and perhaps the viole, to this note. Depending on the hall, the soloist, the piano, and the size of the string section, any of these might be sufficient. Though I am notoriously loath to actually re-orchestrate the work of a master, I admit that I have, on occasion, also added one or both horns, beginning very softly, to this note. When I use both horns I give the second horn the lower octave (written first space F; concert A-natural below middle C) and the first horn the pitch one octave higher, in unison with the violins.

The fact that the trumpets have a half note followed by a *fermata* over a quarter-rest in the final bar while the entire remainder of the orchestra has a dotted half note with *fermata* is something of a mystery. (It could be argued that this is to make their part similar to their "partner" in this style, the timpani, but even if that is true it does not solve our problem.) In cases like this, which crop up frequently, especially in the final bar of works from this period, I try hard to take the composer at his word, not assuming that it is either his sloppiness or an editorial error. Often one will find that such apparent inconsistencies have a basis in some clear musical need or desire. In this case, however, I can find no good reason to release the trumpets while the rest of the orchestra sustains, and I allow them to play the same *fermata* as the rest of the ensemble.

I have purposely saved M.D.'s comments about this piece for last, so that I don't dissuade anyone from reading this chapter or from being enthusiastic about this wonderful and unique work. When I asked M.D. for his insights on this concerto, he surprised me by answering, "It scares the hell out of me. I found it a very dangerous piece, always. I was talking years ago with Horacio Gutiérrez and he asked me what I was playing that week. I told him Schumann, and he said 'difficult, you know, no matter how you play the Schumann nobody's going to like it.' I thought, 'that's harsh.' But then I thought, 'it's too classical, it's too romantic, not enough liberties, too many liberties.' For me, the piece is like walking on eggshells. I never walked off stage thinking, 'hey, that was really fun.'" I've included this rather surprising response only to illustrate that this work is more complex than it may seem on the surface, and that, even to two great musicians like Mr. Dichter and Mr. Gutiérrez, the stylistic and interpretive complexities of a work like this one are never to be taken for granted.

☙

Peter Ilyich Tchaikovsky

Piano Concerto No. 1 in B-Flat Minor, Op. 23

1st movement.

As long as the orchestra is reasonably familiar with the piece, the conductor can begin the first movement with a gentle, out-of-tempo breathing/lifting gesture to the left (in the direction of the rebound from the non-existent first beat) followed by an accelerating gesture to the right, landing on a sharp *ictus* for the second beat that impels the entrance of the horns. In circumstances of unusual orchestral tentativeness or inexperience, the conductor may want to begin with a very gentle and diminutive indication of the first beat before continuing to those gestures described above.

While it is perfectly acceptable to subtly mark each bar of the solo passage beginning in bar 37, it is equally efficient to simply explain to the orchestra in rehearsal that the next downbeat shown will be at bar 51.

There is usually a breath and complete break of the sound on the bar-lines two and four bars before *Allegro con spirito* (bar 108). This approach offers definition and added solemnity to these transitional phrases. The *Allegro con spirito* is, of course, conducted in two.

At bar 204, in addition to the obvious cue for the strings, it is particularly important (and polite) to give a clear look to both bassoons and horns at their respective entrances. Though this passage looks simple enough in the score, entering out of nowhere (particularly for the bassoons that enter first and on the half bar) without a reassuring glance from the podium can feel a bit unnerving when sitting in the orchestra.

I usually dictate each of the two wind chords directly preceding **F**. These chords need a bit of additional musical emphasis that goes beyond simply making certain that the ensemble stays strictly in tempo. In addition, the physical act of subdividing this beat makes a smooth return to *Tempo I* at **F** a simpler and more elegant gesture. Likewise, a gentle subdivision in the second half of the eighth bar after **F** may be necessary to smoothly accommodate a likely bit of *ritard* in the piano, making for better coordination with the orchestra in the final quarter note of the bar.

One bar before **H** it is important to note that the *fermata* falls on the rest after the last note in the piano arpeggio. This silence is intended to be a point of repose, and there is no need to rush immediately into the following phrase. Sometimes this becomes a dilemma when the soloist sustains the final note and seems unwilling to release it. (It is not only noteworthy that the fermata is on the rest, but also that there is not a *fermata* on the final note of the piano.) When this happens, the conductor can either wait a respectable period before continuing into the following phrase, or she can discuss with the soloist her concern regarding the need for silence between the phrases. The latter, of course, should be done in a private moment, out of earshot of the orchestra. Conversely, the bar before **J** does not indicate such a silence after the *fermata*, and the cut-off of winds can serve as the preparatory gesture for the first violins.

In the passage following **J** the composer does not provide any articulation for the first four phrases in the first violins, but the very absence of slurs or dots gives us a good indication of where to begin. "Long dots" or "dot-dash" are effective articulations here. To the extent reasonable and musically logical, this articulation should be reflected in future repetitions of this theme (i.e., trombones at **M** and horns after **M**).

When bringing the orchestra in after the *cadenza*, the conductor can begin with only a gentle indication of the downbeat of bar 612, followed by a cue for woodwinds on the second beat, or he may choose to gently mark the bars beginning at *Tempo I* (bar 611). In either case, the orchestra needs to be informed in rehearsal which method the conductor will employ.

It is not unusual that the penultimate bar of the movement will have a slightly more *pesante* feel. This minor fluctuation of the tempo may require a subtle subdivision for musical weight and emphasis as much as for coordination.

2nd movement.

The *pizzicato* introduction to this movement is an invitation for the conductor to inadvertently select a tempo that is faster than intended. The large silences between *pizzicato* chords unnerve some conductors (and some orchestral musicians) to such an extent that the chords on each beat continue to creep closer and closer together. In such a musical situation, of which there are thousands in our repertoire, it is the conductor's job to calmly discipline the proceedings so that the tempo is set and maintained correctly; it is the conductor's job to be certain he is the solution and not part of the problem. If the soloist does not object, a slight *ritard* in bar 12 (possibly conducted in six) accentuates the delicious flatted sixth of the scale, before returning to *Tempo I* (in two) when the piano enters.

Unless the tempo chosen for the movement is unusually quick, it is often wise to begin beating in six at the pick-up to bar 21. If this method is adopted, the beat should return to two either at **R** or at bar 33, depending on the situation. Bar 49 is usually beaten in six also, to accommodate the *rallentando* in the piano; the following bar returns either to a strict pattern in two or to a hybrid two pattern that subtly hints at the subdivisions for more comfortable coordination with the syncopated figures in the piano.

The beginning of the *Prestissimo*, and therefore the task of bringing the strings in correctly at bar 69, is perplexing to some conductors. The composer's joke is, of course, that the first six eighth-notes of the passage sound like six eighth-notes all in one bar, phrased as a hemiola with accents in the first, third, and fifth positions in the bar. The problem is that if the conductor inadvertently considers this passage in this way he will be perplexed for some time into the future. This is, in actuality, not a difficult passage to follow unless one begins with the wrong mindset, or no mindset at all. Even if the soloist begins the passage in a *prestissimo* blur of sound that loses the conductor's ear before he can think, the fourth and eighth bars of the passage (bars 62 and 66) present a hemiola figure that easily grounds the ear in the correct place. This is, of course, the hemiola of three groups of two eighth note beats that we might have been tempted to hear incorrectly at bar 59. Here, at last, this figure appears at the beginning of the bar.

Because the pianist's *fermata* in bar 145 makes it nearly impossible to give a dotted quarter note preparatory gesture before bar 146, it is sometimes best to begin this passage in six. The conductor can then transition back into two as soon as the tempo is steady. This transition may be possible as soon as the second half of bar 146. Another solution is to give a preparation that is not really either an eighth note or a dotted quarter, but something more amorphous, allowing the orchestra to flow naturally back into Tempo I using their memory of the original tempo and the flow of the rebound from the first beat of the bar as their guides. Using this method, no beating in six is necessary.

It is usually necessary to go into six in bar 160, or perhaps one-half bar earlier. The remainder of the movement, with the obvious exception of bars 161 and 163, usually remains in six.

As often happens when the last note of a movement is *pizzicato* in the strings but some winds (and/or other strings) sustain the same value tied into the bar, the length of the note in the last bar in celli and flutes is something to be considered carefully. Most often, when a composer writes such tied notes over a final *pizzicato* chord (using the same values in both parts of the orchestra) we intuit that the tied note(s) should cut off with the ring of the *pizzicati*, and should not be sustained longer, requiring an additional cut-off for those musicians. This, however, is an unusual situation. In this case, the tempo is so slow, and therefore the correct length of a quarter note so long, that one must wonder if, perhaps, Tchaikovsky wished the flutes and celli to sustain the chord a real quarter-note value in this tempo. I usually do ask those instruments to sustain longer than the *pizzicato* chord, as I find this hanging, *pianissimo* triad quite magical, and not necessarily a contradiction of the composer's wishes.

3rd movement.

This rousing finale does not present extensive or complex problems, but I will deal briefly with a few minor issues. At **W**, a sharp downbeat in each of the first four bars, with the conductor's eyes focused directly on the principal clarinet, helps to keep this passage rhythmically together. After the sharp gesture on the first beat, the second and third beats of these bars should all but disappear. If the conductor should happen to daydream and lose track of the pianist between bars 49 and 55 (not a good idea under any circumstances) the G-flat on the third beat of bar 54 provides an easy point for recovery.

Regarding this same passage (and the parallel passage at bar 134), M.D. related an entertaining anecdote regarding the composer's original ideas. M.D. said, "When I was preparing for Moscow in 1966, Mrs. Lhévinne said [M.D. is now charmingly imitating her voice], 'you know, Misha, Tchaikovsky told my husband, that this section it must sound like a hiccup, with a drunken person walking along the sidewalk, one foot in the gutter.' Of course you can never have that much time in making the hiccup, but it's meno mosso, and I try to be as meno mosso'y as I can in honor of the composer's wishes."

Although not indicated by the composer, a slight *rallentando* in the bar before **Z** provides a smoother transition into the *Sostenuto molto*.

Due to the athletic and *staccato* nature of the woodwind figures between bar 183 and bar 213, these instruments do not usually lag behind the baton. However, the *legato* nature of the string writing here is an open invitation to play slightly behind the conductor's beat. This problem becomes even more severe when the *Molto più mosso* is quite fast.

If the soloist makes a slight *rallentando* in bars 212 and 213, then the pulse for *Tempo I, ma tranquillo* is largely already set by the time the piano arrives at the last note of the downward arpeggios. However, if this is not the case, the conductor must take care to clearly communicate the more relaxed tempo at bar 214 with not only the speed of the baton and the quality of the rebound of the first beat, but with his general demeanor and body language as well.

As before, the composer does not indicate an *accelerando* in the four bars preceding *Allegro vivo* (bars 267-270), but a bit of pressure on the tempo here helps to create a smoother, more logical transition.

The last two bars of the work can be handled in a number of different ways, and we take our cues entirely from the pianist in this matter. Some possible options include the following: (1) continuing directly in tempo through to the last bar, (2) taking a *rallentando*, which might be anywhere from small to extreme, in the penultimate bar, (3) continuing in tempo through the third beat of the penultimate bar and then observing a slight lift on the bar-line, and (4) taking some *rallentando* in the penultimate bar *and* observing a lift on the following bar-line.

☙

Peter Ilyich Tchaikovsky

Piano Concerto No. 2 in G Major, Op. 44

1st movement.

In the manuscript copy of the two-piano version of this work, Tchaikovsky added the words *e molto vivace* in handwriting to his initial tempo marking, *Allegro brillante*. Nonetheless, there is little of *vivace* in the tempo most often selected for this movement, which is usually around ♩ = 112–116. No articulations of any kind are present as guides for the opening theme, so the choices made here are more a matter of personal taste than of right or wrong. I prefer to have the quarter notes in the theme played on the longer side, what might be described as *marcato sostenuto*. This articulation communicates a certain grandeur and *maestoso* quality to the line, as opposed to a more choppy, military quality that may be the result of a shorter articulation. Whatever choices are made, the lack of any specificity in the text makes it particularly important that this information be communicated to the orchestra clearly and completely.

The quarter note that begins the following theme (flutes, violins, and viole on the final beat of bar 16) also has no dot, dash, or slur, and therefore is open to interpretation. I prefer for this note, and others that follow in similar positions within the theme, to be played completely *legato*, connecting as one with the rest of the line. Conversely, some conductors prefer a more "starched" reading, with the quarter note separated across the bar-line.

Tchaikovsky's choices for the piano's first entrance are intriguing. On the one hand, the soloist's first task (bar 25) is to perform a rather unremarkable accompaniment beneath woodwind solos. On the other hand the composer compensates for this lack of a flashy entrance by placing an extended, unaccompanied solo passage (bar 47) immediately following. This opening, unaccompanied solo (and the many other similar passages in this work) is, no doubt, a reflection of the composer's famous distaste for the sound of piano and orchestra together. It is odd that he so brilliantly overcame this "distaste" in the First Concerto, but seems to have such a difficult time with it in this work. No bars need be marked, of course, during this solo, as the orchestra's next entrance falls at a double bar and key change.

At the conclusion of the solo (bar 78), the conductor continues at *L'istesso tempo*, in two. Though the composer specifies a relationship between the two *tempi* as ♩ = ♩ (hence, *L'istesso tempo)*, a somewhat faster tempo, perhaps 𝅗𝅥 = 60–64, is more common.

Even the most delicate string sound at bar 118 can make it impossible for the conductor to hear the movement in the piano clearly. This is surely one of those times when we take the opportunity, with hands still addressing the orchestra, to keep our eyes on the pianist's left hand.

With some acceleration and perhaps too much pedal employed, the solo passage beginning at bar 135 can be a bit tricky for some conductors to follow. For obvious reasons, this is not a good place to get confused, as the orchestra must re-enter in tempo. The voice on which we want to focus here is, of course, the uppermost line in the left hand. This voice creates, and makes most apparent, the melodic shape, while the left hand as a whole drives the rhythmic structure.

If one becomes confused amid the barrage of sound, there are certain points in this passage that are easiest to identify, and these moments can be used to re-orient a confused ear: (1) bar 136, fourth beat; it is entirely clear when this point is reached, and hearing it allows the baton to make any minor adjustment necessary (while marking bars) to coordinate the downbeat of the next bar precisely; (2) bar 140, first and third beats; the repetition of E-flat and D-natural on both major beats of the bar; (3) bar 142, fourth beat; the G-natural followed by F-natural is easy to hear largely due to the repetition of the combination of E-flat and D-natural occurring twice earlier in the bar; and (4) bar 145, fourth beat; this moment is plainly obvious as the G-natural forms the beginning of a new scale downward, and being completely secure from this point onward allows the conductor to cue the orchestra's entrance with complete confidence.

For reasons of texture and rhythmic drive, I move back to a beat in four at bar 175. This choice has nothing to do with ensemble security, which is not in danger in either pattern, but addresses a more muscular, rhythmically intense moment in the piece. Because this reminiscence of the opening theme is placed in a much different musical context here, I do ask the orchestra to keep the quarter notes separated in these phrases. Some *accelerando* is common beginning around bar 170 and continuing through bar 184. (This *accelerando* is also noted by the composer in the two-piano score, and is found in some, but not all, printed full scores.)

Some *ritenuto* is to be expected of the pianist, and followed by the conductor, in bar 195. After the brief solo passage that follows, the orchestra continues, in two, at approximately the same tempo as was established at bar 78. The indication here, *L'istesso tempo*, is almost meaningless, as we have just concluded a passage marked *ad libitum*, preceded by a long passage in *accelerando*. The only "same" tempo we can adopt at bar 201 is the tempo of the similar music earlier in the movement, at bar 78. Perhaps the words *come prima* might have been more helpful here.

The only discussion necessary between this point and the beginning of the solo passage at bar 261 is one that cautions the conductor not to allow the tempo to slow unnecessarily between bar 225 and bar 248. The tremendous energy that is present earlier in the movement slowly drains away during this passage, but Tchaikovsky accomplishes this with a combination of a slowly diminishing orchestral force and a slowing of both the harmonic speed and the fundamental rhythmic structure. It is neither necessary nor desirable for the conductor to make a long *allargando* during this same passage, and the composer does not ask for this. We can best aid the composer's intentions by shaping his lines downward toward their goal, and by making certain that all musicians are conscious of the appropriate color of sound for such a passage. Otherwise, if a long *allargando* occurs, the tempo must be re-invigorated either by the conductor at bar 247 or by the soloist two bars later, and this is by no means desirable.

The scales at the end of the solo passage (bar 289 to 292) are simple to follow and lead logically into the orchestra's tempo at bar 293. Whether this passage (bar 295 and following) is taken in four or in two depends entirely on exactly how *Brillante* this tempo will be, as it can be handled with complete technical and musical success either way. Again, the musical context suggests a somewhat more detached execution of the quarter notes. If this section is taken in two, some brief changes back into four will be desirable artistically when the texture so suggests (e.g., bars 317–318). The composer indicates an optional cut (though it is not reproduced in all editions) from the end of bar 318 to the downbeat of bar 343. In the performances that I have conducted of this work I have never taken the cut, as I fail to see how the removal of 24 bars in a movement of 668 bars aids or tightens the form. On the other hand, I can certainly see the validity of the position that, in a movement lasting twenty minutes, every little bit helps.

Beginning in the second half of bar 496, the conductor needs to take very seriously the tempo being set by the pianist via the scales in sixteenth notes. By the end of bar 500 the soloist should have set the tempo (presumably, the same tempo as the beginning of the movement) for the following *tutti*. This issue is not to be taken lightly, as the conductor must fall in precisely (as to tempo and exact position in the bar) with the soloist's figure that begins in bar 501. If the orchestra enters in bar 502 at a tempo that is even slightly different from the one already established by the pianist, and the soloist changes these constant sixteenths to match the orchestra (or worse, doesn't), the effect is unmusical and unprofessional.

Much of the recapitulation proceeds under the same musical and technical principles as have already been discussed in the exposition. The opening section of the coda (bar 629) is best handled in four, with the rather obvious exception of the first three bars. What follows (bar 641) is in two.

Utilizing the common cadential gesture of broadening the tempo slightly during the last three chords is understandable, but I don't prefer it. While each chord in the final bar needs emphasis, any holding back here feels rather artificial and unsatisfying to me, considering the headlong rush forward that we have experienced during the latter portion of the coda.

2nd movement.

When programming this work, it is vital that a conductor consult with the soloist well ahead of time regarding which version of the second movement will be played. From a conducting standpoint I will only be discussing the original version here, but it is nonetheless quite important that conductors be familiar with the existence and substance of the revised version, just in case a potential soloist expresses a desire to perform the movement in its shortened form.

The revised version of the second movement was created by Alexander Siloti (a contemporary of Tchaikovsky's, though some years younger) after the composer's death. To the best of my knowledge, we do not know the precise reasons that Siloti felt that this movement needed to be "fixed," but we can certainly make some educated guesses. First, the long absences of the piano, combined with extended violin and cello solos, may have been considered irksome to potential piano soloists; or, this construction may have been thought to be off-putting to an audience that would have been expecting something rather different. Second, the original version of the movement is quite long, especially considering that it follows a very lengthy first movement. (I think it is fair to say that audiences in both the 19th and 21st centuries are emotionally and physically prepared for much shorter second and third movements when the first movement of a concerto is of such considerable length.) This latter reason is, of course, no reason at all. Saying that cuts need to be made in the second movement only because it is quite lengthy is like saying that *Lawrence of Arabia* is a bit too long, and perhaps some of the "bits that are just sand and sun" could be cut out. Both works (this concerto and the film) are exactly the length they need to be, and if *Lawrence of Arabia* is too taxing then one should probably watch *Weekend at Bernie's*. The revised version of this movement takes an incredibly unique and beautiful creation, removes more than half the measures and strips it of most of its fundamental uniqueness. At this point, I doubt it even needs to be said: no, I do not think the revised version of the movement should be played.

For the purposes of examination, the fundamental changes found in the Siloti version are: (1) in bars 9 through 45, the solo violin is removed and this material (appropriately re-arranged) is placed in the solo piano; most of the orchestral material is removed entirely, with some orchestral involvement retained, though different from the original, in bars 35 to 42; (2) a cut is made from the end of bar 45 to the downbeat of bar 221; (Interestingly, Tchaikovsky himself suggested a completely different cut, from the end of bar 246 to the downbeat of bar 282. This assumes, of course, that the Siloti cut is not taken.) and, (3) a cut is made from the end of bar 309 to the downbeat of bar 327. (This small, final cut is the only place that Siloti and Tchaikovsky agree, as the composer made the same suggestion. While I cannot say that I'm a great fan of this cut, one surely cannot say that it does fundamental damage to the movement.)

Leaving the issue of the Siloti version behind us, it is important that we stop and take note of the extraordinarily daring thing that Tchaikovsky has done in this movement. The incorporation of significant solos for the concertmaster and principal cello while the piano is mute, as well as extended passages of piano trio, some with orchestra accompaniment and some not, is quite a remarkable idea. The very "newness" of it is probably, and unfortunately, what led to the acceptance of a version that subdues (that is, chokes the life out of) the composer's unique ideas.

The opening violin solo and the following duet with the cello are essentially accompanied chamber music. As such, the two orchestral soloists should be treated like any other soloists, with the conductor accompanying and adapting to their musical direction. It is often reasonable for the conductor to accompany an important orchestral solo, rather than always imposing his musical will on every note, but this moment takes that idea to an entirely different level, virtually elevating the concertmaster and principal cellist into guest artist roles, if only for one movement.

The significance of the cello solo in particular brings up an important question of stage geography. This question comes up in a few other piano concerti, most notably the Brahms B-flat major concerto, but nowhere is it quite as significant as in this concerto, due to the unusual prominence and duration of the cello solos themselves. The issue that needs resolution concerns the fact that, when using a large concert grand piano, the likely position of the first stand of celli is behind (directly upstage of) the piano. The principal cellist's body and instrument are often completely invisible to most of the audience in this position, with the possible exception of those sitting in the extreme audience-right, who view the cellist only from the back. This is not only a question of respect for the musician involved, but it is also a balance problem, as the cellist's sound, in this position, is mostly being enjoyed by the back of the piano and the conductor. Some solution needs to be considered before rehearsals begin to keep the cellist from being subjected to this acoustically disadvantageous, and somewhat disrespectful, positioning.

In the passage that begins at bar 144, there may be a slowly growing balance problem, as the *crescendo* throughout the orchestra takes shape. This needs to be considered even though the pianist is essentially accompanying the orchestra. After all, the same description could be made of the opening orchestral phrases of the second Rachmaninoff concerto, but we would still like to hear the pianist to some reasonable degree.

Between the downbeat of bar 184 and the end of bar 194 I do nothing but mark the bars for the benefit of the rest of the orchestra. I never conduct the two soloists here unless I'm asked to do so, and I've only been asked on one occasion. On the one occasion when I was asked to conduct these bars it was, ironically, the solution to the problem discussed two paragraphs above that created a stage geography causing these two musicians difficulty connecting with one another visually and aurally. There is also, usually, no need to conduct in the duet passage that follows, from bar 199 through bar 205.

The style of conducting for the following "piano trio" passage (bar 221) is a delicate balance between accompanying, as one would in any other concerto, and leading, as one would in an orchestral work. In the best of all possible worlds, this passage can be treated like a moment from the Beethoven Triple Concerto, in the sense that the trio has its own internal musical agreements that the conductor can easily follow. Unfortunately, ensemble limitations imposed by the physical positioning of players on the stage, combined with the relatively short amount of time these three musicians have probably spent together (often, none), usually means that some benevolent central leadership is not only necessary but gratefully accepted.

I can certainly see why Tchaikovsky might have suggested the final cut, as discussed above. However, with all due respect, I cannot agree. While it can be argued that the passage of *dénouement* beginning at bar 286 gives ample closure to the work, I find the cut from bar 309 to bar 327 to be abrupt. And, once again, I find no formal or time-saving virtue in removing seventeen bars out of three hundred and thirty-two. Reviving my *Lawrence of Arabia* metaphor, it seems to me that removing so small yet emotionally important a passage makes about as much sense as removing a brief panorama of the scorching desert: we get short-changed just when we really need to feel the heat.

3rd movement.

Following the considerable length of both preceding movements, as well as the unusual nature and tone of the second, the relatively brief, delightful romp that is the finale of this concerto is quite appropriate and most welcome. Though much of the movement can be handled successfully in one (around ♩ = 144), the rhythmic structure of much of the musical material seems to demand that the conductor remain in two a great deal of the time. Certain passages, however (e.g., bar 132 and following), are well suited to a beat in one.

☙

Ralph Vaughan Williams

Piano Concerto (Double Piano Concerto)

The first version of this concerto, for solo piano and orchestra, was premiered in February 1933. Collaborating with the composer, Joseph Cooper created the two-piano version, and its first performance was heard in November 1946. The orchestral material for both versions is identical. Thus, when attempting to acquire parts for performance of the two-piano version, one acquires parts labeled only "Piano Concerto." To the best of my knowledge, no orchestra materials with the title "Double Concerto" exist. As I recently rediscovered, acquiring the soloists' parts for the two-piano version can be rather difficult. In order to acquire actual, playing sized parts, one must speak to exactly the right person at the rental house. The piano duo with which I most recently performed the work had to speak to four or five different people and return three sets of (incorrect) materials before finally acquiring the parts they needed.

1st movement.

The basic set-up of the $\frac{7}{8}$ bars is, of course, 2+2+3. Some discussion will follow later regarding a few passages in which the conductor may, or may not, want to choose a different pattern. When conducting the beginning of a work, or a new section of a work in which the last beat of the bar is not the same length as the first beat, one must consider (and communicate clearly to the orchestra in rehearsal) what value the preparatory beat will contain. To some conductors it seems logical that the preparatory gesture for the beginning of this concerto would be the value of a dotted quarter note. This is because the non-existent third beat of the preceding bar would have been of that value. While the mathematical logic is laudable, this approach is really not the best solution. A quarter note preparation is best in a situation like this, because it is the value of the first beat that will be played, and because a shorter value choice is usually best and most specifically communicative.

Moving directly from the (slower) opening tempo into the faster, *Poco animato* tempo at **2**, the conductor has no opportunity to indicate the precise new tempo until already in the new bar. As with all such circumstances (in a concerto or not), a precise and comfortable playing of the first several beats will rely on three things: (1) that the tempo is precisely as played in rehearsal, allowing the musicians to accurately predict the pace of the sixteenth notes ahead of time, (2) that the beat is clear, calm, and unambiguous, with the rebound clearly indicating the new tempo, and (3) that the musicians retain at least a reasonable memory of the tempo of the passage from its most recent playing.

A slight *ritard* just before **5**, creating a ♩ = ♩ relationship at Tempo 1, allows for a less jarring transition. This also facilitates a clean performance of sixteenth notes in strings and woodwinds.

The tempo in the sixth bar after **7** is intended to be the same as at the opening of the work (Tempo 1). However, if the opening tempo is taken in the range of ♩ = 72–84, as it often is, one may want to consider a slower tempo here. The reason for this is surely obvious. A somewhat slower tempo here allows the thirty-second-note figures in woodwinds and strings to be played, and heard, to their maximum effectiveness. When this passage is played at a true Tempo 1, much of the beauty and elegance of the harmonies is lost. Though this is certainly a matter of negotiation with the soloist(s) (particularly since the soloist(s) must set the tempo), I have always encouraged a tempo of ♩ = 64–68 for this passage. The more dramatic nature of this passage, from the standpoint of orchestration, harmony, and general musical content, is well suited to this slower tempo. If this approach is adopted, Tempo 1 should return at **9**, re-established by the solo piano.

2nd movement.

As is surely apparent, no bars need be marked from the beginning of the *cadenza* (at the end of the first movement) through the entrance of the solo flute at **15**. In spite of the clarity of the explanation that the conductor will give to the orchestra, "I begin conducting again at **15**," it is polite and professional to clearly cue each new entrance, starting with the flute and continuing with viole/celli, second violins, etc.

In order to allow the piano maximum flexibility in shaping the end of the phrase at **16**, it is most often necessary to subdivide the final beat of the bar (one bar before **16**) for comfortable coordination of the solo and the entrance of viole, returning to beating in three in the following bar. On the final beat of the fourth bar after **16**, a slight subdivision is also advisable. This gesture brings clarity to both the cut-off of strings and the entrance of viole in the following bar. The same applies to the final beat before **17**.

Between **18** and the seventh bar after **19**, the composer gives several indications regarding the use of a smaller string group. This effort at a more transparent sound is important to the mood of the passage, but the composer's precise indications may not be entirely practical. For example, he suggests four desks of first violins and four desks of second violins in his first indications following **18**. While this may be practical in an orchestra with thirty-two violins in total, it does not create nearly enough sonic contrast in a typical American regional orchestra that may be playing with between twenty and twenty-six violins. Slimming the section of first violins down from ten or twelve to eight is simply not enough of a difference to create the effect he is seeking. Therefore, in an orchestra with a string section of roughly 12-12-8-8-6, I suggest the following changes: (1) three desks of first violins, not four; at **19**, only two desks, (2) three desks of second violins; later, two desks instead of three, (3) four bars before **19**, where there is no indication at all, only two desks of viole; the same at **19**, and (4) two desks of celli, not three.

The real musical challenge of the *tutti* passage beginning at $\frac{3}{2}$ (𝅗𝅥 = ♩ *Ma poco animato*) is to insure that the delicate, hushed quality is never disturbed. This is achieved in part by making sure that the strings play a true *pianissimo*, entirely in the upper half of the bow, throughout. This allows the winds to play only *piano* while still clearly dominating the texture. In addition, the strings must take great care with the sound to ensure that up-bows do not inadvertently *crescendo* while down-bows *diminuendo*. Likewise, the winds must not allow expressive swells that the composer does not request to creep into the line. Though not as critical, as the listener's focus is on the solo piano(s), these same principles of musical and ensemble discipline apply between **21** and **23**.

3rd movement.

The main *Allegro* tempo of the third movement (usually around ♩ = 184) is handled best by moving deftly from three to one, and back again, depending on the musical needs of the moment. There are certainly no hard and fast rules, so what follows is a guide in this regard.

Five bars before **29**	in three
Second bar of **30**	in one

At **31**	in three
32 to tenth bar of **35**	in one or in three (depending on the expertise of the orchestra)
Eight bars before **36**	in three (some soloists prefer for this section, through **36**, to be conducted in two; though somewhat easier for the pianist[s], this is not advisable for several technical and musical reasons; see three paragraphs below)
At **36a**	in one (the duplets and quadruplets that dominate this passage make conducting in one virtually imperative)
At **37**	in three
At **39**	in one
Four bars before **41** to **42**	in one or in three (depending on the expertise of the orchestra)
Second bar of **43**	in one
At **47**	in one
Fifth bar of **51**	in three (though it may seem counterintuitive to move from one to three during a *stringendo*, in this particular case it is the best way to control all parts of the texture)

Due to the athletic nature of most of this movement, there is very little accompanying in the traditional sense of the word required from the conductor. Successfully managing a movement like this one is more a matter of keeping control of, and establishing precision with, the orchestra and having a good rapport with the soloist(s) that fosters trust and confidence in one another.

In considering the list (above) of places in this movement that it is recommended to beat in one or in three respectively, one should keep in mind that even one's own solutions to these questions should be flexible. For example, one may decide that the passage from **31** to **33** can be managed in one with no technical problems or musical diminishment. Even so, one may decide that it is preferable musically to show, for example, the second beat of the first bar at **31** for precision, or to go into three for a few bars beginning five bars before **32** to aid the precision of the material in flute and viole.

Also mentioned in that list is the question of beating in two in the hemiola passage beginning eight (or nine) bars before **36**. There is no question that some soloists appreciate this approach, as it may make coordination with the baton through their peripheral vision somewhat less worrisome. Nonetheless, this is not advisable for two reasons. First, it creates an unnecessary complication for the orchestra in an already difficult movement. Second, and perhaps far more important, is the overriding principle of conducting that essentially forbids conducting the hemiola rather than the meter. While there may be necessary exceptions to this rule, this is certainly not one of them. Vaughan Williams was more than capable of writing this short passage in $\frac{6}{8}$, adding ♪ = ♪ for clarity, had that been the rhythmic feel he desired. On the contrary, a figure in hemiola feels very different from this, though appearing the same on the page, and the proper rhythmic "tug" is maintained and reinforced by beating in three with a strongly emphasized second beat.

Whether the beat chosen at **41** is in three or in one, the bar directly preceding **42** is best handled in two, unless there is absolutely no tempo change whatsoever in this bar. Allowing for the expected stretch in this bar, as the music expands toward the end of the phrase, remaining in one can be problematic. Taking this bar in two allows the sudden, duple rhythm on each beat to be executed easily, even in *allargando*, and the low brass can easily coordinate what is now essentially a quarter-note triplet against the two beats shown by the conductor.

The brief orchestral entrance at the beginning of the Finale alla Tedesca (trumpets, trombones, snare drum, and triangle) should be conducted entirely in three. Although not instructed precisely (all that's written is *colla parte*), a nice, broad *allargando*, particularly on the penultimate chord, adds drama and a charming Viennese flavor to this unexpected interjection. Since the bars between this point and **43** will not be marked, it is important to subtly warn the orchestra that their entrance is approaching several bars ahead of time. The first bar at **43** is then conducted in a broad three, before returning to beating in one at *a tempo*.

The *cadenza* between **50** and **50a** exists only for the two-piano version, and is sometimes cut even with two soloists. I have done this piece both with and without this passage, and I am rather well convinced that the piece works better without it, though I am sure not all piano duos will agree. When it is left out of the two-piano version, and at all times for solo piano, the "cut" is to be seamless.

Though not a real concern for the conductor, as it occurs in the middle of the cadenza, one may want to be aware of the following minor editorial issue. Nine bars before **52**, in the right hand of both the solo piano part and piano I of the two-piano version, some performance materials show the F-sharp major chord on the downbeat to be not tied over, but re-articulated. It is clear in the score, in both versions, that the eighth note chord on the downbeat is tied over, but it is equally clear in performance materials (for either one and two pianos) that it is not. I am not aware at this time of a source that completely clarifies the composer's intention, and I have heard it performed both ways.

When the conductor begins beating again at **52**, no more than a clear, but delicate downbeat is needed. Four bars before the end, the baton comes to rest after indicating the second beat, without proceeding further. At this point, the conductor is waiting for the release of sound from the piano(s), indicated by the breath mark. This release should coincide as closely as possible with the preparation for the following downbeat. Once the baton indicates the downbeat three bars before the end, no more beats need be marked through the end of the work. The left hand alone traces the subtle *crescendo-diminuendo*, and then sustains the final chord, *pianississimo*, without any further decay of sound, until the final release.

II. Violin Concerti

Samuel Barber

Concerto for Violin and Orchestra, Op. 14

As any conductor surely knows, R.M. is one of the, if not *the*, foremost interpreters of this work. His experience with the piece spans decades of performances, and he was a close colleague and friend of the composer's. As such, he is uniquely qualified to share his thoughts and ideas about this concerto, one of the most important works in this genre by an American composer. Instead of dissecting this score that he knows so well, R.M.'s comments serve as a general, and very cogent, guide for study, rehearsal, and performance of this piece: "[It is] the most genuine attempt at beauty that anyone's every made. It's the most perfectly imperfect concerto I've ever played. I think that's the basis from which to start, for both conductor and soloist. He didn't know how to write for the violin and he over-orchestrated the piece, but it's still an honest attempt at beauty. We all want to do what the composer wants, and we all want to be great stewards of the composer's work, but what you really want to accomplish can't be accomplished if the sound is too thick. Instead of looking at this masterpiece and trying to follow every marking he made, look at Barber instead as this insecure man who didn't really know what he was doing when he was writing for the violin, and was just trying in his own way to do something beautiful. So, help Barber out instead of being so righteous about what's written in the score. Help him out."

1st movement.

Even though we were ages past the stylistic imperative of a formal introduction by the time this piece was written, the opening of this concerto still strikes one as remarkable for its subtlety, simplicity, and direct, immediate emotional content. If the first, gorgeous sonority does not take our breath away then something is very wrong.

The genius in the construction of the major material of this movement lies in its ability to simultaneously convey the communicative, elegiac feeling of *recitative* (simple melodic line over accompaniment of whole notes) and a kind of almost breathless forward motion (*pizzicato* cello figures and horn triplets). This magnificent duality forms the very heart of the movement, and understanding the importance of allowing neither quality to dominate is one of the principal tasks of both conductor and soloist.

Many soloists will linger a bit over the fourth beat of the fifth bar after **1**. I like to allow the horn the same elegance two beats before, if the soloist does not object too strenuously. The same applies just after **12**. Eight bars after **1**, some violinists continue through the end of the bar entirely, or almost entirely, in tempo, but others take a significant *ritard* before the orchestra re-enters. This is another example of a moment in which the placement of a conductor's preparatory gesture is entirely dependent upon foreknowledge of the soloist's intent. Likewise, the last note of the bar four bars before **2** can slow all the way to a *fermata corta* in some hands, changing everything about the conductor's approach to the next bar.

The violin pick-ups to **4** are nearly always played in the tempo of the bar that follows, and though it is not notated in precisely this way, surely the composer intended this, or at least knew it was the likely outcome. He does not explain, however, how he would like the end of the previous phrase, viole in *poco rall.*, to be coordinated with a violin line, in *accelerando*, on the same beat. I do ask the viole to subtly accelerate with the baton (and the soloist) during that beat, while making a *diminuendo* across the triplet so as not to draw attention to this juxtaposition.

The horn figure one bar before **6** is transcribed rather oddly. The rhythm is not complicated, but you'd never know at first glance. Written more clearly, this rhythm is simply:

Because of the *ritard* preceding **6**, it is easy to make the error of setting the following tempo, with its delicately pulsing celli and timpani, too slowly. Despite the different musical context, this music should flow at the same tempo as its original version at **2**. The same is true of the passage beginning in the third bar after **7**. Here we are left with only a fragment of the original melody, with rather more exotic harmonies, that may seduce one into a slower tempo.

By the time we reach **9**, we are at the fastest tempo in the movement to this point, and moving forward. In spite of that exuberant tempo, the woodwind solos must be played with the utmost delicacy, seeming to float toward us entirely weightless, rather than taking on a clarion quality in their higher registers.

The use of the piano to double the entire wind section at **10** is an unusual touch by anyone else's standards, but very typical of Barber. He wisely places only *forte* in the piano part, while the winds (with the exception of the trumpets, for obvious reasons) are marked *fortissimo*. This is not so much a balance issue (as the piano was unlikely to overbalance all those winds) as one of color. The piano is clearly intended as an added element of percussive color for the wind section, and should not be heard too prominently through the texture.

Most soloists sustain the final note before **10** for emphasis. In order to set up this moment logically, I make a fairly significant *allargando* during that entire bar. One should be careful, however, not to carry this gesture over into the following bar, as the figures in timpani and upper strings that follow should be joyously *più mosso.*

The bar before **11** can be a bit rough on the first reading, for obvious reasons. A quick explanation of who in the orchestra should, and should not, be playing together usually solves the problems on the second playing.

In the second and third bars before **12**, I ask the first violins and viole (only the violins in the second instance) to place a comma after the third beat and a slight accent on the fourth. This helps to give shape to these diminishing phrases, and avoids a sort of musical run-on sentence.

Though the soloist often takes time in the last beat of the fifth bar after **12** (as mentioned above with regard to the horn figure on the second beat), even more time is usually allowed on the fourth beat of the following bar. The conductor does not want to under-anticipate with this gesture, or he will likely end up placing the orchestral string chord on the following downbeat (two bars before **13**) too early.

The solo passage that occupies the five beats preceding **13** can be fairly perplexing for some conductors, causing considerable insecurity in the gesture needed to move the orchestra forward. I have watched a number of performances of this piece in which the soloist had to essentially conduct the downbeat with her scroll and forehead, realizing that the conductor was not going to commit himself without some sort of obvious, physical leadership. This situation (which occurs a lot more than most soloists want to discuss) is completely avoidable by following the top line of the violin part only. Thinking of these five beats as though the lower note of each seventh was removed, one hears groupings of three, two, three, two, and four notes respectively. Training the ear to hear only this part of the line, rather than getting tangled in the entire texture (if that is too confusing) essentially solves the problem, and the preparation can be shown on the G-natural that is the third note of the final grouping of four.

As in the analogous location earlier in the work, there is the possibility that the soloist will slow down essentially to a stop on the final note of the fifth bar after **13**, and the conductor needs be prepared for this so that she neither shows the downbeat early nor gets stuck with the baton around her eyebrows.

In the brief *cadenza* bar directly before **17**, the baton remains motionless after arriving at the third beat. What remains in the bar, and needs to be carefully explained to the orchestra, are three gestures with the left hand as follows: the first gesture indicates the end of the timpani roll and the unification of the bass section to the upper octave, the second gesture indicates the octave movement in the celli, and the third shows the *diminuendo*. The baton only moves again to prepare the following downbeat.

2nd movement.

The sections of this movement that flow in the opening tempo fall into a delightful, but mildly uncomfortable, no-man's land, being not always entirely comfortable in two or in six. Beating this tempo in six often becomes too pedantic, containing many beats that are not necessary and disrupting the flow. However, beating in two leaves room for some inaccuracies, particularly in *pizzicati* and during even a slight *ritard.* The best solution is to consider the passage as fundamentally in two, but to be open to any and all needs or opportunities for subdividing. One of these needs presents itself directly at the beginning of the movement, as clear tempo is best communicated in six in the first two bars, particularly if one takes a slight *rallentando* at the end of the second bar, as I do. One can then move into two in the third bar, subdividing as needed for *pizzicati* and security of ensemble.

Ironically, precisely where the composer writes "in 2" is where we are likely to need to subdivide. The new, *Più mosso* tempo at **3** can be a bit difficult for the winds to read when beaten strictly in two, because this "faster" tempo is still only 𝅗𝅥. = 40. I conduct the first half of the bar in one beat, showing strong subdivisions on the fifth and sixth beats for a clean and confident wind entrance. This may or may not be necessary again two bars later, but the entire rest of the passage can remain in two (in three at $\frac{9}{4}$) as Barber recommended, with the exception of the *allargando* two bars before **4**.

In the *ad libitum* bar, one before **5**, the baton rests on the first beat and goes no further. Changes of pitch for the bassoon and the final cut-off for bassoon and horn are shown with the left hand. As the solo violin moves to the trill in the next bar, the baton marks the downbeat and then dictates the string chord at the appropriate time.

For reasons of both flexibility and ensemble security, I conduct the entire passage from six bars before **7** to **8** entirely in six (returning to a beat in two at **8**). There is so much in this passage that requires subdivision that I simply don't find it helpful to continually vacillate back and forth.

The composer specifies "in 3" at **9**, but the final three notes of the first bar (celli and basses) require the weight of clear subdivisions. By the time the fourth bar before the end is reached, the tempo has slowed to the point that the B-natural in timpani and celli needs to be shown as a subdivision. There is usually a comma, or breath, in all parts, including the solo violin, on the bar-line preceding the final chord.

3rd movement.

Though not even four minutes in duration, the finale of this concerto often absorbs more rehearsal time than the earlier two movements combined. Syncopations at this very quick tempo combined with the virtuosic playing demanded from both the soloist and the orchestra are the ingredients that make this movement both thrilling to hear and nightmarish to conduct with anything other than a very skilled orchestra.

The majority of the movement (in $\frac{4}{4}$) is best taken in two. There are some passages, however, that are best with some orchestras in four, while others would prefer the conductor remain in two. A passage like the one found in bars 3 and 4 is a perfect example of this. For orchestras with excellent inner pulse and ensemble, it is easiest to remain in two in these syncopated bars. Less experienced and/or less confident players, however, may prefer to see the second (quarter note) beat of the bar for security in placing the second chord. Regardless of what occurs directly before a passage in $\frac{3}{4}$ (whether that $\frac{4}{4}$ meter is in two or in four), the triple meter is usually best handled in three, not in one, unless the conductor feels extremely confident in a soloist who will not rush and a wind section that will not play late when seeing the larger value beat.

Eighth note after-beats, such as those found one bar before **4**, are another type of figure that can be handled in two or in four, and the choice is largely a matter of the comfort of the orchestra. Less experienced violins might like to see each beat, giving them a reference point for each after-beat. More experienced players, however, will probably prefer that the conductor stay in two and get out of their way.

The first several bars of $\frac{2}{4}$ (after **15**) are best beaten in one, showing each bar with a gesture that moves clearly downward, being clear to differentiate passive gestures from active ones, to avoid confusion. The seventh and eighth bars before the end, however, may need to be taken in two in some orchestras. When the soloist is ready to release the *fermata* three bars before the end, the left hand shows a cut-off while the baton, simultaneously and knowingly ahead of the soloist, marks the following bar, remaining at rest there. From this position, with the penultimate bar already dispatched, the conductor is ready to respond to the soloist's final arpeggio at any time.

ꕤ

Max Bruch

Violin Concerto in G Minor, Op. 26

1st movement.

A gentle indication of the downbeat, with no sharply defined *ictus*, is sufficient to initiate the opening timpani roll, followed by only the slightest indication of the passing of bar 2. Though the conductor certainly may choose to flow through all the beats of the fifth bar, showing the indicated dynamic swell in this manner, it is really not necessary; after arriving at the downbeat of bar 5, the baton can remain motionless while the left hand alone traces the curve of the *crescendo-diminuendo* figure. This expressive gesture should not crest at a volume higher than *mezzo-piano*, or the gentle, contemplative mood of the opening of the work is spoiled. As the left hand finishes tracing the *diminuendo*, the baton marks the downbeat of bar 6, and again remains still. Once the soloist enters, and a reasonable approximation of two beats of tempo has elapsed, the left hand cuts off the wind chord. No dynamic is given for the beginning of the phrase in bar 7, but we assume it to be no more than *piano*.

The first two orchestral phrases (beginning in bar 3 and bar 7) are often taken at a tempo that is more *moderato* than *allegro*, and this approach helps to set the proper mood. Many conductors take this same, slower tempo four bars before **A**, waiting to set the tempo for the violinist precisely at **A**. But this practice does not, in my opinion, lend the proper character to the *fortissimo* phrase. Immediately setting the slightly faster tempo that will dominate the movement (four bars before **A**) more clearly divides the opening two statements from what follows, as well as giving this phrase a more muscular and energetic character.

The challenges of elegantly and accurately accompanying a work like this one are far different from those found in a more complicated work, such as one of the piano concerti by Rachmaninoff or Prokoffiev. In Bruch, rather than encountering the intellectual and technical complexities that surround concerti by those formidable Russians, the challenge here is to get into the mind and stylistic sense of the soloist so that very subtle changes of tempo and style are adapted to and understood even as they are happening.

The fourth bar after **A** provides the first of many instances, particularly in the first movement, where this awareness of small but important rhythmic subtleties is crucial to good accompanying and detailed music-making. In the fourth beat of this bar, it is common for the soloist to add a bit of extra time between the two final, hooked notes (B-flat and C-sharp). This extra time cannot be managed by the conductor solely through listening to the performance in real time. By the time the conductor, in the midst of the fourth beat, with the baton already descending toward the following downbeat, realizes that there has been a slight stylization by the soloist, it is too late to avoid the sound of the orchestra's downbeat arriving before the D-natural in the solo violin. Knowing beforehand what is likely to happen and dealing with it technically at an earlier point in the bar is the only way to accommodate this kind of stylized phrase. In this case, the baton can pause (ever so briefly) after striking the third beat, moving to the fourth beat at a point that is actually slightly behind the soloist. Thus, when the soloist adds this small bit of extra time, the baton "catches up" and all arrive at the following downbeat together. The other technical possibility is to move to the fourth beat in logical coordination with the soloist, but to then somewhat exaggerate the shape of the rebound after that beat, pausing during that rebound, thus drawing attention to the fact that the baton is not yet descending toward one.

Either of the solutions above can work. Which one is best depends on the comfort and technique of an individual conductor. A significant, but not necessarily exhaustive, list of other points at which such stylization of the rhythm might be employed is as follows: six and eight bars after A; twelve, ten, eight, six, and four bars before B; four, eight, ten, and twelve bars after C. For each of these moments, and any others discovered during rehearsal, the conductor needs to be keenly aware of exactly what is likely to occur, and plan accordingly for good accompanying. The conductor needs to make sure that she takes good notes in the score during this process, as some soloists will take extra time at one point but not at another similar point, and "using the force" is not a good strategy. Just as we expect orchestral musicians to thoroughly write down our stylistic, technical, or musical instructions from the podium, a soloist expects from us the same diligence and specificity of thought and preparation.

Before moving on, I will share one more thought on this subject. By looking carefully at the cello/bass part between A and B, one could certainly draw the conclusion that Bruch was well aware that these stylizations were likely to be employed by the soloist. In every other bar of the passage (second, fourth, etc.), the composer omits the eighth note that should logically follow the fourth beat. This omission can certainly be interpreted as his indication that there is likely to be some liberty taken by the soloist during this beat, and including the final eighth note of the bar would make coordination more complicated than necessary. On the other hand, the omission of this eighth note may be nothing more than his desire to create a series of two-bar phrases in the cello/bass part, rather than an extended pattern in which each bar is rhythmically identical.

Four, six, and eight bars before **B**, it is not uncommon for the soloist to take considerable time in the second half of the bar, often to the extent that the note (or chord) on the second half of the third beat feels almost like a *fermata*. When the bar is expanded to this extent, the baton should pause on the third beat, allowing time for the soloist to sustain the chord, then move forward to the fourth beat, giving the soloist an indication that she is invited to move forward.

Five bars before **B**, some soloists make a slight pause after the first chord, perhaps even sustaining the first chord slightly in a *fermata corta*. When either or both are the case, this considerably changes the conductor's manner of handling the bar technically. It will require a slight pause during, and a somewhat elongated rebound from, the first beat in order to bring to the attention of the orchestra that the second beat will arrive later, possibly much later, than expected.

The delicious bit of orchestrating that begins in the seventh bar after **B** only works to its full effect if the orchestral strings play and maintain a genuine *pianissimo*. The passage hinges sonically on the juxtaposition of the warm expressive lower register of the solo violin against the transparent, somewhat less expressive sound of the orchestral strings in registers remote from the solo voice. Even in very fine orchestras it is often necessary to caution the musicians regarding not only the sonic requirements of this passage, but also that unintended *crescendi* during up-bows are to be scrupulously avoided. Fourteen bars after **B**, one should regard well the pace of the quintuplet: some soloists take considerable time with this figure, while others lean forward swiftly toward the following downbeat.

As mentioned earlier, the final beat of the fourth bar after **C** often contains some *rubato*. This bit of stretch can vary in different hands from inconsequential to considerable, and the conductor must be clearly aware of how the phrase is likely to be shaped.

Five bars before **D**, some soloists take a slight *ritard* at the end of the bar, just before *Un poco più vivo*. This *ritard* runs contrary to the obvious musical intention of the moment, which is to move forward toward the somewhat faster tempo that follows. In addition, such a *ritard* is antithetical to the composer's decision to place measured sixteenth notes in the violins rather than the quarter note arpeggios that are found in the preceding bars.

Catching the end of the G minor scale that leads into **F** is not particularly difficult. Nonetheless, it is certainly not a moment to be taken for granted, as a misplaced orchestral entrance at the top of the scale will be very obvious to virtually anyone in the audience, and makes a soloist quite annoyed. A conductor whose ear doesn't seem to follow the flow of the scale naturally can employ either or both of the following strategies. Most obvious is to follow the shape of the three octaves of the scale, listening carefully to each G-natural. The preparatory gesture can usually be placed with the G-natural that begins the third octave of the scale. In addition to this, one can make sure that the soloist's bowing for the scale is noted in the score, as visual observation of bow use will give extra clues to when the end of the scale can be anticipated. The latter strategy presumes, of course, that the soloist uses the same bowing in performance as in rehearsal, and this is by no means universally the case. Also, while following the upward scale the conductor should take care not to become too complacent with regard to the pace of the scale itself, as many soloists will take the final octave more rapidly than the first two.

2nd movement.

The final two bars (of the first movement) of sustained B-flats in the violins can afford to be played *quasi senza vibrato*, as this adds to the *morendo* quality indicated. As the other strings enter and complete the chord at the opening of the second movement, the sound should be warmed somewhat, but can still be less than completely *espressivo*, as this creates a beautiful contrast with the sound of the solo violin. This technique also allows the conductor to bring forward from the string orchestra those lines most important at any given moment (e.g., viole in bars 4–5 and 7–8) by using the color of the sound (suddenly more *espressivo*) rather than only a higher dynamic. The general sound should continue to warm *poco a poco* until, although still *pianissimo*, the sound is completely *naturale* and *espressivo* by the beginning of the ninth bar.

In the third beat of the bar before **B** (and other musically similar situations) most soloists take some time in the completion of the phrase. How much time is taken will vary from soloist to soloist and from one instance to another within the piece, and the conductor needs to decide which occurrences require a gentle subdivision of this final beat and which do not. For example, one can usually conduct the bar preceding **B** strictly in three, while the third bar after **B** will almost always require the subdivision.

The first violins, who are playing a careful *pianissimo* throughout this passage, may need to be encouraged to play out a bit more in the fourth and fifth bars after **B** and the first two bars at **C**. This important musical material needs to sing easily over the rest of the orchestra at these moments, while still maintaining the feel of *pianissimo*, falling back into the background each time the soloist re-enters.

In the beat preceding **D**, it is really the soloist's responsibility to place the grace note (E-natural) in its proper place before the barline. Nonetheless, after showing the entrance of bassoons, horns, celli, and basses on the third beat, it is appropriate to slightly sustain that beat for safety, carefully observing the soloist in case she chooses to linger a bit over this lovely moment.

The indication *pesante* in the ninth bar after **D** is an invitation to the soloist to take a bit of *rubato* during these sextuplets, particularly on the last beat, and most soloists are only too happy to accept. One of the pitfalls in this bar is the possibility that the conductor will over-anticipate the degree of *rubato* and/or the time that will be added to the bar. When hearing the soloist begin to take some liberty, it is all too tempting to suspend the third beat as a matter of conscientious accompanying, only to find that the time "robbed" early in the beat has already been "paid back" before one can react gracefully and meet the soloist on the following downbeat.

Either or both of the two bars preceding **E** are likely to have some *allargando* that is not specifically indicated, and this musical gesture can be quite extreme. In the first of the two bars, this is likely to occur toward the end of the second beat, emphasizing the change of harmony on the third beat, possibly moving forward again once the third beat is reached. When the stretch in this bar is considerable, the conductor will want to take particular care with the pattern, making certain that the indication of the third beat is clearly floating upward so that the celli and basses are not tempted to play the *pizzicato* F-natural during the extended third beat. In the bar directly before **E**, time is likely to be taken progressively through the bar, with considerable time taken in the third beat, and perhaps even a *fermata corta* added to the final note before the bar-line.

Contrary to our discussion regarding the opening of this movement, the *pianissimo* strings at **F**, while still observing the dynamics, should employ a sound that is emotionally communicative and *espressivo* beginning with the very first note.

The bowing style employed by strings with thirty-second notes, sixty-fourth notes, or thirty-second note sextuplets in the passage from four bars before **H** through six bars after **H** is a matter of personal taste and judgment. (This same discussion will come up again, under rather different musical circumstances, in the opening of the third movement.) Beginning with the thirty-second notes in viole and celli four bars before **H**, and continuing into the sextuplets, I prefer for these figures to remain "on the string." (While it is true that, reaching a certain velocity, this stroke is no longer literally on the string, this is not really the issue. What is important is to differentiate the stroke that attempts to remain on the string from that which is purposefully extremely short and off the string.) As already mentioned, this is a matter of personal taste, but in a passage where the repeated notes form the accompaniment for a lyrical theme I find the sound of this warmer, less athletic approach much preferable. No matter what style is chosen for the viole and celli, the sixty-fourth notes that form the melody in the violins must be played in this way. If the conductor does, in fact, prefer the articulation I have described (for viole and celli), then it should be stated clearly to the section(s) involved, as many musicians will instinctively play a passage like this *spiccato* in the lower part of the bow if not given different instructions.

The shape and expression of the two bars preceding **I** are likely to be somewhat as described just before **E**. The main difference here is that, because of the entrance of the theme in the flute one beat before **I**, it is highly unlikely that any sort of *fermata* will be added during the final beat.

In the bar preceding **K**, some soloists prefer for the orchestral sound to be cleared before they move to the upper B-flat, and not simultaneous with that change of pitch. In other words, they want the orchestra's *fermata* to be shorter than theirs. For other soloists, however, this should sound exactly as it looks. In this latter case, it's a good idea to know the bowing the soloist plans to use here. Some soloists play the bowing as written, slurring from the low B-flat to the upper, and others change bows (usually down-bow in the lower octave) when changing octaves. If the orchestra's cut-off is to occur precisely with the change of octave in the solo violin, then it is rather important that the conductor know which bowing is to be used. This is the only way he can be prepared with the proper gesture at the correct time, unless the soloist supplies the conductor with a considerable amount of body language.

3rd movement.

In the discussion above regarding the second movement (the passage beginning four bars before **H**), I promised a renewed conversation about the bowing style in static harmonies. Once again, the style chosen for the opening of the third movement is a matter of taste, and depends largely on what emotion the conductor would like to elicit in this introduction. If viole and second violins play off the string from the beginning of the movement, there is a certain exciting tension and drama from the first note. If, however, the desired result is to move more gradually from the lyrical expression of the second movement into the more intense drama of the third, then having viole and second violins begin on the string, in the upper half of the bow, works best. If this latter choice is made, most conductors ask these players to move gradually toward the lower half of the bow and off the string as the *crescendo* intensifies.

While some soloists take the bar entirely in tempo, the solo violin chord directly preceding **C** often gets a bit of dramatic extra time. This is another one of those many places in which it is critical that the conductor know ahead of time the soloist's intentions, as the two different scenarios require two entirely different gestures that really cannot be successfully interchanged at the last moment. The bar preceding **E** is also likely to have substantial stretch. This often becomes a moment of such drama that it must be conducted in four.

In the *tutti* passage at **E**, some ensemble balance work is needed so that the separate voices can be heard clearly and with reasonably equal volume. The problem, obvious at a glance, is that the second voice (basses and bassoons) is in such a low register and orchestrated with so relatively few instruments that it can go entirely unheard by the listener if the conductor does not make some dynamic adjustments in the rest of the orchestra. In the first four bars of the passage, the second violins and viole have two slashes across their stems (clearly indicating that they are to play measured sixteenth notes) but also have the indication *tremolo*. This apparent contradiction is not that uncommon in 19th century works, and is often resolved on the side of unmeasured *tremolo*. Here, the desired overall sound is expansive and lyrical, not rhythmically driven, so the unmeasured solution is clearly best. In the fifth bar, these same instruments are clearly marked in measured triplets, so the decision to play unmeasured *tremolo* only lasts for four bars. Further muddying the issue is the fact that the *tremolo* indication (at **E**) is clearly over the second half note in the bar. This bit of poor editing or oversight should be ignored, however, as changing styles in the middle of the bar clearly makes no sense whatsoever. Also to be noted in this *tutti* is the common addition of an expressive *portamento* (or *glissando*, if you prefer) in first violins and celli between the A-natural and C-natural that occupy the end of the fifth and beginning of the sixth bars after **E**. While not requested by the composer, this extra bit of *schmaltz* is now quite traditional, and it's a bit hard to imagine this melody without it. The same applies, of course, in the analogous spot following **H**.

Some conductors take a bit of *ritard* two bars before **G**. I find this puzzling, as the line is clearly driving toward the downbeat at

G, and there is no musical event here worthy of making such a gesture. This *ritard* mostly occurs in performances in which the soloist plans to slightly sustain the first note (D-natural) of the scale before proceeding *a tempo* toward the bar-line. This, also, I find puzzling, as I think it is much more exciting musically when these events drive forward instead of each one slowing slightly.

The *ritard* that is often taken in the one or two bars preceding H (also not indicated) is another matter. The musical material at H is broad, lyrical, and often taken in a tempo that is slightly slower than what precedes it. For these reasons, a slight pulling back of the bar or bars just before, while by no means absolutely necessary, seems quite logical and musical. Though not specified, we are to assume that all half notes with two slashes across the stem (i.e., second violins and viole at H and all upper strings eight to twelve bars after H) will be played as unmeasured *tremolo*, as before.

Two bars before I, the indicated *stringendo* is usually taken fairly modestly by the soloist. Whatever the pace of this *stringendo* may be, however, Tempo I (which, following a *stringendo,* means *meno mosso*) is re-established at I.

The soloist's chord just before K is a point of caution, just as at C. One does not want to run over the soloist with an early orchestral entrance at K, unaware that the soloist planned to take extra time in the pick-up.

Interestingly, the passage beginning at L, marked *stringendo poco a poco*, usually begins *meno mosso*. From a musical point of view, this really does not seem so odd, as one might want to slow down a bit before speeding up, and it is only natural for the soloist to luxuriate a bit over these beautiful first four bars. The *stringendo* usually gets moving around the fifth bar after L, and it intensifies considerably eight or nine bars before *Presto* in order, one hopes, to arrive at the new tempo precisely and logically.

∽

Edouard Lalo

Symphonie Espagnole, Op. 21

1st movement.

In bar 8, it is neither appropriate nor necessary for the conductor to lead the soloist away from the *fermata*, even though the conductor will be leading in most other musical situations like this one. Here, however, the soloist needs to be allowed her own time in this four-bar solo passage, and the pace of the two notes that follow the *fermata* will be slow enough that the conductor can easily follow rather than leading. The conductor simply waits for the violinist to move to the D-sharp, beginning the preparation immediately at that point.

Six bars before **1** (these rehearsal numbers refer to the Kalmus score; the Breitkopf edition has different rehearsal markings), the baton stops immediately after arriving at the downbeat, with only enough rebound to allow the second *pizzicato* chord to be played, allowing the soloist the freedom to take time with the final eighth note in the bar. The baton can lift in coordination with this final quarter note, making entry into the next bar quite easy.

Eight bars before **2**, the note given for the timpani is D-natural; to the best of my knowledge, this is not an error. In spite of this, I ask the timpanist to play E-natural here, instead, for obvious reasons.

Some soloists want the bar preceding **3** to relax somewhat, allowing some extra room for the upward scale. This is by no means universal, but the conductor should be prepared for the request. I prefer it when this does not happen, but accommodating the soloist's desired shape for this line is, after all, part of our job.

Tutti passages in this movement, like the one found at 4, can become choppy and unmusical if care is not taken with both articulation and direction of the musical line. It is noteworthy that the quarter notes contained inside triplets are not marked *staccato*, as are many other quarter notes and eighth notes in this passage. In spite of this difference, it is common to hear this music played entirely *staccato*, which gives the entire affair a more barbarous and angular feel than is really intended. The feel of this music is dramatic and passionate, but not necessarily illustrative of violence. This can be remedied by addressing the twin issues above: articulation and direction of the musical line. When the notes in the triplets, in particular, are given a bit more length, and are executed with direction across the bar-line rather than being executed with equal vertical weight, the overall sound of the orchestra is improved and the music takes on a certain level of grandeur that replaces pure violence.

The extra time that the soloist is likely to take in the fourth bar after 5 makes placing the preparation for the following bar (for the third horn entrance) at the normal half-bar point problematic. It is usually better to wait, placing the gesture with the B-flat at the end of the bar.

I have never had a soloist object to the considerable extra time I (and many others) take in bar 99. Allowing this line in the viole to play itself out with a couple of subdivisions so that it truly achieves *pianississimo* by the time the bar-line is reached can be quite exquisite. The result of this gesture is a tempo at bar 100 that is slower than Tempo I. Tempo I is immediately re-established with the woodwind figures eight bars before 6. These same musical issues come into play at bars 216 and 231.

Some soloists insist on a *più mosso* at 6, and I politely discourage this whenever possible. As has been discussed in at least one other location in this book, the composer's sudden acceleration of the fundamental rhythmic structure of the bar is not an invitation to simultaneously speed up the tempo. On the contrary, the sense of additional urgency is communicated by the sixteenth notes in the violin, as contrasted with the continuing, more earthbound pace of the main thematic material.

In bar 216, some copies of the clarinet parts contain a wrong note. The written G-natural (concert E-sharp, that really should be written in the transposed part as F-double-sharp) in bar 215 becomes written G-sharp (concert F-sharp) at bar 216, and this change of pitch is missing in some editions.

2nd movement.

In spite of Lalo's tempo instruction referring to the eighth note, the movement begins in one, at a tempo of approximately bar = 68. And, in spite of the pattern in one, good style and a proper attitude for this music seem to demand some left hand and/or "body English" subdivisions on appropriate second and third beats of the bar (e.g., bars 10 and 14, and bars 4 and 8, respectively). Once the basic pulse and style for the movement is nicely established, few issues present themselves between the beginning of the movement and **4**.

Between **4** and **6**, each *Poco più lento* section is taken in three and each Tempo I section in one. There is often some *allargando* in the fourth bar, or third and fourth bars, after **4**, leading toward the first *Poco più lento*. This needs to be handled carefully, at least partially in three as the tempo slows, for good ensemble of strings and bassoon. This also helps to ensure that the soloist arrives at the end of the *glissando* on the downbeat of bar 106 in good coordination with the orchestra. The general question that needs to be addressed between conductor and soloist is whether or not each Tempo I section will slow slightly as it approaches the following *Poco più lento*, or if the faster tempo will continue without let-up until the downbeat of each slower section. The first of these two options is nearly always the choice, in spite of the fact that it is not indicated anywhere by the composer.

The first twelve bars at 6 are usually conducted in three, though not beginning as slowly as the previous *Poco più lento* sections. There is sometimes a slight pause on the first note of bar 163. However, this pause is not usually significant enough that the conductor will want to completely stop the motion of the baton. Instead, both phrase and coordination are better served by a gesture that floats away from the first beat but then accelerates toward two, gently leading the soloist forward. The beat returns to one at bar 169.

The *ritard* indicated two bars before 8 is generally not a particularly subtle or gradual affair. In most performances the tempo pulls back rather quickly in the first two bars, usually requiring a beat in three by bar 218. This establishes a tempo similar to the previous *Poco più lento* sections by the time we arrive at 8, and the tempo continues to slow through bar 226.

3rd movement.

The first time I conducted this work was at the Lucius Woods festival in Wisconsin. On that occasion, my soloist was DeAnn Letourneau, a local "girl-done-good" who was often asked back as a soloist. DeAnn is, entirely by coincidence, now the concertmaster of the Las Vegas Philharmonic, where I later served as Music Director and Conductor for six years.

A month or two before the performance at Lucius Woods, DeAnn called me to ask if I did, or did not, intend to include the third movement in the upcoming concert. I was a bit taken aback, as I could not even understand the meaning of the question. What possible reason could there be, I wondered, to think that we would be omitting one movement of a concerto in a professional performance? As I recall, I politely asked something like, "What the hell are you talking about?" Unfazed, she laughed and explained to me some of the history of performances of this piece in the early and middle 20th century, when this movement was frequently omitted. And this is a history of which I was, at that time, entirely unaware. Since then, I have spoken with many violinists and pedagogues on this subject. It appears that when this movement was omitted it was for one, or both, of two reasons. The first reason, and the one(s) most often cited, involves the length of the piece and/or that this movement wasn't "as strong as the others." This doesn't make a great deal of sense to me, as the piece is only around thirty-five minutes long and there's nothing in the substance of this music that is conspicuously less inspired than the rest of the work. The second, more clandestine reason, concerned the tone of this movement. This alleged concern about "tone" was apparently particularly true with female soloists, especially younger women, as it was considered by some that the sexy Habañera feel of this movement was inappropriate for performance by young ladies. Without attempting to speculate which reasons dominated any particular pedagogue's thinking, this tradition was very much alive in the Galamian studio, and extends, also, into the studio of Dorothy DeLay. It is indicative of how entrenched the idea of omitting this movement had become at certain times and in certain studios by noting that DeAnn was rather surprised when I insisted that we include it. And one former Galamian student remarked, "I grew up under his [Mr. Galamian's] tutelage assuming that it was *de rigueur* to skip the third movement." I love this story, and this marvelously old-fashioned tradition, but, as I said, I did insist that DeAnn take her virtue in her hands and play this movement.

The only issue of consequence in the opening passage of the movement concerns the relationship between triplets and sixteenth notes occurring in the same bar. The major inaccuracies can occur in the five bars preceding 1. In the third and fifth bars before 1, it is common (almost universal, in fact) to hear the third part of the triplet (strings and bassoons) played as though it is the final sixteenth note in the first beat, rather than as the final part of a triplet. This is somewhat understandable, as we instinctively react to what is around us. These musicians have just heard the first and second sixteenths of the bar (their own first note and the response in brass and woodwinds) but are asked to divorce that rhythmic structure from their minds and respond with the third part of a triplet. It often doesn't happen. Next, the common problem in the two bars directly preceding 1 is that the earlier figure (two sixteenth notes that open the bar as discussed above) may be unconsciously repeated by the strings, clarinets, and bassoons. In this case, what should be a sixteenth-note triplet within the context of an eighth-note triplet (arriving at the fourth note of the figure on the second part of the triplet) becomes a thirty-second-note triplet. This error almost forces a sixteenth-note response, rather than the correct triplet response, from viole, celli, and basses. In truth, these rhythms and cross-relationships are not that complicated, but these common inaccuracies need to be pointed out and corrected.

A kind of default *fermata* is often employed in the middle of the first bar at 3. Rather than keeping the tempo moving forward precisely, some soloists like a bit of extra time on the horn note, followed by a slight lingering on the two pick-up notes in the solo part that follow. The conductor can simply pause on the rebound of the first beat, not showing the second beat until the soloist's body language indicates that the time is right.

The second half of the bar preceding *Un poco più lento* (bar 101) will usually need subdivisions. The *Un poco più lento* section itself will fall naturally into either two or six, depending entirely on the soloist's tempo. Some soloists take Lalo's instruction (*Un poco*) seriously enough that the passage can be managed in two, with some subdivisions during the *rallentando*. Others take the passage so slowly that beating the entire section in six cannot be avoided, nor should one try to avoid it if the tempo seems to demand it.

One rather well-known violinist with whom I have done this piece chose a tempo that required that I beat in six during this section, but then had trouble figuring out where to place the second note of each duple against that pattern. The result was that the soloist insisted that I conduct the passage in four, making his life a bit easier but creating considerable potential confusion in the orchestra. The orchestra's issues aside, this does not even address the fundamental absurdity of being asked to conduct a fairly simple passage in $\frac{6}{8}$ in four. However, sometimes when the first performance is four hours away and there are only thirty minutes of rehearsal remaining, we do what we have to do.

There are two errors (in some scores) in the third bar after **5**. The cello/bass line has a G-sharp, which should be G-natural, and the second trombone has B-natural, which should be A-natural. In the ninth bar after **5**, the first note in the viole should be C-natural, not B-natural.

The last half bar before **6** will usually require a subdivision to keep the celli and basses coordinated with the solo violin. The question is whether the subdivisions should show the final three eighth notes of the bar (simply allowing the musicians to play the duple where it lies between the fifth and sixth beats) or the two notes of the duple specifically. One instinctively recoils, I hope, from the latter suggestion, as it is thought to be gospel that we conduct the meter, not the rhythm. One can easily make the case here, however, that there is no harm in beating the duple since no other rhythm is present, so there are no other musicians to confuse. In spite of the truth of this statement, and the fact that confusion in the orchestra caused by beating the duple is very unlikely, I hold tenaciously to the position that one beats the meter, not the rhythm, except in what would have to be the most unusual of musical circumstances.

4th movement.

Some scores and some sets of parts contain significant errors in the opening of this movement. First, the clarinet parts that may appear in bars 13 through 15 should not be there at all. Looking at the harmony in these bars it is clear that these parts make no sense. Many conductors have tried to "fix" these clarinet parts to make them into something that fits the harmony, but they are entirely an engraver's error. If you compare the clarinet parts in these three bars with the second and third trombone parts in the same bars, you will see that they are identical, as long as you imagine a bass clef in the clarinet line. It is to be assumed that these are supposed to be bassoon parts and were placed on the wrong line. Second, in the bar preceding **1** the oboes have G-sharp and D, pitches that also make no sense, considering that this chord is supposed to be F-sharp diminished 7th. Once again, attempts to "fix" the oboe parts are fruitless, as the notes are correct, but they are in the wrong line. Though the clarinets are not supposed to be playing in the three previous bars, they are playing in this bar, but their notes ended up in the oboe line in some scores. Once the notes are placed verbatim in the correct line of the score, we end up with clarinets playing (written) D-natural and G-sharp (concert C-natural and F-sharp), completing the correct chord.

The articulations throughout the orchestra during the short *tutti* at **2** are a bit haphazard and can be misleading. Looking at all these separate quarter notes, with no slurs or other helpful indications, one could easily assume that each note is to be executed somewhat separately, perhaps slightly *marcato*, but this is surely not the case. This long, expressive line should be played completely *legato*, regardless of the specifics of bowing or tonguing. Also important is the fact that the *fortissimo* indicated on the last chord of the phrase is not to be interpreted as a sudden, physical blow. This dynamic is only placed there to specify the end point of the *crescendo*, and should not be executed as an accent or *sforzato.*

There is often a pause virtually amounting to a *fermata* two beats before **3**. After arriving at the downbeat of the bar (one bar before **3**), the baton gently drifts to the second beat while the left hand simultaneously traces a sustaining and *diminuendo* gesture, waiting for the soloist to indicate (by body language, bow distribution, and/or the release of sound following the second beat) his intention to move forward to the third beat.

At the end of the first bar at **4**, some soloists linger over each grace note (B-sharp and C-sharp); some even taking a separate bow on each note. Other violinists move forward more rapidly, including the grace notes in the same up-bow as the half note, as written. To properly prepare the following bar, the conductor must have clear knowledge of the soloist's intention here.

In order to communicate the following tempo clearly, it is necessary in some orchestras to beat this passage (second and third bars after **4**) in six. In other orchestras, and depending upon the tempo chosen here, this will not be necessary. In either case, drama and ensemble are both aided by subdividing the first beat in each of the next two bars (the fourth and fifth bars after **4**).

In the passage that follows, beginning at *a tempo*, it is imperative that the soloist does not take unrealistic liberties. Otherwise the funereal figures in the timpani become so rhythmically erratic as to be meaningless. This same principle applies earlier, in bars 62 through 69, regarding the figures in viole and celli. As with the similar example earlier (the fourth and fifth bars after **4**), the first two bars at **5** should be subdivided during the first beat.

5th movement.

The opening of this movement flows happily under its own steam. The only possible pitfall early in the movement is a simple one to avoid. As I have mentioned in other chapters, when the conductor must select the tempo of a movement in which the musical structure is fairly quick and rather inflexible, it is very embarrassing and unmusical when the conductor's tempo for the introduction of the movement does not match the one later adopted by the soloist.

Some soloists insist on taking a bit of extra time at the end of bar 46. In my opinion, this should be politely discouraged. The music in this bar is parallel to the music one bar before **2**, where the composer does indicate a *ritard*. If Lalo wanted this *ritard* in both places he would surely have told us. For the conductor, the bar before **2**, where the soloist does *ritard*, can feel a bit uncomfortable, like a guessing game. The baton must indicate the second beat of the bar, including, by the speed and shape of the rebound, the intended amount of tempo change. This must be done clearly and without any hesitation, or the *staccati* in the viole will not be clean and together. The danger, of course, is that this second beat must be indicated before the soloist moves off the A-natural. This means that the conductor must show this second beat before it is possible for the soloist to give any clear indication of the degree of *ritard* that is coming. As with some other musical situations like this one, the difference between a charming, organic musical solution and a minor train wreck is the fundamental communication between soloist and conductor and their basic confidence in the other's abilities, intellect, and musical integrity.

The indicated *poco rit.* in the bar before **5** is rarely *poco*. Nonetheless, it is both technically efficient and most musical to remain in two. Trying to beat all or part of this bar and a half in six becomes busy, unmusical, and not necessarily all that helpful to the orchestra. All of this applies equally to the bar before 4, but most soloists make a more modest gesture here, saving the larger stretch for the bar before 5.

Six bars before 6, the passage of *spiccato* A-major arpeggios is marked *senza rallentare*. This is almost a comical understatement, as many soloists speed up here, either inadvertently or purposefully. The task of following these rapid arpeggios with the ear flummoxes some conductors, causing the beat to be hesitant and/or inaccurate during these six bars. There are clear aural cues for which to listen as the arpeggio ascends and then descends, usually shifting inversion every three notes. Apart from sharp ears, calm nerves, and a soloist who doesn't go out of his way to make it difficult, there is no magic bullet. Making a passage like this look simple and stress-free is exactly what conductors get paid for.

Though not indicated, most conductors take a significant *allargando* two bars before 7. This allows the new, much slower tempo at 7 to be arrived at logically.

The violin scale in grace notes approaching 8 is a moment that can give any conductor sweaty palms if the soloist cannot be depended on to play the passage as rehearsed. This passage can be performed musically and logically in several different ways that are drastically different from one another. Because of this, there is no possible way, other than being psychic, that the conductor can be properly prepared, and properly prepare the orchestra, if the soloist does not reasonably reproduce the passage as it was rehearsed. Some soloists move slowly up the four grace notes, others rapidly. Some place a *fermata* on the final grace note, others move forward, whether quickly or slowly, in a more consistent tempo. Each of these approaches requires a different plan from the conductor and, for the most part, one cannot be instantaneously substituted for another. For example, if the soloist rehearses the figure moving at a moderate tempo through the four notes and then places a slight *fermata* on the final note, the conductor will not plan to make the preparatory gesture until sometime during the final note. If this same soloist omits the *fermata* at the last moment, and/or moves much more quickly through the figure, it is not possible for the conductor (and the orchestra) to react in time. Fortunately, there are relatively few moments in the literature like this one. But this is certainly one of those moments where the soloist can make the conductor look foolish, if desired. Important lesson: always be nice, accommodating, and offer to take the soloist out for a drink after rehearsal, even if she is someone with whom you have nothing in common, because you do not want her messing with you during the performance.

Some violinists prefer to take a cut in the final section of the movement. There are good reasons to take the cut to shorten the movement, and equally good reasons not to do so. They are both fairly obvious, so I won't dwell on them here. I have done this piece both with and without the cut, but what I find interesting about this cut is that, unlike the situation in some other works, there does not appear to be complete agreement on exactly where the cut should be. Some violinists cut from the end of the second bar after **9** to the beginning of the ninth bar before **12**, and others begin the cut one bar later, cutting after three complete bars following **9**. There is a certain musical logic both ways, and it is waste of time to contemplate which way is better, as the conductor is unlikely to get a vote. I never mix into this issue with the soloist anyway, as a violinist comes prepared to play the piece in a certain way and, barring the most bizarre of circumstances (which I cannot imagine) one does not ask the soloist to alter an intended cut.

Felix Mendelssohn

Violin Concerto in E Minor, Op. 64

R.M.'s only comments about this concerto were simple and to the point, highlighting the most important general issue affecting the performance of this work. He said, "Mendelssohn … Is it Romantic or is it Classical? Once the conductor and the soloist agree on that, then it should be pretty fun." And this is not by any means an arcane or purely academic discussion. In a work that can be interpreted very differently by different artists (in terms of its overall sound, style, and musical direction), a unified, consistent set of choices regarding tempo, sound quality and color, and articulation is vital.

1st movement.

The first movement of the concerto is quite straightforward, and does not present any significant accompanying challenges. Nonetheless, at the outset of the movement it is critical that, even while setting the appropriately gentle mood, the preparatory gesture is so certain and clear that the *ostinato* in the upper strings can lock perfectly together from the first note.

At **A** and just following, the conductor does not need to be terribly concerned if the soloist chooses to play the successive six-note figures with a bit of rhythmic stylization. During these triplets the conductor needs only to focus on marking the passing bars and staying alert for the beginning of the upward arpeggio in eighth notes in the fourth and seventh bars after **A**. No matter what has come before (in the triplets) it is this *staccato* eighth-note figure that sets up the rhythmic structure for the following bar.

From nine through fifteen bars after **B** the *forte* quarter notes in the strings have no articulation marks, but they are generally played quite short.

The arpeggios at **D** are likely to be played with expressive *rubati*, and with some soloists these *rubati* will be somewhat unpredictable. For some, the eighth notes flow forward in a fairly orderly manner until the last one or two notes of the bar, when there may be an unpredictable and/or abrupt pulling back of the tempo. The conductor should be well on guard for this possibility. In order to prepare this rather different mood, the soloist may also take a slight *ritard* in the bar directly before **D**.

Many soloists take some extra time in the third and fourth bars of **G**. When this is the case, the conductor may want to dictate the last quarter note of the fourth bar with a subdivision.

It is extremely important that the conductor know exactly the soloist's desired tempo for the passage beginning thirteen bars before **H**. While this is often Tempo I, it can sometimes be a bit faster, or may begin at Tempo I and then accelerate somewhat. In any case, due to the exacting nature of the clarinet/bassoon figures, even a slight disagreement in tempo between conductor and soloist results in an unpleasant scramble.

Most soloists take some extra time with the two notes preceding **H**. When this is the case, it is best for the conductor to pause after completing the first beat of the bar (one before **H**) without continuing to the second beat. This allows the conductor maximum flexibility to react with precision and calm to whatever extra time is taken in the solo violin.

Twenty-eight bars after **I** the horns need a clear, early look from the conductor, as this entrance comes at an odd point in the phrase from the players' perspective.

Even though the bars of the *cadenza* are clearly delineated with separate bar-lines and bar numbers, it is still to be treated as any other *cadenza*, and the conductor does not mark the bars. Inexperienced orchestras will need to be told, however, that when the conductor begins conducting again the location is the second beat of bar 335. (It should also be noted that in the rarely played, original version of the concerto the *cadenza* is much shorter than the one found in the more familiar, final version.)

Some conductors insist on a slight *più mosso* at **K**, and, when this happens, some soloists respond by taking a slight *meno mosso* (essentially returning to Tempo I) at their next entrance thirteen bars later. Either of these gestures can be a bit awkward, largely because of the *staccato* eighth-note accompaniment, but it is the slower tempo one-half bar before the soloist enters that can be particularly tricky and offers the opportunity for rather poor ensemble. This is for two reasons. First, the clarinets must take a slower tempo *subito*, and they must do so without any guidance about that new tempo. And, second, the conductor must precisely select the new (actually old) tempo that the soloist desires, or else a very uncomfortable negotiation occurs during the first few bars of the solo phrase. All in all, it's both more musical and just plain easier if the tempo stays constant throughout this passage.

For both drama and clarity, I dictate with a subdivision the violin/woodwind entrance six bars after **N**, slightly elongating this note and asking that it be played full length and *espressivo*.

2nd movement.

Two bars before *Andante* ($^{6}_{8}$), the baton should stop after showing the first beat (the cut-off for all instruments except first bassoon). Next, the baton passively indicates the following downbeat, pausing there while the left hand indicates the *crescendo-diminuendo*. Then the conductor continues past the double bar, in six, the first two beats of that bar being quite passive and the third beat more active as a clear preparatory gesture for the change of pitch in the bassoon. The *piano* in the orchestra should be expressive and warm throughout this introductory passage. This is not only because the content of the music demands it, but also so that it is still possible for the *pianissimo* in the eighth bar of the movement to be palpably different in color and character.

Though it may seem like a very minor detail, the first two notes in the first violins at **R** should be played carefully *staccato.* This articulation needs to reasonably match both the horn in the same bar and the parallel *pizzicato* phrase in the following bar. In order to create a very special sonic and emotional moment, some soloists (notable in this regard is Nadja Salerno-Sonnenberg) desire an extreme *ritard* in the second half of the fourth bar after **R**, following this gesture with an extraordinarily delicate *pianississimo* from both orchestra and solo violin at the start of the following phrase. When this gesture is so extreme, it is necessary to subdivide the two sixteenth notes in the celli and basses on the last beat of the bar.

Having mentioned Nadja in the preceding paragraph, I cannot help but think about the indelible connection between great music and the times, places, and people that are involved in our lives as performers. Many works will carry with them in our minds the stamp of a particularly memorable performance, place, or person, and, like it or not, I feel as though that music will always be colored by the circumstances and people surrounding those particularly potent events. No matter how many performances of this work preceded or followed it, the Mendelssohn concerto will always carry bittersweet memories for me because of performances that took place in 2001, owing largely to the character and artistry of the aforementioned Ms. Salerno-Sonnenberg. The opening weekend of concerts in my ninth year as Music Director of the Arkansas Symphony was scheduled for September 14 and 15, 2001, with Nadja as soloist for the Mendelssohn concerto. I hardly need to explain what happened on Tuesday morning of that week, making all plans of all kinds moot. As that week progressed, we struggled with several issues in our attempts to make a decision whether or not to cancel the concerts. Some of the issues we needed to consider are obvious: respect for the state of the nation and the world, the safety of our audience and our musicians, the willingness, or lack of willingness, of people to gather in a public place so soon after the attack, and the appropriateness of a festive concert under such circumstances. Perhaps less obvious thirteen years later is the fact that for several days after 9/11 all air travel in the U.S. was suspended, and Nadja had no way to get to us from New York. Many persons in her situation would have immediately contacted us to cancel, and certainly no one would have blamed her if she had. (Speaking for myself, it was many weeks before I was coaxed to get on an airplane, and I did so then only very unwillingly.) On Thursday the thirteenth, some air travel resumed, but when Nadja went to the airport on Friday the fourteenth (La Guardia, I believe) to travel to Little Rock she found that air travel had again been suspended. She went home and booked a different flight for that evening, but when she got to the airport (JFK, this time, if I remember correctly) she found, again, that flights were not departing. On the third try, she found a flight on Saturday morning, out of Newark and taking a circuitous route of connections, and made it to Little Rock just in time for the final rehearsal. What I did not know until she arrived, tired and shell-shocked, was that she had spent most of the time between Tuesday and Friday volunteering at ground zero. Nonetheless, in spite of being exhausted by her efforts and having endured the trauma and pain that all New Yorkers did during that week, she came and played one of the great Mendelssohn performances ever. The concerts, clearly, went forward, opened by our national anthem and "Nimrod" as a moment of memorial and remembrance. Though perhaps it pales by comparison to what Nadja did during that week, I was proud that our audience turned out for opening night in full force, with almost every seat filled to hear her. Rumors abounded that people were too frightened to come out of their houses, and especially to gather in large numbers in large and obvious public buildings, but it was not true. Attending those concerts was a statement about who we are, and who we refuse to become. I remain eternally grateful to the people of Little Rock for their support and courage that week, and to Nadja for helping to spark something good out of something so tragic. Those impressions will always be indelibly linked to this joyous and emotional music.

The dynamics, and therefore the shape of the phrase, in the eighth and ninth bars after **S** are distinctly different from those in the similar phrase four bars earlier. In this latter instance, the composer asks for one continuously directed *crescendo* lasting two bars. This passage is often inadvertently played as it is written earlier, with a *crescendo-diminuendo* in each bar, and this inattention to detail destroys what is really the climactic moment of the movement. Playing the dynamics as written transforms a rather predictable passage into something far more important, but in order to do this the orchestral strings must overcome the dynamics that are natural to the motion of the bow (avoiding the inadvertent *diminuendo* in each down-bow and *crescendo* in each up-bow). The discipline to make sure that this is carried out with explicit expressive intention must come from the podium.

3rd movement.

The finale begins immediately following the conclusion of the second movement. Following the cut-off of the *fermata*, the conductor must be aware that the soloist is likely to continue to the third movement pick-ups without warning.

The conductor must insist on attention to dynamics in the first two phrases of this movement, since the natural motion of the bow fosters dynamics that are the exact opposite of what the composer requested. The first seven beats, marked *mezzo-forte*, will tend to be lighter in sound as musicians save bow. Conversely, the passage marked *piano* is more active in its melodic and rhythmic content, and the strings have multiple changes of bow direction. These factors contribute to the likelihood that the *piano* passage will be louder than desired. The main portion of the movement, beginning at *Allegro molto vivace*, is, of course, in two.

Most of this movement is not difficult to accompany, nor is it especially difficult for the musicians of the orchestra. However, in the passage between V and W the conductor needs to be concerned with cueing and the direction of the baton. By "direction of the baton" I refer to the idea that his pattern in two actually looks like a pattern in two, and not like an endless series of downbeats. Various entrances of fragments of the major melodic material (such as the entrance of winds and timpani in the first bar at V) occur at the half-bar point throughout this section, instead of beginning on the downbeat of each bar as we hear it originally. Though it may have been of little or no concern in the rest of the movement, in this passage it is important for the confidence and security of the musicians that the first beat looks like "one" and the second beat looks like "two."

When the lyrical theme moves out of the solo violin and into the orchestral strings fifteen bars before X the conductor should be aware of the tendency of the orchestra to lag slightly behind the more active rhythmic figures in the solo line. Here, and again at **X**, this sometimes needs to be mentioned even to very good orchestras.

Eleven bars before **Z** it is usually a not good idea to immediately rebound from the first beat of the bar. The soloist often takes a bit of extra time on the trill and/or the two following eighth notes, so waiting patiently on the downbeat until the soloist arrives at the second beat is prudent.

From six bars before **Z** through **Z** the *crescendo* and resulting *fortissimo* might best be considered metaphors more than actual instructions. Too much *crescendo* and a real *fortissimo* will, of course, obliterate the solo violin. Some *crescendo* is needed to keep the energy of the piece moving forward, but it must be tempered with the obvious necessity for appropriate balance with the soloist. This is also important in the various *crescendi* between **Z** and the end of the movement.

☙

Niccolo Paganini

Violin Concerto No. 1 in D Major, Op. 6

1st movement.

This chapter discusses the original version of this concerto, not the version revised by August Wihelmj. The Wihelmj version makes vast cuts and revisions, essentially changing this mammoth work into a one-movement concerto, and is the version found in the current Dover score. Using this chapter as a guide to this concerto will require the use of the original, and most often played, score.

The opening fanfare figure can be handled in a number of different ways, and each has its own merits and drawbacks. (1) The conductor can give a quarter-note preparation and simply let the orchestra play. The danger in this seemingly obvious approach is the possibility that the musicians of the orchestra will not all subdivide the preparatory beat accurately. That is, some musicians may "over-dot" the rest and play the sixteenth note pick-up late. (2) The conductor can give the same preparation but allow the orchestra to play the pick-up closer to the downbeat, essentially stylizing the figure into a grace note or thirty-second note pick-up. (3) The conductor can subdivide the pick-up (showing beats seven and eight, in eight), giving the orchestra a better opportunity to play a real sixteenth-note pick-up, as written. (4) The conductor can dictate the opening sixteenth note, essentially out of tempo. The downside to this solution is that it does not really reflect the rhythm the composer wrote, but it has the virtue of being nearly foolproof from the point of view of ensemble coordination. (Though not the subject of this book, it should be noted that the same issue, and the same potential solutions, are present in Mozart's Overture to *Die Zauberflöte*, Rossini's Overture to *The Barber of Seville*, etc.)

A slight *allargando* on the fourth beat of the fifth (full) bar gives the cadence a more elegant, less abrupt feeling. The same is true four bars later. Setting the main tempo for the orchestral exposition (eight bars before **A**, and again at **A**) is somewhat problematic. Ideally, a passage like this would be performed at precisely the same tempo that the soloist will take at his first entrance. After all, there is no difference of tempo indicated between these two sections. However, the usual and workable *tempi* of these two sections are quite far apart from one another. The most common tempo at **E**, the first entrance of the solo violin, is in the range of ♩ = 86–90, albeit with considerable *rubato* throughout. The tempo that seems most appropriate eight bars before **A**, however, is something around ♩ = 108, or even faster. So, how to solve this dilemma? No soloist is going to perform the passage that begins at E faster than is appropriate for the material, and no conductor will probably be interested in the entire orchestral exposition being played at ♩ = 90, as this would be purgatorially slow. There is no perfect solution; there are only two imperfect ones. The conductor can simply choose to ignore the dilemma and allow the two *tempi* to be quite disparate from one another (the most common solution). Or, the conductor can attempt to at least soften the discrepancy by not insisting on selecting a tempo for the orchestral exposition that is so quick that it highlights the problem. A tempo of ♩ = 96–98 works well as an imperfect compromise, and, in support of this choice, it should be mentioned that the composer did mark the opening not *Allegro* but *Allegro maestoso*.

Eight bars before A, (and in a number of other similarly orchestrated passages) the orchestra's dynamics need to be adjusted to accommodate Paganini's less than sophisticated scoring. The first violins, first flute, and first oboe cannot possibly dominate the texture as one would like if the rest of the orchestra were truly playing the accompaniment *forte*.

In the eighth bar after B, the first violins should be instructed to play "long dots" on these *staccati*, so that they match what is likely to be the articulation in the solo oboe.

The sixteenth-note pick-ups that begin the solo part need careful attention from the conductor, as they may be performed in strict time or with a slight *rubato*. The fourth beats of the second and third (full) bars of E (and the many similar passages throughout the movement) also contain the kinds of figures to be carefully noted. At these spots there may be *rubati*, including rather sudden pushes and pulls, just before the downbeats where the orchestra re-enters.

Beginning in the ninth bar after E the eighth notes should not be played *staccato*. The composer does not indicate such an articulation even though it is often the fallback approach for a string section that has not been given other instructions. The theme in the solo violin needs a somewhat more lush and stylish accompaniment, so "long dots," "dot-dash," or even "dashes" are more appropriate choices. The articulation should be *staccato*, however, in the passage beginning nine bars before **F**.

Seven bars after **F** (and in other spots like it throughout the repertoire) the soloist usually takes a bit of extra time on the fourth beat of the bar. How much time the soloist takes changes the gesture that the conductor should use in a situation like this. If the soloist flows forward with only a small to moderate amount of *rallentando*, the conductor can continue to flow through the fourth beat of the bar in the usual fashion, simply slowing down the pulse and accelerating toward the downbeat as the solo violin passes the third sixteenth note. If the soloist's *rallentando* is more extreme or *rubato* in character, then an entirely different gesture is required. In a case like this, the conductor should indicate the fourth beat as though a *fermata* for the upper strings, showing that *ictus* by coming in toward the center of the body, but not moving upward out of the *ictus*. In this motionless position, the conductor has the freedom to follow the solo line and will be ready to make a quick gesture upward as the soloist nears the final sixteenth note before the bar-line. Using the previously described ("flow through the beat") gesture in this latter musical situation leaves the orchestra with no real preparatory gesture for the next bar. Instead, as the conductor floats aimlessly downward through a very long fourth beat, the orchestra is left to essentially guess precisely where the first beat of the next bar will be.

Accurate placement the *pizzicato* chord on the downbeat one bar before **G** depends on two things. First, the conductor's ear needs to clearly follow the progression of the three-octave scale, using the second and third E-naturals as signposts. If this is not sufficient for perfect placement of the chord, it is also useful to be aware of the use and direction of the bow during the scale. Some violinists use one down-bow for the entire scale, placing the up-bow on the *fermata*. Others use more than one bow for the scale, however, and it is quite useful to be aware of the soloist's bowing and bow distribution to predict the end of the scale.

Most soloists take some time in the fourteenth and sixteenth bars after G, and the conductor should be aware that, for some soloists, the *rubato* taken is extreme. In some cases this will require subdivisions on the second, or even the first and second beats.

In the ninth bar before H, the third and fourth beats of the bar are usually taken quite deliberately. Often this amounts to a tempo in these two beats that is exactly half of the tempo that will be established in the following bar.

There is often a small lift before the third beat of the eleventh bar after H, allowing the soloist to reposition before the downward scale in harmonics. Careful observation of the violinist's body language between the second and third beats allows the conductor to place the third beat correctly. In the two bars that follow, it is important not to rush the baton into the *ictus* of the third beat, as these three eighth notes will often have some *rallentando*. Too quick a gesture into the third beat (in an effort not to be behind) can result in the orchestral strings executing the eighth notes faster than the simultaneous *rubato* in the solo violin will accommodate.

Nine bars before K, I change the notes on the fourth beat in the trombones into quarter rests. Whether or not these notes on the fourth beat are an error is still up for debate. But, error or not, the trombones sound very much out of place on the final beat of the bar and I believe it is best to omit them.

A slight *meno mosso* at K is traditional, and it allows this secondary theme to sing more lyrically.

Two and four bars before **L**, the orchestra's chord should coincide with the upper part of the soloist's arpeggiation. The soloist needs to be allowed to play the bottom part of the chord before the orchestra enters. This usually works best by allowing the bottom part of the chord to coincide with the conductor's preparatory gesture.

As earlier in the movement, the eighth notes in the strings at **L** form a more stylish accompaniment when executed with dashes rather than *staccato*.

Seven bars after **L** the conductor's gestures on the third and fourth beats should appear as though there are *fermate* on the eighth rests following each beat. This complete pausing of the baton allows the conductor to clearly indicate the fourth beat and the following downbeat, while accommodating the amount of freedom that is likely to be taken by the soloist.

Five bars before **O** there is often a slight break, or breath, before the fourth beat. The baton should pause briefly on the first beat, and then flow passively through the second beat and beyond, pausing conspicuously on the third. Now the conductor is prepared to react confidently and calmly when the soloist begins the triplet on the fourth beat, following the slight pause mentioned above. The next three bars, though not usually played perfectly in tempo, do not require this stopping gesture. In each of these bars the baton, after indicating the downbeat, can flow passively forward in coordination with the violin, giving a more active gesture on the fourth beat.

A slight pause of the baton is helpful on the fourth beat of the bar, six bars before **Q**. This not only allows the conductor to more easily accommodate the extra time the soloist is likely to take during this triplet, but also makes the following preparatory gesture (*meno mosso* and *piano*) easier and less awkward.

Five bars before **Q** it is usually appropriate to set this tempo slightly slower than in the bars directly previous, as mentioned in the preceding paragraph regarding the preparatory gesture. This helps establish the tempo that the soloist is likely to take in the following bar (four before Q).

Some conductors take a substantial cut in the coda following the *cadenza.* While, admittedly, this is not a musically substantive passage, the enormous dimensions of this movement require the balance of a postlude at least as long as the one the composer provided.

2nd movement.

(For a discussion of the trumpet parts and their transposition in this movement, see "Errata" at the end of this chapter.)

This movement is conducted mostly in eight, unless the soloist takes an unusually quick tempo. When a faster tempo is taken, some of the movement can be done nicely in four. The conductor should give a gentle preparation (seventh beat) and then a sharper *ictus* (eighth beat) to impel the triplet pick-ups. Assuming a tempo of something like ♪ = 86-90, there is a considerable musical and esthetic difference between playing the pick-ups exactly as written and playing them at the last possible moment, essentially as three grace notes. For the proper sense of *Maestoso,* it is important that the triplet be played exactly as written.

Four bars before B, five bars before C, and in other similarly marked passages, the strings should be cautioned to play the measured *tremolo* precisely as written, in sets of twelve, and not unmeasured as at other points in the movement.

In the last bar of the movement the composer is clear that the third beat in the strings should be played as a long, *pianissimo* quarter note. This note should not be overlooked or shortchanged, as it provides a beautiful, settling moment following the considerable storminess that precedes it. Also, this reading lines up logically with the *fermata* in the winds, which a shorter note (in the strings) does not.

3rd movement.

Four bars before **B**, and other places like it, the conductor needs to lead (rather than follow) for good coordination into the following bar. When the conductor sees (by the soloist's bow use) that the *fermata* is nearly finished, he should give a gentle second beat to impel soloist and orchestra forward. Waiting for the soloist to begin the final triplet in the bar, and then "following" the soloist is not a good idea, as the conductor cannot possibly prepare the orchestra properly for the downbeat.

In the passage from the sixth bar after **F** through **G**, the conductor needs to be extremely familiar with the harmonies outlined by the solo violin. Because the harmonies change in places for which the logic may not be immediately apparent, it is possible for the conductor to second-guess herself during this passage, and a moment's hesitation or insecurity of leadership during this seemingly simple passage is likely to cause a considerable mess in the orchestra.

There is sometimes a slight lift for the soloist to replace the bow on the bar-line twelve bars before **H**. The conductor needs to be sure that the gesture on the second beat of the previous measure communicates this clearly, so that no musicians move forward to the following downbeat without the soloist.

Many soloists take a cut from **L** to **Q** or from **L** to **R**. The downside of this idea is obvious, as it removes this movement's only real contrasting material. On the other hand, that material is not really a matter of stunning inspiration, and its loss is more than offset by what many would consider a beneficial shortening of the work. Neither of these cuts requires any textual change for the orchestra. It is mostly a matter of making an awkward page turn without unnecessary drama.

Eleven bars before the end, the soloist and conductor must make a philosophical decision that impacts both balance and musical drama. If the orchestra continues to play *forte*, then the soloist will go essentially unheard from this point to the end. The solo part being an octave higher than the orchestral violins gives it some acoustical advantage, of course, but this is not enough to overcome then entire orchestra at *forte*. One solution is for the orchestra to drop to approximately *mezzo-piano* at this point, followed by a *crescendo* nearer the end. This allows the soloist to be heard to better advantage, but some would say that it saps a certain amount of excitement from the end of the movement. The other choice is to continue as written, making the solo violin hardly more than an overtone on the orchestra, but allowing the excitement of the *forte* to continue, undiminished, to the end.

Errata:

1st movement:

- In the first bar at **A**, the first clarinet part, in octaves with the bassoon, is missing in some scores.
- Seven bars after **C**, the pitch in the second clarinet should be (written) B-flat, slurred to the (written) A-natural in the next bar.
- In the eighth bar after **D**, some scores have a spacing error in the percussion parts. Although all the rests are present and correct, the timpani note *appears* to line up with the third beat of the bar, when it is actually on the fourth beat, in unison with the other percussion.
- Eight bars before **I**, the second note in second violins is F-sharp. Many scores and parts have this marked as F-natural, but the correct reading is a cautionary sharp.
- Third bar after **K**, the second and fourth notes in second violins (the upper note of the beamed half note figure) should be B-natural, not C-sharp.

2nd movement:

- No new transpositions are given for the brass at the beginning of the second movement, so it is assumed that both horns and trumpets are still in D. The horns are still in D, but it is clear that the trumpets are not, and that the proper transposition has been omitted from both the score and the parts in some materials. In some performances the trumpets transpose as though they are still in D, and alert players and conductors "fix" those notes that seem to be errors. For example, in the fifth bar the second trumpet, still thinking in D, is often "fixed" from written G (concert A) to written G-sharp (concert A-sharp). This fixes this one chord but fails to address the illogic that the composer would have given the trumpets the third and seventh of a seventh chord. Leaving the written pitch in the second trumpet part alone as G-natural, and reading the part *in B*, the trumpets now have concert F-sharp and C-sharp, which makes much more sense. The entire part works when read in B, which seems to be the only logical solution. Trumpets return to D in the third movement.
- Four bars after **A**, the rhythm in the second violins should be the same as in the first violins.
- Two bars before **B**, the rhythm in violins and viole should be the same as the analogous bar two before **E**.
- Four bars after **C**, the fourth beat in violins should be a rest, not a repetition of the third beat.

3rd movement:

- Ten bars after **E**, the pitch in the second flute is G-natural, not G-sharp.
- Ten bars after **I**, the upper pitch in the viola part is A-sharp, not A-natural.

☙

Maurice Ravel

Tzigane, Concert Rhapsody for Violin and Orchestra

From the conductor's point of view, there is no other work in the repertoire with a construction quite as unusual as *Tzigane*. Quite the opposite of a work like the Dvorak Cello Concerto, in which the soloist must come on stage and then wait nearly four minutes before playing, in *Tzigane* the conductor begins the work by doing nothing for a similar period of time. In this case, not even a glance to the soloist is necessary after arriving on the podium. A very subtle look around the orchestra to make certain that nothing unusual is amiss is all that is required before the conductor completely calms his entire body to set the proper mood, making sure that nothing takes the audience's focus away from the soloist during the opening *cadenza*.

Beyond the obvious task of developing a thorough knowledge of the solo part, there is only one consistent hurdle for the conductor in this piece. This is the ability to remember and accurately reproduce several similar, but not precisely identical *tempi* throughout the piece. Some of these *tempi* are even marked identically, but that does not mean that the soloist will actually want them to be exactly the same. The principal locations where the conductor should be aware of this task are at **5**, at **8**, at **11**, at **14**, and at **20**. As mentioned, these five *tempi* are all very similar, and some may be identical to one or two of the others, but they are not all the same despite how they are labeled by the composer.

The passage from 4 to 5 presents an unusual accompanying situation. As always, the goal is to allow the soloist to set tempo and direct the flow of *rubato*, etc. However, in this case the harp part is so difficult that it is not realistic to assume that the harpist will be frequently looking up at the conductor to acquire new information about subtle changes of tempo. Once tempo is set during the first two beats at 4 the conductor must then listen to the harp and make sure that the baton remains coordinated with that instrument's progress throughout the bar. Because the harpist will be looking at her own hands and/or the music, not at the conductor, moving the beat around, even slightly, to accommodate subtleties in the solo violin, is a recipe for disaster. With the exception of the very end of the passage (when the harp has only *glissandi* and the solo violin has ascending chromatic chords), the soloist really must accommodate the harpist (and conductor) and fit the solo part to the harp. In this same passage, clear cues for horn entrances and for changes of harmony in the strings are vital.

Four bars before 8 the clarinet part is sometimes re-written and simplified into sixteenth notes instead of the sextuplets written. This is unfortunate, but sometimes necessary as the part is extremely difficult even for experienced players.

12 is marked *Allegro*, but one must be rather careful of the tempo being too rapid here. At any tempo even approaching *Allegro*, the technical acumen required of the horns is considerable, and this needs to be a primary consideration when selecting this tempo.

One beat before 19 a subdivision is advisable (whether or not any *ritard* is taken) in order to clarify the last half beat before the *pausa* indicated on the bar-line. The same applies two bars before 20.

The beat preceding 22 requires either a slight *ritard*, a slight pause on the bar-line, or both. This is needed to allow the violin to complete the *pizzicato* arpeggio and also to have time to replace the bow before continuing on the following downbeat. The beat preceding **23** needs only a slight *ritard* for smooth transition to the following tempo.

A rather significant *ritard* is advisable during the first bar at **25**. Once again, this creates a smooth and more musical transition to the following tempo. Contrary to this, it is not necessary or advisable to *ritard* before the *Poco meno mosso* two bars before **32**; the forward movement of the accelerando creates a considerable part of the excitement in this passage, followed by the sudden, unprepared change of both key and tempo.

R.M.'s comments about the final section of the piece would, if taken literally, contradict the first sentence of the previous paragraph. He said, "This is where you find out if a conductor is willing to be slightly blasphemous and not do what the composer wrote. In the *meno vivo* near the end I stay in tempo, playing *sul ponticello, détaché* … it's bluegrass all the way to the end."

Pablo De Sarasate

Carmen Fantasy

Introduction.

There is often a polite difference of opinion between soloist and conductor regarding the tempo of the opening section of this work. Most violinists prefer a somewhat slower, more expressive tempo (circa ♩. = 68). But conductors, for the most part, will gravitate to a tempo that better resembles the one found in this music in the opera itself (circa ♩. = 82). There are two possible solutions. One solution is to simply agree on a single tempo that is either the soloist's preference, the conductor's preference, or a compromise in between. The other possibility (odd though it is) is to begin at a faster tempo, getting the piece off to an appropriately energetic start, and then make a subtle change beginning around bar 13, gently slowing to the soloist's desired tempo. If this strategy is chosen, it must be executed with great care and skill. First, the conductor must be careful that the process of changing the tempo is gradual and, as much as possible, unnoticed by the listener, arriving at exactly the correct tempo at exactly the right moment (bar 18). Second, the soloist must not slow the tempo, yet again, when entering, but should flow naturally into the tempo already established. I have conducted this piece a number of times with soloists who, even though I have given them exactly the tempo for which they asked at bar 18, insist on taking an additional bit of time during their first bar, before returning to tempo in bar 19. In my opinion, this gesture has the effect of sucking the life right out of the beginning of the piece, as it diminishes, rather than enhances, the violin's first entrance. In a similar spot, at bar 34, the soloist may choose to take some extra time, and the conductor must accommodate this in the accompaniment. This is a different situation than at bar 18, since this is the second time this phrase is played, and a little variation is warranted.

Soloists often take some extra time in bars 50 and/or 54. For the conductor, this is managed by letting the baton remain motionless on the downbeat, waiting for the soloist to begin the following sixteenth notes before starting to indicate forward motion toward the following bar. In this way, the soloist can take as much, or as little, time as desired, and the conductor does not risk finding himself stuck in mid-air, moving toward the following bar while the soloist takes more time than anticipated. This same situation might occur in bar 62, but this situation is somewhat different, since two bars played considerably *meno mosso* usually follow this expressive gesture. It is often best to take these two bars (63 and 64) in three, because the accompaniment (*pizzicato* strings, harp, percussion) leaves no room for inaccuracy.

Knowing the soloist's intentions in bar 72 ahead of time is critical, as the violinist's intended pacing for the triplets will alter the conductor's approach entirely. If the soloist takes considerable time in these triplets, then the baton should remain on the downbeat until the soloist begins playing the G-sharp that follows the tied A-natural, placing the preparatory gesture with the B-natural that begins the final triplet. If, however, the soloist takes a very modest *rallentando*, the conductor needs to be braver and somewhat psychic. In this case, the conductor waits for only a moment during the A-natural (the first note of the bar) and then gives a (bar length, but not unnecessarily dictatorial) preparatory gesture that allows the soloist to respond and move forward, arriving at the E-natural harmonic with the bottom of the gesture.

After arriving at bar 75, the conductor should mark the passage of the following bar as soon as is comfortable, not waiting for the soloist to actually finish bar 74 and arrive at the trill. The four notes at the end of bar 76 often come unexpectedly and they are usually *a tempo*, so the conductor must be mentally and physically prepared to respond quickly. Finding oneself in the midst of marking the empty bar when the soloist moves forward is a very awkward place to be, and one is likely to find some members of the orchestra not prepared to enter with so little warning. As I've mentioned in other places in this book, in circumstances like this one it is always wise to mark empty bars and/or beats not *with* but *ahead of* the soloist, as this allows the conductor and the orchestra extra time to prepare for and respond to whatever comes next.

Extra time is often taken in bar 100. As earlier, this is usually a prelude to a slower tempo in the next several bars. For this reason, I usually take bars 101 to 104 in three.

The passage of artificial harmonics (bar 139 and following) will sometimes have a slightly slower tempo than the main tempo of the movement, for obvious reasons having to do with the technical execution of the solo part. This is particularly true beginning in bar 147. Even if the words are never specifically spoken by the violinist, the conductor needs to remain attentive to the possible need for a slight pulling back here as the soloist negotiates this passage.

I. (Habañera)

Some soloists take two cuts to tighten up the form of this movement. The cuts, when adopted, are from the end of bar 205 to the beginning of 222, and from the end of bar 280 to the beginning of bar 297. (Most scores, but not all sets of parts, number the bars consecutively from the beginning of the work through the end. Using this method, the first bar of this movement is bar 179.)

How the *fermata* in bar 237 is handled is largely a function of the pace with which the soloist takes the following triplet. If the triplet is taken fairly deliberately, then the conductor can pause after cutting off the winds and wait for the soloist to begin the triplet before starting his own gesture. If the triplet is likely to be closer to *a tempo*, then the gesture for the wind cut-off can continue seamlessly (with the conductor's eyes on the soloist for encouragement) toward the following downbeat. (The same principles apply, minus the issue of the wind chord, in bar 221, unless it is subsumed within the cut.)

The violin variation at the return to D minor (bar 242) is often played a bit *più mosso*. When this is the case, the original tempo is usually re-established at bar 275.

II.

In most scores (and some parts), the first staff in the horn part is clearly marked "Horn in E-flat." Obviously, this should read, "Horn in E," as the first (concert) pitch must be E-natural. Later in the movement, both horns are marked "Horn in D," and this is correct.

The conductor should be aware of the possible variations the soloist may employ in interpreting the eighth note pick-up that introduces each phrase (bars 304, 316, 320, 329, and 341). It is quite possible that some will be virtually in tempo, others considerably sustained, and others somewhere in the middle. Getting this information ahead of time will keep the conductor from looking silly in the first orchestra rehearsal, finding himself well into a preparatory gesture and then having to wait awkwardly with the baton around his eyebrows while the soloist lovingly sustains the pick-up.

III. (Seguidilla)

Some soloists, but by no means all, take time in bar 386. When any extra time is taken, it can often be enough to require beating the bar in three. The *ritard* in bar 393 extends for two bars, not one, so the conductor needs to allow the tempo to decay even further (probably in three) into bar 394, before returning to tempo (in one) in bar 395. Having read the previous sentence regarding bar 395, one should also be aware that some soloists do not want a return to tempo here as indicated. In such cases the tempo remains approximately as in the bar before, and in three, until returning to tempo (in one) in bar 402. Ironically, this means returning to (approximately) Tempo I just where the composer writes *un poco rit.*, but that is neither here nor there. Equally ironic is the fact that many soloists desire a significant *meno mosso* at bar 411, exactly where *a tempo* is indicated. When this *meno mosso* is adopted, this usually needs to be conducted in three for clarity with horn and celli. No matter what precedes it, bar 418 will be in one, at Tempo I.

The thirty-second notes that occur after the *fermata* in bar 433 are usually played essentially *a tempo*, and with considerable *bravura*. This means that the conductor must move immediately to show the preparatory gesture when the soloist begins these thirty-second notes, or the baton will not accurately indicate the following downbeat.

IV. (Danse Boheme)

Perhaps even more than the passages of harmonics in previous movements, the extended passages of rapid thirds in this movement are devilishly difficult. No matter how much a violinist may love the idea of playing this marvelous music, only those with truly sterling technique can play these passages in tune and reasonably up to tempo. Those who are not up to the task should be steered toward another piece. (I have, on several occasions, done this piece with fine soloists who have made this movement a nightmare because of the intonation of the thirds. On the other hand, it's been my pleasure to do this piece several times with the rather amazing young violinist Giora Schmidt, who makes these rapid thirds look like child's play.) There is really nothing that the conductor can do to assist in this matter, except to be certain that there is no sense of pressure on the tempo within the accompaniment, so that the soloist can settle into his comfort zone (so much as there could possibly be a "comfort zone" in this movement) without feeling rushed by the orchestra.

It should also be mentioned that counseling a younger or less experienced soloist regarding the tempo of this movement is sometimes appropriate. Some violinists who are capable of the technical feats required in this music will nonetheless tend toward a tempo that is faster than their personal technique will allow the thirds to be played *well.* This error stems from the apparent belief that if the piece goes incredibly fast it will dazzle the audience and no one will notice that it's out of tune. This is, of course, wrong. Playing the movement incredibly fast may dazzle a few people who have never heard a really great violinist, but almost no one will be fooled into thinking that it's not out of tune.

The idea behind Sarasate's transition from the previous movement into the *Danse Boheme* is simple, but brilliant. The insistent B-naturals in the last four bars transform themselves before our eyes (through dynamic change, instrumentation change, and a *ritard*) into the supple gypsy dance that follows. But making these two *tempi* meld seamlessly into one another, as the composer seems to be asking, is easier said than done, and it's impossible if we follow his instructions literally. The tempo at bar 454 will be about (eighth note =) 200–220, and the *Moderato* tempo that follows is usually around ([matching] quarter note =) 132–140, and the composer gives us only one bar to make this transition. It is possible, however, to make this illusion work, but only if the *ritard* begins one bar earlier than printed and, most importantly, the soloist subtly begins the upper octave figure (bar 456, second beat) at a tempo that is immediately slower.

Bars 539, 540, and 541 contain an error (in most materials) in the second violin part. The last note in each of these bars should be A-natural, so that they each read exactly like bar 542.

A slight *più mosso* is often taken at bar 543, moving one step closer to the *Pressez* and *Animato tempi* that follow. Nonetheless, a bit, or perhaps a lot, of *rallentando* is often employed in bar 553. The four bars directly preceding *Animato* should take on increased urgency and *accelerando*, allowing the ensemble to reach the new tempo in a manner that feels not just logical, but inevitable.

☙

Dmitri Shostakovich

Concerto for Violin and Orchestra, Op. 99

1st movement.

The major issues for the conductor in this first movement (and the same might be said for the concerto generally) are those of expression, color, and the balancing of various musical elements. These elements are uppermost in our thinking in this work, as opposed to any real accompanying dilemmas. The strings spend the majority of this movement playing *piano* or *pianissimo*, but only rarely should their sound be emotionally or expressively in the background. On the contrary, a considerable challenge in this movement is found in keeping the string sound dark, warm, and expressive, and the string players involved and invested in the piece, despite the non-existent challenge presented by the notes themselves. To this end, I usually ask that the opening passage in celli and basses be played at a dynamic somewhat higher than the written *piano*, in order to ensure that a warm and communicative sound issues from the very first note. I then ask the celli and basses to add a *diminuendo* in the second half of bar 4, settling back to a real *piano* by the beginning of bar 5.

The are many places in this movement where the soloist is likely to take expressive time that Shostakovich did not specifically indicate, and this is certainly to be expected of music in this style. These places are by no means difficult to navigate as long as good communication, both verbal and musical, is maintained between soloist and conductor, so I will not take time enumerating each of them here.

There are also a number of places in this movement where it may be tempting to moderate dynamics in the orchestra in an attempt to avoid any competition with the solo violin. However, this movement is about struggle. The music portrays the struggle of differing emotional and spiritual forces in opposition to one another; so to minimize the struggle of one musical element against another does not, in my opinion, do the piece a service. This piece is largely not constructed (from a solo/tutti point of view) in the manner of a traditional concerto. In addition to the traditional "solo plus accompaniment" textures with which we have become familiar, a work like this one relies also on the genuine partnership, and sometimes antagonism, of the two forces. Look, for example, at the second and third bars after **5**. The line in celli and basses is of at least equal importance with the material in the solo violin here, and the shifting harmonies in horns and clarinets form more than a backdrop for the soloist. In a moment like this, and so many others, I think it is reasonable to let the "battle" proceed, within reason, on its own terms, rather than artificially interfering and inhibiting the orchestral sound.

The figures of accompanying quarter notes and half notes in the strings between **7** and **11** are a bit devoid of specificity in terms of articulation, and some specifics are needed to give this section clear shape and meaning. Passages where these notes are slightly separated from one another offer a very different emotional feel and accompanying style than those in which all quarters and halves are played *legato*. Between **7** and **8**, and including the first chord at **8**, I ask the strings to make a slight separation between each chord, marking each note with a "dot-dash." Beginning with the second chord (fourth beat) at **8**, I ask the upper strings to play completely *legato*, as this forms a better companion to the line in celli and basses, and Shostakovich writes *espressivo* here. In the second through fifth bars after **10**, I ask the strings to return to the earlier, slightly separated articulation. At

11, I once again ask for complete *legato*, as is more suited to the solo line. After **19**, I return to the somewhat detached articulation in the second through fourth bars, with *legato* in the following bars.

2nd movement.

A colleague of mine once used an expression that I love to borrow. (I frequently use this *bon mot* when talking with board members or others who may be new to both the intricacies of a professional orchestra's finances and the subtleties of the lives and work of musicians. The latter is code for the situation that many of us have encountered: being asked, by someone who takes a musician's annual salary and divides it by the number of hours she is actually sitting in rehearsals or concerts, "Why do these people need to get paid so much per hour anyway?" It suffices to say that an appropriate, nuanced response to that question belongs in an entirely different book.) The expression that I love to borrow (at times in response to a question as clueless as the one above) is this: the job of the musicians in an orchestra is to take the nearly impossible and make it look easy. There could hardly be a better illustration of this idea than the duet of flute and bass clarinet at the opening of this movement. While I might not necessarily describe this particular passage as "nearly impossible," playing it perfectly together, perfectly in tune, and with a devil-may-care attitude that implies how easy it is, is fairly close. That sentiment applies to much of this movement, in which nearly every section of the orchestra is given virtuosic material that must not only be played perfectly, but must feel as though it flies forward effortlessly.

The $\frac{4}{8}$ bars between **26** and **27** are, of course, taken in two, as though the composer had written $\frac{2}{4}$. The second time this occurs, when the $\frac{4}{8}$ meter is followed by one bar of $\frac{2}{8}$, is a bit trickier, but only as it applies to keeping those musicians who are counting rests from being confused. It is natural for the conductor to intellectually consider these two bars together as one bar of $\frac{3}{4}$ meter, and there is nothing really wrong with this. However, if the conductor actually uses a three pattern across these two bars, either inadvertently or purposefully, he is opening up the possibility of confusion among some musicians. No matter what may be in the conductor's head during these two bars, the pattern remains one bar in two followed by one bar in one.

What the composer indicates at **37** regarding the transition from $\frac{3}{8}$ to $\frac{2}{4}$ may seem contradictory but it really is not. (It's true that the addition of the word "*ma*" preceding *Poco più mosso* would have been helpful, but we can still make sense of his instructions even if they appear to contradict one another at first glance.) He first makes sure that we understand the basic metric conversion (the previous bar equaling the new quarter note) but then asks that this basic pulse be moved forward from bar = 104 to ♩ = 120. The composer makes clear that the process is reversed when the original meter returns at **49** (the instructions here make even less sense, but let's not dwell on that), the pulse dropping back to the original bar = 104, and the original tempo shift (as at **37**) is repeated at **65**. At **67**, when the $\frac{3}{8}$ meter returns for the final time, the pulse does not change, and the final section of the movement continues at the pace of bar = 120.

3rd movement.

It is curious that, even though the composer is quite clear about his wishes regarding both the basic flow of the movement (*Andante*) and the exact tempo (♩ = 84), most soloists and conductors choose a tempo that is drastically slower. This tempo is usually somewhere around ♩ = 62–66. As is probably already evident from material elsewhere in this book, I am a firm believer in doing as the composer asks unless there are terribly compelling artistic and/or technical reasons to the contrary. This case, however, might well be considered one of those very compelling cases. The more commonly heard tempo allows both the incredibly expressive essence of the music and the dramatic harmonies of this movement to be completely revealed to the listener. I have never heard or conducted a performance at the tempo the composer indicates, but I can imagine that it would seem terribly rushed and would lose a great deal of the unique drama and passion that come with a slower tempo.

The indication *tenuto* found in both the passacaglia theme in the lower strings and in the horns gives us good indication of how to approach these passages in a manner that communicates the kind of intensity of emotion that the composer wished. This question of articulation relates back to the previous conversation regarding the tempo of the movement, as this type of truly *tenuto* articulation would be somewhat awkward at the printed tempo but works perfectly at the tempo most often heard. The indication does not, however, imply that there is never any space between notes, or that the articulation is completely *legato*. Quarter notes in the passacaglia should be well sustained, with little or no decay in the sound, allowing a slight space before the next note is sounded. The triplet figure in the horns (when it remains all on the same pitch) can be quite intense and dramatic when it is played as if with dashes: that is, with virtually no space between the notes. Other triplets in the horns work best with a "dot-dash" articulation, allowing them to sing lyrically without becoming muddy in an attempt at complete *legato*.

In the second iteration of the passacaglia (at **70**), the composer is careful to mark all voices (both the tuba and third bassoon with the passacaglia and woodwinds creating harmonies above) with the same dynamic, *piano*. Although it forms the heart of the piece, the lower line should not be over-emphasized, but should blend as one with what is above. In the next variation (at **71**), the passacaglia falls almost completely into the background, allowing the melancholy air spun by the solo violin to take precedence. At moments like this one, we want the listener to *feel* the presence of the passacaglia more than to be able to point to it and say, "there it is." (This situation is not unlike the one found in the finale of Brahms Symphony No. 4. In both works, we are amazed by the composer's genius when we observe his ability to stay within the confines of the passacaglia form while allowing the listener to be completely absorbed in the passion of the music, and not the craft.) At **72**, it might be tempting to keep the trio of English horn and bassoons in the background, as they imitate the previous material in the violin solo, but this is exactly contrary to what Shostakovich writes. These woodwinds need to play a true *forte*, and *espressivo* as written, as though they are the soloists; once again, we allow the "battle" to take its own shape, rather than interfering and creating a victor artificially. This also applies to the next several variations regarding horns, lower strings, and others.

No beat needs to be shown and no bars need to be marked after indicating the second beat of the second bar after **78**, despite the fact that the ten following bars contain several different meters. From the orchestra's perspective, this is treated as a *fermata* that precedes the *cadenza*. The only gesture that needs to follow the second beat of the second bar after **78** is a gentle cut-off for celli, basses, and timpani that perfectly coincides with the soloist's bow lifting from the string, one bar before **79**.

The tempo relationships found in the final section of the *cadenza* and in the transition to the fourth movement are sometimes not played exactly as written. As printed, there is no tempo relationship between the music at the end of the *cadenza* and the opening of the fourth movement. Following the text exactly, the final tempo in the *cadenza* is 𝅗𝅥 = 108 (♩ = 216), while the finale begins at 𝅗𝅥 = 76. Though there are many valid ways to shape this *cadenza*, what is often played (e.g., David Oistrakh and Elmar Oliveira) is as follows: the four bars at *Allegro* begin well below 𝅗𝅥 = 108, but a considerable *accelerando* brings the tempo above that marking by the time the sixteenth notes begin (fifth bar after *Allegro*); on the bar-line where these sixteenth notes begin, a metric conversion of previous 𝅗𝅥 = new ♩ (plus a modest *più mosso*) takes place, which means that the groupings of four notes (previously eighth notes and now sixteenth notes) will sound roughly the same; the tempo that has been reached at this point is usually around ♩ = 152, allowing a smooth and organic ♩ = ♩ relationship to occur at the beginning of the fourth movement.

4th movement.

Having already made the timpanist and strings aware that the beginning of the finale is near, the baton can gently and passively trace the shape of the final bar of the *cadenza* before a sharp *ictus* on the third beat cues the timpanist. Even though the preparatory gesture for this movement is given as a quarter note, the movement begins in one, as indicated by the tempo marking.

Despite the fact that the basic pattern for the movement is in one, there is no reason that the conductor should stick slavishly to this idea, as there are a number of places in the movement where both musical and technical issues suggest shifting into two. The passage from **84** to **85** certainly qualifies in this category, as both the driving *pizzicato* offbeats and the repeated figures in flutes suggest a certain equality of beats within the bar. It is not quite as clear, musically, that the passage from **86** to **87** demands a beat in two, though one could certainly make the case. If so, the beat should return to one at **87**. The same can be said for the passage from **89** to **90**, again returning to one at **90**. It is not necessary to create a complete list of these passages here, as one's own judgment is sufficient, based on the general discussion in this paragraph.

The sudden appearance of the passacaglia theme at **100**, in the wrong movement and transformed from its earlier *maestoso* feeling to a hysterical canon of clarinets, horns, and xylophone, is as brilliant and wonderful a moment as Shostakovich ever created. The violins have their *mezzo-forte* re-emphasized at this point, specifically in order to keep them out of the fray, and the conductor must sometimes caution them to stay somewhat in the background. The important issue here is the battle between the passacaglia elements and the frantic solo violin, with the orchestral violins providing only the framework for these other events. In a similar manner, it can be a real task of discipline for the celli and basses to maintain *piano* between **102** and **104**, pacing their *crescendo*, when indicated, with considerable patience.

Because the passage in $\frac{3}{4}$ (**99** and following) has been in three, it is most effective to beat in two at **105**. The *Presto* at **107**, however, is in one. In the first bars of this *Presto*, the empty bars should be marked with a combination of clean rhythmic precision and careful passivity. The latter quality ensures that no one in the orchestra is enticed to play in one of the empty bars the figure that (in some bars) appears sporadically on the second beat. This technique of careful passivity creates an unambiguous visual difference between the empty bars and those bars that will receive a sudden, sharp, almost rebound-less *ictus*, indicating the presence of the figure on the second beat. As has been mentioned elsewhere in this book, thorough technical clarity of the type described here is often one of the things that separates conductors whom musicians look forward to working with from those whose appearance on the podium orchestras dread.

In spite of the tempo, I conduct the passage from **109** to **110** in two, as both the drama and rhythmic content of these bars seem to demand it. The penultimate bar can be handled either by remaining in one or changing to two for clarity and drama.

∽

Jean Sibelius

Violin Concerto in D Minor, Op. 47

When asked about this concerto, R.M. summed up his feelings in a rather self-effacing manner. His comments highlight the great complexities of this work for both soloist and conductor, and the extremely high level of technical and artistic excellence that both must bring to a truly outstanding performance. He offered, "That may be the hardest piece, next to Beethoven, ever written for the violin, but for different reasons. I'm just grateful for any conductor that stays with me. When I play it really well I'm always a little surprised."

1st movement.

The conductor faces a significant and rather unique challenge between the beginning of the movement and **1**. That challenge is coordination of the (theoretically steady) *ostinato* in eighth notes (in the upper strings) with the sense of *rubato* often brought to the solo part in this same passage. On the one hand, the soloist cannot logically be asked to play this entire section with absolutely no expressive fluctuations of tempo. But, on the other hand, a constant push and pull in the motion of the eighth notes in the accompaniment threatens to turn what should be a calm, meditative musical idea into something that is likely to make the listener seasick. The solution is two-fold, and requires considerable subtlety. First, any fluctuation of tempo made by the conductor needs to be extremely delicate, and accomplished without over-reacting to the soloist's expressive gestures. The second strategy follows naturally from this idea of not over-reacting. This is one of those relatively rare occasions in serious music (another is the second movement of the *Concierto de Aranjuez*) when the accompaniment functions as a framework for the solo line, allowing the soloist to move, at times, slightly ahead of or behind the accompaniment. In this unique type of passage, the conductor allows the soloist reasonable freedom, but the soloist sometimes has the responsibility to "find us," rather than it always being our responsibility to "find him." This is essentially the same relationship that exists between the singer and the accompaniment in popular song. A singer in this genre will often "back-phrase," and the accompaniment does not necessarily slow down to accommodate the soloist each time this happens. In that unique musical situation, the singer has the responsibility to make up the time later in the phrase and to correctly re-join the accompaniment. (This, as we were all taught at some point, is the real meaning of the expression *rubato*, "robbing" time from one part of the beat, or bar, and giving it back at a later point.) The same principle is at work here, albeit on a far less extreme scale than we often hear in popular song, and the conductor must allow himself to embrace these small, expressive misalignments between the solo violin and the accompaniment rather than panicking or, as mentioned above, over-correcting. When this process works elegantly and with complete trust between soloist and conductor, then this passage acquires both a unique freedom and an expressive tension that pushes the boundaries of the relationship between the solo part and the accompaniment just far enough, but never too far.

The first eight bars following **1** involve a shared responsibility for leadership. While it certainly remains the conductor's task to follow and accommodate the soloist, this cannot be the only principle at work here, and the soloist must remain in contact with, and to some degree follow, the baton. (As is mentioned in other chapters, placing the baton, or a mirroring left hand, in a position where it is easy for the soloist to see it will certainly make the soloist's cooperation more likely.) For example, let's examine the first two bars at **1**. In both of these bars the conductor must commit herself to the placement of the second beat of the bar while the soloist is still sustaining the first note in that bar. If, after showing the second beat, the soloist does not place the next note in correct relationship to that beat, then the rest of the bar, and arrival in the following bar, will be sloppy and uncoordinated. When the conductor shows the second beat but the soloist does not respond in the same tempo, then the conductor must unnaturally elongate that second beat, making correct execution of the clarinet parts nearly impossible. Clearly, the soloist must, to some reasonable degree, stay in a steady tempo and/or play where the baton indicates.

The seventeenth and eighteenth bars after **1** offer the opportunity for either a brilliant demonstration of conducting technique and accompanying skill or some frantic flailing and a small "train-wreck." (I often place the first movement of this concerto on the audition repertoire for prospective students, and it is largely to see them deal with the subtle accompanying challenges discussed in the first paragraph of this chapter and to judge the sophistication of their technique in dealing with the two bars in question here.) These two bars are best conducted in four, but excellent execution of this passage requires considerably more technical subtlety than just choosing not to beat in two. Conducting the downbeat of the first of these bars (seventeen after **1**) without any immediate rebound allows the conductor the technical flexibility to listen precisely to the following violin arpeggio and therefore to place the second beat of the bar accurately. By contrast, if the first beat of that bar is conducted with the usual rebound then the conductor has already committed himself to the (temporal) placement of the second beat, which is very unwise considering that this arpeggio is often taken somewhat out of tempo. After pausing briefly, without rebound, on the first beat, the baton lifts in a separate preparatory gesture once the violinist has begun the arpeggio. (If the conductor knows with absolute certainty that the soloist will proceed from beat one to beat two essentially in tempo, then a normal rebound following the first beat will work perfectly, but that is not the most common circumstance.) After the conductor has accurately placed the second beat of the bar, the left hand indicates the sustained quality of the wind chord as well as its *crescendo*, while the baton flows unnoticed to the right (passively indicating the third beat of the bar). Next, the left hand actively releases the wind chord at the appropriate time, followed by a clear but passive marking of the following downbeat with the baton. As the solo violin continues into this bar, it is polite, but not absolutely necessary, to allow the baton to flow gently and passively through the second and third beats, making it clear to the brass and timpani even before they see it that the next active gesture is the fourth beat of the bar.

From twenty-two bars before **2** though *Largamente* it is only necessary to indicate the downbeat of each bar. The entrance of horns and timpani is indicated gently and soberly, and then the baton slowly marks the following downbeat, with the left hand continuing to indicate the sustained horn chord. The left hand then cuts off the horns at the appropriate point in the solo line, while the baton continues to mark each bar for the timpani. The left hand then cuts off the timpani at the appropriate time, while the baton continues to quietly mark the empty bars between *Largamente* and the entrance of the clarinets at *Tempo I*. The bar directly preceding the clarinet entrance, of course, contains an active second beat as a preparatory gesture to their entrance. It can certainly be argued that the bars between the end of the timpani roll and the clarinet entrance do not need to be marked at all. However, this solo passage is really not long enough to justify such abdication by the conductor. In addition, even subtle and completely passive marking of each of these bars encourages the orchestra to stay rhythmically and intellectually engaged.

Even though the composer clearly indicates ♩ = ♩ at 2, creating a situation where the transition from one meter to another should be simple, it can be helpful (both for accuracy of ensemble and musical intensity) to conduct this first bar at 2 in six. Once the pulse is secure and the proper intensity of the passage is established, the conductor can gravitate into two in the following bar. The necessary intensity of sound is best achieved by making certain that the viole are not playing off the string. Rather, an instruction "on the string, but separate" results in a more appropriately weighty background for the theme in celli and bassoons.

At some point no later than the second half of the third bar after 3 the conductor should have returned to beating in six. How much before this one might wish to gravitate back into six depends upon the progress of the *allargando* and the ensemble skill of the orchestra. I generally move back into six one full bar before 3 because I prefer a particularly relaxed *allargando* in this, the final bar of the bassoon phrase.

In the bar directly preceding *Largamente* (the fifth bar after 3), the style changes to a more passive gesture after arriving at the second beat of the bar, simultaneously cueing the timpani. The baton then flows passively and unobtrusively through the remaining beats, using the left hand to sustain the *crescendo*, arriving at the sixth beat in coordination with the soloist, and at that point using the left hand to delicately cut off the clarinets. This cut-off gesture needs to be fairly modest so that it does not inhibit or interrupt the *crescendo* in the strings and timpani. Once the soloist has reached and briefly sustained the double-stop on the sixth beat, the conductor gives a clean preparatory gesture in the new tempo (essentially showing the sixth beat again) allowing the soloist to move forward gracefully with the orchestra into the *Largamente*.

At *Largamente*, some conductors return to beating in two. This has some advantages and some disadvantages. Obviously, beating in two in this passage solves the dilemma posed for the clarinet and bassoons in executing the quadruplet figures (as some musicians find the quadruplets more difficult when trying to fit them into three beats instead of one), and may also be perceived as more expressive and musical. However, beating in two at such a slow tempo creates potential problems for accuracy of ensemble in the strings; the specific possible difficulties arise from trying to place chords on the second and fifth beats of the bar in the second and fourth bars of *Largamente* and playing consecutive quarter notes (viole and celli) in the fifth bar of *Largamente* and following. Beating in two also gives the conductor far less flexibility to accommodate gentle *rubati* that are likely to occur in the solo violin. Overall, the possible expressive benefits of beating in two are not as great as the dilemmas this choice is likely to cause. Unless the tempo at *Largamente* is unusually quick (making the two main beats of the bar not as far apart from one another), beating in six offers both greater control for the conductor and increased security for the orchestra.

Fifteen bars before **4**, most soloists will take a bit of extra time in the final two beats of the bar. The conductor should follow the soloist's musical direction here by allowing the *pizzicato* chords in the following bar to proceed in an equally unhurried manner. The musical gesture that begins with the soloist's *ritard* carries logically through the *pizzicato* chords, then to the rising arpeggio in the solo violin. However, when the conductor moves the *pizzicato* chords forward, as though trying to return to tempo, these three musical elements have an awkward "slow-fast-slow" quality, rather than being heard as one organic gesture that is passed from the soloist to the orchestra and back to the soloist.

Eleven bars before **4** the conductor encounters a situation that, though it appears very simple on the page, he must be very careful not to underestimate. After coming to rest on the *fermata*, the conductor carefully watches the soloist's bow in order to determine (at least approximately) when she will be ready to move to the second beat of the bar. As the soloist moves forward, the conductor must execute a cue for the timpani and basses, and a cut-off for the horns, all on the second beat of the bar. The clarity of the pattern (in six) is very important here, with the second beat moving conspicuously to the left. This is particularly important in this bar because, following the *fermata*, it is easy for less experienced violins and viole to assume that the next gesture signals the next note in the bar, since it is impossible for them to see that other events occur on the second and third beats. A sustaining left hand (that does *not* mirror the pattern) directed toward the violins and viole throughout the first half of this bar, followed by a clear mirroring gesture as a cue on the fourth beat, helps to dispel any confusion. Clearly showing that fourth beat is very important, leaving no guesswork for the strings as to where the harmony changes at mid-bar. Depending upon the progress of the soloist's *accelerando* (*poco a poco meno moderato*), the conductor can return to beating in two either ten or nine bars before **4**.

After subtly marking the five "empty" bars preceding **4**, the conductor will find that placement of the preparatory gesture for *Allegro molto* depends entirely on the soloist's interpretation of the three grace notes before the double-bar. If the soloist takes the grace notes fairly rapidly, then the preparatory gesture will probably line up well with the first of the three notes. If the soloist takes them more deliberately, then the conductor must place the gesture elsewhere, possibly as late as the final C-natural. This is one of those moments that, by its very construction, cannot be “followed” extemporaneously, and the conductor must be able to rely on the fact that the soloist will execute the figure with at least reasonable similarity to what was played in rehearsal or in pre-performance discussion.

In the second and eighth bars after **5**, the placement of the second quarter note of the bar (trumpets and oboe, later horns and clarinets) is paramount. This is not only important for good ensemble, but also allows the listener to clearly hear that the material in two different parts of the orchestra forms one phrase (D-flat, B-flat in winds, then E-natural, F-natural, G-flat in strings and woodwinds), and are not two disconnected musical ideas.

At **5**, the eighth notes in the basses should remain on the string. During the *fortissimo* sections this articulation creates a more solid foundation for the orchestra, and during the *diminuendo* it allows the basses to remain unobtrusive. In the last four bars before **6**, I generally ask the basses to subtly change to unmeasured *tremolo*. This means two things: first, that each individual changes from measured to unmeasured by simply speeding up the motion over the course of several beats, but not changing suddenly or noticeably, and, second, that the players in the section “stagger” this change so they are not all doing it at the same time. This small bit of sleight-of-hand allows the tempo to be less strict as we approach the entrance of the solo violin, allowing the soloist some freedom in the exact duration of the first note one bar before **6**. At the downbeat of **6**, the basses unobtrusively move from the unmeasured *tremolo* to the written sustained pitch.

The brief orchestral outburst eleven bars after **6** can be managed successfully in four or in eight. The choice depends on the comfort level of both the conductor and the orchestra (regarding the conductor’s own technique and the orchestra’s general level of ensemble sophistication and internal pulse). The opinion or comfort of the soloist is not an issue here, since the brief orchestral interjection occurs entirely outside the soloist's playing. After gently marking the three empty bars following the unison B-flat in celli and basses (marking these bars following the soloist's pace with some reasonable care), the baton marks the downbeat of the eleventh bar after **6**, and then flows passively to indicate the second beat of the bar. The baton should indicate the first two beats of this bar while the soloist is still sustaining the double stop under the *fermata*. If the conductor chooses to conduct the following figure "in eight," then the baton should indicate a passive (but clearly in tempo) third beat followed by an active second half of the third beat (the sixth beat of the bar "in eight") which serves as a clear preparatory gesture for the entrances on and following the fourth (major) beat of the bar. It should be mentioned that the choice to conduct "in eight" in this passage is not usually necessary in a professional orchestra. Assuming that the conductor feels free to remain in four, the baton simply indicates the third beat of the bar as preparatory gesture, continuing through the following two beats in tempo. When choosing to remain in four, the conductor needs to be certain that the preparatory gesture on the third beat is very clear and exactly in the tempo desired for execution of the thirty-second notes that follow. When the gesture on the third beat of the bar is either poorly thought-out or not sufficiently specific, then the musicians' execution of the thirty-second note figure is likely to be messy and unprofessional, through no fault of theirs. It is also to be noted here that the clarinets and bassoons playing this figure are slurred, while the strings are not. This is not an error. The winds are slurred to keep this figure from sounding like a tonguing etude, while the strings play separate strokes (on the string), increasing the dramatic intensity of the moment.

Approaching the orchestra's entrance at **7**, less experienced conductors often address the orchestra (to indicate that the entrance in near) and actually show the preparatory gesture too early. Raising the baton to show the first bassoon and first violins that their entrance is imminent should be done no earlier than two bars before **7**, at *Pesante, ravivando*. In order for the preparatory gesture to be in tempo, allowing the violins to confidently execute their oscillating figure in sixteenth notes, the gesture usually occurs approximately three notes before the double-bar, on the soloist's E-flat. This decision is, of course, entirely dependent on the pace of the soloist's *ritenuto*. The common error is to place the gesture too early, often with the C-natural, four notes before the double bar. This seems logical at first glance, since it is exactly one beat before the orchestra's entrance. However, the final beat of that bar is not in the tempo that follows, making such a gesture essentially worthless. A more sophisticated, and far more helpful, approach is to give the preparatory as discussed above, somewhere in the middle of that final beat, allowing the gesture to actually be in the tempo that follows.

Depending on the soloist's pacing of the final scale approaching **9**, the conductor's job can either be very simple or slightly more intricate. If the soloist takes the final scale before **9** precisely, or very close to, in tempo, then the conductor remains in two, with a slight broadening the final beat to accommodate a similarly mild stretch of the scale. If the entire scale is broadened more than this, then two minor technical adjustments are advisable. First, the first beat of the bar is broadened slightly to ensure coordination on the second beat. Second, the baton should pause briefly on the second beat, rather than moving forward with an immediate rebound. After a very brief pause, allowing for the soloist's stretching of the final beat, the baton lifts sharply from its paused position to prepare the following downbeat. This gesture will look, and feel, something like subdividing the second half of the bar, but should be executed with enough subtlety that the musicians do not feel they are being manhandled with too many gestures.

Approaching the climax of Sibelius' exciting orchestral writing in the following section, the conductor must not get so wrapped up in the obvious drama that he fails (twenty bars before **10**) to properly balance the weight of the *tutti* orchestra with the other extremely important musical element, *crescendo molto* in the trumpets. Although the orchestra is marked variously *fortissimo* and *più forte*, the true thrill of this passage comes not from the general dynamic but from the pressure of the *crescendo* in the trumpets, appearing to burst through a wall of orchestral sound. In addition, the three-note trombone phrase that follows should not be louder than the climax in horns and trumpets, though this is often the case. The trombone phrase, at half tempo, is an after-shock of sorts, and must not overshadow the true climax of the phrase.

Three bars after **10**, the conductor should avoid the temptation to beat these next several bars in three. This is not only unnecessary; it is absolutely contrary to the complex rhythmic idea of these bars. A fundamental pulse in two, divided into three parts by the clarinets, with each third divided in half by the solo violin, is a far different matter from the conductor beating three while the clarinets play on the beats and the soloist plays off-beats. It may seem, in theory, as though the result will be the same, but the resulting performance is not the same. The tension created by the several layers of cross-rhythms automatically creates a different, and much more compelling, musical result.

Though it may seem obvious, the importance of the tempo the conductor chooses at **11** cannot be overstated. This tempo must be precisely the pace where the soloist is comfortable playing the difficult passages in octaves that follow, and the common shift of tempo in this final section of the movement (rather fast in the first twelve bars of **11**, then somewhat slower beginning in the thirteenth bar, etc.) when the conductor chooses a tempo that is too quick, is very comfortable and unmusical. An additional dilemma is presented for the conductor when, ironically, the soloist is the one making a solid tempo choice impossible. With younger and less experienced soloists, it is not uncommon that, when the conductor sets precisely the (soloist's) desired tempo at **11**, the soloist increases the pace in the fifth bar, where the material is rather simple, and then slows down again at the octave passage. This is sometimes followed by another increase in tempo at the arpeggio section and yet another decrease at the next octave passage. Obviously, this unsteady, seasick approach is unacceptable. When the soloist pushes and pulls the tempo this severely then a frank but polite, off-stage conversation is probably in order.

Balance between soloist and orchestra can be a problem between **12** and the end of the movement. The thick (but thematically important) wind writing can be difficult to keep in balance with the solo violin, and the athletic string figures on the last two pages can also be problematic. There is actually not a great deal that can be done about this apart from the obvious: continue to reinforce for the orchestra through both word and gesture the importance of delicate playing throughout this passage; this is most important for winds in the first sixteen bars of **12** and for strings fifteen bars before the end.

2nd movement.

With any orchestra that has not played this work recently, it is usually a good idea to remind the musicians that the opening statement of the clarinets begins in the middle of the first bar. Otherwise, it is likely that those counting rests at the beginning of the movement will be incorrect by a half bar, regardless of how clear the conductor's pattern may be. With this information clearly understood by the orchestra, the conductor is free to begin the movement with nothing more than a gentle preparation representing the fourth beat of the bar, in eight. Even when the first bar has been clearly explained, and the conductor's pattern is flawless, consistent cues throughout the opening of the movement are a polite way to avoid tentative entrances that might be caused by momentary second-guessing. A tempo of around ♪ = 72 works nicely at the opening of the movement.

Some conductors, and some violinists, prefer a slight lift, or separation, in the middle of the phrase following the third (major) beat in bar 6. When this is the choice, the note before the lift should be played delicately, and the lift not prolonged, so that the phrase as a whole still feels intact. This same musical gesture appears twice more in the movement, and its subtle execution here allows for growing importance and intensity later.

Some soloists prefer a slight *ritard* in the final beat of bar sixteen, requiring a coherent slowing of the *pizzicati* in the celli and basses to allow for good placement of the following downbeat. In the following bar, the conductor needs to be aware of the articulation of the rhythmic figure in the strings, making sure that it is unified throughout the orchestra, played in a similar bow position, and is not inappropriately choppy.

Five bars before **1**, a lifting of the sound is inserted for dramatic emphasis and phrase shape following the third (major) beat, as was discussed above. This lift, being at a more intense point in the line, will be a bit more significant than the one found (if so chosen) in the fifth bar of the movement.

The solo figures in the third and fourth bars before **1** are often played somewhat capriciously, with some *rubato*. This is another of those moments when the young conductor needs to calmly continue a steady pulse, providing a framework for the solo line, and not respond inappropriately to these minor expressive fluctuations of tempo. The only point at which the conductor may need to make any adjustment at all will be on the final short scale figure, to insure an accurate and musically satisfying arrival at the downbeat two bars before 1. A slightly more urgent feel, perhaps ♪ = 80, works well at 1.

It may be tempting to expressively stretch the final beat (in eight) of the third bar before 2. But this is, in my opinion, an odd and somewhat unmusical choice. These two notes form the beginning of a rhythmically energetic phrase that follows, and slowing them down saps that energy. To the contrary, an energetic leaning forward here brings excitement to that next passage. In addition, there is the overall rhythmic structure to be considered. The figure in timpani and double basses forms a framework in the final beat of the bar that is then transferred, in the following bar, to the sixteenth-note arpeggios in viole and celli. A *ritard* preceding this bar-line, while not difficult technically, dulls our understanding of the musical connection between the two rhythmic figures.

In the middle of the fourth bar after 4, we place the same lift in the phrase as we have seen earlier in the movement. Here, in its final incarnation, the gesture is at its most profound and musically significant.

Even though the entire movement has been conducted in eight, there is, of course, no need for so many beats per bar beginning six bars before the end. Here, the conductor can beat in four, with a slight lift at the end of each bar that acts as both the cut-off and the preparation for the following bar. The bar five before the end requires only that the first beat be shown, conducted as though a *fermata*, with perhaps an extremely small and subtle motion indicating beats two and three, then a cut-off before moving on to the following bar. Not so much for balance as for correct atmosphere, these bars need to be played truly *pianississimo*, as marked. Three bars before the end, the lift in the strings at the end of the bar works nicely when coordinated with the (high D) anticipation in the solo violin. A similar small lift of the sound should also be made in the middle of the penultimate bar.

3rd movement.

A wide variety of tempi are possible in the third movement. Even when pressed for pre-rehearsal time, it is wise to get a good sense of the soloist's preference, and preferably a metronome marking, to avoid missing the desired tempo by a wide margin in rehearsal. I have conducted this movement with soloists whose *tempi* vary from ♩ = 90 to ♩ = 124, so if pure guesswork is employed it is likely to be very far off the mark.

The only significant challenge in this movement for the young conductor is, as discussed earlier, to avoid the temptation to "fix" things that aren't broken. Once the tempo is set correctly, the driving *cabaletta* rhythm that dominates the movement cannot be subject to any push and pull in response to expressive rhythmic variations offered by the soloist. Slight virtuosic gestures forward and backward, against the steady pulse of the orchestra, are common in this movement, and they are something that we should enjoy but not something to which we should respond.

Seven bars before **4**, the solo cello must sound as an equal partner with the solo violin, even though the cello dynamic is marked as rather delicate. If this passage is played literally in both solo instruments, then the cello will go almost, if not entirely, unheard.

There will be at least some *allargando* one bar before **13**, at *pesante*. If the gesture is quite modest (which it usually is not), then the conductor can stay safely in three. However, under most circumstances the *allargando* is considerable, and the conductor will find safety and accuracy in subdividing the second and third beats of the bar, providing clean placement of the orchestral chords.

ᔕ

Peter Ilyich Tchaikovsky

Concerto for Violin and Orchestra in D Major, Op. 35

1st movement.

It is a matter of personal taste (rather than an explicit matter of right and wrong) whether the opening phrases in the first violins should be performed strictly as written, with no expressive markings, or whether one's musical intuition can be allowed to prevail. These opening phrases are so exposed, and so critical to the overall tone of the opening of the work, that I prefer to give specific instructions to the violins, rather than letting bow direction and "group think" take over. I ask for the following to be marked in the parts: *diminuendo* from the first beat of bar 1 through the first beat of bar 2; *crescendo* from the second beat of bar 2 through the end of that bar; *diminuendo* from the first beat of bar 3 through the third beat of that bar, with a slight breath mark following that third beat; the four consecutive quarter notes in bars 3 and 4 marked with "dot-dash" and another slight *diminuendo* covering all four notes; bars 5 through 7 same as bars 1 through 3; the first two notes of bar 7 in first violins to be played completely *legato* (even though they are not under the same slur); woodwinds in bars 7 and 8 play the same articulation as strings in bars 3 and 4 (dot-dash).

I do not concern myself with the fact that the tempo in bar 9 is usually slightly faster than the one I conduct in the first eight bars. I want to be sure that these opening phrases have room to breathe musically, while the passage beginning at bar 9 requires a sturdier, steadier tempo.

Though not indicated by the composer, a small *ritard* in bar 22 is by no means unstylish. And this gentle slackening of the tempo provides for a more graceful transition to the opening phrases of the solo violin, which will certainly be taken at a tempo slower than the one utilized in bars 9 though 21.

In bar 25, there is a common misprint (in scores) in the solo violin part. The first grace note (before the fourth beat) should have an accidental natural, not another sharp. (This also has the result of confirming that the note on the fourth beat is A-natural.)

The approach to bar 28 is a matter of shared leadership. The soloist usually approaches the *Moderato* with two notes taken under the same or consecutive down-bow(s) (A-natural, G-natural). When the soloist arrives at G-natural (usually somewhat sustained beyond its printed value), the conductor gently shows the preparation for the following downbeat, allowing the soloist to play the grace note without haste before arriving at F-sharp in perfect coordination with the orchestral strings.

The conductor will want to listen carefully after arriving at the third beat of bar 30, as many soloists will choose to take a bit of extra expressive time during the sixteenth notes in beat four. These four sixteenth-notes will commonly slow down at first, but then speed up slightly just before the bar-line.

Many scores reproduce an error in bar 35. The pitches on the second half of the third beat in the solo violin are both B-naturals, not B-sharps.

In judging the timing of the preparatory gesture leading into **A**, the conductor must be aware of two issues. Most obvious, she must follow the preceding chromatic scale carefully, placing the preparatory gesture precisely on D-natural, the first of the four sixteenth-notes in the beat preceding **A**. Second, the preparatory gesture must be made with the understanding that, between that gesture and the downbeat, the solo violin will play not only the four chromatic sixteenth notes but also the double-stop (D and A), in the manner of a grace note before the beat. Conducting as though unaware of this is likely to have the result that the *pizzicato* chord on the following downbeat sounds well ahead of the upper F-sharp in the solo violin.

The conductor takes the tempo for bar 50 from the soloist's tempo in bar 49. In bar 50, there is often an extra, sometimes considerable, stretch of the last beat. This stretch may be so considerable that the conductor will want to subdivide for clarity and control. Unless the tempo in the following bar is unusually slow, the conductor can return to beating in four in bar 51.

In both of the two bars preceding **B** it is the fourth beat of the bar that is most important. While listening carefully to the soloist's sextuplets in each of these fourth beats, some conductors fail to adequately prepare the orchestra for the following downbeat, thus compelling the musicians to arrive at that downbeat more surprised than prepared. A clear, confident *ictus* that is perfectly lined up with the soloist's fourth beat is absolutely necessary.

The tempo is usually somewhat more deliberate in bar 63. In order to instantly communicate this sudden change (and in order to avoid a "train wreck" on the second beat caused by some individuals playing that chord ahead of the conductor and the rest of the orchestra), the look of the conductor's beat needs to change radically at this point. What was, in preceding bars, a small and concise beat with a rather small rebound, here becomes slightly larger, but with a noticeably larger rebound that hangs motionless in mid-air for a split second. The first and second beats in these bars (63 and 64) get the immediate attention of the orchestra when they are preceded by a slight, but absolute stop on the *ictus*. This slight stopping motion, followed by the somewhat larger rebound, feels something like subdivided time, but it is not exactly that. This quality of hanging in mid-air creates both the ensemble awareness and the extra time required to wait for the soloist to finish the figure in each of the first two beats of the bar.

Unless the conductor is aware (by previous experience) that the soloist intends to sustain the final note (F-sharp) of bar 68 for an unusually long period, the conductor can usually show the fourth beat of the bar where it would normally fall (after the soloist's F-natural), moving forward within the soloist's tempo to the following bar. This may require some "leaning backward" to sustain the soloist's *allargando*, but it generally does not require any subdivision or other such manhandling of the phrase. However, if the conductor is aware that the soloist is likely to sustain the final F-sharp to any considerable degree, then he may wish to wait and place the preparatory gesture precisely with the final note of the bar. Although this latter solution will result in a preparation that is equivalent to neither an eighth note nor a quarter note in the following tempo (being somewhere in between), it is nonetheless perfectly intelligible to the orchestra when executed logically and musically.

The fourth beat of bar 80 usually requires a subtle subdivision. This allows the soloist time to take some *ritardando* during the last two notes of the bar while still giving the conductor the flexibility to show a clear cutoff for the strings.

To signal the conclusion of this eight-bar episode, the first note in bar 95 serves the phrase and the energy of the moment best when marked *staccato* in strings and horns.

Bars 97 and 98 are best handled with patience rather than anxiety. While exact coordination between the soloist's triplet on the third beat and the orchestra's answer on the fourth beat is to be desired, it cannot be denied that a split-second late (for the orchestra's entrance) is substantially preferable to a split-second early. However, precise coordination is not difficult to achieve as long as the conductor does not anxiously anticipate the third beat. After arriving, passively, at the first beat (of bar 97), the baton flows with similar passivity into the second beat, waiting for the soloist to arrive at the first note of the triplet on the third beat. As the solo violin approaches the end of the scale, the baton, without *ictus*, moves with accelerating speed toward a sharp *ictus* on the third beat, being careful never to arrive at the third beat ahead of the violin. The following bar (98) is handled in nearly the same manner, the only difference being that in bar 98 it is possible to flow with more predictability through the opening beats of the bar, as it is likely to rhythmically resemble bar 97.

Excellent handling of bars 99 and 100 requires both confident, sharp *icti* on beats one and three, impelling clean performance of the off-beats, and calm attention to the pace of each triplet on the second and fourth beats, to be certain that one does not anticipate the beginning of each scale that follows. After indicating, with a sharp *ictus*, the third beat of bar 100, however, the baton should pause, not flowing forward into the fourth beat. Most soloists take a slight lift on this bar-line, and, when this is the case, the conductor uses this slight silence as the location of the preparatory gesture. If the preparation is placed, instead, where the soloist plays the fourth beat, then the conductor has no flexibility to allow time for the desired *pausa* on the bar-line. If, however, the soloist is one of those relatively few who move strictly in tempo from the triplet to the following downbeat, then none of these considerations is necessary, and the baton can flow naturally from one bar to the next.

Some *allargando* is usually observed in bar 126, moving logically from the preceding *più mosso* to the following *Moderato assai*. This is not usually a matter of extremes, however, and is best (both musically and technically) when it is treated modestly, remaining in four. The grandeur of the passage beginning at bar 127 is best served when the *allargando* leads gently and logically toward it, rather than slowing down to such an extreme that the new tempo is actually faster than the end of bar 126.

In bars 128, 130, 136, 138, 189, and 191, I ask the violins and flutes to mark the following items: slur the first three notes of the bar together (strings under one down-bow) with a slight *diminuendo*; place a breath mark following the third beat; and add a slight *crescendo* on the fourth beat (up-bow). In this way the melody is given more direction and shape as it flows above a less nuanced accompaniment. Obviously, I make the same request in the parallel music later in the movement (bar 188).

At bar 160, most soloists take a slightly slower tempo than the one heard in the preceding *tutti* section. When this is so, it is appropriate to make a slight *allargando* in the end of bar 159 for a smooth and more musical transition.

In the passage beginning in bar 162, it is quite common for the middle beats of each bar (particularly in the first four bars) to be treated with considerable *rubato*. This often takes the form of a pulling back of the tempo in the second and third beats, returning toward tempo at the end of the third beat and into the fourth. When this is the case, the conductor's gesture indicating the third beat of the bar must reflect these changes with considerable specificity, showing no real *ictus* on the third beat and then accelerating clearly toward the fourth as the sixteenth notes accelerate.

At *Allegro giusto* (bar 304), some scores show the first note in the solo violin as G-natural. Clearly, this is correctly an F-sharp. At this moment the conductor must sometimes be quite cautious, as some soloists take a bit of *rubato* in the first several beats of this bar, accelerating from a suddenly slower tempo toward the real intended tempo of this passage. It is also common that bars 321 through 324 accelerate somewhat, leading more smoothly to the following "*Più mosso.*"

2nd movement.

The composer's metronome marking for this movement presents something of a dilemma for the conductor. The two issues of choosing an appropriate, musical tempo for the movement that does not grossly intrude on the composer's stated wishes and that of finding a tempo that can be acceptable to the soloist stumble over one other in considering this question. The printed tempo, ♩ = 84, is problematic at the outset from a practical standpoint, as virtually no soloists play the movement as quickly as that. The most-often heard tempo is something closer to ♩ = 64, and it is not uncommon to hear it played substantially slower than that. Obviously, with the possible exception of the circumstance when one is working with a very inexperienced or student soloist, the tempo that the soloist wishes is the tempo at which the movement will proceed. If this tempo is slower than the conductor can bear to conduct the introduction, then he does have a dilemma. On the one hand, he can, for the sake of unified interpretation and performance, submit entirely to the soloist's tempo and conduct the orchestral opening at that tempo. On the other hand, the conductor can lead the opening of the movement at a tempo that is more palatable in his view, allowing the motion to slow naturally when the soloist enters. Neither of these is a perfect solution, but they are really the only options that we have under such circumstances. Some may wonder why I have not mentioned the obvious third option, that of endeavoring to convince the soloist the wisdom of performing the movement at, or at least close to, the composer's tempo. The reason I have not bothered to mention it among the realistic options is that, apart from when dealing with a younger soloist as mentioned above, such a discussion is unlikely to have a good result.

Two issues regarding dynamics need to be addressed in the first four bars of the movement. First, considering the atmosphere of the movement, the climax of the first phrase at the beginning of the fourth bar should be no more than a luscious *mezzo-piano*. Any more sound than this makes the phrase into something that it is not, and ruins what it is intended to be. Second, the beginning and ending dynamic of the phrase, *piano*, must not be so soft or so lacking in a core of expressive sound that a substantial change of dynamic and color at bar 5 is no longer possible.

The unintentional addition of (unprinted) dynamics in bars 5 and 6 should be carefully avoided. These two bars create a momentary oasis of meditative calm as contrasted with the phrases both before and after, and the common addition of little swells in each bar completely defeats this purpose.

The change of dynamic indicated at **A** is quite important, as it represents a complete change in tone in the orchestra. The preceding eight bars should be played exceptionally quietly and with a minimum of vibrato. By contrast, the passage beginning at **A**, while still only *piano*, needs to be suddenly warm and expressive.

It may be necessary to subdivide the third beat of bar 33. If the soloist's *ritardando* at the end of the phrase is at all significant, the subdivision may be necessary to coordinate soloist, principal flute, and strings.

The printed *ritenuto* one beat before **B** should be taken rather modestly, as the tempo at **B** is usually a bit faster than the original tempo of the movement. Because of this, taking a larger *ritenuto* feels quite awkward when immediately moving forward at the beginning of the next phrase.

The woodwinds have no articulations in the passage from bar 53 to bar 58. Usually "long dots" are intuited from bar 53 to bar 56. Some conductors ask for this articulation to continue in the next two bars, and some want a more *legato* tonguing in bars 57 and 58.

In bar 72, it is often advisable to subdivide the third beat. The soloist usually takes some time during the seven-note turn, and subdividing allows the clarinet to place the final note of the bar accurately and without guesswork.

Being familiar with the soloist's intended pacing and bowing is important in bar 95. The two grace notes at the end of the bar can be performed in a variety of tempi and with several different possible bowings. Only by being forewarned, and therefore forearmed, can the conductor calmly lead the orchestra into the following downbeat with the soloist.

3rd movement.

The composer's indication *attacca subito* is not to be taken lightly. This is more than a request to avoid an instrument-cleaning break between movements, as the composer is trying to highlight the enigmatic conclusion of the second movement by moving directly from what feels like the dominant (E major) to what feels like the tonic (A major). In order to achieve this close proximity of the two movements, and the two important harmonies, the cut-off of the final chord of the second movement functions as the preparatory gesture for the downbeat of the third movement.

The soloist is usually allowed to lead at bar 53. However, if the conductor is completely uninvolved physically until she actually hears the first note of that bar then she has no way to respond calmly, quickly, and accurately. When the soloist arrives at the C-sharp in bar 52, the baton can begin to float gently upward while the conductor also engages the soloist visually. In this way, and without any need for discussion, the baton mirrors the motion of the bow (no matter what bowing is used), and conductor and soloist are wordlessly in sync. Once in sync in this way, when the violinist moves to begin the next phrase the conductor is already part of that motion, and can drop the baton to indicate the downbeat at bar 53 with clarity and security but without haste or panic.

A number of small cuts are often taken in this movement. As a whole, they serve to trim down a movement that can become somewhat repetitive when played as written. The most common set of cuts is as follows:

From the End of Bar	To the Beginning of Bar
68*	81
258**	271
294	299*****
304	309
422	431
475***	488
579****	584

[* When this cut is taken, the last note of bar 68 in viole, celli, and basses is omitted.]

[** When this cut is taken, the last note of bar 258 in viole, celli, and basses is omitted.]

[*** When this cut is taken, the last note of bar 475 in viole, celli, and basses is omitted.]

[**** Some soloists play these four bars even when taking all other listed cuts.]

[*****When the abovementioned cuts are taken, violins and viole will need to mark pizz. in their parts at bar 300, as the printed indication is now inside the cut at bar 296.]

Knowing ahead of time whether or not the soloist intends to take a slight *ritard* in bar 144 can save the conductor from some embarrassment. The conductor must commit himself to a clear preparatory gesture in this bar, and if the soloist slows down from the headlong rush of sixteenth notes precisely when the conductor makes the (in tempo) gesture, then the result is either an accurate orchestral chord that arrives ahead of the soloist or an orchestral "train wreck" as the conductor attempts to suddenly change the meaning and pace of the gesture.

At **D**, the oboist must usually figure out the new tempo from what has occurred in rehearsal, as a preparatory gesture in the new, slower tempo is not possible in the preceding bar. This is true even when the soloist takes a slight *rallentando* in the preceding bar, as the tempo at the end of that *rallentando* is usually not slow enough to be the desired new *meno mosso* tempo.

In some editions, the articulation in the celli in bars 210 and 214 is either inconsistent or simply completely inaccurate. In both bars, the eighth notes on the second beat should have a slur with dots, not a slur with dots in one case and only a slur in the other.

In order to accommodate the passage in harmonics and the generally delicate texture, a slight *meno mosso* is often observed seven and a half bars before **H**. When this is the case, the printed *molto meno mosso* at **H** will be less significant because the tempo has already slowed somewhat.

Many scores, and some parts, contain a misprint at bar 409. In this bar the basses should play on the first beat, not on the second eighth note of the bar with the remainder of the string section.

The solo passage from bar 452 to bar 459 is usually not played as printed, as most soloists play the Leopold Auer version of this short *cadenza*. While the rhythm remains the same in the Auer text, conductors who are new to the performance of this work should acquire the exact Auer text. In addition, even more experienced conductors should be aware that some soloists play a version of the Auer *cadenza* that is one bar longer than the version most commonly heard. I had conducted this piece many times before a soloist threw me this curve during an orchestra rehearsal, though his curve throwing was entirely unintentional. This violinist (who will remain nameless, since he is both an extraordinary violinist and a good friend) assured me that "everyone" plays nine bars of sixteenth notes following the two bars of triplets. It suffices to say that this is not correct. (R.M. concurs.) Most violinists play a version with eight bars of sixteenth notes, the same number of bars found in the original, just not the same pitches. But forewarned is forearmed, and now I always ask before the first rehearsal which "version" the soloist plays.

Four bars before **M**, many soloists like the tempo to pick up slightly. This is usually not a continuing *accelerando*, but only *poco più vivo* precisely at this point. At bar 632, exactly where the composer indicated *fortissimo*, it works well for the orchestra to mark *meno forte* or even *mezzo forte* in order to allow the soloist to be heard. A slight *crescendo* can then accompany the rising line in the solo violin, arriving back at *fortissimo* four bars before the conclusion.

III. Cello Concerti

Samuel Barber

Concerto for Violoncello and Orchestra, Op. 22

1st movement.

Being careful that the preceding upward gesture contains no discernible *ictus*, the baton descends sharply to dictate the empty downbeat of the first bar. In the second bar, the second beat can contain virtually no rebound at all, allowing the third beat to be indicated by a gentle lift of the baton that nicely communicates the new dynamic and the more lyrical feel of the third bar.

Many passages in this movement (the eight bars preceding **1** are a good example) contain a simultaneous contrast between a highly lyrical line that dominates the texture and a subtle, but highly rhythmic, figure below. The baton must reflect both of these qualities simultaneously by elegantly maintaining *legato* and style for the melody without ever sacrificing complete accuracy and solid mathematics.

Even though Barber does not specify it, the first note in the fifth bar after **2** should be played rather short and quite delicately. This note functions as the final note of the previous phrase, and for this reason it needs to be executed as a logical part of the *diminuendo* just preceding it; a small space follows this note, helping to define the beginning of the next phrase.

An accurate and confident cue for the English horn entrance in the fifth bar after **5** does not appear, on paper, to be an issue. It can, however, require a deft touch from the conductor, as it is not unusual for the cellist to make a slight expressive *ritard* at the end of the previous bar. This can make perfect coordination between the English horn and the soloist slightly trickier than it looks.

Because the next orchestral entrance is at a rehearsal number, there is no need to mark any of the bars during the extended solo preceding **6**. As has been discussed in other chapters, merely mentioning in rehearsal that the next downbeat will be at that point is sufficient. This entrance of horn and clarinets at **6** can be slightly tricky (mostly for the clarinets), depending on the precise shaping of the line by the soloist. In order to ensure that the clarinets are able to enter cleanly and confidently, the preparation must be clearly in tempo. However, the soloist's *allargando* in the previous bar can make that gesture uncomfortable and/or inaccurate. If the *allargando* is fairly substantial, then the preparatory gesture can be coordinated with the final two notes of the bar, as the eighth note value there will be at least fairly close to that of the quarter note in tempo. If the *allargando* is more modest, then the preparation, in order to be accurate, must be placed somewhere just after the E-flat on the second beat.

While marking the two empty bars before **9**, the conductor should be aware that a slight pause is common after the first note of the bar directly before **9**. Even though the conductor is using a passive gesture to mark empty bars, it is tempting to immediately follow that final passive, bar-marking gesture with an acceleration that shows more musical intention, knowing that one is headed toward a more active beat. In this case, however, the baton should pause passively, still in a lowered position, after marking the bar, waiting for the cellist to begin the upward scale before coordinating the (still rather passive) upward gesture with the sound of the second beat in the cello. The first real *ictus* will, of course, be on the downbeat at **9**. A somewhat similar situation occurs in the bar before **27**, but because there is one considerable difference in the orchestration, I will discuss it separately later in the chapter.

The composer offers a parenthetic "a tempo" at **11**, even though there is nothing specific in the music just before it that demands something different. Presumably this is because a bit of *rubato* during the three preceding bars is rather likely.

Though it is not absolutely necessary for ensemble, I prefer to conduct the second bar after **12** in three. This decision not only adds rhythmic drive to the bar, but also removes any potential tentativeness in violins and viole entering in the following bar. For similar reasons (rhythmic drive and general drama, not because it is required for ensemble), I prefer to conduct all the $\frac{3}{8}$ bars between **13** and **14** in three. Conducting these bars in one feels too much like a waltz to me, and this music is anything but that.

While one does not ever want to dismiss the soloist's music from one's perception, it is neither necessary nor musically desirable for the conductor to be overly concerned with "following" the cellist at **15**. Within reason, both conductor and soloist are aware that the cello is accompanying the woodwinds, not the other way around.

Some cellists take a bit of *ritard* in the bar before **16**. I try to discourage this, but I can only do what I can politely do. I discourage this for two reasons. (Three reasons if you count the fact that it's simply not written there, but that's really not fair.) First, the composer goes out of his way to create a charming transition, linking the equal eighth note in two different meters, and the *ritard* muddles this relationship to a considerable degree. Second, it is a bit difficult for the first violins to play the quarter note triplet mathematically correctly and with good ensemble if a *ritard* is added to the bar. Contrary to the rationale in some earlier passages containing $\frac{3}{8}$ meter, there is no reason to beat the bars at **16** in eighth-note pulses, and there is every reason not to do so: the charming hemiola figures in the clarinets and flute need to flow naturally and without any sense of angularity.

Three bars before **17** it is easiest to control all elements of the orchestra by immediately going into eighth note beats. This continues through **18**, where it is safe to return to beating in two. A comforting look at the bassoons on their entrance one bar before **17** is very much appreciated. The sudden switch to beating in six two bars earlier, combined with the off-beats in violins, flute, and clarinet directly before their entrance, can cause just enough second-guessing for the bassoons' entrance to be missed or insecure.

The bar directly before **19** requires a beat in nine, and one may wish to show some subdivisions in the second half of the previous bar so that the change to the eighth note pulse does not seem so sudden. In spite of the clear indication *a tempo, giusto*, there is sometimes a slight breath between the first *pizzicato* chord and the beginning of the next phrase (*arco*) in the solo cello (at **19**). When this is not the case, the conductor can simply move forward easily in two. When this slight pause is taken, the result is that at least the first half of the bar, if not the entire bar, will probably need to be subdivided. In addition, violins and flutes need to be warned not to jump in early, as their first note of the new phrase will arrive quite a bit later than they expect. If subdivisions are necessary, the beat returns to two in the following bar.

I conduct all the $\frac{3}{8}$ bars between **24** and the end of the movement in three. As previously mentioned, this is for reasons that are more of style than ensemble. I simply cannot bring myself to float along amiably in one during music of such intensity and rhythmic diversity.

One bar before **27**, many cellists take a slight pause after the first note, therefore not slurring downward as written. When the conductor is aware of this, the baton should pause in an upward position after marking the downbeat two bars before **27**, not moving again until the pause (in the next bar) is complete and the soloist begins the scale in octaves. At this point the baton moves swiftly to indicate the downbeat, then cueing the woodwinds, catching the soloist's second beat of the scale.

I have discussed in other chapters the technique of occasionally keeping the baton purposefully ahead of the soloist (when the orchestra is not playing) so that the conductor and the orchestra are better prepared for their next entrance. The situation one bar before **27** is exactly the opposite. Here, even though the soloist has reached the first note of this bar, the baton remains paused in the previous bar. This is because indicating the downbeat as it occurs, and then pausing before the soloist begins the scale in octaves, would mean having to indicate the first beat a second time, as a preparatory gesture. While it is true that sometimes this double indication of the same beat is necessary, the point is that it is *not* necessary here, and avoiding it by disciplined technique will help avoid any possible confusion for the woodwinds.

2nd movement.

Barber's intriguing melodic shapes are an important part of the beauty and intricacy of this movement, and they also form its most significant conducting and interpretive challenge. The $\frac{8}{8}$ meter that occupies the majority of the movement lends itself to various melodic subdivisions (3+3+2, 3+2+3, 2+3+3), and the composer's simultaneous use of more than one of these possibilities creates a unique kaleidoscope of interweaving rhythms and melodies. Sadly, the conductor cannot accommodate more than one of these choices in any given bar, so she must choose one pattern to conduct, allowing those with a contrary construction of the bar to work somewhat on their own. C.B. commented on this same subject less technically but far more artfully, remarking on how important it is for the conductor to establish a good flow and shape for each of the musical components in this movement so that "the feeling of Siciliana and the feeling of $\frac{4}{4}$ can coexist successfully."

No matter which pattern is chosen in a given bar, someone's music will be at cross-purposes, so there are no perfect solutions. See, for example, the second bar of the movement. The second violins and clarinet will be content with a simple divided four pattern (2+2+2+2), but the solo cello is shaped as 3+3+2. Even more complicated is bar 5, where the strings are as before, but the shape of the oboe line is 3+3+2, and the solo cello's construction is 2+3+3. While there is, as mentioned, no perfect solution, there is also no absolutely best solution, and different musicians will see the optimum choice differently. Since I cannot accommodate everyone at any given moment, I prefer to remain in divided four (2+2+2+2) for all such bars, with a very few exceptions. My reasoning for this is two-fold. First, it is easiest for the musicians if there is some consistency to the pattern throughout the movement, rather than changing the pattern constantly when this still does not accommodate all musical "points of view." Second, it makes no sense to adopt a default pattern that is in unequal parts when it does not consistently serve the entire orchestra. The only time I alter this is for those bars in which the music is clearly shaped in a unified manner throughout the orchestra, but does not conform to the 2+2+2+2 pattern. The following is a summary of those bars:

First bar at **2**	3+3+2
Third bar after **2**	3+2+3
Third bar after **6**	3+2+3
First bar at **8**	3+3+2
Third bar after **8**	3+2+3
First bar at **9**	3+3+2

Fourth, fifth, and sixth bars after 9	3+3+2
Three bars before the end	3+3+2

Even though most of the bars are beaten as 2+2+2+2, or perhaps particularly because of this, it is of the highest importance that both the baton and, especially, the left hand create musical shape in each bar. For example, in the first bar of the opening oboe solo the left hand should be used to encourage the 3+3+2 shape of the bar, even though the baton moves symmetrically in divided four. Such shaping gestures are even more important two bars later, where the shape of the oboe line contrasts with both the baton and the solo cello. Without moment-by-moment attention to these interpretive and expressive issues in this movement, the conductor, shackled with a static pattern, becomes no more than a traffic cop who hopes that someone else will make some music.

In the bar directly preceding 6, it may be impossible for the bass clarinetist to sustain the final note in the bar long enough to accommodate the amount of liberty taken by the soloist. If the bass clarinet fades out early, this is really not a crisis, as the orchestral celli double the same pitch. If, in rehearsal, this appears likely to happen in performance, the bass clarinetist may need to be advised not to repeat the note after taking an extra breath.

Though some conductors add a bit of *incalzando* in the last two beats of the bar preceding 8, I prefer the opposite approach. I find it more dramatic to take a touch of *allargando* across the arpeggios of strings and woodwinds that lead into the *tutti*.

In the fourth through sixth bars after 9, the sonorities in trumpets and horn are critical in the journey toward the final cadence. The first two chords must not be played too softly, as they sometimes are, as this may cause them to lose beauty of sound and to leave no room for the *pianissimo* (though muted) that follows.

3rd movement.

C.B.'s comments on this movement were global, rather than site specific. After we commiserated for a few moments over our shared opinion that the third movement is by far the least successful part of the composition, he mentioned more specifically his concern that without a clear concept about this movement (from the conductor) the music tends to "atomize": that is, to break into small component parts intellectually, musically, and interpretively, at the expense of a clear vision of the whole. He is, in my opinion, exactly correct in this. The music in this movement, not Barber's most inspired material from the outset, seems to come at us in fits and starts, so a clear and mature concept of how different *tempi* and diverse musical materials flow together and work together is vital to keep the movement from feeling like a patchwork of unconnected ideas.

Following a moment of complete stillness, a sudden, dramatic drop of the baton prepares the entrances on, and following, the second beat of the first bar. The conductor (and musicians of the orchestra) should be careful to avoid any inadvertent *accelerando* during these first four bars, as the composer has built this quality into the rhythmic structure, and further pressing of the tempo only undoes his efforts. Though it is a bit more difficult for flutes and celli, I prefer that there be no extra space between the *fermata* in the fifth bar and the downbeat at **1**. Though this may be acoustically imperfect in some concert halls, as the remaining sound in the hall may somewhat obscure the beginning of the next phrase, I find the added drama and surprise to be a reasonable trade-off.

The $\frac{6}{4}$ bars that appear throughout the movement are conducted in two, the $\frac{9}{4}$ bars in three. This adds the appropriate, unexpected swing to each phrase.

The solo passages between **6** and **7** are not usually a challenge to follow. These are rather difficult for some soloists, however, so if some inconsistency of intonation makes the passage unnerving for the conductor, then simply following the bow changes simplifies everything. At **9**, the conductor does not need to be concerned about a minor discontinuity, if any, between the soloist's syncopations and the theme in the orchestra. Some soloists position the chords in the syncopated bars with an extra bit of stylization, and attempting to "follow" the soloist is a recipe for chaos.

Some soloists prefer the passage at **10** to be taken a bit *meno mosso*. This will, of course, be dealt with in pre-rehearsal discussion, and those cellists who do want a slower tempo here will probably want the same tempo at **24**. If so, the original tempo is partially revived during the *animando poco a poco* beginning at **12**, and completely re-established at **14**.

It is rather important that the conductor be aware of the soloist's intended bowing for both the *fermata* that precedes **14** and the following downbeat. Some soloists take the *fermata* in one down-bow, pause at the tip for the breath mark, and then begin up-bow at **14**. Others will take both a down-bow and an up-bow in the *fermata*, beginning the F-sharp trill down-bow. Either way, prior knowledge of an issue like this is important, since, without it, neither the conductor nor the woodwinds will be ready for the following entrance and are likely to be taken off guard.

If the conductor gets aurally turned around during the solo passage in the first two bars of **15**, recovery is easy when the soloist reaches the slurred double-stops in the third bar. The only real danger here is if, in concentrating on keeping track of the soloist in the first two bars, the conductor fails to continue marking bars clearly. This accidental disconnect between hand and brain (the "brain/hand schism") is not an uncommon failing, and one should be on guard for it at all times when aurally navigating a more complex solo passage (see Introduction: Conducting Concerti, paragraph 4).

Depending on the degree of *calando* agreed upon by the soloist and the conductor, the last three quarter-notes preceding **16** might demand some subdivision. This not only provides additional clarity for placement of the last note in the bar (oboe and clarinet), but also more effectively sets up the quarter note pulse that follows.

Staying coordinated with the soloist's *accelerando* after **16**, and keeping orchestral forces in sync with her, is not generally difficult. Minor difficulty may occur, however, in the *rallentando* before **17**. The potential awkwardness lies in the combination of the pace of the last four eighth notes (before **17**) of the solo cello and the gesture needed for the entrance of the flutes. If the *rallentando* is not too severe, and, more importantly, if the soloist does not take a bit of extra time on the last two notes, then the baton can flow forward fairly easily in half-note beats. In this case, even though the last half note before the flutes' entrance is not in exactly the same tempo as the music at **17**, adapting to this is fairly easy as long as the point of entrance is clear to them. On the other hand, if the soloist does take some extra expressive time across the last two or three eighth notes (as is not uncommon), the conductor may want to allow the baton to rest on the first beat of the bar (one bar before **17**), refraining from giving a preparatory gesture for flutes until the soloist reaches the last two notes of the bar. Utilizing the earlier solution in this latter musical situation (which is what happens when the conductor is unprepared or the soloist does one thing in rehearsal and another in performance) leaves the conductor awkwardly hanging on the second beat, waiting for the soloist to finish the bar, and with no remaining resources (other than another up-beat) for clearly showing the following downbeat.

Bars of $\frac{3}{2}$ meter between **19** and **20** are beaten in three, contrary to the $\frac{6}{4}$ bars earlier in the movement, with which they have nothing in common musically. The real question arises in the $\frac{6}{4}$ bars between **22** and **24**. From a musical (not technical) standpoint, these bars are of the same fundamental content as those found earlier in the movement (e.g., eight bars after **1**), and those bars are to be beaten in two. The obvious difference here is the addition of orchestral forces with eighth notes grouped in fours. These musicians very much appreciate seeing these bars in three, but we should not accommodate them except in the most unexpected circumstances. While it would do no real, overt damage to these bars to take them in three, there is the intent of the composer to consider, and that must take precedence. Consideration of the composer's intentions must be the primary concern except, as alluded to above, in a circumstance when the bar simply will not hold together in two, and this is extremely rare. The composer's clear intent is for these bars to feel as they did earlier in the movement, as a sudden moment of swing with three quarter-notes per beat instead of two, with the new addition of a hemiola laid on top. Beating in three turns these bars into $\frac{3}{2}$ meter, which is exactly what Barber didn't want.

Since rehearsal numbers conveniently bookend the solo passage between **28** and **29**, there is no need to mark the bars. During the last two bars of the solo, the cellist moves us easily back into the correct tempo for the orchestra's entrance. During these last two bars, the only indication for moving forward toward the *Allegro molto* is an arcane *poco a poco*. Clearly, this is meant to indicate *poco a poco accelerando*, or perhaps more specifically a *poco a poco* movement toward that new tempo.

The indication *Doppio lento* four bars before **33** can be a bit confusing. The composer gives a metronome marking of ♩ = 66 here, half of the marking at **29**, ♩ = 132. Though this seems clear enough mathematically, the expression *Doppio lento* fails to take into consideration the preceding, often quite extreme, *allargando*. Four bars before **33** the composer wants the tempo "twice as slow" as the tempo at **29**, but not necessarily having anything to do with the tempo in the first four bars of **32**. The good news (for the conductor) is that the soloist is going to set the tempo here anyway, so we are pretty much absolved of dealing with this issue. After giving the downbeat at *Doppio lento*, each of the next three bars (until **33**) can be marked with only a downbeat, while the conductor is carefully following the solo line, thinking in four (not in two). In particular, the conductor must intently follow the pace of the quintuplet and sextuplet in the bar preceding **33**, as these set the basic pulse for the following bar, even though some soloists take a slight pause on the bar-line for the purpose of clearly setting a new tempo. At **33**, the beat resumes, in four; the tempo here is usually approximately ♪ = 116 (despite the fact that the composer says ♪ = 132).

The three sextuplets at the end of the first bar at **34** are usually executed in a reasonably predictable manner, often beginning a bit more deliberately and then accelerating downward. This usually allows the conductor to place the preparation for the following bar at the beginning of the final sextuplet. At *A tempo*, the beat is still in eighth notes, as before, though a considerable portion of this first bar should contain a beat that is quite passive, so it may resemble a beat in quarter notes at some moments. The beat remains in eighth notes through the end of the first bar of **35**, shifting to a beat in one at $\frac{3}{16}$, with the 𝅘𝅥𝅯 = 𝅘𝅥𝅯 relationship observed precisely as indicated. Reaching the final $\frac{3}{8}$, we return to a beat in three for this one bar.

Antonin Dvorak

Cello Concerto in B Minor, Op. 104

My conversation with C.B. began, not surprisingly, with this work. While he shared a number of very specific ideas that you will read throughout this chapter, he began by talking about his general approach to a new Dvorak collaboration. "This piece more than any other, along with Elgar, is a piece where you have to develop a concept in tandem with the conductor. The first thing I do is to show the conductor all the places I'm going to be with him, instead of him following me, and that's a lot of places in this piece. I like to develop a concept, as much as time allows, and that depends on the conductor's comfort level with that approach. There's a certain amount of dictating, from cellist to conductor, that has to happen, but ideally I like it to be equal … each person giving it [i.e., a cue, etc.] at the same time."

1st movement.

After the conductor and the soloist come on stage before any concerto, the conductor always glances around the orchestra, and then to the soloist, before beginning. I have always done this same thing during the Dvorak concerto, but now whenever I am onstage and about to begin this piece I cannot help but think of a conversation that I had with the wonderful cellist, and my dear friend, Zuill Bailey. Just as we were about to go onstage for a performance of this piece he mentioned that, considering that he was about to sit there for nearly four minutes before playing, it didn't really matter if he was "ready" when I started. Consequently, he really didn't care if I checked in with him before I began. Now, whenever I do this piece with Zuill, I only cast a surreptitious glace in his direction to see if I can get him to laugh. On a more serious note, the lengthy orchestral exposition of the first movement is a substantial orchestral work on its own, and not to be taken lightly interpretively.

As we all know, many of the great concerti have become filled with "traditions" that now seem to be handed down from one generation of conductors and soloists to the next, mostly by experience in live performance and exposure to recordings. And this blind adherence to "traditions" that have little or nothing to do with the composer's intentions inhibits each new generation of musicians from considering a great work with fresh eyes. Much of my conversation with C.B. focused on this idea of getting "back to the score" in a work like this one, and the opening bars of the piece provide our first opportunity for re-evaluation of current practice. The first statement of the theme is often played at a tempo much slower than the following, *fortissimo* statement (at 1). Not only is this not indicated in the score, but the composer obliquely hints at exactly the opposite relationship, giving us a tempo for the opening but then writing *Grandioso* for the second statement of the theme. There is no reason for the opening statement to be paced more slowly than the *Grandioso* statement, and a slower tempo does nothing to increase the mysterious content of the opening of the work. A lower dynamic level and/or a smaller orchestration does not equal "slower"—we all were taught this as children, but sometimes any one of us may have a hard time remembering.

The *crescendo-diminuendo* in the third and fourth bars (clarinets and bassoons) should not be overdone. The zenith of this phrase should not reach more than *mezzo-forte* because this drama is just beginning, and there is considerable narrative territory ahead of us. In bars 7 and 8, the woodwinds should be careful not to imitate this expressive gesture, which the composer indicated in bars 3 and 4 but conspicuously not here. In the ninth bar, there is more than just a difference of dynamics to be observed. The tentativeness and delicacy of the first eight bars is now entirely changed, requiring a color of sound that is expressive and rich with emotion. A slight *rallentando* is natural and graceful a half bar before 1, leading logically into *Grandioso*.

The horn solo (twelve bars after 2) can be phrased in a number of different ways, and different hornists will want to phrase and breathe in different places. In most circumstances, it is best to allow the principal horn to phrase (and breathe) as she wishes at the first rehearsal. This is, after all, a major solo in the instrument's repertoire, and orchestral musicians should be allowed personal artistic expression in such a passage, as long it does not materially interfere with the conductor's and/or soloist's overall view of the work.

In the clarinet and oboe solos that follow, the situation is quite different. Although it would be nice to allow these musicians the same freedom, it is completely impractical considering the *misurato tremolo* sixteenth notes, which must be kept at an absolutely consistent tempo. Violins, viole, and celli should, of course, play this passage at the tip.

After the chord in the bar preceding the first entrance of the solo cello has sounded, and the baton has rested there a moment, the right hand should subtly lift to a raised position awaiting the first note of the cello. This baton position allows for complete calm, but also places the conductor in a position from which he is able to respond immediately. As the first note of the solo is played, the conductor drops the baton for the downbeat, and then cues the *pizzicato* in the celli and basses on the second beat, adding the left hand to this cue for clarity. This process is essentially repeated for the second bar of the passage. The downbeat of the soloist's third bar usually arrives approximately in tempo, but the conductor cannot count on this being precisely so. The soloist's use of the bow in the half note preceding this bar, as well as his/her body language, provides the best information for coordinating the *pizzicato* A-natural with the beginning of the soloist's next phrase.

Both thirteen and fourteen bars before 4, it is imperative that the conductor be familiar enough with the solo cello line that his ear does not get turned around in the repetition of these three-note phrases. The conductor is, of course, listening for the beginning of the downward scale on the fourth beat of the bar preceding the woodwind entrance, and the passage can be made somewhat less perplexing by concentrating on the rhythmic element rather than the repetition of the same three-note scale. A conductor who may have a tendency to get turned around in the soloist's *rubato* would do well to think only of the groupings of four sixteenth notes, rather than focusing on the melodic element. These two bars are a perfect opportunity for an appearance of the "brain/hand schism" discussed in the introduction. All that is required following the downbeat thirteen bars before **4** is for the baton to remain paused in the position of that downbeat, followed by a clear, passive indication of the following "empty" bar, and then a gentle lift of the baton so that the conductor is geographically prepared to indicate the following downbeat and entrance of the bassoons. But, in spite of the fact that these gestures are quite simple, it is not uncommon to see less experienced conductors neglect them altogether, or to have the right hand wander incomprehensibly, because the conductor is so involved mentally in following the solo part. Once the two preceding bars have been calmly and successfully negotiated, the conductor should be careful not to set the tempo at the entrance of the woodwinds too rapidly, as the cello is likely to pull the tempo back somewhat in the next bar. Too rapid a tempo for the woodwinds, followed by a much slower tempo in the solo cello, results in a jarring and disorganized reading to the passage.

C.B. shared an interesting thought about the figure thirteen bars before **4**. To create the most interesting phrasing and musical shape, he suggests thinking about this figure (as he does) as four consecutive bars of $^{6}_{16}$ meter (rather than continuing to thinking slavishly about the actual pulse of the bar) that are then followed by the final eight sixteenth-notes of the passage. He credits Edgar Meyer (with whom he has worked closely) for inspiring this way of thinking about a passage like this one. I can certainly see how, from the soloist's point of view, thinking about this passage in this way will add a certain nonmetric, jazzy sparkle to its performance. But, as I told C.B., I do not necessarily recommend that conductors think about it in this way.

The cello's two-note turn directly preceding 5 has been the subject of questions from students on more than one occasion. The question concerns how the conductor can accommodate this turn, and coordinate perfectly at the downbeat of the following bar, when the sixteenth-note motion in the woodwinds doesn't give the conductor any real room for a sudden change of direction. The concern is quite valid, because if the soloist extends those two notes unpredictably the conductor cannot possibly slow the woodwind scale, and the downbeat in the orchestra could be well ahead of the soloist. The only solution (and it's really not a solution at all) is to listen carefully to this turn in rehearsal, and to slightly slow the woodwind scale during the third and fourth beats of the bar on the next playing if the soloist seems to want extra time in the turn. In addition, I always look the soloist in the eye somewhere near the beginning of this bar, keeping my attention there. This communication is important, as it benignly and kindly indicates, "We're going to play together here, right?" Once this downbeat is successfully reached, a slightly slower tempo is usually set at 5.

Many scores (and parts) reproduce an error in the twelfth bar after 5. The correct rhythm in the first violins is quarter note (E), dotted quarter note (C-sharp), quarter note (B), eighth note (A). A delicate subdivision of the fourth beat of this bar allows for better control while the soloist continues the *ritard* into the first note (A-natural) of the new phrase.

The passage that begins nine bars before 6 presents a situation similar to the one found ten bars before 3. The difference here is that instead of the solo line (which must be played without any *rubato* due to the nature of the *misurato* accompaniment) being played by the clarinet, it is here played by the solo cello. This presents not only a technical challenge but also one of a more sociological nature. If, at the first rehearsal or pre-rehearsal meeting, the soloist insists on playing this passage with any substantive *rubato*, then the conductor might politely remind the cellist that this plan will make an accurate and stable reading of the accompaniment almost impossible. If detente cannot be amicably reached on this subject, then the conductor must choose a tempo for the passage which she believes will allow the soloist to move forward and backward within that tempo, eventually meeting at the downbeat three bars before **6**, where the composer *does* indicate a change of tempo.

In spite of the triplet in the flute on the fourth beat of the first bar at **6**, this beat must often be subdivided (in two parts) to accommodate the end of the *ritard* in the solo cello.

The passage that begins in the second bar of **6** is daunting to some conductors, but simply attuning the ear to follow only the upper voice in the solo cello makes it quite simple. When one attunes the ear to nothing but the first and sixth notes each sextuplet, then the ease of staying with the soloist becomes clear.

Eleven bars before **7**, a slight subdivision is sometimes needed on the fourth beat to accurately follow the solo line during the usual *poco ritard* here, leading into the *meno mosso* that often follows. Arriving ten bars before **7**, coordination between soloist, conductor, and second violins is critical. Achieving good ensemble here depends on the conductor giving a clear, confident, steady pulse for the second violins, despite the more expressive nature of the solo line. If the baton hesitates even slightly, attempting to adapt to the solo cello, then ensemble in the second violins is nearly a lost cause.

Transitioning into the usual *poco più mosso* six bars before **7**, the conductor should be attentive to the bottom tone (C-natural) in the cello that generally acts as a sixteenth-note pick-up to the following downbeat. This de facto sixteenth-note pick-up allows the conductor to accurately set the tempo for the following bar.

In the simple-looking bar eight after **7**, two issues need to be addressed. First, while concerning himself with listening to the solo cello and preparing for the following bar, the conductor needs to be attentive to the horns, leaving the left hand extended to support their sustained chord after the rest of the orchestra plays the downbeat. Second, the baton is best left paused after indicating the downbeat, while the conductor uses only the left hand to indicate the cut-off of the horns on the third beat. Using only the left hand avoids any possible confusion in the rest of the orchestra, and also keeps the right hand free to passively lift just after the third beat, in preparation for a swift motion downward to cue the first violins' unexpected entrance in the next bar.

Six bars before **8**, and in each of the three bars following, the baton should proceed as quickly, but unobtrusively, as possible to the fourth beat, pausing there. By doing this, the conductor is prepared to respond quickly, moving toward the downbeat as the cello proceeds out of the two-note turn at the end of each fourth beat. Each of the three following downbeats (as well as the third beat three bars before **8**) should be dictated sharply with little or no rebound, allowing the chords in the winds to following logically and accurately.

The eighth-note pick-up to **8** is usually dictated at the pace of a quarter note in the tempo that follows. The baton should remain completely at rest (in the third beat) during the cellist's B-flat, and the preparatory gesture does not begin until the cellist releases the B-flat. The final two notes (A-natural and D-natural) are usually taken with repeated down-bows. The "tradition" of playing the eighth-note pick-up as though it is a quarter note in the new tempo sparked another discussion with C.B. about "getting back to the score." (By coincidence, our conversation took place one day before C.B. was leaving for Vail to play this piece [as soloist] with the New York Philharmonic, where he was continuing his practice of removing this and other "traditions" from the piece.) There is, of course, no reason whatever to play this pick-up in a manner other than as written, except that, again, that's just how everyone seems to do it. Playing the passage literally (which also means that the soloist plays the pick-up up-bow) drives the music forward, while this "tradition" drains the energy from the following orchestral passage.

In less skilled and/or less experienced orchestras, the interaction between flute, oboe, and first violins beginning eight bars after **8** will require both explanation and rehearsal. As musicians are, of course, unable to see each other's parts, musicians less familiar with the piece will assume these arpeggios are supposed to be played together, and they will be. Even after the conductor has explained the rhythmic relationship it may take a few moments of rehearsal to make sure that the opposing voices do not accidentally become one unison line.

One bar before **9**, the second and third beats of the bar should essentially disappear from view. This half-diminished seventh chord functions as a mysterious point of transition from one set of musical ideas to another. As such (and whether or not the conductor actually adds additional time to the bar) it should *feel* as though the pulse of the work has stopped, and time itself has been suspended.

Eight bars before **10**, a gentle, expressive *portamento* is appropriate between the G-natural and the C-flat in the violins. This passage is often played *meno mosso*.

In the passage from six bars after **10** through the following *Animato*, the conductor must achieve a delicate balance between two tasks: (1) following the various *rubati* in the solo line and (2) providing sufficiently clear technical and musical leadership for the orchestral celli and, especially, the solo flute. The most common mistake made by inexperienced conductors in this passage is to wait too long between certain beats while waiting to hear what the soloist will do next with the phrase. When this is the conductor's approach, the flutist is essentially left to fend for herself, which is by no means a desirable result. The conductor must be attentive to the various pushes and pulls of the soloist's phrasing, while still moving forward to provide clear leadership for all orchestral musicians at all times, helping to create a unified and musically logical whole. The potential problems in this passage can certainly be described as resulting from the "brain/hand schism": although the solo material here is not complicated, we may nonetheless find the baton not moving forward confidently and clearly at all times, while the conductor's brain is entirely focused on the soloist's musical direction at that moment.

A slight *rallentando* in the bar preceding **11** is common. This is usually not enough to require subdivision, but needing a subdivision to clarify the fourth beat for the flute and oboe is a possibility.

Four bars before **12**, an alternative version of the solo part is most commonly performed. Conductors who have not conducted the work should be certain to acquire a printed copy of this alternate passage in order to be completely prepared for their first experience conducting the work.

For some conductors, coordinating the cello's scale in octaves with the violin entrance on the fourth beat (six bars after **12**) can be perplexing. Although the composer is not specific about this subject, it is best when the first note of the violins coordinates with the solo cello's highest F-sharp in the chromatic scale. For those to whom this does not come naturally, there are several strategies that can be employed either separately or simultaneously. (1) Be sure to know how the soloist bows the scale. Some soloists change bows on or just before the F-sharp in question. When this is the case, watching the bow can help those who may feel insecure about their ability to accurately follow the scale aurally. (2) After the orchestra plays the chord on the downbeat of the fifth bar of **12** ($F^{\sharp 7}/_{\flat 9}$) the conductor must keep F-sharp securely in his ear. This attention to the F-sharp, while continuing to follow carefully the soloist's progress up the scale and, perhaps, the direction of the bow, should easily allow the conductor to begin a preparatory gesture at an appropriate moment to bring the violins in with perfect coordination with the cello scale as earlier described.

After reading the preceding paragraph, C.B. commented that he thought it was surprising that I felt the need to go into such detail about the conductor's responsibility at this point, since, in his opinion, "it's really the cellist's job to make it work." While I appreciate this perspective immensely, it is still important to remember that few cellists with whom one plays this piece have his level of experience, technique, and perspective ... so forewarned is forearmed.

In addition to the aural skills and coordination issues just discussed, there is also the matter of pure technique to be addressed in these same two bars. After arriving at the downbeat of the fifth bar of **12**, the baton should stay paused in that position for a moment. Next, the baton passively marks the following downbeat, immediately moving (with a fairly large and obvious, but still entirely passive gesture) to the left, pausing conspicuously at the second beat. As the baton is now ahead of the soloist (as it should be in this musical situation), the conductor is now prepared to respond immediately to the progress of the chromatic scale, with the baton already in the correct position to initiate the preparatory gesture that occurs on the third beat of the bar.

The passage beginning nine bars before **13** presents many of the same musical and negotiating issues as described earlier regarding the passage nine bars before **6**. The only major difference between the two passages, in this regard, is that the passage before **13** presents fewer challenges because the orchestra is less rhythmically involved throughout.

In the fifteenth bar after **15**, the conductor's beat must stay scrupulously with the soloist's scale, but without inadvertently impelling any activity in the orchestra. Thus, the beat should be precisely in tempo in order to be ready to cue the low brass accurately in the following bar, but without showing any clear *icti* on the second, third, or fourth beats; in other words, this is one of the less common situations, where it is best if the baton stays precisely in tempo but still remains completely passive in character. Any hesitation or falling behind the solo line in this bar will most often result in the conductor being forced to show the following downbeat without proper preparation, and this will most often cause the low brass entrance to be late and uncoordinated with the solo cello.

One bar before *Tempo I*, the winds most often need to see a subdivision on the fourth beat, and sometimes on the third beat as well. The soloist usually places the two-note turn precisely on the final eighth note in the bar. However, the conductor needs to be keenly aware of exactly how the soloist intends to place the turn, and how she intends to bow it. As in some passages earlier in this movement, the final eighth note in this bar, within the *molto ritard*, will usually be roughly equal to the following quarter note.

In my opinion, the final note of the movement should be played as a full, dignified, quarter note (or perhaps held even slightly longer than this). A sudden, abrupt tone at the end of the movement, in spite of the composer's *sforzato* indication, does not seem to me to lend proper dignity to the end of so grand and important a composition. This being the desired result, I show a weighty (rather than a sharp) down beat in the final bar, with no rebound, followed by a clear cut-off.

2nd movement.

In addition to problematic intonation, one of the most uncomfortable possibilities in the opening woodwind passage is the potential for some musicians, particularly double reeds, to play too softly, making a truly beautiful sound nearly impossible. The passage is marked *piano*, not *pianissimo*, and even *piano* in such a case is relative to the size and acoustics of the concert hall, as well as other factors. Extraordinary beauty of sound and stunning intonation are the paramount issues in this passage. The impression of *piano* will mostly take care of itself through the nature of the instrumentation.

The composer's use of quintuplets in the fifth and sixth bars is especially elegant and beautiful. It is very important that the musicians with this figure play it lyrically and accurately. This, as opposed to playing the most commonly heard variant: two sixteenth notes followed by a sixteenth-note triplet.

Unlike the expressive, warm *piano* that we desire from the winds in the first eight bars, in bar 9 the lows strings and clarinets must take on an entirely different character. Here the sound should be extremely *pianissimo*, with a character that is light and transparent.

The third beat of the third and fifth bars after **1** may require a slight, subtle subdivision to follow the likely *rubato* in the solo cello. In the eighth bar after **1**, some conductors make the mistake of adding excessive time to the third beat, believing that they are helping the soloist by "following" him. While a slight bit of extra time may be desired in the third beat, allowing the *diminuendo* to have room and not rushing the phrase generally, in reality the soloist is waiting for the conductor to go on to the following downbeat, trying desperately not to run out of bow in the process.

One bar before **2** (whether or not subdivision of either or both of the first two beats is found to be musically desirable) the third beat must be subdivided for the benefit of both flute and bassoon. After arriving at the second subdivision of the third beat, placing the C-natural for the bassoon, the baton pauses for the *fermata*, and then shows that second subdivision again, as a preparation for the movement downward in the flute and the entrance (or cadence) of other instruments.

Even if the *ritardando* in the fourth bar after **2** is not particularly extreme, the last beat should be subdivided in order to accurately prepare the downbeat for the *tutti* orchestra with sufficient weight and drama.

Beginning in the ninth bar after **2**, asking the viole to play out more than the indicated *pianissimo* helps for a lovely duet between that section and the solo cello.

One bar before **3**, some editions (score and/or parts) show an F-natural in the first violins. This note should be D-natural.

Five and seven bars before **4** it may be advisable to change the dynamic in celli, bass, and all winds to *subito piano*. In this disadvantageous register, it is not easy for the solo cello to be heard clearly when the orchestra literally executes the dynamics given. While I have always asked these instruments to play their written *diminuendi* rapidly in order to get out of the way of the solo line, the request to specifically play *subito piano* came to me in rehearsal from Janos Starker. Whether one instinctively agrees or disagrees, one must consider the source. And, considering this source, it is certainly a request to be taken seriously.

The passage that begins in the fifth bar after **4** is another one that is daunting for some inexperienced conductors. The passage is really not particularly difficult to follow, however, as long as the conductor is properly familiar with the arpeggio figures and can focus her ear to follow only the melodic line in the solo cello that appears at the bottom of the arpeggios.

The "correct" bassoon articulation at **5** is a matter of opinion. Whatever choice is made, however, it should be clearly defined by the conductor for the bassoonist, as this choice is very important to the sound of this entire passage. The composer writes only *semplice*, which really tells us nothing specific about the articulation desired. Most bassoonists default to a rather *staccato* reading which, to me, is rather intrusive on the highly lyrical nature of the lines in solo oboe and solo cello. While this is certainly debatable as a matter of taste, I prefer that the bassoonist play "long dots" as the very shortest possible choice, in order to intrude less on the entire texture.

Four bars after **5**, and in other similar spots, the oboes should play the grace notes on the beat, as this is generally what the soloist does on the following beat. In the event, however, that the soloist makes a different choice, all winds throughout the movement should reflect that same choice in their execution.

Five bars before **6**, on the third beat, many soloists take a significant *rallentando*, often combined with *subito pianissimo*, and the conductor should be on alert for this moment.

In the horn chorale that follows **6**, several issues present themselves. The first and most ubiquitous subject concerns the thirty-second note triplets in celli and basses. Subtle subdivisions are sometimes necessary in the beats where these triplets occur, to be sure that they are executed cleanly, accurately (without rushing or being treated like grace notes), and *pianissimo*. Having read an earlier draft of this chapter, C.B. remarked on this passage, even though the solo cello is not involved. Though he didn't specify, I suspect he felt motivated to comment both because, as a principal cellist, he has played the section part many times and because, as a soloist, he has probably been forced to sit quietly through this passage while the cello/bass part was playing inaccurately. He mentioned (and I concur) that a beautiful, subtle, and accurate performance of this passage is the result of more than brilliant subdividing; it is also the result of all cellists and bassists playing and feeling the phrase with the horns, and participating in the totality of the music-making at that moment.

The other important subject in this passage concerns the phrasing in the horns. There are several possible options regarding where the horns will breathe, and therefore how they will phrase. An important spot for considering this subject is found in the seventh and eighth bars after 6, as this phrase can be played logically in at least two different ways. The first possibility is to play the entirety of these two bars as one phrase, with a breath on the bar-line at end of the eighth bar after 6. Making this choice, the phrase is carried through the resolution of the suspension in the first horn, and some *diminuendo* during the half note will be needed for an elegant phrase. Another choice is for the breath to be taken after the half note, making the quarter note at the end of the bar part of the following subphrase. Yet another possibility is to continue the phrase that began in the seventh bar after 6 all the way through the following cadence, without any obvious, coordinated breath from the horns. This requires clandestine, staggered breathing from the three horns, but it can be quite effective when executed skillfully.

Following this cadence, the conductor waits and gently marks the passing bars during the brief *cadenza*. As the bar containing the entrance of the clarinet and flutes approaches, the conductor should take care not to anticipate the arrival of these entrances. As the cellist approaches the third beat of the preceding bar, the conductor must show great patience so as not to rush, or worse anticipate, the following bar. In this particular case, better a trifle late than a trifle early.

Thirteen bars before 7, some scores have a misprint in the solo part. The upper line should read half note, eighth rest, eighth note, not half note, quarter note. The passage beginning in the following bar and continuing until three bars before 7 is another in which, though the conductor must be extremely attentive to keeping the baton moving precisely in coordination with any tempo variations the soloist may make, constantly waiting and allowing the baton to become vague or uncommunicative is a recipe for disaster. As much as the conductor wishes not to rush or get ahead of the soloist, leadership of the orchestral musicians is equally important, and this responsibility cannot be abdicated simply because one is attentively listening to the soloist.

Beginning at **7**, it usually best to beat entirely in six, as this improves the control and coordination of the viole and celli, as well as aiding in the task of following any *rubato* that occurs in the solo cello in the second and fourth bars.

The grace note pick-ups before **8** are usually played slowly enough that they need to be individually dictated (with the left hand only) for the second clarinet, with the soloist and conductor working as a team of equals, neither one precisely "following" the other. This is another example of the importance of the conductor being highly aware of the soloist's use of the bow at all times. Even though the conductor will most likely lead this passage more than the soloist does, he cannot begin the gesture for the two grace notes until the soloist has arrived at the desired moment to play them.

The five-bar passage that begins ten bars before the end of the movement can easily be conducted in three. Beating again in six is best five bars before the end, allowing the conductor to follow precisely the descending line in the solo cello while providing clear leadership for all woodwinds.

3rd movement.

The third movement generally begins *attacca* from the second movement. In the seventh bar, the *sforzato* in the horns (and later in oboe and clarinets, though it is nowhere near as serious a problem there) should be played, as always, in terms of the prevailing dynamic, *piano*. When this effect is overplayed then this moment becomes nearly a comedy, rather than a moment of mystery and breathless anticipation.

Five and six bars before **3**, it is very effective when the violins' quarter notes on the second beat are played long (with a slight break after each), rather than the safer articulation, played nearly *staccato*.

After all, Dvorak went out of his way to give the horns and violins different values here, so giving the quarter notes their full value seems to better execute his intentions.

The cello scale one bar before **6** can be performed in several different ways. In order to perfectly coordinate both the pick-up to **6** and the following downbeat, the conductor needs to give considerable attention to this scale and its intended execution. Here are some possible variations. (1) The bar is played precisely in tempo, occupying exactly two beats of the former (and following) tempo. In this case, the conductor really has no difficulties all with which to wrestle. (2) The bar is played precisely in tempo, but the scale utilizes three beats of the prevailing tempo. In this case, the conductor must be very careful not to beat three beats, no matter how delicately, as it is quite disconcerting for the orchestra. The baton pauses at one, allows the extra beat to pass, and then gives an energetic second beat to impel the following eighth note. (3) The bar is played in the printed two beats, but with the *ritardando* indicated by the composer. This is the most difficult version for the conductor, but once the soloist's sense of pacing up the scale has been heard once or twice it should not be particularly difficult to follow.

The passage beginning fifteen bars before **8** (at *in tempo*) is often played at a tempo more deliberate than Tempo I. When this is the case, Tempo I is usually restored at the following violin entrance.

The balance problems inherent in the passage that begins at the key change following **11** are obvious. A solo violin, marked *piano*, will, of course, not be heard clearly over the *tutti* orchestra, even though they, too, are marked *piano*. Add to this the solo cello marked *fortissimo*, and it is apparent that the passage cannot be performed exactly as written. The solutions are simple, however. Most soloists know instinctively not to actually play *fortissimo*, though a younger cellist might need a word of advice. In addition, the concertmaster's solo needs to be played at a solid *mezzo-forte*.

Four bars before 13, some sets of parts have a misprint in the (orchestral) cello part. The note should read F-natural, the same printed pitch as the double basses.

Between the trill seventeen bars before 15 and the following bar, it is customary for the soloist to insert a passing A-sharp. This tone usually occupies the space of approximately an eighth note in the following tempo, and the conductor should be careful not to rush toward the following bar without allowing sufficient time for this deliciously expressive moment.

Beginning eight bars before 15, as the tempo continues to slow, the conductor will need to subdivide at some point. Precisely where this subdivision begins depends on the progress of the *rallentando*. Five bars before 15*, the conductor usually needs to dictate the final sixteenth note of the bar for the first violins (with the left hand only) in order to achieve precise coordination between the violins and the solo line. This final sixteenth is usually sustained slightly before continuing on to the next bar. Three bars before 15, each note should be dictated, without haste.

[*In some materials, the first note of the solo part in this bar is erroneously missing the necessary natural sign, losing the critical D-natural throughout the bar in the solo cello. The final note of the bar in the first violins, however, is still D-sharp.]

∽

Edward Elgar

Cello Concerto in E Minor, Op. 85

1st movement.

On a few occasions, a soloist has thrown me a curve of some sort just before we've stepped on stage. For example, just as we were about to walk on stage before a performance of the Beethoven concerto, Itzhak Perlman curtly cautioned me not to drop his violin. I really wasn't giving the possibility of dropping his violin a lot of thought until that moment, but after that remark I could think of nothing else during the entire, interminable walk to the podium. Before his retirement, it was my privilege to share the stage on several occasions with the late, great cellist Janos Starker, who tossed me a knuckleball just before our first Elgar concerto together. When the final sounds of the orchestra's tuning have died away and the stage manager is about to give me the signal to go, I usually say something to the soloist like, "ready?" or, "shall we?" Until that evening with Janos I'd never given that innocuous question much thought, but I've never asked it again without thinking of him. With the hall silent and the stage manager giving me the "go" sign, I asked Janos, "ready?" He turned to me straight-faced, and in his charmingly gruff voice said, "no...." My heart was up in my throat. What was wrong, I wondered, and how do I fix it in the next ten seconds? Before I had even the time to think, he took his first step on stage, looked over his shoulder at me, and quipped, "... but I'm not getting any readier."

After delivering the *forte-piano* downbeat, all that is required in the first bar is to indicate the cut-off at the appropriate time. No other beats need to be shown in this bar, and the second bar is gently marked following the cut-off of celli and basses.

Because Elgar is so specific in placing the breath mark at a point that both follows the wind phrase and precedes the string entrance, three bars before **1**, simply subdividing the second beat and then flowing directly forward to the string chord is not specific enough. After showing the fourth eighth note in the bar, the baton lifts to indicate the breath mark; having made the required space, the baton can continue to the strings on the third beat. This gesture may feel as though the second half of the second beat has been shown twice, because that's exactly what is required to create the space necessary between that subdivision and the third beat of the bar.

The indication *Moderato*, combined with the elegant melancholy of this tune, can lead one to initiate too slow a tempo at **1**. It is not uncommon to hear the conductor indulge a bit in this passage, only to have the soloist take an entirely new tempo at **2**, and this is certainly to be avoided. An average desired tempo at **2** will be around ♩.= 60.

A slight subdivision (of the duple) will sometimes be advisable in the beat directly before **4**. This extra gesture allows the conductor an added measure of control in a performance when the soloist seems likely to take some extra time making the cadence.

The *poco allargando* in the bar before **5** is often more than *poco*, and usually requires some subdivisions in the third beat for excellent accompanying of the soloist. The same is likely to be true one bar before **16**, in spite of the clear parenthetic admonishment "in tempo" covering the entire bar.

In some scores, the bar preceding **7** contains several errors in the celli and bass parts. The two parts should be identical in this bar: dotted half note (E-natural below the staff) tied to a dotted quarter note (with a *fermata*); the dotted quarter note is then tied across the bar-line to a quarter note. Upon examining this bar in some scores, one may find various permutations of missing dots and added rests that make no sense at all.

The indication *tenuto* on the third beat of the woodwind phrase at **7** is intended to indicate a bit of expressive pressure at this point in the phrase, but not any actual "holding" of the note.

The *ritard* two bars before **11** is not indicated until the third beat, but it is fairly common for the conductor to begin pulling the tempo back nearer the beginning of the bar. The soloist often wants to extend the F-sharp at the end of the second beat, beginning her part of the *ritard* at this point, and this feels more logical and organic if there is also a slight pulling back in the orchestra on the first beat. This sense of pulling back usually becomes fairly intense from that point forward, and the first half of the bar before **11** will usually require some subtle subdivisions for clarity, even though the material in the orchestra contains only two notes. With some soloists, the *ritard* in the first half of this bar is so intense that the baton will need to come almost to rest on the first beat, waiting until the cellist is further into the bar before moving forward. In the similar passage two bars before **13**, the indications in the score are somewhat different. This time we have *ritard*, *tenuto*, and *largamente* all on the first beat of the bar. Nonetheless, it is not uncommon for the soloist to begin the process one beat earlier (on the arpeggio preceding the G-natural), and sometimes even this figure will be stretched to the point of requiring subdivisions for coordination with the first violins.

It is fairly obvious that the first half of the fourth bar after **13** must be taken in subdivisions. What may be a little less obvious is what the conductor should do after reaching the *fermata* in the middle of the second beat. After the soloist arrives at the F-sharp on the second beat, the conductor continues forward, still in *largamente*, to the *fermata*. Then, carefully watching the soloist's bow and body language, and judging the intensity of the cellist's sound, the conductor understands when to move forward to the sixth eighth note, in a sort of simultaneous "following" and "leading" scenario. Arriving at the third beat, the piece flows forward again without subdivisions.

Some soloists will take a bit of time in the beat preceding **17**, both delaying the arrival of and elongating the length of the final note in the bar. This choice may or may not involve the need to subdivide the bar for the celli and basses, but those instruments are not those most at risk here. In accommodating the soloist here, if necessary, and making the appropriate technical adjustment to coordinate celli and basses, the conductor needs to be most concerned that the bassoons and horn are not shown the following downbeat without sufficient preparation and breathing time.

2nd movement.

The baton marks the downbeat of the first bar of this movement when the cello strikes the uppermost note (B-natural) in the opening *pizzicato* chord, establishing the *Lento* tempo from that point. The fourth beat of this bar is often subdivided, as are the second and third beats of the following bar. Some conductors will prefer not to subdivide the third beat, but that is dependent upon both the intensity of the *accelerando* and the ensemble skill of the orchestra's strings.

After a respectable *fermata* one bar before **19**, the baton drops sharply to indicate not only the cut-off for the horn but also the first beat of the following bar. In this gesture, which is largely for the lower strings, it is important not to turn one's back to, or hide the baton from, the soloist. After arriving at the downbeat of the third bar after **19**, the motion must be immediately arrested to adapt to the suddenly slower tempo that will be taken by the soloist in the second and third beats of the bar. The baton stops after showing the first beat, flowing passively through the second beat as the soloist enters, coordinating the preparatory gesture with the soloist's *sforzato* half note.

The only general accompanying dilemma in the main body of this movement (following **20**) is one that is rather well known. This possible dilemma principally involves keeping the shape of the cello part always in mind, and not allowing the ear to be fooled into placing each beat one sixteenth note later than is correct. This happens, of course, when the conductor complacently allows the beat to fall with the first of each group of four notes on the same pitch, placing the beat (and therefore the orchestra) always one note behind the solo cello. Even C.B. confessed that, when listening to a student play this piece, for example, he could let his own ear drift into hearing the sixteenth notes incorrectly grouped in this way. More importantly, though, he emphasized the importance of phrasing these bars toward, and then away from, the third beat, so that the shape of the figures feels easy and natural.

The lyrical theme at **22** is marked only *cantabile*, but not *meno mosso*. Nonetheless, it does follow a bar of *poco allargando*, with no instruction to return to Tempo I, so the more luxurious tempo appropriately prevails in this passage. After beating the first bar at **22** easily in lyrical four, the baton stops sharply on the second beat of the following bar. What follows is another, sharply shown "second beat" of the bar, this time in Tempo I, allowing the soloist to find the correct placement for the last two notes of the phrase. Though it is not indicated in the score, the fifth and sixth bars after **22** are traditionally shaped in the same manner, with *meno mosso* in the fifth bar and Tempo I returning half way through the sixth. These same musical shapes and conducting techniques repeat themselves following **27**.

At *animato* (the third bar after **28**), there is no reason not to begin beating in two. There are no ensemble issues here that require a beat in four, and the musical flow of the *animato* is enhanced in two. In addition, this allows for a smooth transition at **30** (in three), even though the preceding one or two bars may have been in four (at *colla parte*). One can return to beating in four at **32**, or not, as one sees fit from both musical and technical perspectives.

3rd movement.

The fact that string mutes are removed, rather than added, at the beginning of this movement seems a bit counterintuitive at first glance. When we look further, however, we see that the warm and expressive sound the composer desires for this music is more easily communicated *senza sordino.* In addition, this creates a beautiful sonic contrast when the opening phrases are (essentially) repeated at the end of the movement, this time *con sordino.*

The composer's metronome marking of ♪ = 50 feels perfect for this music, and most soloists do play the movement at approximately this tempo. There are places where considerable, unmarked liberties are taken with the tempo, and the conductor should be aware of these common practices before meeting with a soloist. The bar before **35**, where the two eighth-note chords are often spaced with great care, completely changing the tempo, is a good example of this.

The placement of *fermate* in the third bar after **40** is a bit ambiguous. The solo cello has the *fermata* on the third beat and the orchestral celli and basses have it placed on the rest following the third beat, all of which makes perfect sense. What is puzzling is that the clarinets have a *fermata* on both the third beat *and* the following rest. This may be an error, or it may be a subtle signal from the composer that the final note of the bar in the solo cello is likely to be sustained somewhat in spite of the fact that no *fermata* or other indication appears there. These subtle incongruities aside, the *fermata* in the clarinets can be sustained for slightly longer than one (eighth note) beat and then released (with the left hand), with the baton still paused in the position of the third beat of the bar, awaiting the soloist's move to the final note and into the next bar.

4th movement.

As tempted as the conductor might be to begin the fourth movement *attacca*, this is really not practical, as the strings must remove mutes before being prepared to begin. The opening passages of the movement do not present any serious accompanying challenges, as even the ebb and flow of the expressive solo lines tend to fall into logical and musically predictable paths. After striking the final chord preceding 44, with hands still addressing the orchestra, the conductor's eyes move immediately to the soloist, allowing the cellist's body language and bow preparation to make coordination at the beginning of the following bar easy and logical.

First-time conductors of this work will want to be wary of the indications *colla parte* and *ad lib.* in the bar preceding 45, as the pace taken by the soloist is likely to be immediately slower by as much as a factor of one half. In this common "half tempo *subito*" scenario, the baton stops on the downbeat, moving to prepare the second chord in the orchestra (in a gesture that is something like a subdivision) only as the soloist plays the first of the two sixteenth notes.

Citing the many *fermate* in this movement like the one in the second bar of 47, C.B. reinforced the importance, to him, that the conductor knows when to lead rather than follow. For him, this isn't just a matter of avoiding "train-wrecks," but, as I discussed in the introduction to this book, a matter of seamless, easy, and elegant music making. Even more specifically, he remarked that if the cellist leads out of the *fermata* in this situation (which is repeated many times throughout this movement) the result will be a musically unintended lengthening of the sixteenth note, the result of the cellist giving the conductor time to respond.

A slight stretching of the phrase is to be expected during the one or two bars before 49. This expressive gesture sometimes results in a somewhat slower tempo being established at 49. Though this is not indicated precisely, this bit of freedom allows the several changes of tempo between 49 and 50 to feel less jarring.

A bit of *accelerando* can be anticipated with some soloists in the three bars preceding 55. This gesture creates a smooth, logical, and almost unnoticeable transition into the *animato* tempo.

Some cellists also take extra time five bars before **59**. When this occurs, it is best for the conductor to follow the soloist's lead and take a tempo in the following bar that is a bit slower than Tempo I. This avoids the discomfort of moving back to Tempo I (four bars before **59**) only to slow down again two bars later. The tempo at **59**, though marked "Tempo I," is often played more ponderously, at a tempo more in the neighborhood of ♩=80. When this slower tempo is taken at **59**, a slight *accelerando* is usually made during the five to eight bars preceding **61**, re-establishing Tempo I at **61**.

The combination of a slightly slower (though unprinted) tempo at **63**, followed by indications of *allargando* and *poco rit.* usually results in a tempo one bar before **64** that is so slow that subdivisions are required. This does not have to be the case, of course, and it is really not what the composer indicates, but it is the most common outcome.

Both soloist and conductor should be careful not to indulge in too slow a tempo at **66**. The composer writes only *Poco più lento*, and gives a metronome marking that matches this idea (♩ = 88). An even slower tempo is ahead (*Più lento*, two bars before **68**), and too lugubrious a pace at **66** dilutes the differences between these two sections. Leading into this *Più lento*, a passionate *portamento* across the bar-line, from E-natural to C-sharp in the first violins, adds a beautiful vocal quality to the phrase, and is certainly not unstylish for this music.

The *rit.* indicated in the bar preceding **74** usually amounts to something more like a *fermata* on the final (orchestral) rest of the bar. After indicating the second beat of the bar without rebound, the conductor then allows the soloist to move to the final eighth note, often sustaining this note (as mentioned) as a short *fermata* before moving forward to the next bar.

❧

Camille Saint-Saëns

Cello Concerto No. 1 in A Minor, Op. 33

In spite of its minor key and tempestuous triplets, there is a playful and youthful quality to the opening passages of this concerto that should not be overwhelmed by too much force in the opening chord. This chord is marked only *forte*, and might be played as one would play such a chord in Mozart or Beethoven, but not as one might in Tchaikovsky or Rachmaninoff. It is important in these opening phrases that the second violins and viole take quite seriously the task of playing exact measured sixteenth notes. When these figures are played haphazardly by even a few members of the section, then not only does the passage lose its rhythmic drive, but it is quite likely that changes of harmony (in the second violins) will not be executed with precision.

Though not indicated in any way by the composer, the secondary theme that begins in bar 59 (seventeen bars after **B**) is usually played considerably slower than Tempo I. This section is usually played at around 𝅗𝅥 = 68, as contrasted with the original tempo that is most commonly around 𝅗𝅥 = 80. Tempo I is re-established at bar 75 (16 bars before **C**). The *Animato* tempo at **C** is usually played at around 𝅗𝅥 = 96, with the strings strictly measured in sixteenths.

While the doubled eighth notes that trace the melody in bars 116 and 117 (the sixth and seventh bars of *Allegro molto*) are played on the string, the scales that follow (in all strings) need the vibrancy and scherzo-like quality of an off-the-string stroke.

As before, a slower tempo is usually employed at bar 178 (fifth bar after **E**). This time, however, the original tempo is never re-established, and the tempo usually continues to slow, to a greater or lesser degree depending on the soloist, throughout the passage, until **F**.

After marking the passage of each of the six bars before **F**, it is imperative that the baton marks (benignly but clearly) the downbeat of the first bar of $\frac{3}{4}$ before moving forward to prepare the entrance of the upper strings. Once again, the issue is not confusion among the upper strings, who will doubtless respond to a clear cue regardless of having seen or not seen the downbeat of that bar. The danger lies in the possible miscounting by other musicians who must enter later. The stylistic challenge in the passage beginning at **F** lies in ensuring that all notes marked *staccato*, particularly all quarter notes and any notes played down-bow, are played equally *staccato*. In such simple music, it is easy for musicians to lose concentration on such details, and just one musician playing one note slightly longer than *staccato* is heard clearly through the texture.

At bar 271 (twenty-seven bars before **G**), neither the winds nor the upper strings are given any specific articulation. These quarter notes are not necessarily *staccato*, though one might intuit this by observing all of what comes earlier in this section of the piece. However, one could just as easily assume that these chords should be played long, as though with dashes, as contrast from the earlier section, justified by the absence of any articulation. Whatever conclusion the conductor reaches, it needs to be explained clearly to the ensemble, or these notes may be executed with a wide variety of articulations.

In the first fifteen bars at **G**, I always ask the violins to bow every upward arpeggio down-bow, beginning in the middle of the bow. In this way, each figure has the same delicate decaying quality. I prefer this result, as opposed to having the figures inadvertently alternating between the quality of decay and that of a slight *crescendo* that may occur when the figure is played up-bow.

In some scores, the new system that begins at bar 333 contains the wrong clef in the viole. Clearly, this is supposed to be alto clef, not tenor. The position of the notes in the staff is correct; only the clef needs to be changed. Several bars later (bar 339 and following), the previous *staccato* string figure is now augmented with *pianissimo* quarter notes in winds on each downbeat. I prefer that these quarter notes have a bit of length, while other conductors like them to agree with the *staccato* in the strings, or nearly so. This is a matter of taste, but needs to be mentioned for reasons outlined earlier. The repetition of the *staccato* theme in celli and basses at bar 346 again raises the issue that every note, whether up-bow or down-bow, must be executed equally *staccato*. Because of the size and resonance of these instruments, attention to this detail by all cellists and bassists, as well as to maintaining a delicate *pianissimo*, is essential.

The new section that begins at **K** is taken in a rather wide variety of *tempi*, and this possible variation means that the conductor often has to decide at the last minute (when meeting with the soloist for the first time or at the first rehearsal with orchestra) whether to take this section in two or in four. It is somewhat ironic, considering contemporary interpretations, that the composer writes *Un peu moins vite*, since a performance where this section is truly only "a little slower" than what precedes it is hard to find. The preceding tempo will have been approximately 𝅗𝅥 = 80, and I have tried on a number of occasions to persuade a soloist to try this section actually *un peu moins* vite (perhaps 𝅗𝅥 = 60) but generally I have no success. All of that notwithstanding, a tempo of 𝅗𝅥 = 40-42 is not uncommonly slow here, and this tempo can be managed remaining in two, with some subtle subdivisions when necessary. In some hands, however, the tempo can descend well below this, particularly in various *ritardandi*, and these cases virtually demand treatment in four for clarity and good ensemble control. As with any decision regarding pattern choice, the best, most musical choice is nearly always to beat in the largest possible value that is technically manageable and effective (in this case, two rather than four, if possible). This principle certainly applies to the present situation, and it is best to stay in two unless forced into four by circumstances beyond one's control.

Though there is no tempo change indicated, the fact that the *Un peu moins vite* passage is usually played as slowly as described above means that an abrupt tempo change must be made at bar 436 (four bars before **L**). I think of this unprinted tempo as *Allegro moderato*, and it is usually played around 𝅗𝅥 = 70. (The fact that there is no new tempo indicated here, when it is clear that this music would be nonsense at the previous tempo, only reinforces the idea that the composer never intended the *Un peu moins vite* section to be played as slowly as it usually is.)

In the *recitative* passage beginning at bar 468 (the ninth bar after **M**), the composer gives the second violins and viole whole notes with two slashes over each note. At first glace, this appears to be a clear instruction to play measured sixteenth notes, but the *rubato* nature of the solo part means that the only workable solution is for these musicians to play unmeasured *tremolo*. (This raises the larger subject of the slash nomenclature during this period. In repertoire from this part of the 19th century, it is not uncommon to see the marking of two slashes through the stem used interchangeably to mean unmeasured *tremolo* or measured sixteenth notes. Therefore knowing that the text may be unclear, we have to use our best judgment, influenced by factors such as tempo, style, and musical meaning, to make a decision in any given circumstance.)

Clearly, it is very important that the chords in first violins, celli, and basses are precisely synchronized with the top note of each scale in the solo cello. For those who find these rapid scales hard to follow, this is another situation in which knowing, and following, the soloist's bowing can be helpful. Most soloists take the scale in two bows, sometimes slurring the final note into the second bow, and sometimes not. Knowing precisely what the soloist will do, and following the use of the bow in addition to the pitches of the scale, can help greatly with coordination, as it is often possible to place the preparatory gesture exactly with the beginning of the second bow of the scale. While knowing, and carefully regarding, the soloist's bowings is also helpful at bar 479 (one bar before **N**), it is important to re-emphasize here that there is no substitute for excellent ear training skills, and this bar amply demonstrates this fact. This bar of chromatic octaves often flies past the eye so rapidly that following it by keeping up with the bow can be, at times, impossible. There simply is no substitute for having the final G-sharp clearly in one's ear before the bar begins. It is also very important to keep D-natural in mind while hearing B-major on the downbeat, as this flatted third will sound where the preparatory gesture needs to be placed.

The passage beginning at letter **O** is often played slightly *meno mosso* as compared with what comes earlier; usually around 𝅗𝅥 = 66. The *a tempo* at bar 526 should bring a return of the mythical *Allegro moderato* from bar 436. Though indicated nowhere, it is entirely logical that bar 552 (twenty-four bars before **P**) is played at the same tempo as the earlier passage of the same music.

One often encounters some *accelerando* beginning six bars before **P**, and particularly two bars later, as the music requires more urgency nearer to the cadence. The composer asks for the tempo at **P** to be *Tempo I* (the opening tempo of the entire work), and it is important that this indication is carefully observed, saving room for the *Molto allegro* that is just ahead. The two bars preceding *Molto allegro* are sometimes given a bit of *accelerando* to create a more exciting, more organic transition. The *Molto allegro* is usually given a tempo around 𝅗𝅥 = 144. In addition, the tempo at **R** is sometimes slightly invigorated with a modest *più mosso*.

⁂

Dmitri Shostakovich

Cello Concerto No. 1, Op. 107

1st movement.

Once the cellist and the orchestra are seated and the soloist indicates that she is ready to begin, I clearly but passively touch the baton to the score, marking the first bar of the piece. Having done this ahead of time, I can now simply wait upon the soloist's pleasure to begin whenever she wishes, lifting the baton (without *ictus*) as the first notes sound and proceeding into the second bar with a small, tight, appropriately sarcastic beat. It is possible, instead, to simply inform the orchestra ahead of time that the first downbeat shown will be the second bar, but this opens up the possibility that someone who enters later than the second bar (which is most of the orchestra) will forget this instruction and miscount the first set of rests, making a missed or tentative first entrance much more likely.

The subtle changes of dynamics following **3** are very important to the forward flow of the music and to providing proper support for the increased intensity of the solo line. With this in mind, the first several pages do not present any balance issues, as the orchestration is rather spare and most of the orchestral playing falls during sustained tones from the solo cello, but a little care is sometimes needed when the winds begin to have *legato* phrases of consecutive half notes (now marked *forte*), as in the sixth bar after **3**. Though there are relatively few winds involved, and the cello is in a high register, one should not take this too much for granted. The seriousness of this issue, or lack thereof, will depend on several things, including the acoustic qualities of the hall, the placement of the winds on stage, and the size of sound produced by the particular soloist.

The two bars in $\frac{5}{4}$ meter, directly preceding **5**, present an interesting analytical, and therefore technical, question. The question presented is, of course, whether these two bars should be taken (in two) as 3+2 or as 2+3. There are good arguments on both sides. The three quarter notes at the end of each bar are clearly a variant of the opening motive. As such, there is logic to having the second beat of the bar fall on the second quarter note of the motive, exactly as it does at the beginning of the movement, beating the bar as 3+2. Though it really should not be part of the equation in this decision, beating these bars as 3+2 has the added benefit of making the following string entrance easier, since it means that the last beat before **5** is equal to a half note. 'Ihe virtues of choosing to beat these two bars as 2+3, on the other hand, are more subtle and subjective. This choice purposely misaligns the opening motive, placing the first of the three consecutive quarter notes on the beat, as if mocking the seriousness of the motive itself. In addition, this choice places the final note of each woodwind phrase on the beat, creating a more dramatically punctuated, and less waltz-like, feel to this motive. The latter of these two options is my personal choice, but neither can really be considered "wrong."

Obvious though it may be, cueing the string section at **5**, with ample warning, is an issue not to be overlooked. The strings have not yet played in this piece, and their entrance follows a passage containing eight meter changes in twelve bars.

Specificity and consistency of articulation are key issues in this movement. It should be made clear that in the string figures at **5** (and all other similar passages, regardless of orchestration) that the quarter notes are played the same length (very short) as the eighth notes. In order to achieve both the desired dramatic effect and a mature variety of articulations, the conductor should continue to be very specific throughout the movement, as much of this information remains unmarked by the composer. For example, the successive quarter notes in passages like the one beginning five bars before **7** are most effective and dramatic when played on the string, *martelé* and not *staccato* and off the string.

Even in a relatively good orchestra, the third and fourth bars after **11** may require a second look in rehearsal, or at least a meaningful "pay attention" glance when someone plays in a rest here, where the string pattern changes. The two bars directly preceding **14** will also sometimes need a moment in rehearsal, as this figure seems to come out of nowhere for the viole and celli, and can be tricky in terms of both intonation and creating an appropriately stealthy atmosphere in such rapid playing.

The conductor may want to avoid any rebound on the downbeat of the bar before **16**, as some cellists take a bit of time in this bar. Though the amount of extra time taken, if any, is usually modest, it is just enough to allow one or two members of the string section to enter early if their attention is not forced to the baton by this rebound-less gesture.

Some cellists will take extra time before proceeding into the downbeat at **30**. Even when this is the case, this does not present any problems since the orchestra is absent for the first four bars of this passage. After delivering the dramatic chord preceding **30**, the conductor can choose, if she wishes, to pause momentarily in that position, gently dropping the baton into the first passive marking gesture only when the cellist has actually proceeded forward.

The first six bars following **32** are another passage where the string figures fall in charmingly irregular patterns, so the conductor should be prepared for the possibility of a few "extra" notes, where rests are printed, in the first reading.

The five bars directly preceding **34** may need some rehearsal, even as simple as they look on the page. A more experienced conductor will see this problem coming a mile away: while the soloist proceeds vigorously in tempo with the repetition of this short motive, the slurred chromatic figures in the violins may tend to drag well behind the beat.

2nd movement.

It is important to note that the tempo given by the composer is *Moderato*, and he further supplies a metronome marking as a guide. I mention this first as a matter of overall tone and meaning, to musically differentiate *Moderato* from indications like *Adagio* or *Lento*. But I also mention this as a matter of musical continuity. It is not uncommon to hear the first fifteen bars of this movement (everything before the cello entrance) conducted in a radically different, considerably slower, tempo than that employed by the cellist at **40**. This opening passage is not the conductor's own personal, emotional wallowing pit, with which he can do whatever he pleases. It is the same piece, with the same emotional content, as the rest of the movement, and its tempo and musical substance should be communicated as such.

In some orchestras, the soli passage in viole between **40** and **42** will need some rehearsal. Though it is not, technically speaking, a difficult passage to play, intonation can be tricky within a section that is not equally skilled from the front of the section to the back.

The issue of balance between the solo clarinet and the solo cello at **42** is one that can be successfully handled in more than one manner.

From an overall musical and textural perspective, the ideal solution is to do exactly what is found in the score: the cello plays *piano* and clarinet *mezzo piano*. Conditions in the hall, among other things, may not make this possible, and not all cellists will be comfortable playing truly *piano* in the register near and below middle C in a large hall. This is not an enormous problem, but it does mean that the dynamics need to be carefully adjusted to achieve the desired musical effect.

One can easily lose oneself in the string orchestra's music between **45** and **47**. Indeed, one should lose oneself if at all possible. The only danger in doing so is if the conductor loses track of the forward motion of the music, as already discussed regarding the opening passage of the movement.

The expressive dynamics in the second violins found in the third and fourth bars after **45** and the second and third bars after **46** are very significant both expressively and structurally. While it is important that the conductor leads and encourages these expressive gestures, it may be necessary to caution other sections not to follow along that same path so that the composer's effect is not spoiled.

The cellist's entrance at **49** often comes at us out of tempo as compared with what occurs directly before it. And this is as it should be, since the first several bars of **49** require a recitative-like freedom from the soloist. Because the first note of this phrase will occur at a moment that is somewhat unpredictable, after cutting off the finale chord in the previous bar the baton should gently and passively indicate the first beat at **49**, with no rebound whatsoever. This choice, to place downbeat in this manner, allows the conductor to respond immediately when the soloist plays the first note of the bar, easily placing the *pizzicato* chord accurately and without undue haste or a sudden, distracting gesture.

In some performance materials, the music for the second violins in the two bars directly preceding **50** is missing from the parts.

At **50**, and following, Shostakovich tells us just enough about his desired articulation in the winds to open up debate. His instruction, *non staccato*, can, of course, mean anything from "play each note full length to the following rest" to "play minimally longer than *staccato.*" On the first reading, this often results in a smorgasbord of articulations. Obviously, the conductor needs to specify precisely what he wants. I prefer something that is clearly long enough to satisfy the instruction, but is by no means full length. This instruction is usually clear enough to satisfy all musicians and create a unified articulation.

At **54**, it is easy to become a bit self-indulgent in matters of phrasing and expression. The composer writes *molto espressivo*, but this is a characterization of the sound he desires, not an invitation to add gratuitous *crescendi* where no dynamic other than *piano* is written. Remaining thoughtfully and expressively *piano* throughout this passage is not principally a matter of balance, however, as the solo cello is playing *fortissimo*. It is a matter of color, texture, and, most of all, meaning. In this passage, the solo cello, supported by the orchestral winds, rages violently, while the strings patiently spin their melancholy air. It is a miraculous moment that, like so many others, is made so in part by doing precisely what a master composer asked.

The placement of the downbeat at **56** is not at the conductor's sole discretion, or at least it should not be. The moment is most effective when this note is placed precisely with the moment of greatest drive in the cello's sound, which means that the conductor should carefully follow the motion of the bow, coordinating the orchestra's downbeat with the release of sound at the frog.

The passage between **57** and the end of the movement is one of the more sonically stunning moments in the composer's output. The combination of the soloist's harmonics, celesta, and muted strings, *pianissimo*, is magical. The key to bringing his sonic vision to reality is the color, intonation, and disciplined *pianissimo* of the strings.

Neither the tone color nor dynamic of the soloist or celesta are particularly flexible here, so it falls to the strings to make or break this passage with their control of dynamic and color, use of the bow, and attention to details of intonation. It is fair to say that the most difficult things musicians do often pass unnoticed, as our goal is to make them look (and sound) easy. This is certainly the case in this passage, as the goal of the strings is to provide a miraculously transparent and mysterious framework for the duet of celesta and solo cello while having their presence hardly noticed.

4th movement.

In the closing portion of the cadenza, the soloist sets the tempo for this movement, and the conductor needs only to join in by marking the first two bars (in one) at the appropriate time. The $\frac{3}{4}$ bar near the beginning of the movement is most elegantly, and least stressfully, handled in one. However, if the four woodwinds in question seem unable to make a secure, correct, coordinated entrance, the conductor may need to resort to beating the bar in three. The first timpani entrance (as well as several that follow) is marked both *coperti* (literally "covered," meaning "muted" or "dampened") and *secco*. The first indication really takes care of the second, but I suppose the composer thought it was better to be safe than sorry. Student players, or other less experienced timpanists may miss or not understand what is asked for here, and the conductor needs to be able to explain the issue and be sure that the correct type of sound results.

The new material at **65** is sometimes taken slightly *meno mosso*. In this case, and depending on how much change of tempo there will be, the conductor may want to continue in one, or may change to beating in two. Either method can work, and the decision is largely a matter of style, rather than technical need. I have usually conducted the section from **65** to **68** in two (returning to beating in one at **68**), regardless of any tempo change, as I find that this gives me more flexibility and variety in driving the rhythm forward, cueing, etc.

The indication ♪ = ♪ at **69** is often not observed strictly. The idea is a wonderful one, but the literal execution of this instruction results in a hair-raising tempo to follow. As is often the case when moving from a faster pulse to a slower one, there is no opportunity in this situation for the conductor to give any preparation that communicates the new tempo precisely. The success of this transition, therefore, depends on three things: (1) the musicians' reasonable memory of this tempo from rehearsal, (2) the conductor accurately reproducing the tempo from rehearsal, and (3) the conductor's ability to transmit clear information via the rebound in the first bar of the new tempo. The adjusted tempo here is usually around bar = 88. C.B. and I discussed this transition and its ramifications at some length. He plays the transition literally, regardless of the tempo created for the $\frac{3}{8}$ passage, and I applaud this approach: it means that the passage is played as the composer asked while simultaneously avoiding the awkward and potentially messy transition I've discussed above. In all humility, C.B. was quick to point out that the composer was present at the recording sessions that resulted in the landmark Rostropovich-Ormandy-Philadelphia Orchestra recording of this piece, and the tempo relationship is not strictly observed there. Nonetheless, he eloquently pointed out the dilemma posed by the availability of documents like this one, saying, "The presence of that recording, as phenomenal as it is in every sense, robs current performers of the opportunity to take Shostakovich at his word."

While there is little of specific conducting or rehearsal technique to be discussed, it is certainly worthwhile to note the extraordinary inventiveness of the orchestral material at **79**. Here the composer transforms the original woodwind motive of the finale into a *scherzo* in $\frac{3}{8}$ meter, in phrases of five bars in length, "accompanied" in four disparate key areas by the rest of the strings. The effect of what appears so simple on the page is riveting, as he transforms the fairly doggerel first version of the theme into a moment of pure genius.

The tempo relationship at **79** is usually observed as written, the previous bar equaling the new quarter note. The only caveat to this strict observance is that the soloist will sometimes add just a bit of *più mosso* to this supposedly equal mathematical relationship in order to keep the tempo from feeling stodgy. This liberty actually makes sense as it relates to the earlier transition, at **69**. If some tempo is lost in the earlier transition, then it makes sense to take it back where the meter changes at **79**.

In the three bars preceding **80**, the bassoons respond to the solo cello with their own statement of the theme fragment. In order to keep this interjection from seeming impotent and draining energy from the piece (the woodwinds being much further from the listener than the solo cello), the bassoons must do everything they can to create the largest sound possible. This is not a "phone it in" kind of moment, but needs to be played with a true and committed *fortissimo*.

The conductor's best instincts will tell her to keep careful track of the soloist's scales and bow changes between **81** and **82** to make sure that coordination with the orchestra remains perfect. While the conductor should certainly not "tune out" the soloist in this passage, the highly rhythmic and disciplined nature of the orchestral material here does not allow for any adjustments if there is a slight discontinuity with the soloist's scales. As will be the case in some passages in nearly every concerto, here it is the job of the soloist to make sure that he remains coordinated with the orchestra, and not vice versa.

Though it is a bit more difficult for the strings, I handle all four $\frac{5}{8}$ bars between **82** and the end of the piece in the same way: 2+3. For the first one (seven bars before **83**), this is entirely obvious and causes no one any stress. It is the three other instances (five bars before 83, and both six and three bars before the end) that might be up for debate. However, I still maintain that it is best to keep them similar to one another, in addition to the fact that there are structural reasons for handling them in this way. The only argument for handling these latter three examples as 3+2 is that it is easier for the strings (and because it is easier for the strings, it may end up being easier on the conductor and the audience). Handled in this way, the strings play their first chord in the middle of the grouping of three but *on* the beat in the grouping of two. This method allows for a greater sense of security and promotes better ensemble in the second chord. However, what's most expedient is not always the right thing to do. (That is true in life as well as in music, but that's not the subject of this book.) It is clear when observing both the beaming in the solo part and the rhythmic values in the winds that Shostakovich heard these bars as 2+3, and therein ends the debate.

Peter Ilyich Tchaikovsky

Variations on a Rococo Theme, Op. 33

At the outset of our conversation about this piece, C.B. mentioned that he no longer plays the Fitzenhagen edition. Like a growing number of soloists, he has played only the original version for some years. Nonetheless, this chapter discusses the Fitzenhagen edition, since it is still the most commonly heard version as well as being the score most readily available to young conductors. Forearmed with this knowledge, it is wise to consult the soloist well ahead of the performance to be sure which version of the work she intends to play.

The introduction (bars 1-21) is conducted in four, as are most passages in the work that are in $\frac{2}{4}$ meter. During the horn solo that ends this passage (bars 16-21), the conductor does not need to be overly concerned that the pulse remains perfectly steady throughout. Quite to the contrary, this passage reflects the dying of the energy with which the piece began. As such, the longer tones are most effective when they feel (to the listener) as if they are without rhythm and suspended in time.

Soloists often take some *rubato* in bars 32 and/or 33. But the conductor should be careful not to make too many assumptions, as some soloists make these expressive gestures in the first repetition of the passage but not the second, or vice versa. Eye contact with the woodwinds, especially the principal bassoon, is critical when approaching the second ending. The violin and viola articulation in bars 42 and 43 is best played as very long dots, as this better matches the remainder of the phrase, which is slurred.

In bar 45, having arrived at the *fermata*, one needs to be aware of the bowing employed by the soloist, as this will give the conductor the proper clues regarding when it is appropriate to begin the preparatory gesture that will provide leadership for both the soloist and the orchestra. In bar 69, after the *fermata*, the conductor must again lead out of the bar, and not follow. Also, when arriving at the *fermata* the conductor's eyes should be glancing significantly at the principal horn, as she has not played in some time, and it is polite to reassure that musician that the time is near.

In bars 96–98, a longer articulation, "dot-dash" with just a bit of space between the eighth notes, helps to carry the phrase and *crescendo* forward. A shorter articulation makes the accompaniment feel too vertical and not musically supportive of the direction of the solo line.

The passage beginning at bar 140 is a good example of a texture found frequently in the repertoire that offers the opportunity for rhythmic discontinuity between orchestra and soloist. The strict rhythm of the triplets in the woodwinds is in stark contrast to the lyrical line in the solo cello. The common tendency in such a passage is for the solo line to take some freedom (even if inadvertently) that will force the woodwind figures to either follow the *rubato* (causing an ungainly push-pull feeling in what should be a stable rhythmic pattern) or be at odds with the solo line in some places. Neither is a good situation, and occasionally the soloist needs to be politely reminded that it is really better for the overall musical effect if the expressive qualities of this beautiful passage are created with color and dynamic, and not with expressive fluctuations in tempo. C.B. commented specifically about this passage, saying, "There's a lot of push and pull, but the soloist has to allow the triplets to remain constant. The triplets are the structure, and the soloist [even considering some *rubato*] has to fit two against three."

Bar 171 is usually best accomplished in six, so as not to rush the soloist. Variation IV is once again in four. C.B. mentioned the fourth bar of Variation IV as a hazard, which it certainly can be. The downward *glissando* that follows the *fermata* is easy to follow if the cellist is dependable and leads with good body language. But if the cellist begins the gesture unpredictably, it is certainly a moment that can, as C.B. so colorfully put it, "drive a conductor to the bottle."

As the conductor's ear follows the soloist in bar 192, it is usually best if the preparatory gesture does not coincide with the fourth beat of the bar. Any significant *ritard* by the soloist here will cause such a gesture on the fourth beat to be too long and uncommunicative to be helpful to the orchestra. A better approach is to give the gesture on the final D-sharp of the bar. While this does not precisely communicate the new tempo, it is much more efficient for creating good ensemble on the following downbeat, and tempo can be established during the following bar without mishap.

A similar situation presents itself in bar 210. However, in this case it is common for the soloist to take little or no *ritard.* If so, then the normal preparatory gesture on the fourth beat will be the most efficient solution.

Due to its melancholy and highly expressive nature, Variation VI is usually taken considerably slower than the main tempo of the work. A metronome marking in the neighborhood of ♪ = 54 is a good place to begin study of this section.

Whether the strings play the *pizzicato* chords in bar 315 *divisi* (taking one note per person, or two with two fingers) or unison (strummed) is a matter of taste, as the composer does not tell us which he prefers. There is a lyrical elegance to the strummed version (if beautifully executed *pianissimo*), but playing the chord *divisi* puts a more convincing, final punctuation mark on the phrase.

Though the composer does not indicate it, there is often an *accelerando* beginning at or near bar 384 and continuing until four bars before the end. As often occurs in such cadential gestures, there is usually a slight lift or breath inserted on the bar-line preceding the last note of the piece.

IV. Other Works

Ludwig Van Beethoven

Concerto in C Major, Op. 56 (Triple Concerto)

I will begin this chapter by making a confession, and it is one of which I am not proud: as a young musician, I hated this piece. I found it long, repetitious, and unsatisfying as musical narrative. I don't know if this was because I had never heard a really compelling performance of the piece or because I was simply not mature enough to appreciate its unique elegance and beauty. Perhaps both. In spite of this rocky start to our relationship, I have come to love this piece over the years, and have enjoyed many satisfying performances with wonderful colleagues. In spite of this love, or perhaps because of it, I can also honestly assess the work's shortcomings. As a more mature musician, I can now reflect more soberly on the fact that, as a younger person, I was not entirely wrong. The piece *is* long, and it *is* rather repetitious. One's relationship with a great work of music, especially one as important as this, has similarities to our relationships with other human beings. We don't love the people who are dear to us because they are perfect; we love them because of their good qualities, their positive effect on our life, and in spite of their shortcomings. As we mature, we may even learn to embrace some of those imperfections as endearing qualities. And, perhaps, we may work subtly to help our loved ones overcome them. Much of this philosophy can be applied to music, and, for me, it certainly applies to this concerto.

A performance of this work lives or dies on the expertise and mature, elegant music making of the trio of soloists and the musicians of the orchestra. This is, in large part, because of some of the issues discussed above. The first sentence of this paragraph may seem an obvious statement with regard to any concerto, but all concerti are not created equal. For example, a performance of the Mendelssohn or Tchaikovsky violin concerto with a soloist who is not outstanding in literally every moment of the piece may not be one's dream evening in the concert hall, but the performance may still have many redeeming qualities, as the works themselves are quite compelling beyond the question of the soloist alone. By contrast, a performance of the Beethoven Triple in which the soloists are anything less than brilliant throughout (both as individuals and as a trio) makes for a very long, rather dreary affair. Consequently, one chooses soloists (or trios) for a performance of this work with great care. Obviously, it is often best to work with a group who plays together as a trio regularly (and, preferably, has played this piece together previously), but sometimes like-minded colleagues who are not a regular trio can come together specifically for this piece and make something wonderful happen.

In this latter case, it is important that the individuals involved approach the piece stylistically in a reasonably similar fashion. Though this can be a bit hard to assess unless one gives each potential soloist a survey of stylistic issues, one can surely know the playing and temperament of a colleague well enough to know if she is likely to be a good fit with other soloists you have in mind. While I have been very fortunate to perform this work with several trios and groups of individuals who created stunning and beautifully organic performances, I have recently, on more than one occasion, re-learned the lesson of being more selective and careful about combining musical personalities (or just personalities) for this work. In one instance (in which I distance myself from the result, as my selection of soloists was not entirely within my control), the trio of soloists was as follows: (1) an excellent pianist with considerable classical era expertise, (2) a fine cellist who was not pushing any particular stylistic agenda, and (3) a violinist of the "old school" in whose deft stylish hands Bach sounds like Tchaikovsky. As you can imagine, the result was, at best, a mixed affair. The trio, when playing together, often sounded as though three different pieces were being performed. Ensemble among the three, usually not a difficult issue in this piece, was very problematic: the pianist tried to keep the tempi clean and stylish, the violinist knew no bar that didn't need some sort of *rubato*, and the cellist tried his best to work between them, attempting to negotiate. I re-hash this dreary story, one that I'd like to forget, only to illustrate in the most ghastly manner possible the realities of the first sentence of the preceding paragraph: unlike perhaps any other piece in the repertoire, this piece lives or dies on the performance of the soloists.

The physical positioning of the three soloists relative to one another, and of all three relative to the conductor, is a subject of considerable importance. This is a matter to be discussed with the trio ahead of time, and not one to be left to the whim of the stage crew, who (except in the most expert of situations) are unlikely to have a clue how to manage the issue properly. The general issue to be addressed is one of "line of sight." The goal is to find a set-up where all soloists have a reasonable line of sight, directly or peripherally, to both the other soloists and to the conductor. When keeping the soloists downstage of the conductor, it is virtually impossible to achieve this goal with complete success. (I mention the subject of downstage vs. upstage only to make sure the subject is covered thoroughly. Positioning the soloists directly upstage of the conductor, between the podium and the first stand of strings, essentially solves the issues I have mentioned. Unfortunately, this choice also causes a considerable number of other problems, including orchestra/soli balance and sight lines for the front stands of strings.) In general, this is usually a matter of choosing the imperfect solution to which the group objects the least. There is, to my knowledge, no perfect solution to this question. If there was, I imagine we'd all do it the same way. Since there appears to be no perfect solution, we have to accept that there are only several different, imperfect solutions, and each unique quartet of soloists and conductor will choose the solution best for them at that time. In the next paragraph, I'll outline three (of the many) ways in which the soloists can be positioned with some comments on the pros and cons of each arrangement.

(1) In the most traditional arrangement, the piano sits in its normal concerto position, with the cellist directly stage right and slightly downstage of the pianist and the violinist (standing or seated) stage right of the cellist. Advantages: the pianist can see the conductor off her left shoulder and the cellist off her right; the cellist can see both other soloists off his left and right shoulders; and the violinist has eye contact with both the cellist and the conductor just beyond the scroll. Disadvantages: the pianist has no eye contact at all with the violinist; even angling her position slightly stage left, the cellist has virtually no line of sight to the conductor and vice-versa; and the violinist, for the most part, only sees the back of the pianist's head. (2) Piano and cello as in #1, with the cellist angling more strongly toward stage left, but the violinist standing stage left of the piano (directly downstage of the cello section). Advantages: the pianist has good line of sight to both the conductor and the cellist off each shoulder, and looks directly at the violinist; the cellist has good line of sight off his left shoulder to both other soloists, but as before, only fair to poor contact with the conductor; the violinist has good line of sight to both soloists and the conductor. Disadvantage: considerable ensemble problems can result with this arrangement, as both

the pianist and cellist may have problems hearing the violin, and the violinist is likely to have severe difficulty hearing the solo cello. (3) Piano as before, the violinist standing stage right and slightly downstage of the pianist, the cellist upstage and slightly stage right of the conductor (between the conductor and the first stand of second violins). Advantages: the pianist has good line of sight to the violinist off his right shoulder and to the conductor off his left; the cellist has excellent line of sight to the conductor and the pianist; the violinist has good line of sight to the conductor and the pianist off her left shoulder. Disadvantages: the pianist may get whiplash looking to such extremes right and left for the two other soloists; the cellist has virtually no eye contact at all with the violinist, and vice-versa; the cellist may go virtually unseen by a considerable portion of the audience seated downstairs (this may be helped by removing the piano lid and giving the cellist an extra tall platform, but even these things are not a complete remedy); the cellist is likely to inhibit the view of some orchestral strings; the cello sound may penetrate to the audience unequally as compared with the other soloists.

R.M.'s comments about this piece ranged from personnel to style to an anecdote about the landmark Richter-Oistrakh-Rostropovich-Von Karajan recording, illustrating that even legendary musicians can have an off day. He remarked, "Don't play it too slowly, it can get so bogged down, and pray for a great cello soloist, or a great principal cellist if that's the route you take." "I played it with Rostropovich's daughter, at their home. Rostropovich told me about Richter in the recording being unable to switch accurately from triplets to sixteenths [in the transition to the coda of the third movement]; he said it took many, many takes … he just couldn't do it." "Do it fast and make it exciting. Be careful of both minutiae and inertia: once the excitement and joy and energy are lost it's very difficult to get everyone re-inspired."

1st movement.

Various portions of this movement are handled best in two and others in four. (I will not even attempt to create a complete guide for this issue, as it would be a chapter unto itself. I will, instead, only mention this subject occasionally, if it seems particularly important. Using one's own good judgment regarding texture, cues, and the rhythmic structure of the music should be a sufficient guide.) The gentleness and grace of the opening figure in celli and basses demands to be conducted in two, with possibly a bit of subdivision for clarity in bar 9. Once bar 11 is reached, a fairly consistent four pattern might be selected if necessary to maintain clarity of tempo. However, the further past bar 13 one moves, the more one may wish to gravitate back toward a more elegant and *maestoso* two pattern, making obvious musical exceptions in circumstances like bars 31 and 32.

At **A** (bar 33), and in other similar passages, strings with the accompanying triplet arpeggiations need to be concerned with uniformity of stroke and ensemble (both are served by staying as near to the string as possible) and dynamic (keeping this rather athletic figure well into the background).

Contrary to what one often hears, there is no reason to believe that the *crescendo* in bar 46 should rise above *piano*, requiring that the following bar be played *subito piano*. On the contrary, it is obvious that the *crescendo* bar (46) serves as a mirror image of the *diminuendo* bar (44) that moves smoothly from *piano* downward to *pianissimo*. Therefore, bar 46 should gently *crescendo* only as far as the *piano* that is reached in the next bar.

Though it appears to be child's play on paper, the first entrance of the solo cello can be modestly challenging to coordinate with the orchestral strings. This is often due to the cellist's inability to see the baton, the cellist's inability to clearly hear the orchestral strings while playing, or both. If both difficulties are present simultaneously, then at least one of them needs to be solved in rehearsal so that this first solo entrance is not stressful to anyone concerned.

Throughout this movement, Beethoven makes use of the soli-ripieno tradition in concerti of an earlier era. Strangely, though, he confines his request for a limited string section to only celli and basses, wishing to thin out specifically the lower end of the texture in certain parts of the score. Another oddity is the wording of his request: *uno Basso e Violonc.* Because he uses an abbreviation for the word for cello/celli, and the dispositive part of the word is that part that's omitted, we cannot be precisely certain if he wants one double bass (*uno Basso*) and one cello, or one double bass and all the celli. Most conductors assume that he means one of each instrument, though some performances do execute this instruction as one double bass and the entire cello section.

For the conductor, one subject that cannot be avoided in this piece is the question of which solo instrument to follow if there is a slight (or not so slight) rhythmic discrepancy within the trio at any point. The basic answer, though by no means catholic in its scope, is that we follow the piano whenever possible. See, for example, bar 138 (eleven bars before **E**). While the cello has the main melodic material and the violin has the musical material of secondary importance, it is clear that the piano creates structure for the entire texture, and is therefore the voice with which the conductor must coordinate if such a choice has to be made.

At **H** (bar 277) and following, woodwinds playing their solo lines at the dynamic indicated are simply wasting their breath. In order to be heard with any clarity whatsoever through the *forte* solo piano and solo strings these woodwinds also need to play a solid *forte*.

The arpeggios in the solo piano at bar 494 are not hard to follow, as they easily outline F major. However, a conductor new to this piece needs to be cautious of the fourth bar of the passage, as there is often a significant *ritard* in the last beat. Here, the conductor's gesture needs to not only account for the extra time that will be taken, but should gently alert the strings (with the left hand, facial expression, and/or body language) to what is coming so that no one blindly moves forward to the following C major chord.

In the meeting or trio rehearsal that takes place before the first orchestra rehearsal, a decision needs to be made regarding the trills in bar 505 (nine bars before *Più allegro*). More specifically, decisions are needed regarding how the soloists will finish the trills, who is leading, and who is following. If the soloists wish to play the two grace notes at the end of the bar fairly swiftly (approximately equal to two eighth notes in the tempo that follows), then the conductor needs to lead the trio out of the trills with a (half-note length) preparatory gesture that the trio can then follow with their grace notes. If, as some trios do, the group plans to linger slightly on each of the grace notes, then the trio guides itself and the conductor follows the logical flow of these two notes. It is often best to begin the following bar in four, as the lack of specific tempo in the preceding bars can cause a lack of uniform ensemble in some orchestras if the new tempo begins in two. A comfortable transition into two can easily follow.

Even though the final passage of the movement is *Più allegro*, and earlier passages at a slower tempo have been conducted in two, this coda is most effective in four. After the first several beats this is no longer necessary for reasons of ensemble, but both the tone and texture of the passage lend themselves to this somewhat more athletic approach.

2nd movement.

As we all know, *Largo* covers a wide variety of tempi, and in this case it leans heavily toward the slower end of the spectrum. A usual tempo for this movement is around ♪ = 36–40. With such a slow basic pulse, subtle subdivisions that do not disturb the basic flow in three, where needed, are important to an elegant and musical handling of this movement.

The opening of the work is marked only *piano*, not *pianissimo* as it is often played. This distinction is of particular importance because the strings are playing *con sordino*, and will already be producing a more subdued sound. The string sound at the beginning (and through most of the movement) needs to remain warm and expressive, never glassy or hollow. Dynamic control and specificity in the opening bars is also quite important because it allows the *pianissimo* halfway through bar 8 to have real importance and meaning. In spite of the strongly classical roots of this piece, there is usually at least a modicum of freedom allowed to the cellist in the opening solo. This is particularly evident in bars 4, 6, and 12. The pianist also sometimes takes a bit of time in the last beat of bar 20, but I try to talk pianists out of this, as I feel that it disrupts the flow of the new musical idea.

A glance at the bassoons for their entrance in bar 29 is polite, as it is easy to miscount or second-guess oneself when the pulse moves this slowly. (This is also true at bar 21 for clarinets and bassoons, and at bar 12 for the second horn.) The second horn also needs clear attention at the end of bar 32 and following. This is not, of course, because he is likely to have gotten lost in the one beat during which he didn't play. It is simply polite to acknowledge for security the individual playing of a non-principal. After the first horn joins, there is often a bit of time taken by the soloists in the final beat of bar 36, and the horns need clear, calm leadership through this moment.

Dynamics, as a function of the desired musical expression, need to be carefully considered and crafted in the passage from bar 40 to bar 43. First, the initial bar of woodwinds must be an absolute whisper in order to differentiate it from the more substantial and expressive, but still *piano*, sound two bars later. This applies equally, of course, to the strings in these same bars. Of great importance, though, is the volume and sound quality of the strings in *forte* at bars 41 and 43. I am fond of saying to both conducting students and orchestral musicians that not all *fortes* are created equal; that the *forte* we want in the slow movement of a Beethoven concerto is by no means the same *forte* we'll desire in a dramatic moment in one of his symphonies, or in a work by a later composer. The *forte* of these string figures should feel like a rapturous sigh or an exhalation of breath that one has been holding in anticipation, and they should not feel like one has been poked with a stick. These ideas about the interrelationship between color, expression, and meaning, at any dynamic level, often need to be communicated clearly to younger or less experienced orchestras.

The length of the note on the first beat in bars 44 and 45 is clear. The eighth note, occupying the same amount of time as the soloist's first two triplets, seems too long to some conductors, and some release it earlier than written. Whatever decision is made, it needs to be communicated clearly and followed up with a gesture that reinforces the instruction. Failing both a clear instruction and a clear gesture, this moment can become a confusion of various string players stopping at different points in the note, as each tries to avoid being the last one still playing.

After marking the passing of the penultimate and antepenultimate bars, the baton gently traces the path of the first two beats of the final bar, with or without some gentle subdivisions, allowing the strings that may not be familiar with the intricacies of the cello solo to easily follow the progression of the bar. The fourth sixteenth-note (beat) of the bar (in the solo cello) is then coordinated with a clear *ictus* as preparation for the *pizzicato* chord that follows.

3rd movement.

Most cellists take a brief pause, as for a breath, after the final triplets of the previous movement, in order to set the bow and cleanly establish the new tempo. When this is the case, the conductor can use the placement of the pause and the cellist's body language as clear guides for the gesture preparing the downbeat of this movement.

The orchestral sound at the opening of the movement needs to be of the most delicate sort, allowing the solo cello to float easily above it without effort. All strings need be playing well into the upper half of the bow.

It is not uncommon for some playful *rubato* to be employed in the solo violin's entrance (third beat of bar 8), and the conductor should be prepared for a downbeat in the next bar that comes slightly later than expected. Other places where this same phrasing is common are bars 33, 61, 126, 151, 254, and 306.

Though it does not look complicated, the articulation in bars 18 and 19 can pose a bit of a problem in some ensembles. The dotted eighth notes are marked *staccato*, but the result is often that these notes are played longer than the sixteenths in the same phrase, and this should not happen. All notes in the phrase should, in my view, be equally short. When every string player is not playing the dotted eighths as short as required, this may be simple inattention to detail, a bowing issue, or both. Addressing the latter subject (the bowing) can often solve much of the problem. By starting the passage up-bow (third beat of bar 18), taking those five notes "as it comes," then placing another up-bow on the third beat of bar 19 (playing down-bow on the last note of the phrase), the tones that are likely to be inadvertently played too long are all now on up-bows, making the error less likely.

Slight accents are helpful on each of the thirty-second notes (first violins) in the passage beginning at bar 49. This helps less expert players avoid the error of accenting the second note of each pair, making the figure sound like an eighth note with a grace note preceding it.

The F-sharp grace note that is found at the end of bar 118 (cello solo) is usually taken with considerable time. When it is played as approximately the length of a quarter note, which is quite common, the conductor follows the cellist's lead. When the cellist prefers the grace note to be the length of an eighth note, or some shorter indeterminate duration, then she must either show the third beat with her body language (so that the conductor can place the preparation at that same point) or allow the conductor to lead by showing the third beat on his own.

There is sometimes a bit of stylish *allargando* on the final beat of bar 170 requested by the violin soloist. When this is so, this is often followed by a tempo that is slightly *meno mosso* as compared with Tempo I of this movement.

The transition into the *Allegro* (bar 333) is almost always simple, as the violin soloist sets the tempo and the conductor follows. Only once has this passage been made difficult for me. In that performance, the violin soloist insisted on playing the beginning of the *Allegro* in tempo and then stopping abruptly four notes into bar 336, playing the triplet and one sixteenth note in that bar before making a pause. After this pause, he wanted to start again with the final three sixteenths of that bar, the orchestra and the two other soloists entering one sixteenth later. Although I found this idea stylistically ridiculous (as did his two soloist colleagues), I told him that I would try to accommodate him, but that I would have to lead, not follow, after the pause, as there was no way for me to catch him and bring in the orchestra with only one sixteenth-note's warning. Try as he might, he could not seem to come back in correctly coordinated with the orchestra after the pause. After trying it the other way, with *him* leading, which was a total disaster, he finally agreed to abandon the idea and simply played it as written. We managed, in the process, to waste ten valuable minutes of rehearsal time and thoroughly frustrate everyone on stage. Though our job is to be accommodating and helpful to soloists, sometimes the correct answer is just, "no."

The grace notes at the end of bar 442 are clearly marked *adagio*, so it is easy for the conductor to follow the soloists' lead. The Tempo I that follows is sometimes taken at a somewhat more deliberate tempo than an actual Tempo I, giving a more *maestoso* feel to the coda of this magnificent work.

☙

Leonard Bernstein

Age of Anxiety—Symphony No. 2

In the preface to the score, the composer offers substantive comments about this work, the poem upon which it is based, and the relationship between the two. Any conductor or pianist who studies this work should, of course, read Bernstein's comments thoroughly. Central among his comments is the explanation that this is not a "concerto," as he constructed the role of the solo piano quite differently from what is found in most concerti. It is out of respect for this explanation that I have not placed this chapter in the section on piano concerti, but in this section instead.

In his prefatory notes, Bernstein briefly outlines the four characters, their interactions, and the events and important ideas in each of the six major sections of the work. This serves well as extended program notes, but no one should consider serious study of this work without first carefully reading the entire Auden poem. It is not hard to understand why this poem so caught Bernstein's imagination, and interpreters of the work owe both the poet and the composer the respect of at least attempting to understand the original source material. Surely, no one would consider conducting Strauss' *Don Juan* without exploring the most important literary versions of that story, or *Pelleas and Melisande* (Schönberg or Faure) without understanding the story from which they are drawn, and this work certainly deserves equal respect and study.

Part I. a) The Prologue.

The clarinet duet that opens the work is marked *pianississimo* and, more to the point, "Echo tone." This expression is the Americanization of an older term used by Mahler and others, "ecoton," meaning the same as "sub tone." What, though, does this mean? And exactly what, other than "play extremely *pianissimo*" is being requested of the player? This is a subject of some debate, as even many fine, professional players of my acquaintance either disagree with one another or find it impossible to specifically define the term. Nonetheless, a conductor should be familiar with the subject, as he will not want to be asked by a less experienced player what to do here and have no answer at all. The best, most coherent answer is that, in addition to being very soft, this particular tone is to be nearly unsupported, and therefore inexpressive and "white." It is very important to the expression of the opening passage that this be accomplished skillfully, or the sections marked *naturale* (play with a regular, supported *piano* sound) will not be sufficiently different in their color and expression.

Three is an appropriate number of players for the section in the bass part marked *la metá*, even if three is not precisely half of the section. The celli are marked "3 desks only" beginning in the third bar after **B**, which means two players per part, violating the cardinal rule that two is the only number of strings one never wants on a single part. "Rule" violation aside, this passage in the celli is so subdued and easy to tune that one can take his instructions at face value.

Part I. b) The Seven Ages (Vars. I to VII).

The remainder of Part I, sections (b) and (c) combined, contains a set of fourteen variations. The first seven variations, *The Seven Ages*, describe the stages of life through which modern human beings progress. These "variations" are quite unusual, however, from a formal point of view. If one searches diligently for the theme that holds them together, one will search in vain. This variation set is novel because, rather than varying one theme in fourteen different ways, as one might expect, the composer introduces a new (or reasonably new) musical idea at the end of each variation, using that new idea as the principal material for the next variation. In this manner, he brilliantly reflects, through the use of form, the narrative idea within both the *Seven Ages* and *Seven Stages* sections: that each stage of life is built on what comes before, rather than being a through line from birth to old age in which our lives carry similar "themes" along the entire journey.

Variation I describes "Infancy," as reflected by the simple statement in the solo piano. The descending harp line, already foreshadowed by the flute in the Prologue, becomes the downward theme in the piano at the beginning of the next variation. Variation II is "Youth," described by the delicate playfulness in both piano and woodwinds, becoming momentarily more dramatic, but only as a child's game. A subdivided pattern is best for the second and third beats of the penultimate bar in this section, *Quasi lento*. This theme of rising fourths becomes the material for Variation III, "Sexual Awakening." Even though the previous bar (*Quasi lento*) was partially subdivided, the entire final bar should have a beat in three, to set the tone and tempo for what follows. The rising perfect fourth motive of this variation becomes ponderous falling perfect fifths three bars before the end ("Broadly"), creating the material for the following variation. Variation IV is "A Clown's Cosmos." Its musical circus imagery illustrates the folly of young men and their irrepressible self-confidence. After arriving at the bar before this variation begins, the conductor should lead with a preparatory gesture, as a soloist proceeding on his own will not allow enough preparation time for the orchestra. As the "circus" music reaches a climax, the composer hints at the following variation's theme in the final beat of the variation, where four sixteenth notes in trumpet, trombone, and first violins become the motive for Variation V. The transition into Variation V, describing "Man as 'Astonished Victor'," must be handled carefully and clearly, as it is quite easy for those musicians who count rests early in this section to lose count due to the initial "G.P." bar. Directly following the final beat of the previous movement, the baton moves clearly, but as passively as possible, downward, marking the empty first bar of the next variation. Because the composer has instructed that ♩ = ♩ as we cross the double-bar (really ♪ = ♪, but the result is the same), the tempo of the beat containing the four sixteenth-notes is precisely the tempo of Variation V. Having marked the G.P. bar passively but in tempo, the baton then lifts (again, in tempo because the G.P. has no *fermata*), clearly cueing the solo clarinet. Each subsequent entrance needs a clear cue (beginning with percussion, then lower strings, etc.), as it is quite easy for any musician to be off by one bar in counting rests despite any explanation given in rehearsal regarding the G.P. Man's "victory" music takes a slightly different form eight bars before the end of the variation, where the figure in upper strings, flute, piccolo, and horns first changes shape and then loses its enthusiasm, creating the theme of the next section. No beat should be given during Variation VI, "The Scars of Time (Man is impotent, aged, successful)." A simple explanation that the next downbeat will be at Var. VII, *L'istesso tempo*, is sufficient. Having so explained, the downbeat in the first bar of this variation, "Death," should be passively indicated before flowing with more expression into the third beat, the cue for solo oboe.

Only the smallest hint, the final, falling half step from C-natural to B-natural in the piano, shows us what the musical content for the final variation in this section will be. The closing series of chords in flutes and clarinets often needs some intonation work, even with very fine players. With the exception of the final C major harmony, all of these chords contain "added" tones ($E^{6/9}$, $F\#^{6/9}$, $E^{\#7}$, B-flat$^{6/9}$, F^9, B^9). Tuning these chords can be a bit frustrating for the players, but some guidance with intonation, as well as help with analysis (which voice has the root, which voice is an added tone, etc.) is usually quite helpful and welcome.

Part I. c) The Seven Stages (Vars. VIII to XIV).

The variations that comprise *The Seven Stages* describe the journey of these four characters through their time together on this one, fateful night. Their personal and spiritual journeys, detailed for us by Auden, are outlined by these next seven variations.

The final bar of Variation VII ends with a breath mark covered by a *fermata* for the orchestra while the solo piano sustains, with the additional indication *attacca*. At the desired end of the *fermata* of flutes and clarinets, the left hand cuts off the winds in a gentle, upward gesture, the right hand moving unobtrusively slightly upward as well, so that the baton is in position to move only downward for the following bar. Both hands remain calm and still in this position, allowing for the breath mark on the bar-line. Next, the baton moves downward in the new tempo as preparation for the entrance of viole and English horn on the second beat of the bar. The melancholy chromatics of Variation VIII describe perfectly, but delicately, this first part of the group's journey, "each isolated in his own thoughts." The waltz of Variation IX, "Pairings, hopeful and not hopeful," is foreshadowed not in its thematic material but with a rhythmic preparation that begins three bars before the conclusion of Variation VIII. Only the falling fifth in the final bar (of Variation IX), A-flat to D-flat, gives us a hint of the material for Variation X, "Travel by Air and Land." The $\frac{3}{4}$ bars in this multi-metered variation can be handled successfully in one or in three. It is preferable to remain in one if the orchestra and soloist can remain rhythmically in sync without the extra beats in the $\frac{3}{4}$ bars being indicated. Though sometimes chaotic on the first reading (no matter how the $\frac{3}{4}$ bars are handled), once a coherent rhythmic flow is felt throughout the orchestra, this variation is not really as difficult as it might first appear. The real ensemble dangers of this passage are found in the solo piano (sixteenth note figures that may rush) and lower winds (the repeated figure containing an eighth rest followed by three eighth notes, at this tempo, is an invitation for poor ensemble). By the time we arrive at the abrupt conclusion, the fundamental motive of this variation, the falling fifth, has morphed almost unnoticed into the shape of the opening motive of Variation XI, "The City Degraded." After pausing for the *fermata* that concludes Variation X, but before the pianist continues, the conductor should unobtrusively, but very clearly drop the baton to indicate the passing of the first bar of Variation XI. By doing this, the conductor is ready to mark the second bar when the pianist chooses to begin. In this way, the marking of these solo bars can be done calmly, without having to "catch up," which can be confusing for the orchestra and distracting to the audience. Even working with such calm and clarity, the cues given by the conductor at, and just after, **V** must be extremely clear and well prepared. (It is also possible to conduct nothing between the beginning of the variation and the pick-up to **V**, but this requires a completely different approach and explanation.) At the beginning of Variation XII, "The Trolley Ride, discussing the 'Big House,'" the composer notes both *Poco più vivace* and ♩ = ♩ so we are to assume the same tempo but a bit faster. This is really not an issue for the conductor anyway, as the soloist sets the tempo from the first note. The tempo remains the same moving into Variation XIII, "In a 'Forgotten Graveyard.'" The only possible difficulty here is that the slurred, *piano* and *pianissimo* half notes in winds may appear a bit late by the time their sound reaches the podium, and it is a considerable problem if this wind sound appears to be behind the rapidly moving solo piano. This melody in half notes, a variant on the previous piano solo but slowed to one-quarter speed, now appears to be a variation of the *Dies Irae* melody, quite appropriate for the subject of this variation. The same beat and basic tempo continue into Variation XIV, "Realization that their world has no meaning, and the dream comes to an end," with the pianist once again selecting exactly how much *Poco più vivace* is appropriate.

Part II. a) The Dirge.

From the beginning of this stunning and very dramatic portion of the work through **3**, it is not incumbent on the conductor to "follow" the figurations in the piano in any way. The Dirge tempo must, by its very nature, remain absolutely constant, and the pianist fits his figures into that framework.

The rhythmic and tempo transition from the end of the solo passage at **6** into the orchestral entrance at **7** should work easily, but this is only the case if the soloist does precisely what the composer asked. The clear intent is that the eighth note pulse in the final bar of the solo slows down to exactly match the quarter note pulse at **7**. (The composer expresses this as [old] 𝅘𝅥𝅯 [at the end of the *allargando*] = [new] ♪, but I find it more useful to think of this exchange as I've expressed it above.) When this is executed as written, the conductor simply gives the preparation on the final eighth-note pulse before **7** and brings the orchestra back in perfectly in tempo. This does not work when the soloist insists on taking a broader, final *allargando*, stretching the final two sixteenth notes, and therefore slowing down below the desired new tempo. If this occurs in rehearsal, or in pre-rehearsal meeting, all that can be done is to politely point out to the soloist the clear musical goal at this point (that the *tempi* should match seamlessly), and hope for a good response.

Part II. b) The Masque.

It is clear to anyone, at the slightest inspection of the score, that this portion of the work can present considerable ensemble challenges. Although the music here involves a number of syncopations and cross rhythms, these are not the principal challenges of the passage. The difficulty here is largely geographic rather than musical. The six percussionists will be together, usually either stage right or far upstage center, the solo bass (in American seating) will be stage left, the celesta and harp could be anywhere depending on the particular set-up of the orchestra (and these two may or may not be anywhere near each other), and the solo piano is, of course, all the way downstage center. Imagining this in its environment, one can begin to see how the coordination of syncopations and other fast and/or complicated rhythms that offer essentially no "elbow room" at all at this tempo can become troublesome. Other than correcting obviously errant individuals, all that can be done about this (other than rearranging the orchestra for the entire work) is to repeatedly and clearly bring issues of late response, late sound, and lack of coordination across the orchestral space to the attention of the musicians in this movement until the group achieves a more coordinated and stylish ensemble sound.

Although it is an extra expense, it may be advisable (in some orchestras) to have a rehearsal of those musicians involved in *The Masque*, preferably with the soloist as well, without the rest of the orchestra. In this way, all issues can be worked out calmly, thoroughly, and without the haste, without the rest of the orchestra sitting and watching. While some may view this extra rehearsal time as an expense that should not be extended, it is also fair to say that this strategy saves money, or at least controls fiscal waste, as the entire orchestra is not sitting idle being paid for the considerable rehearsal time that this movement may absorb.

The largest localized problem in the movement is likely to be the passage at **10**, and others with similar rhythmic construction. The most likely dilemma is the combination of percussion instruments sounding late (by the time the sound crosses the space from percussionists to conductor) and the pianist jumping in slightly early at the exact same points after eighth or sixteenth rests (see the first and second bars at **10**). These two issues, when they occur simultaneously, form a perfect storm, and make nonsense out of the passage, destroying the tight, jazzy feel intended. Again, the only solution is to state the problem clearly to both percussionists and soloist so that all can make the slight adjustments necessary at these critical moments.

At **24**, and in similar passages, the conductor must not become distracted by the tremendous display being put on in the pianist's right hand, but should focus her attention on the left hand, keeping the stick in clear view of the solo bassist for perfect ensemble. As the pianist's right hand is likely to be more sonically prominent than the left at this point, it is a good idea to be sure one is looking directly at the keyboard from the beginning of the passage, in case the sound of the left hand becomes completely obscured at any time. In this way, the conductor's head facing to left (toward the keyboard) and baton to the right (toward the bass soloist), one theoretically sees all, hears all, and controls all.

Just as one is surely fastidiously cueing all members of the small ensemble throughout this movement, the conductor needs to be aware that the rest of the orchestra is not counting bars at this time. In addition to needing the obvious, big cue at the beginning of the final movement, and notwithstanding the fact that the conductor is a bit busy during *The Masque* with more immediate concerns, they need an indication (with the eyes and facial expression) somewhere around **40** that the time has nearly arrived. Without this assistance, the cue for the downbeat of the last movement is pointless for obvious reasons.

Part II. c) The Epilogue.

The entrance of the pianino at the end of the fourth bar needs a clear cue. This is not only for obvious technical reasons, but also because the musician playing the pianino is usually the same one who played the celesta part earlier. This musician has changed seats and possibly re-arranged music in the thirty-three seconds since the last note in celesta, so it is entirely possible that counting rests during the move was not feasible. When a real pianino is not available, a small upright piano will do. It provides the best contrast with the sound of the solo piano if this instrument (the pianino substitute) is fairly well upstage, at a point as far distant from the audience as is reasonable. By doing this, the *fortississimo* dynamic sounds appropriately desperate and frantic without being too present to the ear.

Between **H** and **I**, in the passage featuring solo upper strings, the winds must be extremely transparent in order to allow these solos to be heard sweetly and without forcing the sound. What is a bit puzzling is the composer's decision to indicate *a2* in the viole three bars before **I**. At this same point, both other octaves of the same line (first and second violins) use only one player each. Having two viole here makes no sense to me, and it is a potential intonation problem. I prefer to have the assistant principal viola play the lower line in the fourth and fifth bars after **H**, as indicated, then drop out until the following *tutte*.

I do not indicate any tempo for the pianino solo interjections within the soloist's final *cadenza*. Each time the pianino enters, I only give a gentle cue (one that neither distracts from the soloist nor alerts the audience to the pianino entrance before it happens) and allow the orchestral pianist to play in the correct tempo that she will well remember.

On the bar-line preceding **K**, the entire orchestra observes a breath mark, with the exception of those musicians with a tie across the bar-line. The gesture for the breath should not be the same gesture as that which indicates the seventh beat of the bar. If the composer had wanted the "breath" in all other instruments to coincide with the C-sharp in the lower part of the orchestra, then he would have given them a rest on the seventh beat instead of a breath mark on the bar-line. The baton, with a sustaining gesture, shows the seventh beat; next, the left hand clears the sound for the rest of the orchestra while the baton moves upward. The baton then falls toward the downbeat at **K**. (Even with such clear physical communication and a tie in the part, it is sometimes necessary to explain to some of the sustaining instruments that they are, indeed, to sustain through the cut-off.) At the end of the second bar after **L** there is also a breath mark, and this time it applies to the entire orchestra with the exception of the timpani. Due to the nature of the rhythmic values in this bar, this cut-off can be made on what appears to be the third beat, simply stretching the time of the first two beats, without doing any damage to the desired result. The timpani continues and intensifies its *crescendo* through the empty space created by the breath mark. The same musical result is desired in the fourth and sixth bars after **L**.

∽

Johannes Brahms

Double Concerto for Violin and Cello in A Minor, Op. 102

The complexities of conducting any double concerto are unique. They involve all of the issues usually presented in concerto conducting, but also offer the potential additional complication of negotiating differences of tempo, rhythm, interpretation, and leadership between the two soloists. Unless one's soloists comprise a duo that has played this piece together many times, it is even more important than usual that a significant pre-rehearsal meeting/rehearsal take place. In this way, the many specific issues of leadership, phrasing, and style that are central to successful performance of this work can be largely dispatched without taking orchestral rehearsal time for such discussions. (For further, though somewhat different, discussions regarding multiple soloists, readers may wish to refer to the earlier chapter on the Beethoven Triple Concerto.)

R.M.'s comments on this piece also took on several subjects, including two great conductors and the realities of live performance vs. the more academic consideration of a work. Regarding the latter, his comments highlight the important and delicate balance between our duty as scholars and stewards of the composer's wishes and making a live, modern day performance exciting, inspiring and relevant. "I've done it with Dutoit and Blomstedt. Dutoit had a plane to catch and he wasn't into it. With Blomstedt, on the other hand, it was a really nice experience: [he was] a great colleague who really cared. This [piece] and Beethoven Triple both work better on recording, so it's up to the conductor to make sure that they are exciting in the hall; if everyone is trying too hard things get bogged down. [Advice for conductors in both this work and the Beethoven], don't get too excited about the 'wishes of the composer,' keep it interesting and exciting."

1st movement.

This movement has no real introductory material, but only a forthright statement of the head-motive. This statement ends abruptly, with a purposefully enigmatic quality, at the end of a quarter-note triplet. A tempo of ♩=104 feels natural for this passage. The quarter notes on the third beat of bars 1 and 3 should be mentioned to the orchestra concerning both articulation and phrasing. These notes are often played quite short, and although Brahms does mark the passage as *marcato*, playing these notes very short does not lend the passage a proper grandeur and dignity. It is also important to avoid accenting these same notes, as the emphasis in these bars should be on the first beat, with the third beat somewhat de-emphasized, to create a more shapely phrase. Placing equal accents on beats one and three of these bars creates an unpleasant atmosphere of heaviness and brutality, which is not in keeping with the tone of the work.

It is completely unnecessary to mark the empty bars of the opening cello *cadenza*; it is less distracting to simply inform the orchestra that the next downbeat will be at bar 26. The same is true of the duet *cadenza* that follows, in this case explaining to the orchestra that the next conducting gesture will be at letter **A** (bar 57).

Similar principles of phrasing as were applied in the first two bars of the movement should be applied to the first two bars at **A**. In the fifth and seventh bars after **A**, it is important not to treat each half note as an independent entity, with space after each note. It is best if these notes are lyrically grouped together, along with the note that follows, so that the two half notes always lead logically toward the next bar. Bars 71 through 74 are effectively conducted in two, to emphasize the change of texture and mood, returning to four in bar 75.

One beat before **C**, the motive from the introduction (bars 26 to 30) appears as a more matured phrase. Although Brahms does not specifically indicate it, it is important that the emphasis in this part of the theme occurs on the fourth and second beats, more importantly de-emphasizing the first and third beats (of the first and third bars at **C**).

Though some conductors will already be in two before this point in the piece, texture and mood indicate a beat in two from measures 120 through 125.

There is usually a slight *rallentando* in bar 131, sometimes commencing as early as the end of the previous bar. This is a passage in which the conductor should take particular care, as he is following both soloists while all strings are playing *pizzicato*, so the margin for error is essentially zero.

The first nine bars of **E** are handled nicely in two. Though some conductors continue in two after this passage, I return to four in the last beat of bar 152 for clarity, control, and phrase shape.

Though bar 189 should proceed (through the second and third beats) exactly in tempo, and therefore present no significant problems, it is possible for some discontinuity to occur between the two soloists and/or between soloists and orchestra on beat four. Though the conductor's beat should be gentle and without particular emphasis on the *ictus* during the preceding six beats, beat three of bar 189 should have a sharp, clear *ictus* to allow for good ensemble on the fourth beat. This should be accomplished, however, without the beat becoming too large or athletic in nature, as this may encourage the strings and horns who enter here to play *forte* instead of *piano*.

Four bars before **I**, the string sound needs to be particularly delicate and transparent to allow the exquisite solo writing to soar without effort. Simply *piano* will not do.

Unlike other passages where this same rhythm occurs, the articulation of violins and viole at bars 242, 246, 250, and 252 should be more *legato*. Here, the syncopated motive needs to sing more than it needs to bounce.

In the *tutti* passage preceding **K**, a more elegant and engaging phrase can be created by asking the first violins (last note of bars 265 and 267) and celli and basses (last note of bar 266) to make a slight *crescendo* across the bar-line, thus continuing the phrase with more urgency. The opposite approach, creating a slight break after each tied note, creates a choppier and less dramatically compelling phrase.

During the first eight bars at **K**, the conductor should be mindful that her gestures do not intrude on the general atmosphere of the moment. The beat should remain quite small, with beats two and three of each bar virtually disappearing. All that is required for orchestral precision is a clear fourth beat followed by a clear, gentle downbeat. It is also polite during this passage to indicate with one's eyes, and/or a subtle change of the angle of the baton, which parts of the string section change pitch in any given bar.

The *sforzato* in bar 330 should be, as at all times in all works of music, interpreted relative to the prevailing dynamic. The overall dynamic at this moment is still *piano*, and the volume, weight, and color of sound in this string chord should reflect this fact.

In order to coordinate perfectly with the solo cello in bars 414 and 415, it is important to be aware of what bowing the soloist will use. Brahms marks the G-natural slurred over to the A-natural, but it is not always performed this way. In order to anticipate precisely when the A-natural will occur, and therefore to accompany with precision, the conductor must watch the motion of the bow at least as much as he is listening to the playing. If the soloist performs these two notes in separate bows (up, down), it is a very different matter than if they are performed slurred, as written, and the conductor must anticipate this difference of phrasing and pacing.

2nd movement.

In the first two bars of the second movement, dynamics, both expressive and general, are of paramount importance. In the second bar, Brahms adds six winds and places the horns in a higher register than in the first bar, but this bar is marked *piano*, while the opening bar is marked *forte*. This sometimes needs to be rehearsed and pointed out to the ensemble, as the natural result can often be the opposite of what Brahms wrote.

It is neither important nor necessarily desirable that the listener hears the soloists as independent from the orchestra in bars 3 and 5, and in attempting to achieve this result the orchestral strings would not be able to play *poco forte* as Brahms indicates. As long as the orchestra is not playing a real *forte*, but *poco forte ma dolce* as marked, the solo voices will magically and clearly emerge from the orchestral texture in bars 4 and 6, exactly as the composer intended.

In the fourth bar before **B**, it is sometimes necessary to begin adding some subtle subdivisions, continuing this through one beat before **B**. The combination of triplets in the soli and duple offbeats in the orchestra, combined with the gentle *rallentando* that sometimes appears here, can make accurate placement of the string chords treacherous when conducted entirely in three.

Less experienced conductors should be aware of bars 52, 55, 58, and 61, as they each present a similar potential pitfall. In each of these bars, the solo violin usually makes a *ritard* as the line descends, passing the phrase to the solo cello already in *rubato*. Accommodating this elegant but possibly unpredictable gesture requires the conductor to "float" the rebound of the second beat of each of these bars, accelerating toward the third beat as the cellist (who may choose to expressively sustain the first sixteenth note) begins the sound, but no sooner.

In some editions, *arco* is missing in the viole in the sixth bar after **B** on the third beat.

Four bars before the end of the movement, the baton pauses on the second beat, waiting for the soloists to complete the final two triplets, which are usually taken with considerable *allargando*. For greatest security and clarity, the preparatory gesture for the next *pizzicato* chord is placed with the soloists' final note before the bar-line.

3rd movement.

If the soli take anything more than the slightest *ritard* in bar 64, it may be necessary to make a slight subdivision to clearly cue the orchestral entrance at the end of that bar. Four bars later, as the phrase concludes with the *diminuendo* in viole, celli, bassoons, and horns, the conductor should avoid the temptation to make any *ritard*. The phrase can be nicely shaped using only elegant control of dynamics and color of sound, and anything more than the slightest *ritard* here saps the energy from the beginning of the following phrase and impedes the forward motion of the piece generally.

Seven bars before **C**, the conductor does not need to be in a hurry to show the second beat of the bar. Pausing briefly after indicating the *pizzicato* on the first beat allows the cellist to complete the phrase without feeling rushed. Equally important is the slight bit of breath needed after the cello finishes, before the orchestra returns *fortissimo*. Six bars later, at **C**, Brahms solves the problem for us by beginning the next phrase following a quarter rest. Only the slightest *ritard* precedes *Poco meno Allegro* (bar 297), in order to gracefully acquire the new tempo of approximately ♩ = 56.

Nine bars before the end, it is curious that Brahms places *piano* on the second eighth note of the bar in all parts, as the dynamic at that point is already *piano* (marked several bars earlier in all winds, and remaining at that dynamic in the strings after the most recent ***sfp***). We can only assume that this indication is placed here as a reminder, to begin the following four-bar *crescendo* at a modest dynamic level so that the soloists are not overwhelmed by the orchestral sound before the end of the phrase.

Some soloists take a modest *ritard* six bars before the end, on the second beat of the bar. If this gesture is anything more than infinitesimal, it is wise to show a subtle subdivision in this beat, to make sure that the two *staccato* chords that conclude the phrase in the orchestra are executed cleanly.

☙

Alberto Ginastera

Harp Concerto, Op. 25

1st movement.

Because the composer gives us a dual time signature, the major issue in this movement from a purely technical point of view is the question of which bars will be taken in two and which in three. In most of the movement, the choice is obvious; in other places, it is a bit subjective and certainly open to personal preference. This is so much the case, in fact, that I have not always done each section the same way from one experience with the work to the next. In preparing for a performance that is taking place after considerable time has passed since my most recent encounter with the work, I have sometimes thought differently about the musical needs of a certain passage. In order to dispatch this subject entirely in one location, I will deal with it in the following paragraph in its entirety, rather than piecemeal throughout the discussion of this movement.

The vast majority of the movement is taken in three. With this as a preamble, I will deal here with only those passages that one should, or may wish to, take in two. Bar 35 should be in two, moving back into three with the entrance of the harp at bar 39. I like to take bars 47 through 49 in two, as this is clearly the shape the composer wishes. This decision (bars 47 through 49), however, drives some harpists to distraction, and one may need to negotiate. If one must stay in three for the harpist's sanity and security, then those musicians in the orchestra with moving eighth notes need to make a slight accent at the half bar, emphasizing the $\frac{6}{8}$ structure of their figures. I go into two at bar 132 and return to beating in three in bar 142. My preference is to do what is plainly obvious from bar 146 to bar 149: to alternate between two and three in successive bars. I have never actually done this, however, as I have never had a soloist who didn't beg me not to. In all fairness, this passage is quite difficult for the soloist, and the last thing she needs is to be catching a different meter out of her peripheral vision. Regardless of the disposition of the previous four bars, I am in two at bar 150, returning to three at bar 188. In this passage (150 through 187), there are a number of bars that clearly lend themselves to a beat in three, but here I prefer to stay in a fixed pattern and allow those bars to feel like hemiolas. Two places where the conductor might choose to make an exception are bars 167 and 175. In both of these bars the soloist may feel more secure with a beat in three, and there is certainly nothing wrong with accommodating the harpist in this way.

Proper balance can be a major headache throughout this piece. While Ginastera is quite skilled in thinning out the orchestral sound for the harpist, there are limits to how much sound the harp can make and how little sound an orchestra can make. Negotiating this thin line often occupies considerable time in rehearsal, and it is vital that the conductor have an extra set of ears in the hall that will deliver reliable feedback throughout the process. As I have learned the hard way, it is not a good idea to entrust this task either to an orchestral musician (who does not happen to be playing this piece) or to the harpist's significant other. In the former case, one may not be getting quite the precise feedback one desires. In the latter case, there is the high likelihood that the feedback will contain nothing but "the orchestra is too loud," even when that's not precisely the case. The presence of a trusted assistant or apprentice conductor is always an asset at rehearsal, particularly in a concerto, but in this piece it is vital.

Toward the twin goals of good balance and an appropriately dashing beginning, I ask the orchestra to play a bit more fully in the first two bars, pulling back a bit in bar 3. It may appear that there is no need for the winds, percussion, second violins, upper celli, and basses to make this adjustment, since they always make their interjections when the harp is not playing, but this is not at all the case. The eighth-note interjections in these instruments, though *staccato*, will have more than enough ring to interfere with the following notes of the harp, even in an average hall. Contrary to how things may look on the page, these chords are the major balance issue, not the arpeggio figures in violins and viole.

Bars 44 and 46 can pose considerable balance problems, depending on how much one cares whether or not the harp arpeggios are heard clearly. Even a modest *crescendo* in second violins and (lower) celli will often obliterate the harp sound entirely. The *forte* at bar 47 is, of course, a very considerable problem. Any orchestral playing here that even resembles *forte* will mean that the harp is inaudible. Though it can be very frustrating for the orchestra, the default position for this concerto (particularly in this movement) often ends up as, "play *piano* all the time, no matter what's written on the page, unless I tell you or show you something different."

The looming balance problem between bar 95 and bar 103 is self-evident. All that can be done is to politely remind the winds to keep the *crescendo* to a minimum and to remember that *forte* doesn't exist. Balance in the following passage (bar 103 through 127) works nicely as long as the woodwind solos play a bit more than *piano* and the strings do not get bored and allow their sonorities to continually increase in volume.

To the great joy of most orchestras, they can finally play *forte* beginning at bar 130. Unfortunately, at bar 142 the *forte* in celli and basses and, most likely, the *mezzo-forte* in horns are wholly unworkable, and these dynamics must again be moderated. One would think that the passage beginning at bar 150 would not present problems, but it often does. After all, the harpist is striking the soundboard with the knuckles and fingertips here, so how much of balance problem can it be? The potential difficulty here lies, in part, in how much the harpist desires the knocking on the soundboard to be heard. Though I find this passage delightfully unique, I have always thought of the harpist's figures here as part of the percussion section, and not really a solo role that needs sonic prominence. Some harpists agree with this, and others do not. As one harpist put it to me (quite politely) during rehearsal, "I'm getting bloody here and I'd kind of like it to be heard."

The passage beginning at bar 188, *appena meno mosso* alternating with passages marked *a tempo*, can be a challenge to navigate for the harpist. (Actually, those are the exact words of one harpist colleague who, after reading this chapter, suggested that I address this subject.) The two keys to making these tempo changes less stressful for the harpist are (1) making sure that the baton (or a mirroring left hand) is explicitly within the harpist's line of sight, and (2) being careful that the *a tempo* sections are, in fact, at precisely the tempo expected by the soloist, and no faster.

Contrary to the *cadenza*-like look of the solo passage beginning at bar 229, it is rather unwise to fail to mark these bars for the orchestra. Even a clear explanation to the orchestra that the next downbeat will occur at bar 251 is somewhat likely to result in some confusion and/or insecurity. As I am fond of repeatedly telling my students, sometimes to no avail, one must view a decision like this from the players' perspective, and not from the conductor's. We must remember that it is quite likely that many musicians will find themselves in the middle of a multiple-bar rest at bar 251, forcing those musicians to do extra math on the fly, which is itself an invitation for errors and insecurity.

The solo passage beginning at bar 277 is rather easy to follow, as the melodic line (in eighth notes moving from one hand to the other) is easy to hear in the uppermost register. At bar 283, some conductors will find the solo a bit more difficult to follow. The important and most audible line in the harp still moves in eighth notes, alternating from hand to hand, but the combination of the register and the fact that it is at the bottom, rather than the top, of the texture can deceive some ears. As with all parts of all concerti, thorough familiarity with the part itself will go a long way to making the conductor's job easier. Also, as with piano soloists, watching the harpist's hands, in this case the fourth finger of the left hand, can also provide considerable help and security.

At bar 296, the composer gives a metronome marking of ♩ = 88, but this *Andantino* is usually taken a bit more slowly than that. If the tempo set by the conductor in bar 296 is too fast, the harpist will certainly make a correction in the following bar, as the harmonics can only be played accurately at or under a certain tempo. However, as should be obvious, it would be nice if the conductor simply set the tempo correctly in the first place.

As he does throughout this work, in bars 314 to 317 the composer notates the resulting pitches he desires in the string harmonics, but does not describe the execution. Though all conductors are expected to be thoroughly familiar with execution methods for harmonics, this is particularly important for conductors who find themselves in front of university, community, or hybrid professional orchestras, as it is far more likely in these situations that the strings will actually need on-the-spot instruction in a passage like this one.

As with many other similar passages in the repertoire, bow distribution is quite important, and often overlooked, at the end of this movement. The most likely bowing for violins and viole in the last three bars is simply one down-bow, beginning at mid-bow, placed at the beginning of the three-bar tie. The problem presented by this bowing is that, by the time the beginning of the *fermata* is reached, most players will be on the last couple of inches of bow. When this happens, no real *fermata* (even one that has the required *diminuendo* to *niente*) is possible, and the conductor is forced to release the chord shortly after the harpist's final note sounds. In addition to reminding the string section that their arrival at the last bar is only the beginning of the *fermata*, two solutions, neither one perfect, are most common. First, the violins and viole can begin up-bow, changing to a down-bow *ad libitum* somewhere near the beginning of the last bar, or they can start down-bow but be asked to "recycle" the bow before arriving at the tip.

2nd movement.

At the beginning of this movement, the composer solves all potential balance problems within the orchestra for us, but it is then up to us to actually do as he asked. The celli are marked *pianis-*

simo, and the basses must play fully and expressively, allowing the listener's ear to move immediately to their line. Intonation in this chromatic passage in the basses can sometimes be problematic, and may require a moment's work even with a professional section. This is particularly true regarding the augmented second at the end of the second bar. In bar 10, the baton pauses on the fifth beat, which serves as a cut-off for the second violins and viole, with the left hand still assisting the flute to continue sustaining. Approximately two beats later, the left hand cuts off the flute and the baton then marks the first bar of the harp solo at some point after the soloist continues, thus not visually marring the pause before the solo with any further movement.

Some harpists want the conductor to accommodate what may be a bit of extra time for the completion of the arpeggio in the second half of bar 32. This is, however, to be avoided if at all possible. This is not because one doesn't want to accommodate one's soloist, of course, but because the figures in the celesta make any tempo variation rather awkward.

Repeated figures of widely spaced trills in the strings (bars 42 to 44 and 47 to 48) can be misinterpreted in terms of articulation. There are no ties between the bars, but this does not imply that we want to hear each new bar sounded, whether there is a bow change or not. These bars should sound as though they have ties between them, flowing seamlessly together, no matter what the bowing may be.

The final string *tutti* (bars 51 through 58) is marked *molto espressivo* but also both *pianissimo* and *con sordino*. For reasons concerning these latter markings, neither the strings nor the conductor should interpret *molto espressivo* to mean that gratuitous swells are appropriate. On the contrary, the expressive nature of the passage comes from the sheer beauty of the sound and the breathless quality generated by the sustained, disciplined *pianissimo*.

3rd movement.

Having already subtly alerted the orchestra that the *cadenza* is nearing completion, the preparatory gesture for *Vivace* can be given when the harpist is approximately halfway up the final *glissando*. Though this seems ridiculously obvious, it is strangely worth mentioning that, while being happily lulled into a trance during the preceding *cadenza*, the conductor needs to carefully and specifically consider the tempo to follow. It is quite easy to inadvertently fall into the tempo of the first movement, which is considerably slower than the *Vivace* required here. Even though the first note in the strings is marked *sforzato-piano*, the *piano* portion that follows the first note needs to continue with a sound containing considerable intensity and "bite." This is angular, vicious music, even in *piano*, and it is important to maintain that intensity in both the expression and the sound quality throughout.

The extra beam on the bottom note of the *glissandi* in horns and xylophone (bar 13 and following) is a bit confusing. I assume that the figure is transcribed in this manner as an extra indication of the *glissando*, but it's both unnecessary and an invitation to execute the rhythm incorrectly. Looking carefully at the rests in the beginning of the bar, as well as the note's position vertically relative to the melodic line, it is clear that the figure occupies a half beat (sixteenth note) and not the space of a thirty-second note. These three musicians might need clarification so that this very important figure is executed together and at the correct point in the bar.

There is a discrepancy regarding the dynamics beginning at bar 25. Some materials show *piano* for the strings at bar 25, then *forte* at bar 27, and *piano* again at bar 31. In other (piano reduction and/or orchestral) materials these indications are missing entirely. Whether or not these indications should be there as a matter of editorial correctness, the addition of *piano* for the upper strings in bars 25 through 26 and 31 through 33 is a prudent addition.

During passages containing both angular syncopations and periodic meter changes (e.g., bars 45 through 62), it is particularly polite for the conductor to position the baton (or mirror the left hand) so that it is always within the easy view of the harpist. Though the soloist is coordinating mostly by listening to the orchestra, this bit of security in a complicated passage is much appreciated.

This issue of keeping the baton visible to the soloist cannot help but raise the question, "where does a harp soloist sit?" While the answer is obvious (because the answer is, "wherever she wants to"), a quick overview of the pros and cons is probably in order. I am most used to the harpist being positioned in the normal soloist's location (somewhere just off my left hand, stage-right of the podium). Most harpists with whom I have worked also wish to be in that location because this means that, while playing, the soloist's head is on the same side of the harp as I am. While this is true, it also means that the soloist's head is inclined toward the right (toward the strings) and therefore away from the conductor. Due to this problem of angles and sightlines, some harpists prefer to be on the other side of the podium (my right, stage left of the conductor), because even though this means that the harp is between the soloist's head and the conductor it also means that while looking at the harp strings the soloist is looking the correct direction, i.e. directly at the conductor, through the strings the of instrument.

A passage like the one mentioned two paragraphs above (containing frequent meter changes while always maintaining the same pulse) should be a red flag for any conductors who may have the habit of playing fast-and-loose with the direction of the beat and/or the specificity of the pattern. Without losing musical and rhythmic drive or the general drama of the piece, the pattern must continue to be very specific in such passages, allowing orchestral musicians to have complete security and confidence in every entrance.

Though the overall balance issues in this movement are not quite as serious as those presented in the first movement, the passage from bar 70 to bar 83 will require moderation on the part of the orchestra.

Observing the composer's beaming choices between bar 114 and bar 121, one may wish to beat in two during this passage. There is no compelling right or wrong choice here. It is simply a matter of whether one hears the passage as truly falling into two lilting beats per bar or if one prefers the idea that the passage remains in three with strong syncopations. The question could also be asked regarding bars 126 through 129 and 132 through 133. Though some of the same structural issues present themselves in bars 136 through 139, I never conduct these bars in two, as it makes life very uncomfortable for the soloist, for obvious reasons. I return to beating in two at bar 150, and back to three at bar 170.

The one bar of $\frac{3}{16}$ meter (bar 173) forms an important signpost in the movement, and its drama should be emphasized. To that end, I remove the *piano* portion of the strings' indication ***sffp***, keeping all notes in that bar equally savage, placing *piano* on the second note of bar 174 instead. As the composer indicates by his notation choices in the string parts, all of the $\frac{5}{16}$ bars are taken 2+3.

Even if we have reached an important musical climax, it is still important to remember that *glissandi* in the harp also have a finite upper dynamic level. In the third beat of bar 191, I ask the entire orchestra to mark this note as *forte-piano*, with their *crescendo* beginning from that point.

While it is not difficult for the tom-tom to play quite softly at bar 197, it can be much more difficult in bar 199 and following, as the process of moving rapidly from one drum to another makes a careful *piano* much more problematic. This, combined with the disadvantageous register in which the harp is playing, can present problems. As the harp writing moves higher up the instrument (bar 205, and more effectively at bar 211) this becomes a bit less of a problem. Each brass and woodwind entrance in bars 226 and 227 is best played with a *forte-piano* on the second note, as otherwise the accumulated sound becomes much too intense for the harp to be heard with any clarity, as well as making it difficult to hear wind entrances that follow. The winds can then *crescendo* at bar 230 so that the sense of drama is not ruined because they have remained *piano*. As difficult as it might be for the harpist to be heard between bar 232 and the end, it is hard to justify much moderation in the orchestra, or we risk emasculating the end of the piece. One accommodation that does not do damage to the drama is to ask the strings to begin (at bar 232) less than *fortissimo*, still playing the *crescendo* where indicated. This thins out the texture slightly without taking away the desired force of percussion and brass.

Joaquin Rodrigo

Concierto de Aranjuez

Though it may seem antithetical to the traditional orchestral concert experience, it is usually not feasible to perform this work (or most other guitar concerti) without the aid of some amplification for the guitar. Modern orchestras and, in particular, modern concert halls, being what they are, performing this work with no amplification for the soloist will most often result in an orchestra strangling itself attempting to play softly enough, while the solo guitar is still not heard to the audience's satisfaction. The microphone for this piece is usually placed on the floor, on a very short (4 to 6 inches) stand, just in front of the soloist and pointed upward at the guitar. The level should then be adjusted to give the guitar just enough reinforcement to be able to be heard in reasonable balance with the orchestra, but not so much prominence that the experience resembles a rock concert. This electronic help should be subtle, and is by no means a substitute for careful control of dynamics and balance when the guitar is playing. It is only an aid to make that balance actually possible.

1st movement.

Though it seems tedious and a bit unnecessary, with only the basses sustaining, the conductor should usually continue to delicately mark each bar between the beginning of the piece and the first entrance of the woodwinds. Rodrigo is charmingly enigmatic in his choices of beaming at this point. The bassoons are beamed as though in $\frac{3}{4}$, emphasizing the hemiola nature of their figures, guitar and strings are beamed logically for $\frac{6}{8}$, but the upper woodwinds are really beamed for neither. This issue is not a major concern, but I mention it both as an illustration of the composer's delightfully quirky rhythmic structure and as a caution, lest any conductor consider beating any of this movement in a pattern other than two, which would be quite wrong.

The passage that begins a half bar before **3** is marked *con talone* (at the frog) for the strings, and needs to be played with considerable joy and gusto. This is not a piece for the emotionally stand-offish, and each new sonic and expressive element that the composer presents should be executed with complete commitment: *staccato* must be extremely *staccato*, *spiccato* is flamboyantly *spiccato*, trills and accents played with unabashed bravura, etc.

Neither this movement, nor any part of this particular concerto, presents real conducting challenges on a technical level. Its challenges are those of style, articulation, clarity, ensemble, and, of course, balance. Oddly, the only place in the movement where one could have a coordination problem with the soloist is in the penultimate bar. On paper, it's hard to see why this would be the case. However, some soloists take the slightest *ritard* in the second half of the bar, and this can make coordination with the bassoon something more than a no-brainer. This deviation in tempo is usually so minor that subdividing for clarity is not an option, but remaining in half-bar beats may not communicate quite enough information for perfect ensemble every time. One must hope that the acoustics are such that the soloist and bassoonist can hear each other for added security, and the slight bump of a subdivision on the last eighth of the bar never hurts.

2nd movement.

Achieving the appropriate feel and style for this movement depends on a delicate balance between two opposites: a sense of freedom and improvisation on one hand, and a strict sense of pulse that allows the soloist's "improvisations" to exist within a clear musical framework, on the other. Even though some later passages in this movement may need to be conducted in eight, the opening should always be in four, allowing the English horn to play expressively with the guitar, without the musician feeling that she is in a rhythmic straitjacket. The passage at 1, however, and considerable portions of the rest of the movement, needs some further, subtle assistance for good ensemble and security. This is not the same as saying that the passage is conducted in eight, of course. The beat is still fundamentally in four, but instead of a style that flows directly from beat to beat, each *ictus* is "placed" with a slight pause following, after which the baton lifts to move toward the next beat. This gesture resembles, but is by no means the same as, a subdivided pattern.

This work was among the first ten or twelve concerti that I conducted as a professional, and it was my privilege in that first encounter with the piece to be working with the great guitarist Angel Romero. I wanted, of course, to impress an artist of this caliber with my careful attention to the details of his part and my ability to easily accompany him through the twists and turns of the seemingly improvised portions of the piece. When we arrived at **1** in our first rehearsal with orchestra, I knew I was in for my first real accompanying test in the piece, but the further we got into this section (between **1** and **4**) the more uncomfortable I became, and the more uncomfortable Angel appeared. By the time he stopped playing at **4**, he was looking even more uncomfortable. I couldn't figure it out, because I knew that solo part like my own name and I had every *pizzicato* placed exactly where he was. Even that long ago I tried not to have conversations with a soloist in my "rehearsal voice," since, to me, those are private conversations and not necessarily exchanges that the entire orchestra needs, or wants, to hear. So, I stepped off the podium and leaned fairly close to him to ask if there was something he would like me to do differently in that passage. He was very kind and gentlemanly, and said, "stop trying so hard … you keep the beat and just let me play. OK?" I had "accompanied" him so well that I had ruined the piece. In this kind of music, of which there is not a great deal in our standard repertoire, the goal is to establish a framework upon which the soloist can appear to improvise. The result of my attempt to vigilantly "accompany" him in this passage was a *pizzicato* bass line that, instead of creating an even, pulsing framework, sounded like someone in the early stages of a heart attack. I was so attached to the idea that every note needed to line up vertically that I had overlooked the obvious: this is popular music, and great popular artists will always "back-phrase" somewhat and create a kind of stylish *rubato* that sets them rhythmically apart from the accompaniment for brief periods.

Conductors who tend to be too detail oriented for their own good need to get comfortable with the fact that, even though the solo part is written out note for note, this does not mean that every note will be placed *exactly* where it is written, because to do this will result in a stilted and unstylish performance.

Exceptions to the "just keep the pulse and let the guitarist do his thing" rule occur three bars before **9** and in the analogous musical situation at **9**. In both these bars, the baton should remain still after showing the second beat, allowing the soloist to take some time with the four grace notes that precede the third beat, as most guitarists do.

Three bars before **10** there is a question of articulation in wind instruments that the conductor must resolve. Sixteenth-note triplets in flutes, oboes, and English horn in the latter part of the bar are marked *staccato*, while the similar figure in clarinets, bassoons, horns, and trumpets is not. The absence of dots, plus the curved line over (or under) the "3" that appears to be a slur, often leads these winds, rather logically, to slur their triplets. There are two reasons, however, that believing the composer intended these to be slurred makes no sense. First, the curved line is not a slur; it is merely a grouping mark for the triplet, and it occurs in the upper voices where the *staccati* also occur. Clearly, the upper woodwinds are not both *staccato* and slurred, so the curved line cannot be interpreted as a slur, as some people insist on doing. Second, the figures that are missing the dots occur as part of the same sequence of voices as those that are marked *staccato*, making the only logical conclusion that the dots are simply missing and all voices should be *staccato*.

Two bars before **10**, the whole note(s) in the first violin part contain no indication to *diminuendo*. It seems illogical, however, that this octave is literally to be sustained *fortissimo* to its conclusion, particularly when it would be sounding at the same time as the clarinet that is marked *piano*, making the solo clarinet inaudible. A gentle, natural decay of sound should simply be allowed to occur as the bow moves into the upper half.

Though the composer gives us no clues whatsoever, the tempo at the *tutti* following the *cadenza* (nine bars before **12**) is not the same as that with which the soloist concludes. By the time the soloist reaches **11**, he is usually at a tempo of approximately ♩ = 80, and the following passage often flows, quite conveniently, at around ♪ = 80. In spite of this easy transition, I usually pause slightly on the bar-line after the guitar finishes, rather than launching into the F-sharp minor passage strictly in tempo. Though not everyone would agree, I find that this moment of breath after the guitar has finished adds anticipation and meaning to the dramatic orchestral entrance that follows.

I take a considerable, almost embarrassingly large amount of stretch across the seventh and eighth beats of the second bar of this passage (eight bars before **12**). I find that the passionate move to the ninth of the scale on the eighth beat needs almost a *fermata*. Though this is quite self-indulgent, I figure if you can't do it in this music, where can you do it?

Even though entire sections of violins and viole cannot rhapsodize with quite the same freedom as a soloist, this final statement of the theme needs stylish *rubato* and personal musical input in order to keep it from feeling stodgy next to the soloist's version of the same music. I have already mentioned some (significant) stretch in the second bar is something I advocate and highly recommend. Other touches that help keep this passage fresh and singing are (1) *diminuendo* and a subtle relaxing of the tempo in the first half of the fifth bar before **12**, followed by an athletic *crescendo* and return to tempo in the second half of the bar, and (2) two bars before **12**, a bit of rhapsodic *accelerando* in the first half of the bar, followed by a considerable breath between the two down-bows that follow, using that extra space to return to tempo.

Three bars before the end, even though the soloist may employ some *rubato* that sets the guitar minimally apart from the string orchestra's chords in the first three beats, the conductor will need to pause on the eighth beat, as soloists usually delay the downbeat of the next bar, often considerably. Following the downbeat of the penultimate bar no beats need to be shown: the chord is simply sustained without any sense of pulse until well after the soloist strikes the final note.

3rd movement.

The charming awkwardness of the changing meter, combined with the fact that the first entrance of most of the orchestra is nowhere near a rehearsal number, means that it is entirely appropriate to passively mark all bars from the beginning of the movement. Even doing this, the opening of this movement is sometimes a minefield of lost musicians. Knowing this, the conductor should be scrupulously polite about giving a cue to every section and/or individual of the orchestra at their first entrance of the movement.

Apart from what is mentioned in the paragraph above, this incredibly charming little movement offers virtually no challenges of note for the conductor or the orchestra. The only place that the conductor can get himself into a real jam at this point in the piece is if he forgets to give the English horn player a solo bow when it's over. Though it may seem ridiculously simple, it is easy to forget an important orchestral soloist when a performance, particularly a concerto, is finished. Toward the goal of never appearing to be a puffed-up Maestro who doesn't care about a bow for soloists within the orchestra, I write a note to myself on the last page of every score regarding who should be acknowledged in this way. When I conduct from memory, a note is taped to the floor just upstage of the podium.

Henri Tomasi

Concerto for Alto Saxophone and Orchestra

1st movement.

Even though the harmonies of the first bar are not unusual or complex, Tomasi's orchestration choices can make intonation a bit difficult. The combination of so many voices clustered in such low registers (low strings, bass clarinet, and bassoons) and three woodwinds of unlike timbres in unison on the melodic line (English horn and two clarinets) creates an unusual sonic scenario that may need a few moments of rehearsal.

In the second and third bars, the musical atmosphere requires the violins to interpret the quarter notes written with both dashes and a slur as completely *legato*. We need to hear a gently pulsing attack for each new quarter note, but it is best if there is not space between the notes. In these same measures, the dynamics in all instruments must be carefully observed. Even though it is marked *mezzo-forte*, the solo horn playing *sons bouchés* will not be particularly penetrating, and the hornist should not have to force the sound in order to rise above other instruments that are not playing with appropriate subtlety.

It is important at 1 (lower strings), and again at 2 (all strings except basses), that the string sound is suddenly warm and emotional. The listener needs to perceive the *piano* at 1 as markedly louder than the previous *pianississimo*, but the sound should also be newly warm and expressive, with just a hint of the indicated accent. The same is true at 3 (now including the basses) taking it to the next level in *forte*.

The bars directly before 7 and 8, both marked *cédez*, should be subdivided. This not only clarifies the *cédez* itself, but also allows the accents on the second and fourth eighth notes of the bar to be shown clearly. Despite the *fermata* on the bar-line, the conductor can proceed from the final eighth note to the following downbeat without hesitation, as the time needed for that *fermata* will be taken by the soloist, as desired, before proceeding.

Though it is not indicated, I take a slight pause on the bar-line preceding **10**. I find that this short silence helps to nicely set up the new tempo and mood that follow, rather than proceeding directly. At **10**, the score contains one misprint and one bit of missing information. The lowest percussion line (directly above the harp) appears to be tam-tam, as it remains in percussion clef and no new instrument is designated. However, there should be a treble clef here, and an indication that this line is xylophone from **10** to **12**. One bar before **12** the error is corrected, and the correct clef and instrument name appear. Also, the note on the downbeat at **10** in the saxophone part is only to be played when the cut from **9** to **10** is taken, and this is not explained in the score. One hopes this would never come up, however, as why anyone would take this cut in the first place is a mystery. This brief restatement of the opening material directly before the *Allegro* is necessary to close the opening section of the work, and moving directly into the *Allegro* feels abrupt and awkward.

The new *Allegro* tempo at **10** is marked *env.* (in the neighborhood of) ♩ = 144. While there is certainly no interpretive or orchestral impediment to strictly adhering to the composer's tempo, it takes a considerable virtuoso to play some of these figures cleanly at that tempo. In addition, a slightly more modest tempo adds a certain degree of charm and mystery that flies away at a more rapid tempo. It's been my privilege to both perform and record this piece with the legendary Eugene Rousseau, and even the Maestro himself plays this section at ♩ = 132.

The three beats marked *Suivez* in the fourth bar after **11** can be interpreted a number of different ways. Some soloists interpret this as a genuine *rallentando*, so the conductor must accommodate with the tempo of the orchestra. Others make a genuine *rubato*, not just slowing down but also "robbing" from one part of the bar and giving the time back somewhere else. When this is the case the soloist slows down but then catches up, and the conductor needs to make little or no change in the tempo.

In the passage from two bars before **24** to two bars after **25**, there are several small, but rather important things missing from the score. The following indications need to be added to score (and parts where necessary):

Two bars before **24**	Second violins *arco* on the first beat and *pizz.* on the fifth beat
One bar before **24**	Second violins *arco* on the first beat
At **24**	Viole *pizz.*
At **25**	Viole *arco*
Second bar of **25**	Violins *arco*

The glockenspiel part at **28** is unplayable unless executed by at least two players working together. Even when played by two players, the passage is quite difficult, and the two musicians are likely to be very much in each other's way if playing on the same instrument. Even if technically possible, the result of so much sound, which cannot be well controlled at this tempo, is even more chaotic than this moment really requires. I have always had this passage played on celesta, sometimes with the top voice played on glockenspiel for color. The glockenspiel passage at **32** requires another judgment call from the conductor. The instrument in octaves at *fortissimo* will be quite penetrating, but if that is the desired sound, then so be it. As before, one may wish to consider having this passage played on celesta.

The accompanied *cadenza* (fifth bar after **34**) is a unique and wonderfully mysterious creation. After sustaining the *fermata* on the fifth beat of the previous bar (note that the *fermata* in the harp is misplaced, and should be on the fifth beat), the conductor sets a slightly less hectic tempo, in five, for harp and cymbal. After two or three repetitions of the pattern, the conductor can cease beating through the remainder of the *cadenza*, allowing the harpist to sustain the tempo. Even though it is not indicated precisely, I always ask the soloist to wait for at least two repetitions of the pattern before beginning to play, as this allows the mysterious and meditative mood to be established. In the score, the first note of the solo part lines up vertically with the first note of the harp, but I have always considered this a convenience of transcription, rather than being something that is at all dispositive of the question of when the soloist must begin.

As the soloist begins the last phrase of the *cadenza* (*Lent)*, the conductor should give a warning look to the harpist and percussionist, to let them know the end is near. As the final note of the saxophone dies away, the conductor gently brings the *ostinato* to a logical close, allowing the last note of the harp to linger, without any dampening of the sound.

Rather like the previous *Allegro*, performing this section cleanly at the printed metronome marking takes extraordinary technical prowess. The printed tempo is ♩ = 132, but most soloists take a tempo of ♩ = 120–126. Even this relatively small change in tempo is often just enough to allow for the awkward sixteenth note arpeggios to sound cleanly. At **40**, the *Poco meno* flows nicely and lyrically at around ♩ = 72. Although Tomasi does not ask for this, some soloists begin the *accelerando* back toward *a tempo* as early as the middle of the first bar of **40**. In this way, a longer, more dramatic line is created, as opposed to a more sudden rush back to tempo. The *rallentando* leading into the slower tempo (at **40**) should be only enough to arrive logically at the desired, new tempo. What should be avoided, as always in similar musical situations, is a *rallentando* so extreme that the tempo slows down below what is desired at **40**, and then speeds up again at *Poco meno*.

At **42**, the composer writes only "*Tempo*." Fortunately, he also gives us a metronome marking to let us know that this is, in fact, not a duplication of any of the three most recent tempi. Here he writes ♩ = 146, but if other fast tempi in the work are moderated downward by the soloist, then this one usually gets a similar modification. The modified tempo will often be around ♩ = 132. On the other hand, some soloists who moderate earlier tempi take this one at face value, or very nearly.

Editing out the three bars between **49** and *Lent* is not optional. The composer removed these bars, preferring the version with the *fermata* on the bar-line, and then going straight into *Lent*. These three bars still appear in most scores, artfully scratched out.

In the final bar of the movement, after showing the first beat, the baton should move gently, and without impulse or *ictus*, to the second beat, pausing there. When the soloist moves to the (written) E-natural eighth note, the baton coordinates with this note as a preparatory gesture. This penultimate note in the saxophone will usually be executed within such a significant *ritard* that using the eighth note as preparation still gives the conductor and the orchestra plenty of room for response.

2nd movement.

Clarity, articulation, and ensemble are not the only things about which the conductor needs to be concerned in the opening woodwind passage of this movement, though they are the most obvious issues on the page. This passage will often pose intonation problems that need to be sorted out, particularly in the second and sixth bars, especially concerning the (concert) E-flats and F-naturals. Different conductors interpret the breath mark on the bar-line at **1** in different ways. Some conductors ignore it altogether and some actually stop on the bar-line for approximately the length of a quarter rest. I have done it both ways and have come around to enjoying the quirky and unexpected pause. In either case, but especially if the pause is taken, the oboe and clarinet must be sure to avoid any *diminuendo* as they approach **1**. These instruments are left essentially alone on the last beat and the drama should not diminish, nor the pause be telegraphed ahead of time, by allowing the sound to decay as the line descends.

In some orchestral materials, the trombone parts are missing (in the parts only) from the third and fourth bars after **9**. These two bars should be precisely the same as the two that precede them, with the obvious exception that the final tied note is a dotted half note, not a half note. (Some saxophonists and conductors argue that the error is precisely the opposite from what I have just described: that the trombone parts in the score are in error, and should be removed. However, failing any evidence from some higher authority, I cannot bring myself to agree with this. Everything else about the orchestration of these two two-bar phrases is identical, so I don't see any logic in removing the trombones without compelling evidence.)

At **26**, the *pizz.* indication is missing from first violins, and all strings are missing the *arco* indication in the third bar after **27**.

After a brief *fermata* to allow for the *diminuendo*, the conductor proceeds from the bar before **28** directly into **28**. There is no need for any break of sound on this bar-line. And, for musical reasons, such a break should be avoided, allowing the sound of the trills to blend logically into the beginning of the next phrase. This passage, from **28** to **31**, is often played at a more moderate tempo than what is directly before, perhaps ♩ = 100. This allows the "whirling" triplet passage to have its necessary charm without feeling rushed, and also gives weight to the music at **29**. The bar that closes this passage, one bar before **32**, should be beaten in eight. Flutes and clarinets often need a reminder that this is *pianissimo* and *mysterioso*. The bi-tonal harmony sometimes elicits an increase of volume and lack of attention to color and expression, as individuals struggle with intonation.

The composer's indication of 𝅗𝅥 = 80 works perfectly at **32**. The conductor must show discipline about setting this tempo, however, as the relative simplicity of the orchestral texture in the first four bars can lead one to overshoot the tempo. Once this happens, the soloist is stuck with a tempo at which the complicated saxophone figures that follow may not be playable as one would like. Between **38** and **40**, the conductor needs to keep a sharp ear for any tendency in bassoons, low brass, and also trumpets, to be chronically behind the beat as compared with the rhythmic position of strings, harp, etc. The nature of the instruments (for low brass), the musical material, and the distance from the podium makes this slight disconnect fairly common in the first rehearsal, and it needs be addressed immediately. In the second bar after **38**, the *arco* indication is missing in celli and basses.

The tempo indicated at **40**, ♩ = 144, is blindingly fast by the standard of most saxophonists. While a performance at or near this tempo is very exciting when done well, conductors who are performing this work for the first time should be aware that a tempo of ♩ = 112–126 is more likely to be requested. It is not so much the solo figures at **40** that are at issue regarding tempo selection, but those just following **42**. Looking forward, at **45** we have the indication to begin an *accelerando* through **47** (*pressez légérement jusqu'á* **47**), so a more modest tempo that may be chosen at **40** can be made up for here.

At **42**, *arco* is missing from the second violins, and *pizz.* is missing from viole and celli. At **46**, the change back to alto clef is missing (in the score) from the viole, and *arco* is missing in the celli.

While no soloist with whom I'm familiar actually omits the passage from **47** to **49**, there is a clear indication in the score (at **47**) that the *fermata* on the bar-line is only to be observed if one does, in fact, take the cut. Nonetheless, most conductors, including me, make this brief pause on the bar-line to better set up the following passage, in direct opposition to the instructions. When this pause is observed without making the cut, violins, viole, and solo saxophone should still omit the note on the downbeat of **47**, since this note only makes sense when played as the conclusion of the previous phrase, without a pause on the bar-line.

Depending upon the desired degree of *rallentando*, one or both bars at **48** will be conducted in eight. After indicating the first beat of the final bar, the baton moves passively to the second beat, pausing there. Once the conductor hears the first note of the final arpeggio in the saxophone, the baton moves to begin the preparatory gesture for the final chord.

William Walton

Concerto for Viola and Orchestra (1962 Version)

1st movement.

The opening duet between (orchestral) viole and first violins is marked *forte* and *espressivo*, but *con sord.* This seeming contrast (which is not really a contrast at all) lends a unique hyper expressivity to this opening passage, but only if these lines are truly played *forte* as the composer asked. It is all too common to hear these lines played shyly, and this not only defeats the composer's goal in creating a unique sonic environment, but also allows far too little room for the following *diminuendo* to *pianissimo*.

The basic *tempi* of this movement are quite manageable in dotted quarter-note beats, and subdivisions should only be needed for *ritardandi*, etc. It is common for the tempo to take on a bit more liveliness, perhaps ♩. = 56–60, at **1**.

Some soloists want the tempo to push forward again at **3**, but this is unnecessary and rather contrary to the composer's ideas at that point. After all, Walton increases the fundamental rhythmic motion (in the solo viola) by 100 percent (moving from basic motion in eighth notes to motion in sixteenths), so there is no logic in increasing the tempo as well.

The soloist will pull back the tempo, as marked, four bars before **4** (and not always *ritmico*, as indicated). There is, however, no need to subdivide in this bar or either of the following two bars, as one might be tempted to do. The majority of the *allargando* will probably be taken on the third beat (four bars before **4**), so the baton should pause on that beat, waiting for the soloist to complete all three eighth notes. When the violist reaches the final eighth note of the third beat, a quick preparation leads to the harp entrance on the fourth beat, with the baton also pausing slightly there. Again, when the soloist sounds the final note of the bar, the conductor moves forward to the first beat of the following bar. The baton then pauses slightly on this downbeat, rather than flowing through it, repeating the same process on each beat of this and the next bar, to allow for maximum physical control and musical flexibility. The last bar before **4** should be taken in six, as this allows for complete control of the *rallentando*, but also makes the following transition quite easy. The beat then moves at essentially the same tempo both before and after the bar-line, with the $\frac{3}{2}$ meter being taken in six, following the composer's instruction of (old) eighth note equals (new) quarter note.

A look toward the second horn, followed by cues for bassoon, trombones, and harp, is always appreciated five and six bars after **4**, since it has been a while since any of these musicians have played.

A bit less information, or perhaps just differently worded information, would have been helpful when we arrive at the three bars of $\frac{7}{4}$ meter. When introducing a passage with unusual or mixed meters, it is always a helpful gesture when the composer tells us plainly his thoughts regarding the rhythmic construction of the bar. But these bars are not one bar of $\frac{3}{4}$ followed by one bar of $\frac{4}{4}$, as the parenthetic note attempts to explain. While it is helpful that the composer told us what musical shape he intended for these bars, this is not to be taken literally. These are simply bars that are to be divided 3+2+2, and this explanation would have made things simpler and clearer. Anyone who actually beats these bars as one measure of $\frac{3}{4}$ and one of $\frac{4}{4}$, using the traditional patterns for those meters, is courting confusion in the orchestra, no matter what explanation is given ahead of time.

In the second bar after **5**, if the soloist lingers considerably over the sextuplet on the final beat then subdividing this beat (into two eighth notes) may be necessary. This is not, however, particularly common, and most soloists take only as much time as can be easily accommodated with the conductor remaining in a quarter-note beat.

The instruction *risoluto* in the bar preceding **7** does not necessarily have any effect on the tempo of this bar. On the contrary, it is most likely placed here to discourage the conductor from any radical shift of tempo. While the written instruction may imply a certain "stiff upper lip" approach to this bar, that will only shade the tempo downward by two to four metronome points, at the most.

Intonation can be tricky in the four bars preceding **10**, particularly as it applies to the relationship between the E-sharp in the celli and basses contrasted with the E-natural in the solo viola (four bars before **10**), and the opposite relationship two bars later. It is not uncommon to see cellists and bassists who may be unfamiliar with the complete harmonic context puzzling over how to play in tune with the soloist, when the goal is solely to play in tune with their own sections.

In the passage of shifting tempi that follows **10**, the conductor faces a delicate challenge in each of the first eight bars. Fortunately, each two-bar phrase is nearly a technical repetition of what comes before it, so once the problem is solved in the first two bars it is essentially solved for the entire passage. The first issue here is to coordinate the figure in the first bar between soloist and orchestral strings. The success or failure of this is, in each separate case, entirely dependent on understanding what the soloist will do in the last several sixteenth notes of the preceding bar. Contrary to what I said above, suggesting that "once it's solved, it's solved," the four approaches to this figure will probably not be identical to one another. If the soloist's *ritard* in one instance is fairly modest, then the preparation can be confidently placed two (sixteenth) notes before the following downbeat. In a more extreme phrasing, the preparation has to be placed with the last note before the bar-line. The second issue involves coordinating the two *pizzicato* notes in celli and basses in each following bar. The root of the problem here is that, in order to give a clear preparation (on the first beat of the bar) for the celli and basses, the conductor must show that downbeat before the soloist moves off the tie (i.e., the conductor is leading, not following). This means that the conductor must commit herself to the celli and basses with neither any "real time" information about the soloist's intentions regarding the pace of the sixteenth notes that follow, nor any information about the possibility of any extra time that might be taken during the tie. There is no perfect, specific solution to a situation like this one. The solution is global, rather than incident specific, as it is rooted in the good musicianship, knowledge, and mutual respect and trust between the conductor and the soloist. When these qualities are in place, the conductor has come to understand the soloist's musical personality, and the soloist has come to trust the conductor's instincts and will follow appropriate and studied musical leadership when necessary. Likewise, the conductor has come to trust that the soloist will not (to use this example) suddenly place a *fermata* on the tied note, ignore the conductor's indication of the first beat of the bar, and leave both conductor and orchestra in a very difficult position.

Because the composer has placed a comma on the bar-line at **11**, this junction can feel awkward. But this does not need to be so. The conductor should feel free to mark all three empty bars preceding **11** ahead of the soloist, while carefully following the soloist's current location with the ear. Unless the soloist has specifically asked that the comma be interpreted as unusually lengthy, the conductor can give the preparation immediately following the final note before the bar-line. This has the effect of the comma occupying the space of roughly a quarter note in the new tempo.

How many times have most conductors remarked to an orchestra that expressive markings such as accents and *sforzati* are always to be executed within the context of the prevailing dynamic? That number is too many to count, I'm sure, if the number of times it has already been mentioned in this book is any indication. This subject is particularly important for the marking ***sfz***, as it is so easy to assume by looking at the ***f*** in the marking that *forte* must be some part of this event. It is rare that a composer is so diligent and specific as to specify the details of this issue, and we are in Walton's debt, yet again, for doing so. The markings in horns and trombones following **13** have specific instructions that these expressive gestures are within the overall context of *piano*, so no explanation or waste of rehearsal time should be necessary.

It is clear, both by the nature of the preceding figures and by the lack of any contrary instructions, that the relationship when moving to $\frac{6}{8}$ meter two bars before **14** is ♪ = ♪. Unfortunately, this often turns into something quite different, usually a sudden *meno mosso* in which the meters have no relationship to each other. In some cases, this may be no more than a failure to thoroughly think through what is on the page. At other times it is the result of the conductor insisting that the new meter be taken in six. The pace of the preceding eighth notes is such that, if one conducts the new meter in six, one will almost inevitably begin the bar at a slower tempo. There is no reason whatever to handle the $\frac{6}{8}$ bars other than in two, and this will allow for both the correct metric relationship and an actual *poco ritard*, instead of *subito meno mosso.*

The last beat of the bar preceding **15** needs to be subdivided to facilitate an accurate, confident entrance of the oboe. The following bar moves back into three. The final beat preceding **16** is to be subdivided into two parts, one for each dotted eighth note. This allows the pulse to remain exactly the same crossing the bar-line (as specified by the composer), without any new mathematics being required when arriving at **16**. Toward the goal of executing the metric relationship precisely as Walton asked, no *ritard* should be added to the final beat before **16**, or the intended relationship is stretched and mangled. Sometimes this is a hard sell with the soloist, who may wish to linger on the trill. Whether or not this negotiation is successful is a matter of the personalities of a particular soloist and conductor, and their relative negotiating skills. The movement continues in beats of eighth notes to its conclusion.

2nd movement.

Any complexities of the technique of conducting or accompanying in this movement are virtually non-existent. This joyous music, much needed following the dark and intense emotions of the first movement, flows entirely in one tempo and essentially "plays itself." The conductor's major concerns in this movement involve balance and rhythmic integrity.

Unlike the first movement, where the transparency of the orchestration, combined with the *tessitura* of the solo viola, makes balance virtually a non-issue, some care needs to be taken during the portions of this movement in which the orchestral writing is more athletic and indicated at higher dynamic levels. My remark about rhythmic integrity refers to the discipline of the sixteenth note throughout the movement. Even with very fine orchestral musicians (and very fine soloists!), attention needs to be given to consistency of the sixteenth-note pulse and its possible effect on the general stability of the tempo. This is all a nice way of saying that this movement has the potential to rush forward for both orchestra and soloist. In this matter, the conductor must strive to find a delicate balance of control and leadership that keeps the rhythmic and tempo issues in check without dampening the exuberant spirit of the work or those involved in performing it. If the subject of rhythmic control becomes too rigid and demanding, this movement becomes four and half minutes of math instead of a joyous romp.

3rd movement.

The jaunty opening theme of this movement is often taken a bit slower than the composer's metronome marking, but this is (almost) entirely a function of the soloist's desired tempo. Though it seems an obvious thing to mention, in a type of music in which any fluctuation in tempo will be immediately obvious, it is critical that the conductor begin the movement at exactly the tempo in which the soloist intends to enter. A shift of even two to four metronome points at the soloist's entrance in this movement is jarring and unmusical.

Even though the indication *poco rall.* appears at **40**, the violin entrance preceding the bar-line should proceed smoothly and in tempo, without hesitation or any reference to what follows. Though subdivisions will probably be necessary in the third bar after **40**, gracefully slowing to Tempo II, the passage of *meno mosso* returns to a beat in two. If the new tempo is not easily manageable in two, then the tempo is too slow. Both bars preceding **42** usually need to be taken in four, placing the last beat before **42** (in the clarinet) as though on a *fermata*. This allows the baton to show a precise preparation, in exactly the desired new tempo, just after the soloist has playing the final G-natural in that bar.

Even though the composer is very specific regarding the tempo in the fourth bar after **45** (the same metronome marking as at the opening of the movement), this section is often played considerably slower than Tempo I: often in the neighborhood of 𝅗𝅥 = 60–62.

Both conductor and soloist should be careful not to let the *Animato* tempo at **51** (and following) accelerate beyond what is intended. When this happens, the soloist is often forced to pull the tempo back suddenly at **54** in a most awkward fashion. Another issue regarding care and specificity of tempo often comes up at **55**. If the tempo at any point preceding **55** is faster than intended, then no *Più mosso* is really possible here, leaving this new passage without the needed, sudden boost of energy. This is particularly important because the fundamental rhythmic motion slows at this point, so without an upward change of tempo the piece actually feels as though it slows down at **55**, precisely the opposite of the composer's intent.

Two bars before **59**, a precise, dramatic subdivision of the second beat finishes the phrase nicely. After a very small, very passive gesture for the third beat, the baton then delicately marks the following downbeat, utilizing the least motion possible in order to continue the illusion of a grand pause. Next, the baton sharply indicates the second beat, as preparation for the final three chords in the bar, each of which is dictated individually, as subdivisions. The precise meaning of the dashes over these chords will always be subjective, and the conductor must be certain to specify the precise articulation desired, with particular attention to agreement between strings and winds.

There is very little difference between the tempo in the two bars marked *più allargando* (at **60**) and the one intended at *a tempo* two bars later. The *a tempo* refers to the tempo at **59**, which is only four points faster than the "𝅗𝅥 = c. 80" indicated at **60**. Nonetheless, there should be a certain sense of re-invigoration here, so that the third bar after **60** does not feel like a continuation of the *allargando*.

At **61**, the composer specifies a beat in nine. Though there are portions of this passage where this is good advice, beating in nine is not necessary or desirable at all times during this portion of the piece. After beginning the passage in nine for security, an orchestra with good internal pulse will allow the conductor to expand into three during some portions of the music that follows.

The first bar at **62** resembles the bar directly preceding **16** (first movement) in the sense that, during a final portion of the bar, the conductor must show a beat that is no part of the current meter in order to create the proper metric relationship with the following bar. Here, the conductor beats the first six (quarter note) beats as one would expect, but then beats two beats (each the value of a dotted quarter note) to cover the final one-third of the bar. The first of these two final beats falls on the *forte-piano* in viole and second violins (coinciding with the dotted eighth rest in flute and oboe and the tied F-sharp in celli) and the second gesture lines up with the lower F-sharp in flute and oboe (coinciding with the slurred F-sharp in celli and the space before the last note of the bar in first violins and solo viola). This pulse then continues into the next bar as instructed, equaling the new quarter note. For some reason, Walton places the meter $\frac{2}{2}$ here, even though he specifically instructs that he wants a beat in four, so we will oblige.

Even though it is not the soloist's job to follow the conductor, but the other way around, it is polite in the fifth bar before **63** to indicate the placement of the second beat within sight of the soloist. This allows the soloist to place the final F-sharp where desired, but with complete knowledge of where the conductor believes the second beat to be. This simple courtesy helps a soloist who may not hear the orchestra clearly while sustaining the high A-natural, and avoids the possibility that the soloist and the clarinetist may reach the F-sharp at nearly the same time, instead of two beats apart.

Nothing is to be taken for granted between **63** and the end of the piece. As simple as the relationships appear on the page, the conductor needs to be constantly aware that any note in the solo viola may be given considerable expressive time, as fits this epilogue. Being aware of this, the baton is never moving forward irrevocably from one beat to the next during music such as this. Instead, the conductor needs to carefully utilize the space that exists at the zenith of each rebound to assess the musical situation before accelerating toward the following beat. In this way, the conductor/accompanist is always allowing space for the soloist, never inhibiting a musical gesture or causing stress or discomfort.

Index